THE KERRY WAY

THE KERRY WAY

The History of Kerry Group, 1972–2000

James J. Kennelly

Oak Tree Press
Dublin

Oak Tree Press
Merrion Building
Lower Merrion Street
Dublin 2, Ireland
www.oaktreepress.com

© 2001 James J. Kennelly

A catalogue record of this book is
available from the British Library.

ISBN 1-86076-184-4 Paperback
ISBN 1-86076-205-0 Hardback

Printed in Britain by
MPG Books, Bodmin, Cornwall

Contents

The Author

James J. Kennelly, PhD, is an Assistant Professor of Management and Business at Skidmore College in Saratoga Springs, New York, where he lectures on topics in International Business, Management and Business Ethics. He has also been a Visiting Assistant Professor of International Business and Management at the Stern School of Business at New York University. His research interests centre upon the social and environmental performance of multinational corporations, and the "rootedness" of multinational firms in their home countries. He has a particularly keen interest in the evolution of indigenous Irish-based multinationals. This is his second book.

He is married to Linda Fauth, and they have two children, Brendan and Terence. They live on a converted dairy farm near the Village of Salem, in bucolic Washington County, New York.

Acknowledgements

I am grateful to have been given the opportunity to write this corporate history of the Kerry Group. As a management scholar and a student of multinational corporations, it has afforded me the chance to study a remarkably successful enterprise, founded and still rooted in a place that I love well, County Kerry, Ireland.

It is not intended to be solely a history of one organisation, although it is primarily that. Rather, I have tried, with what little wisdom that I have, to paint a portrait of a people, a place and a time, and the short (in terms of time span) but eventful story of a highly successful enterprise that arose from it. Although I hope that business academics and practitioners will find this book informative and useful, I am even more hopeful that the general reader, that endangered species, will find it accessible and interesting.

Since beginning this book, I have accumulated a host of obligations, which I am pleased to acknowledge. I would like to thank Skidmore College for a Faculty Development Initiative Grant that permitted me to embark upon this project, and for a sabbatical leave that permitted me to complete it. I am also grateful to my colleagues on the faculty, who gave me their support, encouragement and wisdom throughout the process.

I would like to acknowledge the support of the Kerry Group, without which it would have been impossible to complete this project. Our "rules of engagement" were simple, and generally accepted by scholars writing company histories. Choices of subject matter, themes and interpretations were left to me. Kerry Group provided access to its files and to its personnel, and was given the opportunity to review the text and correct factual errors. For my part, I agreed to maintain the confidentiality of proprietary financial, operational and strategic information.

At Kerry Group, I wish to acknowledge the assistance and encouragement of Frank Hayes, Director of Corporate Affairs. From the beginning, his commitment to the project never wavered, and his efforts in support of it never flagged. Also in the Corporate Affairs Office, Noreen Sugrue and Orla O'Doherty were always helpful, patient and good humoured. Denis Brosnan, Hugh Friel, and Denis Cregan were most generous with their time and knowledge in many interviews. Michael Griffin and Michael Drummey in the UK, and Jack Warner and Stan McCarthy in the USA, were very helpful in painting a portrait of the Kerry organisation around the world. Michael Rice in Tralee graciously read the entire manuscript To these, and all the Kerry employees throughout the world whom I interviewed in the course of writing this book, I offer sincere thanks.

Many people outside the Kerry organisation have assisted me in the preparation of this book. A few deserve special acknowledgement. Jim Moloney, former Director General of the Irish Co-operative Organisation Society and the current chairman of IAWS, submitted to a number of interviews, read the bulk of the manuscript in draft form, and willingly shared the fruits of his broad experience and knowledge. I would also like to thank Bill Sweeney for his interest and support, and for his hard work in ferreting out old documents, minutes and correspondence. Ned O'Callaghan was very helpful with his recollections of a long period of association with Kerry Group and provided incisive comments on an earlier draft of this manuscript.

I would also like to thank Padraig Kennelly of *Kerry's Eye* and Kevin Coleman of The Kerryman for their help in locating early photographs.

At Oak Tree Press, I thank David Givens for his early encouragement, Senior Editor Brian Langan for his professionalism, insight, and good humour in editing the manuscript and Maureen McDermott for overseeing the production of this book.

I also wish to acknowledge the assistance of two men who passed away before they could see this book in print, Pat Lyons and Seamus Murphy.

Finally, I offer humble thanks to my wife Linda, for her constant support and encouragement, and my children Brendan and Terence, for reminding me always of what is truly important in life.

Dedication

To my wife Linda, and my sons Brendan and Terence

*To my father Jim Kennelly, a proud son of Finuge, County Kerry,
and my mother Helen, who like so many before her,
became more Irish than the Irish*

*To my mother-in-law Dorothy,
and in fond and loving memory of my father-in-law Helmut*

Foreword

Ivor Kenny

To be discontented with the divine discontent . . . is the very germ and first upgrowth of all nature. — Charles Kingsley, 1874

Possunt quia posse videntur.[*] — Virgil, 70–19 BC

This is the story of an Irish multinational food company. It began in a rented caravan in the muddy Canon's Field in Listowel in 1972 and is now a world leader. It is a story of leadership: of the Kerry Group and its team; and of its chief executive for 28 years, Denis Brosnan.

The author writes warmly about Eddie Hayes and his "utterly unwavering leadership" that brought into being North Kerry Milk Products, the forerunner of the Kerry Co-op, and of Frank Wall, the Co-op's first chairman. They blazed the trail. Denis Brosnan and his colleagues brought Kerry to where it is today.

Fifteen years ago, when I first got to know the Kerry Group, a friend said to me, "I hear you're working with Kerry Co-op. That's a one-man-band, isn't it?" A moment's thought would have stopped him fantasising that an organisation which even then was big, complex and political could be run like a village shop, never mind the multinational group it is today.

What is leadership anyway? Warren Bennis said that books on leadership are often as majestically useless as they are pretentious.

---

[*] They can because it seems to them they can.

Chester Barnard said that leadership has been the subject of an extraordinary amount of dogmatically stated nonsense.

The only definition of a leader is someone who has followers. Without followers, there can be no leaders.

Leadership is a combination of knowledge and intuition, of position and personality, of constraints and human will, of time and chance. Leaders engage issues on the level of both fact and feeling. While I believe in the usefulness of management science, the future cannot be met with more and better systems. You will not get leadership from managerial mechanics — enraptured with technique, never asking questions of meaning and purpose, captives only to the bottom line. You will not get leadership from people clothed in power and status, but lacking in heart, mind and vision.

Vision is the first quality Denis Brosnan brought to the Kerry Group. In 1986 he said,

> I don't like talking about myself in Kerry Co-op but, if I say we are going to get to that goal, when all the advice has been given, when all the pitfalls have been pointed out, we still get there. It is the goal that has to be right. I can see where we will be three or four years hence. Ten years ago, I might have led people there. I will, I suppose, still lead them, but now I will let them work it out for themselves.

There are two qualities there: Denis Brosnan the visionary, who, in his own words, can "sense" the future; and Denis Brosnan the leader, who lets them "work it out for themselves".

Leadership, however, is contingent on the circumstances of the time, the constraints and opportunities, the culture or sedimented attitudes of the people we have to work with. Any lessons to be learned from this book must be seen *in context*, in the unfolding drama of the Kerry Group. While the Group has now more multinational than Irish employees, you will not understand it unless you understand the *Slí Ciarraí*, the origins of the company in the Kingdom of Kerry. A wag once put it: "There was Denis Brosnan with his back to the sea."

A characteristic of the Kerry culture is its lack of pretension, its warm, if at times astringent, humanity. The posturings of suburban Dublin are anathema. Or the Kerry humour, where a senior Kerry manager quotes Dan Paddy Andy to the very serious Group Planning Conference: "There'll be no peace in the county until every man has five more cows than his neighbour." And it's helpful if you understand farmers. I asked Den McCarthy, a senior manager in the Agribusiness Division, to tell me, an urbanite, about farmers. Den knows every farmer in Kerry. The first thing he said was, "Ivor, they're fierce lonely." I recounted this to a farmer. He said, "That's right — but do you know what's great? Funerals. You don't need an invitation and you don't have to bring a present."

Denis Brosnan casts a long shadow, but the Kerry Group is not a monolith. To understand that you would first have to feel the muscles of the barons who report directly to him. Hugh Friel and Denis Cregan, deputy managing directors, were with him in that caravan in Listowel. Hugh Friel is in charge of the multi-disciplinary lean Head Office in Tralee. Denis Cregan is Group head of human resources and chairman of Kerry Ingredients Europe, Kerry's most complex division. Stan McCarthy, a Board member, who did pioneering work in the US, now heads Kerry Ingredients America, which takes in all the Americas. Michael Griffin, a member of the Board, built Kerry Foods in a fiercely competitive market. It is now a leading UK consumer foods company. John O'Callaghan, who epitomises Kerry wisdom and wit, heads up the Kerry Agribusiness division.

These divisions have a high degree of autonomy. It is the key ingredient in their energy and enthusiasm. There is a corps of over 80 senior managers. They come in all shapes, sizes and, increasingly, nationalities. To a greater or lesser extent, they share the predominant Kerry characteristic: the will to win.

To be autonomous, paradoxically, you must have boundaries. To attempt to do without them is to become entrapped in a web of accommodations. For change, you need clarity of direction. Without that clarity, people pursue their own survival and, after ructions, return to square one or worse. Anyone who has watched children grow up knows they need boundaries to grow towards true autonomy. If you throw them in the deep end to toughen them for their encounter with a hard world, they do learn to swim and fast, but the legacy is a lifetime of drowning nightmares. If you over-protect, they push clumsily to find their proper limits and end up alienated.

The right balance is a boundary like a chalk line on the ground rather than a stone wall. You are free to cross it, but you are also very clear where it is and what the consequences of trespass will be. Management is always about balance, about freedom *and* order. Kerry managers seem to me to have achieved that balance.

The late Tom Barrington, who loved and wrote about Kerry, once said to me, "How can you believe this place? You look at a mountain and next minute it's disappeared." This may account for Kerry managers' ability to embrace change and ambiguity. One of them told me he was in his job for two years before he was appointed. This can make people uneasy — but management is about the necessity of imperfect choice. It means the acceptance of paradox, the acceptance of contradictory phenomena, without trying to resolve them. Most Kerry managers understand that. Most of them know that the test of intelligence is the ability to hold two opposed ideas in mind at the same time and still to retain the ability to function. These qualities give Kerry a unique flexibility faced with a market place in constant ferment. Kerry managers have an aversion to bureaucracy.

The author talks about Kerry's preoccupation with planning, with SWOT analyses and with Kami and Argenti planning systems. These are useful and may bring necessary order into the always messy job of management. But real — as distinct from textbook — strategising is a complex process that requires insight, creativity and synthesis. These are the very things that defy formal processes and schedules. And how can you measure courage?

The Kerry story is well worth the telling. Do what the King says in *Alice in Wonderland*: "Begin at the beginning and go on until you come to the end and then stop." You will participate in a rich Kerry odyssey, the tale of a leadership that believed nothing was impossible — it just took a little longer.

Chapter 1

Historical Background

The Irish Question is . . . of paramount importance, the problem of a national existence, chiefly an agricultural existence, in Ireland . . . it is the question of rural life. What is migration in other countries is emigration with us, and the mind of the country, brooding over the dreary statistics of this perennial drain, naturally and longingly turns to schemes for the rehabilitation of rural life — the only life it knows. — Sir Horace Plunkett, 1904[1]

Business organisations, like people, do not issue forth fully fashioned and engineered *de novo* according to the antiseptic plans of some master draftsman. Rather, their own birth and development is shaped and coloured by the social and economic context of their times. In this, the founding and growth of the Kerry Group is no exception. Its founders, leaders and supporters were themselves products of a legacy of economic and social stagnation that characterised much of the first five decades of independence in the Republic of Ireland. To properly apprehend the story of Kerry Group and its people, one must appreciate the soil from which it sprang, the times that shaped it, and the legacy that it has carried. In Ireland, for the greater part of the twentieth century, social and economic life was dominated by agriculture, and dairying and cattle dominated agriculture itself. This is where the story of Kerry Group must begin.

Central to many of the myths of Irish prehistory, the sagas, the wars, the heroes, and the epics, were cattle. Cattle were regarded as the primary form of wealth, the most valuable of possessions, and assets to be gathered, hoarded, stolen, guarded, and accounted for continually. In the epic *Táin Bó Cuailnge* (the "Cattle Raid of Cooley"), Ailill and Maeve compared their riches in terms of cattle, before Maeve led her warriors in a bloody attempt to carry off the prize bull of the King of Ulster. In later days, when Mountjoy and his lieutenant Sir George Carew wished to be done with the men of Munster who had supported the Desmond rebellion, they simply destroyed their herds, such that "scarcely a cow could be heard lowing from Dunquin in Kerry to Cashel in Munster".[2] Throughout its history, climate and geography have conspired to give Irish agriculture a predominantly pastoral cast. The lush grasslands have provided the platform for the production of dairy and cattle products that came to form the foundation of agriculture in Ireland. Given such centrality, it is little wonder that the trade in live dairy and cattle products, particularly butter, came to figure so prominently in Irish economic and social history. Some will suggest that this heritage has also come to imprint itself upon the collective psyche of the Irish nation. Doubtless, as well, this legacy has coloured the histories of those agricultural enterprises that have emerged from the soil of this small island economy.

Agriculture in Ireland — Years of Stagnation

The history of agriculture in Ireland, at least until the decade of the 1960s, was not on the whole a happy one. Although agriculture had dominated economic life from long before Ireland even recognised itself as a nation, the economic returns to most farmers had been miserly at best. At the creation of the Irish Free State in 1922, agriculture accounted for more than half of the nation's employment, about three-quarters of its exports and about one-third of GDP.[3] Even as late as 1989 nearly 5.7 million hectares of Ireland's total land area of 6.9 million hectares remained devoted to agricultural production, with roughly 90 per cent of that in grassland.[4] Until the most recent of modern times, Ireland remained a largely rural and agrarian nation, dependent upon agriculture and fully exposed to the shifts of agricultural policies and the whims of agricultural markets, particularly in its biggest market, the United Kingdom.

Despite occasional forays into tillage (for instance, the compulsory tillage schemes during the Second World War), Irish agriculture retained a predominately pastoral character, due as much to the economic policies of successive governments as to the advantages of land, climate and simple economics. The image of a bucolic green countryside, well favoured for production of cattle and other livestock for export on the hoof to England or the continent, is not entirely inappropriate. In essence, Irish agriculture has always been based upon a straightforward objective: to convert efficiently the grass with which it has been so richly endowed into milk and meat.[5] The practice of dairying and the raising of beef cattle remain to this day the bedrock of Irish agriculture. Historically, this competitive advantage provided by the rich grasslands that characterise so much of the country was not lost upon the landowners of the Anglo-Irish Ascendancy, who in the eighteenth and nineteenth centuries increasingly converted land from tillage to the more lucrative production of livestock. This led to increasingly keen competition for even the most marginal land, as the native Irish population scrambled for access to enough land to eke out a bare subsistence. Inevitably, their holdings grew smaller. The greater part of the Irish population existed on these small farmsteads, tenancies, or for the most unfortunate, conacre.[6] Indeed, the possession of even a small plot of substandard land could and did make the difference between life and death. Even this meagre existence, however, crumbled in the face of the cataclysm that was the "Great Hunger", the famine of 1845-1849. Those on the smallest holdings suffered terribly during the famine, as they grew their main source of food, the potato, on these small plots, and a blight had devastated nearly the entire crop. The possession of land, and the desire for land ownership, was a passion increasingly manifested in the wake of the Famine. The land agitation that followed, and the rise of Michael Davitt and the Land League, led to the reforms and redistribution of land that began at the end of the nineteenth century. Land ownership became widespread, but holdings tended to be small, particularly in the "congested districts" of the western seaboard of the country. Nevertheless, by the founding of the Free State, most Irish farmers

owned their own farms, small and dispersed as they may have
been.

It would take a full history in itself to begin to do justice to the
story of Irish agriculture before more modern times. For our purposes, however, it may suffice to simply reiterate that, for trade in
cattle and livestock, tillage and dairy products, there were cycles
of boom and bust as prices for cattle, grain, and butter rose and
fell on the international (primarily UK) markets. A depression in
farm prices characterised the end of the nineteenth century. The
First World War brought good times to Irish agriculture, but this
ended abruptly around 1921. In the years after the founding of the
Free State, the Irish economy in general performed poorly.
Throughout these times, of course, Ireland remained economically
tied to and, in fact, substantially dependent upon the United Kingdom. That this dependency did not decline in any meaningful way
subsequent to the founding of the Irish Free State in 1922 remained
a source of disappointment for many Irish nationalists. Political independence did not bring simultaneous economic independence,
and Yeats, in this as in so much else, captured the feeling well:

> Parnell came down the road, he said to a cheering man:
> "Ireland shall get her freedom and you still break stone."[7]

A suffocating stagnation permeated the national economic and social environments, and reflected itself in the agricultural situation
at the time. Farm output scarcely increased in the first decades after independence. Productivity increased only marginally, due as
much, perhaps, to the emigration of farm workers as to any improvements in efficiency. Emigration itself remained the most
visible sign of the nation's failed economic policies, a national
tragedy made all the more caustic by its apparent inevitability.
Economic historians of this period have not suffered from a dearth
of explanations:

> Most accounts [of Irish economic history] have concen-
> trated on explaining "The Irish disease".[8] Plausible rea-
> sons for that poor performance — tariff protection, mis-
> guided fiscal policies, a bloated public sector, the power
> of sectional interests, a poorly-functioning labour market,
> the wrong investment mix, the lack of competition, emi-

gration and the brain drain, an anti-success cultural ethos
— were not hard to find.[9]

Agriculture, tied as it was to the markets in the United Kingdom,
was held hostage to what seemed an endless cycle of trade disputes and negotiations with the UK regarding reciprocal market
access, quotas and other trade restrictions, and trade policy generally. In fact, agriculture in Ireland typically was a matter of
moving cattle, and cattle products, gradually from south and west
to east. Cattle would be bred in the province of Munster in the
south-west of Ireland, where dairying was the primary agricultural
activity, and moved north-east to the "ranches" of the Midlands
and the eastern part of the country where they were finished for
export, typically on the hoof, to England. Exports of butter followed a somewhat different migratory pattern, proceeding primarily south (to Cork) and south-east (to Waterford) for export.

England had long followed a "cheap food policy" that subsi-
dised its own farmers directly, while leaving its own agricultural
markets open for the rest of the world, including Ireland, to fight it
out. Anglo-Irish trade negotiations became even more difficult as
the UK began to move towards greater self-sufficiency in its food
supply. Ireland itself had begun a similar journey, following the
"self-sufficiency" goals of the ruling Fianna Fáil party. Self-
sufficiency, in fact, was as much an article of faith for Fianna Fáil as
was the revival of the Irish language. It was also similarly, and fa-
mously, unsuccessful. This economic policy played a key role in
the shaping of an inward-looking Ireland that was economically,
socially and culturally parochial in its orientation. It fostered the
numerous protective tariffs put in place to protect such indigenous
industry as then existed. It led to the "economic war" with Britain
from 1934–38, which was waged largely on the backs of Irish farmers. It was clearly manifested in the bias towards tillage exhibited
by Fianna Fáil in the 1930s and 1940s. It exacerbated the trade-
impairing effects of the Great Depression, and reinforced the isolation of neutral Ireland during "The Emergency" of the Second
World War. All through this period, Irish agriculture remained
largely dependent upon access to the UK markets. Market access
to the UK for butter, beef, and other agricultural commodities became a matter of continual negotiation and a revolving door for

delegations to London. Meanwhile, access to continental markets was out of the question, at least from the mid-1950s, as the new Common Market began to expand its own internal market and erect external trade barriers.

Given the prevailing circumstances, agriculture up to the early 1960s remained in the doldrums. Individual farms tended to be small and fragmented, new technologies such as tractors and other equipment were relatively rare, and farming methods were generally unenlightened. Smith and Healy (1996) noted that "Farms were undercapitalised; livestock breeding was unsatisfactory; marketing was chaotic."[10] Although Ireland's natural advantages allowed its livestock exports to retain some measure of commercial viability, the general state of agriculture was backward. For most of Ireland's farmers, working their small, dispersed holdings, and engaging in mixed farming, survival remained the primary objective during the first half of the twentieth century. Yet, they were engaged in their modern struggle using farming practices and tools that would have been easily recognisable to a farmer of the eighteenth century. It was not a recipe for success. Into the 1950s, Ireland itself remained largely a traditional agricultural economy, and the image of a sleepy backwater of an island, separated from Europe and forgotten by time itself, was not entirely inappropriate. By the end of the decade, however, the economic window was at long last to be opened, and four decades of dramatic change would begin.

The Dairy Industry in Ireland to the 1960s

If agriculture had long been the centrepiece of the Irish economy, dairying represented the central focus of economic life for a majority of the small farmers in Ireland. Unlike the relatively large farmers of the midlands, the milk cow and its produce occupied a far more exalted station among the smaller farmers of the rest of the country. For them, the influence of the milk cow was, and always had been, pervasive. At home, it provided milk for consumption and for churning into butter, both of which when combined with potatoes came to comprise a major portion of the staple diet of the people. The surplus milk and butter were sold, providing many farmers with much needed participation in the monetary economy. The geography of Ireland itself allowed for the vital place of dairying in the everyday life of the people:

> From the beginning, Ireland was well endowed with natural advantages for the development of what was to be a uniquely successful dairy industry. Good soil and a position in the path of warm, moisture-bearing south-west winds, together with the influence of the Gulf Stream, put the country in a particularly good position for dairying.[11]

The cow became so indispensable to the people of Ireland that it became strongly associated with the accumulation of wealth; in fact, historically one was wealthy in proportion to the number of cows one owned. This was not by any means confined only to the very wealthy. It was at the centre of life in ancient Ireland, as cows and dairy products functioned as currency and social "status symbols", as well as, like so much else, raw material for poetry.[12] One need only read the first stanza of Mangan's translation from the Irish of the poem "The Woman of Three Cows" to gain a sense of the centrality of the cow to Irish life:

> O Woman of Three Cows, agra! Don't let your tongue thus rattle!
> O, don't be saucy, don't be stiff, because you may have cattle.
> I have seen — and, here's my hand to you, I only say what's true —
> A many a one with twice your stock not half so proud as you.[13]

But the economic importance of dairying in Ireland can be reflected in one product: butter. Its manufacture in Ireland can be traced back thousands of years. Traditionally, it was made in the kitchen, churned by the women of the house, for private use. Butter may originally have been churned by agitating the cream in an animal skin container, and then only later in small wooden churns. These churns, called "dash churns", had a conical body and a splayed top into which fitted a lid, and a staff or agitator that passed through a hole in the lid to agitate the cream.[14] Although the Irish were prodigious consumers of milk products, the surplus butter was traded, giving rise to a growing export trade in butter for England and the continent. It was Ireland's principle export for many years and indeed, Ireland was the world's dominant exporter of butter in the seventeenth and eighteenth centuries. Increasingly, as grains and the potato achieved a more dominant place in the Irish diet, more butter was redirected from the home to the export market.[15] Butter was also an increasingly valued source of cash necessary to pay the rent. As commercial dairy operations developed throughout Munster, an economic "ripple effect" ensued: calves were increasingly sent east for finishing and final export, and skim milk left after butter manufacture was used to feed pigs, leading to growing interest in, and interconnections with, both the beef and pork meat export markets.

Butter for export was highly salted to survive long voyages and was primarily shipped from Cork and Waterford. Indeed, the Cork Butter Mart became world famous for its trade in butter. The profits of the butter merchants of Cork helped to fuel the growth of the city and the construction of many of its grand buildings. They also pioneered steps to standardise the grading of butter as to quality, and generally to improve the marketability of the product. By the 1880s, however, the butter trade declined precipitously in the face of competition from Holland, France, and Denmark, who were employing both new technology and better methods which produced a more lightly salted, standardised, hygienic product. The development of the centrifugal separator also led to huge advances in the countries of Scandinavia, which were the first to adopt this new production method. Combined with their adoption of the co-operative form of organisation, Scandinavians and other European followers revolutionised the production and trade in butter, decimating Ireland's export trade. As noted in a recent history of the Irish co-operative movement:

> Ireland had remarkable natural advantages for and a long tradition of making butter, but in terms of scientific innovation, education and business organisation, Irish farmers had fallen far behind their Continental counterparts. The development by Laval in 1878 of the centrifugal cream separator and the steam-powered churn was revolutionising European dairying. Denmark, where co-operative dairying had been in full swing since 1882, was providing very stiff competition. In 1848, 379,000 packages of Irish butter had entered the port of London as against 576,000 from overseas. By 1884 Irish butter had declined to 5,618 packages exported via London compared to 1,703,772

from elsewhere. The average price in that year was £6.10.0 (£6.50) for Danish butter as against £4.19.0 for Irish. It looked as if Ireland's English market would disappear, while, even in Dublin, Danish butter had taken the lead.[16]

The days of heavily salted, farm-produced butter were over. Ireland had to catch up, and creameries — factory-like facilities for the intake of raw, whole milk, its separation into cream and skim through the use of the centrifugal separator, and the processing of cream into butter — were part of the answer. But change did not come easily, or quickly, and there was considerable criticism of Irish farmers who either would not, or could not, adopt these new technologies. Ó Gráda, for instance, notes that:

> Doubts were expressed about the ability of the Irish dairy farmer to meet the challenge: his industry was seen as inflexibly organised and inefficient, and he was frequently accused of producing butter of inferior or inconsistent quality.[17]

Nevertheless, the economic dictates were clear, and the first creameries began to appear in Ireland, owned by butter traders and private investors. New creameries spawned by the farmers' co-operative movement of the very late nineteenth century later joined them, although proprietary creameries continued to dominate until the beginning of the Free State. Although the benefits of these creameries were quite evident, they could operate economically only if a sufficient supply of milk was available within a radius of a few miles, since transportation was primitive and cooling facilities for the milk were non-existent.

In the context of the overall agricultural economy, however, dairying declined in importance from the 1870s, as some farmers moved into other enterprises such as beef cattle (if they had enough land) or various tillage enterprises (for example, sugar beets were encouraged by various government schemes).[18] Still, this was only a relative decline. The dairy industry remained, along with the beef industry, a large and formidable component of the overall Irish agricultural economy. By the end of the nineteenth century, proprietary creameries were contending with the new co-operative creameries that were spreading rapidly throughout Ireland, in many cases competing for the same milk pool. It was a sign of hope for Irish dairy farmers, for indeed the agricultural cooperative movement was to dominate the Irish dairy industry in the next century.

The Irish Co-operative Movement

The face of Irish agriculture was changed forever by one man's vision, perseverance and passion for the right of Irish farmers to control their own enterprises and their own economic destiny. Sir Horace Plunkett was a most unlikely revolutionary. A leading member of the Anglo-Irish aristocracy, a Member of the British Parliament (from Dublin), a Protestant and a Unionist, Plunkett had been inculcated with the utopian and co-operative ideals of Robert Owen, a British factory owner and social reformer who had pioneered experiments with industrial co-operatives in England. Observing the condition of the Irish dairy industry in the 1890s, Plunkett saw the demand and prices for Irish butter continuing their decline in the face of superior Danish production. He judged the formation and development of farmers' co-operatives in the dairy sector as an essential component in the modernisation and development of a successful, farmer-controlled industry.

The co-operative movement in Ireland can be said to have begun with the founding of the first Irish co-operative organisation at Dromcollogher, County Limerick, in 1889. Over the next ten years, a total of 64 co-operatives were organised throughout the province of Munster, an average of over 10 creameries per county. The co-operative movement then spread first throughout Ulster, and then other parts of Ireland.[19] This rapid diffusion of the radical ideas of co-operation after decades, even centuries, in which the social structures of farming had been relatively unchanged remains even today a remarkable achievement. It stands as a testament to the vibrancy of this revolutionary message, the inspired idealism of its promoters, and the fact that, clearly, here was ground upon which such a message would quickly yield a harvest.

Although Plunkett was the founder of this movement in Ireland, a capable cadre of full-time organisers ably assisted him in the hard work on the ground. Men such as R.A. Anderson and the mystic and writer (but surprisingly pragmatic) George Russell

(A.E.) travelled the country, addressing farming meetings, planting the seeds of co-operation, and contending with a largely hostile class of merchants, traders and shopkeepers. It was not a task for the faint of heart or the thin-skinned. Nor was it a job for wild-eyed idealists with their heads in a cloud-cuckoo land of communitarian and co-operative ideals. It involved hard graft of the most practical and pragmatic sort. R.A. Anderson recounts an incident that illustrates the difficulties they faced:

> It was hard and thankless work. There was the apathy of the people and the active opposition of the press and the politicians. It would be hard to say now whether the abuse of the conservative *Cork Constitution* or the nationalist *Eagle of Skibbereen*, was the louder. We were "killing the calves", we were "forcing young women to emigrate", we were "destroying the industry". Mr. Plunkett was described as a "monster in human shape" and was abjured to "cease his hellish work". I was described as his "Man Friday" and as "Roughrider Anderson". Once when I thought that I had planted a creamery within the precincts of the town of Rathkeale, my co-operative applecart was upset by the local solicitor, who . . . gravely informed me that our programme would not suit Rathkeale. "Rathkeale," said he pompously, "is a nationalist town — nationalist to the backbone — and every pound of butter made in this creamery must be made on nationalist principles, or it shan't be made at all". This sentiment was applauded loudly and the proceedings terminated.[20]

Despite such setbacks, the co-operative movement, particularly in the dairy sector, continued to gather steam. By the turn of the century, there were 840 co-operative societies, of which approximately 350 were creameries.[21] There was also, by this point, a co-ordinating body, the Irish Agricultural Organisation Society (IAOS),[22] formed in 1894, as well as, in 1899, the formation by the government of the Department of Agriculture and Technical Instruction. Horace Plunkett had championed both of these institutions, and indeed he served both as the first President of IAOS, and later as the first Minister for Agriculture.

What was this co-operative "philosophy", and why did it find such fertile soil among the dairy farmers in Ireland? Even though "co-operative principles and practices are not fixed, immutable sets of standards carved on stone",[23] the foundations of co-operative thought can still be traced to the Rochdale Principles first developed by an early co-operative set up in Rochdale, England in 1844. An updated version adopted by the International Co-operative Alliance Commission in 1966 cites the following:

- Membership should be open and voluntary for all persons using the co-operative

- There should be no discrimination based on racial, social, religious or political grounds

- Member/users alone should be owners

- One member, one vote — members control equally

- Share capital should receive only limited interest

- Members should benefit in proportion to use. Profits should be distributed in proportion to a member's transactions with the society.[24]

These elements comprised the essential gospel message of those first organisers of the co-operative movement, and one that resonated with farmers. It must be remembered that, at the time, virtually all creameries were privately owned, many in fact by English joint-stock companies. Typically, there would be only one creamery serving any particular geographic area. A farmer had little choice in deciding where he would market his milk; he would take it to the local creamery, and accept what he was given for a price. He had little by way of alternatives. The creamery owners and managers ruled their monopsonistic (single-buyer) domains with impunity, with no worry of countervailing power in the hands of farmers. For their part, the farmers had to endure an enforced bondage to the local creamery, within the context of the overall whims and cycles of the larger markets for dairy products in the UK, over which they also exerted no influence. It was a very precarious business, with farmers increasingly reminded that they had little or no say over their own economic destiny.

The arrival of co-operatives on the dairy scene, however, provided a viable and realistic alternative, a revolutionary overthrow of what had gone before. Under the slogan of "better farming, better living, better business", co-operative creameries were organised and the Irish co-operative movement gained worldwide attention.[25] Co-operative retail stores and trading societies, credit unions, and other co-operative enterprises grew dramatically in number in the decade before World War I. Meanwhile, colourful characters like Patrick (Paddy the Cope) Gallagher added to the stock of co-operative success, as well as mythology, as they began at last to break the hold of the dreaded "gombeen man" in rural Ireland.[26]

The period during and immediately after World War I provided farmers in Ireland with what has been described as "seven years of plenty"[27] as agricultural markets for products from wool, to beef, to grains, to butter, to horses remained very strong. An air of optimism and achievement permeated the Irish co-operative movement. This euphoria quickly evaporated, however, by 1921, as war-disrupted supplies (from America, the Commonwealth and Europe) began to come back on line and agricultural prices went into a sudden and dramatic decline. To compound this, Irish creameries were singled out and suffered greatly during the Irish War of Independence, as British military units such as the Black and Tans targeted co-operative creameries in retaliation for IRA attacks.[28] Given the centrality of the creameries to local farmers, such retaliation had extensive consequences that reverberated throughout the local farm community. Such disruptions also had negative impacts on the export butter trade, which never recovered to its pre-war levels. With political independence and the end of "The Troubles", Ireland found itself deep in an economic depression, and many co-operative enterprises were in severe financial straits, having borrowed prodigiously during the halcyon days of prosperity. Competition for milk among the creameries, both co-operative and privately owned, drove down profits even further. The financial condition of many creameries was tenuous, and worsened as the decade of the 1920s unfolded. There were simply too many creameries, and too few that were of an economic size. Some form of rationalisation was desperately in order.

The Irish co-operative movement, particularly in the dairy industry, had grown explosively. The 1920s on, however, called for a period of retrenchment. Plunkett himself, surveying the situation in 1923, appraised it this way:

> It may be that we have attempted to go too fast with our movement. We made a few understand it thoroughly. These, not our membership as a whole, applied the doctrine to their industry, their business, and in some cases their social life. Then others said, "we won't want to hear about the theory, we want to practice the system and to make money". So we kept dotting the map with new societies, most of which did make money. But too few of the members had the co-operative spirit, and when things went wrong — when times were bad — they were helpless. There is less evidence of the real co-operative spirit in agricultural Ireland today than there was 20 years ago. Works without faith are no more use in agricultural co-operation than in religion.[29]

The situation for many creameries, particularly in the peripheral areas where milk collection and assembly were less economically viable due to the land, the climate, and transportation distances, was desperate. This was an industry caught in the twin pincers of excess capacity and a fiercely cut-throat export market, with poor prospects for any improvement. As creameries and co-operative societies began to fail, the new government of the Irish Free State was called upon to take action to stabilise the situation and buffer the dairy farmers served by these enterprises from complete ruin. In modern-day terminology, we might call it a "bail-out". In 1926 the IAOS published a memorandum that focused upon the ruinous competition that then existed between private and co-operative creameries, and the existence of far too many creameries than could be economically justified. The government responded with the passage of the Dairy Disposal Act by the new Irish Parliament, Dáil Éireann, in 1927, which set out the creation of the Dairy Disposal Company, the first of many "semi-state" enterprises to be created in Ireland over the next 40 years.[30] The Dairy Disposal Company was to play a critical role in the very survival of the dairy industry in Ireland, and particularly in the more peripheral, uneconomic regions like Kerry, for nearly 50 years.

The Dairy Disposal Company

The proliferation of small co-operative creameries and privately owned creameries created an urgent need for rationalisation. Much of the competition was leading to uneconomic results as proprietary creameries and co-operatives competed for milk supplies. Farmers reaped no benefit from this competition; if anything, they received lower milk prices as creameries, unable to cover their high operating costs, had to reduce the price they paid for milk. The Dairy Disposal Company (DDC) was intended to be the instrument to end this "undesirable situation" and accomplish a full-scale economic rationalisation of the creamery system.[31] The DDC would purchase these proprietary creameries, or, more accurately, would *facilitate* their purchase so that they might be transferred quickly to co-operative organisations. In many cases, that happened. But the DDC was left, unexpectedly, with roughly 15-20 per cent of the nation's milk supply, an event for which the DDC and its government sponsors were not prepared. In fact, the government, through the DDC, was left with the ownership of some 113 of the surviving 180 proprietary creameries (the remainder were successfully transferred to co-operatives).[32] Given the *laissez-faire* orientation of the government at that time, the idea of having the state in the creamery business was anathema. The Department of Finance was, no doubt, similarly horrified.

Why did more farmers, and their co-operatives, not step in to purchase these creameries? The lack of economic viability on the part of many creameries was a large part of the reason, combined with a natural reluctance on the part of farmers to invest in any enterprise with such dubious prospects. Creameries located in remote areas, with land, and climate and infrastructure that were inhospitable to efficient dairy production, were not attractive candidates to be taken over by co-operative societies. As economic enterprises, successful (or at least viable) co-operatives did not relish the opportunity to subsidise the uneconomic activities of failing creameries. Nor would farmers in those areas themselves join together to form new societies. In many cases, there was neither knowledge of, nor a tradition of, co-operatives in the area, or if there were, it might have been of co-operative enterprises that had failed during the early decades of the century. Additionally, to

form a new co-operative, farmers would have to put up at least
some capital. In those times, the investment was on the basis of £1
per cow (later increased to £3), but people lived in very poor circumstances, incomes were very tight, and many farmers refused
the opportunity to buy these creameries. Thus, the Dairy Disposal
Company, which had intended to finish its job of "disposal" of
creameries within a period of months or, at most, a year, found itself in the creamery business for the next 50 years.[33] Ironically, its
primary task was to become the "disposal" of the milk and milk
products generated by its businesses rather than the disposal of
the creameries themselves.

During more than 50 years of existence, however, the DDC
evolved into far more than an organisation devoted exclusively to
the "disposal" of a commodity. In effect, it became a semi-state
body that was *de facto* charged with the development of the Irish
creamery industry as well as other related (and even unrelated)
agricultural activities. By the mid-1960s, in fact, the DDC was
among the largest business organisations in Ireland, with nearly
1,400 employees and a turnover of £11 million. A brief inventory of
its activities is telling: 17 central creameries and 131 branch
creameries, several AI (artificial insemination) stations for cattle
breeding, a condensed milk, milk powder and cheese factory in
Limerick, pig production activities, a bacon factory, and other activities. Six of the central creameries and 66 of the branch creameries had in fact been erected by the DDC itself, primarily in areas
of County Clare, the Dingle peninsula and the southern half of
County Kerry, and parts of West Cork. They had also pioneered
the use of the "travelling creamery", vehicles that travelled out to
the more remote areas and collected the milk, separated it on the
spot, returned the skim to farmers and brought the cream into the
central creamery. Such activities not only protected the creamery
system, and dairy farming itself, in areas where it had been economically troubled, but also propagated it in remote areas where
it had never been economically viable.

Aside from the initial grant from the government for the buy-out
of proprietary creameries, the DDC was expected to be a "self-
funding" organisation. In this sense, it had to function like any private enterprise, and was limited in its activities by capital constraints. It was, however, also run directly by the Department of

Agriculture, which held the controlling shares in the company and appointed its chairperson from "the Department". In this sense, it functioned very much as a government body. Thus it retained its peculiar status as a "semi-state" body, and only the first of the 55 that Garrett Fitzgerald had counted in the early 1960s.[34] Of course, in a formal sense, only the DDC Chairperson and one other director were civil servants; nevertheless, the DDC was, in everything but name, effectively a government department.

Given its resources, its peculiar organisational status, and the broad responsibilities vested in it, it is easy to see how it became a target of criticism. At times, it seemed, blame for virtually all the problems and inefficiencies endemic to the dairy industry in Ireland was visited upon its doorstep. Yet, the DDC's contribution towards the preservation of the dairy industry in many parts of Ireland was significant. Civil servants generally make poor heroes, but clearly the role of the DDC in the very survival of the industry in Ireland should be acknowledged.

Congested District Boards

In any summary of the recent history of agriculture in Ireland, it would be wrong to overlook the impact of the creation and administration of the Congested Districts Board, set up by the Land Purchase Act of 1891. Generally, the purpose of the Board was to offer assistance to those areas, primarily in the more remote parts of the west of Ireland, whose inhabitants were clearly unable to eke out any more than the most meagre subsistence. At its inception, the Board had responsibility for over 3.6 million acres in parts of counties Donegal, Leitrim, Sligo, Mayo, Roscommon, Galway, Kerry and Cork, but over time its jurisdiction expanded. In attempting to improve the viability of these local economies, the Board focused upon four primary areas of activity: 1) land purchases designed to facilitate the combination of small shareholdings into larger, more viable farm enterprises; 2) resettlement of tenants to more viable landholdings; 3) promotion of native crafts and enterprises; and 4) promotion of instruction in more modern farming methods.[35]

Until its dissolution in 1923, the Board played an important role in the redistribution of land and the consolidation of landholdings in some of the most extremely distressed areas of the country, including County Kerry. It has been estimated that, in total, the board spent £10 million on the purchase and/or redistribution of some two million acres of land, as well as on attempts to improve farming techniques.[36] The Land Commission succeeded the Congested Districts Board after its dissolution, and was charged with continuing the work of redistribution, albeit in a way that did not conflict with property rights in the new Irish Free State. Obviously, greater sensitivity to property rights limited the scope of such activities significantly.[37] Nevertheless, the new Land Commission succeeded in distributing a further 450,000 acres to 24,000 families by 1932.[38]

Development Issues through to the Late 1960s: From Stagnation to Revival

Agriculture remained the single most dominant industry in Ireland after the creation of the Irish Free State in 1922, with most farmers engaged in mixed farming with an emphasis on dairying and the rearing of livestock.[39] These activities accounted for three-quarters of overall farm output and more than half of national exports, almost all of which went to England.[40] For the first 40 years of the new Free State, productivity in farming was virtually static, remaining at an abysmally low level (about half that of Denmark, for example).[41] The "economic war" with the United Kingdom (1934–1938) further squeezed the already small incomes of Irish farmers, and demonstrated yet again the economic dependency of Ireland upon the English market.

Although the first administration of the Irish Free State, that of Cumann na nGaedheal (later to be known as the Fine Gael party) took a predominately free market approach to agriculture, it only lasted until 1932. The Fianna Fáil party, led by Éamon de Valera, then came to power for nearly 30 years of uninterrupted rule, bringing with it de Valera's own vision of a self-sufficient Ireland. His St. Patrick's Day Broadcast in 1943, known later as his "dream" speech, perhaps illustrates best his vision of a free and prosperous Ireland:

> The Ireland which we dreamed of would be the home of a
> people who valued material wealth only as a basis of right
> living, of a people who were satisfied with frugal comfort
> and devoted their leisure to the things of the spirit; a land

whose countryside would be bright with cosy homesteads, whose fields and villages would be joyous with
sounds of industry, the romping of sturdy children, the
contests of athletic youths, the laughter of comely maid-
ens; whose firesides would be the forums of the wisdom of
serene old age.[42]

In attempting to accomplish at least part of this vision, that of a
countryside "bright with cosy homesteads", de Valera pursued a
policy of Irish self-sufficiency in agriculture and manifested a significantly "pro tillage", "pro small farmer" orientation. But, as
Professor J.J. Lee has written about this and other similar visions of
an "ideal" Ireland:

However attractive they may have found their images of
the ideal, they were all vitiated by a fatal flaw. They had no
grasp of economic reality . . . his address contained not a
solitary hint as to how the country could get from the real
to the ideal.[43]

Certainly, there were subsidies and incentives, but few initiatives
in the direction of productivity improvements, modern farming
methods, or responsible approaches to agricultural trading in
world markets. Although the hand of the state was everywhere,
with power highly centralised and decisions made by civil servants in the government ministries, there was little substantive improvement in agriculture.

There were few centres of power, other than the church and the
state. In the dairy industry, many co-operative creameries were
just hanging on, and the dairy business in general was just "ticking
over". Mere survival was an achievement. Farm organisations had
yet to emerge, and farmers suffered from a lack of strong, unifying
leadership. On a larger social level, lack of opportunity, social re-
pression, and all the absurdities of censorship combined to fuel a
stifling feeling of hopelessness. For many, their only hope was to
escape from the country of their birth. Not one to sentimentalise
about the joys of "Old Ireland", James Joyce wrote bitterly:

Oh Ireland my first and only love
Where Christ and Caesar are hand in glove![44]

And so Irish life, and Irish agriculture, remained in the doldrums, and Ireland itself remained a land in a state of suspended animation. This was a boon, perhaps, to a tourist industry that could market this bucolic, scenic, unhurried, pastoral image to great effect, but a curse to those who had to endure its economic reality of hopelessness and cynicism. Ó Gráda notes the "corrosive pessimism" that characterised the early 1950s, and recalled that:

> The July 1956 issue of the satirical monthly, *Dublin Opinion*, bore a cartoon on its cover showing a map of Ireland, with the caption, "Shortly Available — Underdeveloped Country . . . Owners Going Abroad".[45]

But the beginning of the end of the era of economic stagnation came in 1958 with the introduction of the *First Programme for Economic Development*. Already, from the early 1950s, serious political thought had been moving away from the romantic notions of "self-sufficiency" and towards the idea of Ireland in an international context. Crafted by T.K. Whitaker, a career civil servant and at that time the Secretary of the Department of Finance, the *First Programme* proposed a cohesive series of measures to develop industry, reduce emigration, attract foreign capital, and develop productivity in those agricultural areas that were profitable. The initiative was given added impetus with the accession of Seán Lemass, perhaps the ablest man to ever serve in de Valera's cabinet, to party leadership. Ironically, Lemass had also been the Minister most responsible for the introduction of many of the protectionist measures that characterised the Irish economy during the years of de Valera's leadership. It was Lemass's overturning of those very measures that he had installed that helped to shake the foundations of the moribund national economy. The windows were opened, and the winds of change began to air out the dusty mansion of Irish economic life. Although the Lemass era would last only until 1966, it did serve to imprint an entire new orientation on Irish economic life: a commitment to membership in the global economy, outward-looking economic policies, the courting of foreign direct investment, and an orientation towards industrial development. It also had the secondary effect of changing Ireland increasingly from a rural to a largely urban country. This new economic regime reflected a radical sea change in Ireland's fundamental economic and social orientation. That it was generally accepted so willingly, so quickly and so completely is very telling of the frustration that must have accompanied the original ideology. The *Second* (1964–1970) and *Third* (1969–1972) *Programmes* for economic expansion followed. An outward-looking Ireland, eager to reshape itself in the mould of Western capitalistic democracies, had quickly succeeded the self-sufficient Ireland of economic nationalism.

Among the actions taken by the Irish government were the creation of a number of semi-state bodies intended to take the lead in attracting foreign capital and creating markets abroad for Irish produce. The Industrial Development Authority (IDA) had already been created in 1950 with the purpose of attracting foreign direct investment into Ireland. It was singularly successful in this effort, thanks to the generous incentives it could offer such as tax holidays, low corporate tax rates, training allowances, and various grants, particularly in the electronic and pharmaceutical industries. Of more importance to the Irish dairy industry was the establishment, in 1961, of An Bord Bainne (the Irish Dairy Board). Bord Bainne took the place of the old Butter Marketing Committee and served as a central marketing organisation for Irish dairy products being offered for export. Its first Managing Director was Anthony (Tony) O'Reilly, who quickly became one of the new breed of leaders on the Irish business scene. Although only 26 when he took the reins of Bord Bainne, O'Reilly quickly shaped it into a professionally managed, outward-looking, entrepreneurial organisation. With the advent of the Anglo-Irish Free Trade Agreement in 1965, the quota for Irish butter to the United Kingdom was increased dramatically, and Bord Bainne took advantage of this opening by marketing the first *branded* Irish butter to be exported, *Kerrygold*, which was to meet with considerable success.[46] Bord Bainne quickly became a highly influential player in the Irish dairy industry as the prime outlet for the butter manufactured by Irish co-operative creameries, as well as the Dairy Disposal Company creameries. Bord Bainne followed up its success with *Kerrygold* in the UK by augmenting the range of dairy products that it marketed abroad to include skim milk powder, cheese, and other products as well as by expanding its geographic focus. *Kerrygold*, in fact, later became a best-selling brand of butter in Germany. At a minimum, both the IDA and Bord Bainne brought a new activist orientation, and new hope, to Irish business and agriculture. The old mindset of "let's hope for the best and let God do the rest" was changing, and rapidly.

Similarly, change was occurring in Irish farming organisations, which were developing a new militancy of their own. Macra na Feirme (Young Farmers' Clubs) was founded in 1944 with the goals of providing opportunities for young farmers to educate themselves in modern farm techniques, and generally to further their knowledge of agriculture. It also aimed to provide social and cultural activities. Importantly, many of the young people who had begun with Macra na Feirme in the 1940s had, by the 1960s, assumed leadership in the various farming organisations. They brought with them a fresh, new perspective, a willingness to change, and a determination to be heard on issues important to farmers. Smith and Healy, in their book *Farm Organisations in Ireland*, made the point that:

> The impact of these clubs in training leaders can hardly be exaggerated. They taught the skill of organising and identified the people who could get the work done. Debating contests made farmers articulate and taught procedures of debate — as well as spreading farming knowledge.[47]

Macra, in turn, spawned the National Farmers Association (later to become the Irish Farmers Association, or IFA), founded in Dublin in 1955, as a national association intended to represent the interests of farmers. Already, the Irish Creamery Milk Suppliers Association (ICMSA) had been founded in 1950 as an association of dairy milk suppliers, largely in reaction to frustration over low milk prices. From its beginning, it was a militant organisation, "concentrating on forceful presentation of the farmers' case, supported by strike action, rather than technical or market development, which it left to the IAOS [the Irish Agricultural Organisation Society]".[48] These three organisations, along with the IAOS, would remain the most influential farming organisations in Ireland to present times.

This new militancy in Irish agriculture was demonstrated on many occasions during the decades of the 1950s and 1960s. Milk strikes, marches and demonstrations became more common. The new activism culminated in a well-organised march on Dublin in October 1966: "Marchers, 10 to 15 in number, were selected from each county — men fit to walk 15 miles a day, of good national background."[49] The total of 400 marchers timed their journeys to converge on Dublin on the same day, as they joined a mass demonstration of some 25,000 farmers who marched to the Department of Agriculture offices in Merrion Street. This march was followed by protests including picketing, sit-downs and machinery blockages, all in support of the "Farmers' Rights Campaign". It appeared that the days of farmers as a poorly organised, fragmented, leaderless segment of society were coming to an end.

Finally, perhaps the most dramatic change for the Irish economy, and Irish agriculture, was just beyond the horizon. Ireland had made its first application to join the EEC in 1961, when Prime Minister Seán Lemass's attempt to gain admittance was scuttled by President de Gaulle of France. Although Ireland was turned down again for membership in 1967, it had become clear that it was only a matter of time before Ireland would be admitted. This finally came to pass on 1 January 1973. With this, Irish agriculture, and particularly the Irish dairy industry, would never be the same again.

Notes

[1] Sir Horace Plunkett (1982), *Ireland in the New Century*, Dublin: Irish Academic Press Ltd., pp. 39-40. This is a reprinted edition of Plunkett's 1905 Popular Edition. It was reprinted to commemorate the fiftieth anniversary of Plunkett's death.

[2] Roger Chauvire (1965), *A Short History of Ireland*, New York: The New American Library, p. 58. This work was originally published by Devon-Adair in 1956. The quotation is from the *Pacata Hibernia*.

[3] W.J. McCormack (ed.) (1999), *The Blackwell Companion to Modern Irish Culture*, Oxford: Blackwell Publishers Inc., p. 14.

[4] Department of Agriculture and Food (n.d.), *Ireland: Agriculture and Food*, p. 2. This publication contains summarised agricultural statistics through 1989.

[5] Department of Agriculture and Food, op. cit., p. 3.

[6] A small piece of land, leased for a period of less than one year, for cultivation of one crop, particularly potatoes. Labourers, artisans, and other landless

people would often lease land in conacre to gain some ability to grow their own food.

[7] William Butler Yeats (1938), "Parnell", in M.L. Rosenthal (ed.), *Selected Poems and Two Plays of William Butler Yeats,* New York: Macmillan, 1962.

[8] Cormac Ó Gráda (1997), *A Rocky Road: The Irish Economy Since the 1920s*, Manchester: Manchester University Press, p. 2. Ó Gráda cites a number of studies that describe "the Irish Disease", e.g. J.J. Lee (1989), *Ireland 1912–1985: Politics and Society,* Cambridge: Cambridge University Press; K.A. Kennedy, Thomas Giblin and Deirdre McHugh (1988), *The Economic Development of Ireland in the Twentieth Century*, London: Routledge, chs. 1–2; C. Johns (1993), "Last in the class?", *Studies*, 82(325), pp. 9–23; David Johnson (1991), "The economic performance of the independent Irish state", *Irish Economic and Social History*, 18, pp. 48–53; C. Ó Gráda and K. O'Rourke (1996), "Irish economic growth, 1945–88", in N. Crafts and G. Toniolo (eds.), *European Economic Growth*, Cambridge: Cambridge University Press, pp. 388–426.

[9] Cormac Ó Gráda (1997), op. cit., p. 2.

[10] Louis P.F. Smith and Sean Healy (1996), *Farm Organisations in Ireland: A Century of Progress*, Dublin: Four Courts Press, Ltd., p. 11.

[11] National Dairy Council (1982), *A History of the Irish Dairy Industry,* Dublin: National Dairy Council, p. 3.

[12] National Dairy Council (1982), op. cit., p. 9.

[13] James Clarence Mangan's translation from the Irish of "The Woman of Three Cows", in Diarmuid Russell (ed.) (1946), The *Portable Irish Reader,* New York: The Viking Press, p. 657.

[14] National Dairy Council (1982), op. cit., p. 12.

[15] National Dairy Council (1982), op. cit., p. 24.

[16] Irish Co-operative Organisation Society (1994), *Fruits of a Century*, Dublin: The Irish Co-operative Organisation Society, p. 8.

[17] Cormac Ó Gráda (1977), "The Beginnings of the Irish Creamery System, 1880-1914", *Economic History Review, Second series*, 30(2), p. 286.

[18] National Dairy Council (1982), op. cit., p. 9.

[19] Liam Kennedy (1983), "Aspects of the Spread of the Creamery System in Ireland", in Carla Keating (ed.) *Plunkett and Co-Operatives: Past, Present and Future*, Cork: Bank of Ireland Centre for Co-operative Studies and University College Cork, p. 97.

[20] Irish Co-operative Organisation Society (1994), *Fruits of a Century*, Dublin: Irish Co-operative Organisation Society, p. 9.

[21] Irish Co-operative Organisation Society (1994), op. cit., p. 13. The number of co-operative societies indicated reflects those societies that were affiliated with the IAOS (see note on the IAOS in the text).

[22] The IAOS was re-christened the Irish Co-operative Organisation Society (ICOS) in 1979. This organisation played a critical role in the development, and later the survival, of the Irish co-operative movement. It also was to play an important role in the formation and development of Kerry Co-operative Creameries Ltd., as detailed in Chapters 2–4 of this book.

[23] Bob Briscoe, Susan Grey, Paul Hunt, Mary Linehan, Hugh McBride, Vincent Tucker and Michael Ward (1982), *The Co-operative Idea*, Cork: Bank of Ireland Centre for Co-operative Studies and University College Cork, p. 14.

[24] Bob Briscoe, et al. (1982), pp. 40-44.

[25] Patrick Bolger (1983), "The Dreadful Years", in Carla Keating (ed.), *Plunkett and Co-Operatives: Past, Present and Future,* Cork: Bank of Ireland Centre for Co-operative Studies and University College Cork, p. 111.

[26] "Gombeen man" is the name for certain traders and merchants who had plagued the smaller market towns in Ireland for decades. These merchants charged high prices for their goods and usurious rates for their credit. Since these merchants typically had monopoly positions in their markets, their customers had little choice but to deal with them. Even when there was no monopoly, once in debt to such a merchant, customers were frequently "trapped", in that if they could not pay off the debt, they could not take their custom elsewhere.

[27] Patrick Bolger (1983), op. cit., p. 111.

[28] Co-operative creameries, of course, were of the utmost economic importance to the farmers of any area, and were in many cases their only lifeline to the monetary economy. Of equal importance, perhaps, was the apparent belief that they were also symbols of Irish nationalistic aspirations. As such, they were ideal targets.

[29] Irish Co-operative Organisation Society (1994), op. cit., pp. 58-60. This letter from Horace Plunkett was read by Father Finlay, Vice-President of the IAOS, to an IAOS Committee meeting in 1923.

[30] It was the first such semi-state body by only a matter of a few hours. The Electricity Supply Board (ESB) was created by legislation passed by the Dáil later that same day.

[31] John Hennigan (1965), "The Dairy Disposal Company Limited". As Chairman of the Dairy Disposal Board, Hennigan prepared this short summary of the history of the DDC in September 1965.

[32] National Dairy Council (1982), op. cit., p. 32.

[33] I am indebted to Jim Moloney, Director General of ICOS from 1983–1989, Jimmy O'Mahony, former Secretary for Agriculture and John (Jack) Hennigan,

former Chairman of the Dairy Disposal Company, for their recollections and insights concerning the formation and operation of the Dairy Disposal Company.

[34] John Hennigan (1965), op. cit.

[35] W.J. McCormack (ed.) (1999), op. cit., p. 130–131.

[36] Peter Newman (ed.) (1991), *Companion to Irish History: 1603-1921*, Oxford: Facts On File Ltd., p. 35.

[37] Cormac Ó Gráda (1997), op. cit., p. 145.

[38] R.E. Foster (1988), *Modern Ireland: 1600-1972*, London: The Penguin Press, p. 522.

[39] Cormac Ó Gráda (1997), op. cit., pp. 144–145.

[40] Cormac Ó Gráda (1997), op. cit., pp. 144–145.

[41] R.E. Foster (1988), op. cit., p. 523.

[42] Patricia Craig (ed.) (1998), *The Oxford Book of Ireland*, Oxford: Oxford University Press, p. 13.

[43] J.J. Lee (1999), "A Sense of Place in the Celtic Tiger?", in *Are We Forgetting Something: Our Society in the New Millennium*, Harry Bohan and Gerard Kennedy (eds.), Dublin: Veritas, pp. 72-73.

[44] James Joyce, "Gas from a Burner", in Harry Levin (ed.) (1947), *The Portable Joyce (revised edition)*, New York: The Viking Press, p. 660.

[45] Cormac Ó Gráda (1997), op. cit., p. 27.

[46] Of course, not all the credit should go to O'Reilly. The quality of Irish creamery butter was improving as well, largely as a reflection of improvements in the quality of raw milk being delivered to the creameries. Irish farmers had responded well to the government's Clean Milk Campaign, and to the incentives (bonus payments) offered for successfully passing the more stringent Methylene Blue tests on three out of four monthly surprise tests of their milk supply.

[47] Louis P.F. Smith and Sean Healy (1996), op. cit., p. 42.

[48] Louis P.F. Smith and Sean Healy (1996), op. cit., p. 45.

[49] Louis P.F. Smith and Sean Healy (1996), op. cit., p. 187.

Chapter 2

Kerry Clay and Rock:
Dairying in Kerry through the 1960s

Since every moment of the clock
Accumulates to form a final name,
Since I am come of Kerry clay and rock . . .
— Brendan Kennelly[1]

The Kingdom of Kerry: Location and Climate

Location, geography and climate profoundly influence the history
and experience of a people and a place, and the County of Kerry
in the south-west of Ireland is no exception. It is bounded to the
east and south by Counties Limerick and Cork, to the north by the
wide estuary of the Shannon River, and finally, to the west, by the
wild waves and pounding surf of the Atlantic Ocean. Perhaps this is
the genesis of the notion, peculiarly strong in people from Kerry,
that their "backs are always to the sea", figuratively as well as literally. In Kerry, there is a story attached to every place name.
Kerry itself, spelled *Ciarraí* in the Irish, derives from the Irish epics
and means "'the territory of the people of Ciar', the son of Fergus
Mac Roighe and Queen Maeve of Connacht."[2] It is considered a
relatively remote area; that is, it is far from the Pale of Dublin. In
the parlance of the bureaucrats in Brussels and Dublin, it is a "peripheral area"; to a cosmopolitan Dubliner Kerry might be "the
back of beyond". It is easy to see, and feel, why. One need only

stand on the rocky headland at Slea Head at the tip of the Dingle
peninsula, overlooking the dark, humpbacked shapes of the now-
deserted Blasket Islands, to realise that, as the locals are so fond of
relating, "the next parish is America". Yet it is, perhaps, a matter
of perspective. A visitor who spends a few days in Kerry mixing
with the locals may quickly be converted to the view that Kerry is,
in fact, the very centre of the universe. It is, after all, the only
county in Ireland with the temerity to call itself a Kingdom.[3] In fact,
to quote from a less than objective observer, Kerry writer John B.
Keane (simply John B. to most people in Kerry), "there are only
two Kingdoms, the Kingdom of God and the Kingdom of Kerry."[4]

Usually caressed but sometimes buffeted by the Atlantic winds,
watered by copious amounts of rain, but also warmed by the ocean
waters of the gulf stream, Kerry enjoys a pleasantly equable climate with few extremes. An area of nearly 1,200,000 acres, Kerry
is characterised by lowlands and gently rolling hills in the north
and by rugged, craggy hills and mountains in the south and west.[5]
Blessed with a long and wildly indented coastline, no place in
Kerry is very far from the sea or its influence. These attributes,
combined with the mountains of the Dingle and Iveragh peninsulas
that seem to fall off into the sea, provide some of the more stunning
scenery in the world and have provided at least a part of the
county with a busy and growing tourist trade in recent decades.
Another native Kerry writer and national school teacher, Gabriel
Fitzmaurice, has written of Kerry and its people:

> What sort of place is Kerry? Look to the landscape —
> ocean, river, lake, mountain, hill, bog, pasture and plain.
> Some believe that a landscape explains a people, defines
> them. I don't know. But I do know that landscape influ-
> ences people — who can not but be influenced by break-
> ers in a gale charging the cliffs in Clochar or Ballybunion;
> who can not but be pared down to bare essentials by the
> mountains of Corca Dhuibhne or Uíbh Ráthach; who can
> not but be awed by a stippled sunset over Cnoc an Fhóm-
> hair or a silver moon tinselling a bog in Sliabh Luachra or
> Oidhreacht Uí Chonchubhair?[6]

Overall, perhaps ten per cent of the land is good enough for tillage, with the remainder of more limited use in grazing. Much of

the southern part of the county is a boggy, craggy landscape that, while stunningly beautiful, is of far less utility than the lush grasslands of the midlands of Ireland or of the "golden vale" that cuts through Limerick, Tipperary and Cork. The growing season in Kerry is rather longer than in most of Ireland (although the grazing season is not), and late spring frosts are rare. With a combination of substantial rainfall and relatively marginal soil, the county in general is best suited for livestock farming and dairying. Mountain sheep are also raised in the west and south of the county. These natural constraints of the soil leave few other opportunities for economically viable agriculture.

In 1971, three-quarters of Kerry was considered rural.[7] Agriculture had always, until only quite recently, dominated the economy of the county. Even at the end of the 1960s, there was still only one sizeable town, Tralee, with a population of greater than 10,000. Tralee, the capital of the county, Killarney, Listowel, and other smaller "urban" centres had all developed to cater to the agricultural trade in farm inputs and in marketing farm produce.

Through the 1960s, mixed farming was the rule, and dairying was the predominant farm enterprise. Most holdings were small and often fragmented, with the average farm size totalling 38 acres and with two-thirds of the farms having less than 50 acres.[8] Consequently, farm incomes in much of the county were relatively low, even in the context of generally low farm incomes throughout Ireland. It would not be hyperbole to suggest that the economy of Kerry in the 1960s, which means of course the agricultural economy of Kerry, was crippled. Like a patient anaesthetised upon a table, the economy was in a coma, and the only questions were whether it would ever wake up and, if so, when?

Social and Economic Conditions in Kerry

Kerry's troubled agricultural economy gave rise to very high levels of emigration, far higher than most other parts of Ireland. In 1841, the population of the county was nearly 294,000, while by the end of the 1960s, the population had shrunk to about 113,000.[9] In the period 1961–1966, net emigration out of Kerry was twice as high as the national average. As a survey on agriculture in the county put it, rather dispassionately, in 1972:

> Chronic decline in total numbers, and a disproportionate
> decline in numbers in the different geographic regions,
> has been a feature of the history of our population[10] ... the
> county has experienced a protracted emigration of young
> people for many decades. This emigration has been
> greater in absolute terms than the natural increase of
> births over deaths. And so the total population of the
> county has declined.[11]

It was not the mere promise of adventure and excitement that
drove this exodus, but the desperation that poverty and an utter
lack of economic opportunity brought. This was fuelled by a sense
of hopelessness that conditions would change; indeed, to many
they appeared to be part of the permanent nature of things, no less
enduring than the glorious landscapes that surrounded them. This
Diaspora of Kerry people around the world had its roots in the sad
reality of economic conditions at home.

Opportunities for agricultural employment were declining
throughout the 1950s and 1960s. Although farm mechanisation and
modernisation in Kerry were taking place at a rate far slower than
elsewhere in Ireland and Western Europe, improved methods
were filtering in and farm employment was declining. Unfortunately, there was insufficient off-farm employment in Kerry to absorb the influx of workers leaving farm employment, and
emigration remained, as it had for decades, the sole path to economic opportunity for many young natives of the county. Although
there was some growth in non-farm employment opportunities in
the 1960s, as jobs opened up in manufacturing and, particularly for
women, in service industries, they were clearly insufficient to absorb the excess labour supply. Prospects for economic growth in
the county, and thus for additional off-farm employment, were
generally dismal even at the beginning of the 1970s. There was
hope that jobs could be secured, but there was no *plan* and probably no expectation that they would ever materialise.

To an economist, such labour mobility would, no doubt, be
commendable, demonstrating the operation of those inexorable
laws of supply and demand, and of a world where everything must
balance and markets must eventually find their equilibrium. For
the suppliers of this surplus labour, that market equilibrium would,

unfortunately, not be found in Kerry, but in Dublin, the UK, the United States, or further abroad. Such economic logic, however, does not take the edge off the human cost, and does not measure the psychological damage done to a region, a locality, or a community who have seen their sons and daughters fly away, in their turn, as they reached maturity. This sadness of emigration is captured poignantly in the local tradition of the holding of the "American wake", a party given emigrants the night before their departure for the new world, a farewell from friends and family and from the community of their birth. It was a "wake" because, as in a wake for the dead, the emigrants would rarely, and sometimes never, be seen again, as they set down roots across the ocean. A memoir by Mary Colum captures this feeling well:

> I remember still with emotion the emigration of the young people of the neighbourhood to America. In those days the farmer's children were raised for export. . . . The night before their departure there would be a farewell gathering called an American wake in one of the houses of the emigrating boys or girls. There would be singing and dancing interlarded with tears and lamentations until the early hours of the morning, when, without sleep, the young people started for the train, the mothers sometimes keening as at a funeral or a wake for the dead, for the parting would often be forever and the parents might never again see the boy or girl who was crossing the ocean.[12]

If seen again, it was often only in old age, when, returning as tourists to the places of their youth, the returned emigrants would wander, virtual strangers to the once familiar fields, searching for faces from their past.

It should again be emphasised how closely agriculture and the remainder of the county's economy were linked. Growth in farm productivity and in farm incomes might have fed increases in the many supporting industries, such as fertiliser and feed sales, transportation, equipment sales and maintenance, and the positive impacts on consumer spending. These, in turn, would have created increased employment opportunities. As the 1960s wore on, officials in the county looked at the "virtuous cycle" promised by improved farm productivity with hope and anticipation, as a way for the county to find its way out of the economic wilderness. Such growth, however, was proceeding far more slowly than was needed. With agriculture still accounting for almost half of the labour force, more than one-third of the income, and nearly all of the usable land, county officials conceded that "it is difficult to imagine Kerry without its farming industry".[13]

The demographic implications of this malaise were even more sobering. The majority of workers leaving farming, as well as most emigrants leaving the county, were young. With this exodus, the average age of Kerry farmers began to rise markedly. Between 1951 and 1966, "the proportion of the farm labour force of 45 years [of age] or more increased from 42 per cent to 57 per cent".[14]

For a county that was badly in need of modernisation of its farms and its agricultural practices, the ageing of its farm population suggested that there would be significant impediments to change. The county survey noted that:

> The ageing of farmers as a group has important implications for farm development. Elderly farmers are usually not change conscious. They are unable or unwilling to adopt new techniques, to engage the services of agricultural advisors or develop co-operative activities.
>
> The elderly farming community is not equipped, physically or otherwise, to introduce changes of the magnitude required to achieve this objective. As a result, only a minority of farmers can contribute to progressive farm improvement and, in turn, to general agricultural development.[15]

The fact that many of these older farmers (41 per cent of farmers over age 50, in fact[16]) appeared unlikely to leave heirs who would maintain the farm as an economic unit also clearly militated against any impetus for change and improvement. A high percentage of these farmers had never married, due (among other factors) to the high emigration rate among marriageable-age girls. The lack of heirs to whom they would pass along their farming enterprises not only raised serious questions about the viability of farming in Kerry into the future, but also cast considerable doubt upon the continued viability of rural communities in general.

A Kerry Dairy Farm Circa 1970

In 1970, there were approximately 10,200 milk suppliers in County Kerry. Certainly, for the typical Kerry farmer of the time, dairying took primacy of place as the most important farm activity and income producer. Over 90 per cent of all farmers in Kerry maintained a dairy herd.[17] Yet dairy farming in Kerry, even more than in other parts of Ireland, was characterised by extremely small herd sizes. In 1970, some 27 per cent of all farmers delivered an annual milk production of less than 2,000 gallons, the output of approximately four cows, while 28 per cent had slightly larger herds of five to ten cows. When it is considered that a herd size of at least 14 cows at the time (approximately 7,000 gallons) was considered necessary to maintain an economically viable farm enterprise, the problem is clear. To gain or maintain an adequate farm income, either off-farm income was necessary, or herd sizes would have to be expanded. If herd sizes were to grow, more land would have to be put into production, or existing land would have to be used far more efficiently. As already noted, however, Kerry farms were generally not large enough in size to achieve these economies, and often fragmented, in the sense that the fields and pastures would not be contiguous and farmers would have to travel some distance between their various holdings.

Although mechanisation was creeping into farming in Kerry, by and large the tenor of farming life remained relatively unchanged from what it had been for decades. Except on the larger farms, hand milking was still predominant and bucket plants (use of a vacuum pump for milking into a bucket — a "semi-automatic", still labour-intensive operation) represented the extent of any automation. Rotary milking parlours were scarcely imaginable. Even on farms where mechanical milking systems had been installed, service and maintenance of the equipment was often an issue, and a proper appreciation of cleaning and hygiene was not well developed. For that matter, refrigeration on farms was nearly nonexistent, and refrigerated bulk tanks for chilling and holding milk were unheard of. Lack of chilling capability had serious impacts on the quality of milk coming off the farm. To maintain its freshness, and to avoid souring, it was necessary for milk to be cooled, and stored at a low temperature. Some farmers with a good water supply were able to cool their milk somewhat, but a substantial number of Kerry farmers were not. Lacking such facilities, milk had to be transported to the creamery or collection station as soon as possible. This was easier said then done, for transportation and distribution in the farming sector in Kerry were still primitive, by any standard. As farmers queued outside the creamery, waiting their turn to unload their milk churns, the milk, which may have been sitting since the previous evening and now sat in the metal churns baking in the sun, could well be "turning".

Given this, the quality of some of the milk entering the creamery was often suspect, certainly from the perspective of present-day standards. Stories are readily told of the day, typically once a month, when the creamery manager would announce that there would be testing that day of the milk being delivered to the creamery. Knowing this was the day for "the dirty man" (actually, the Inspector from the Department of Agriculture's Dairy Division), some numbers of the waiting farmers would simply pull their carts out of the queue and go home. They well knew the quality of their milk. Adding water to increase volume was not unheard of. The addition of lime to reduce the acidity of the milk was also among the many tricks of the trade not uncommon in the cat and mouse game between farmers and creamery.[18]

That there were quality issues with the milk ought not to be surprising, for Kerry reflected a farming economy that was only now emerging from the era of the horse and the plough. Only in the 1960s was it becoming uncommon to see horses rather than tractors on the farm. The advent of the tractor notwithstanding, the majority of farmers still brought their milk to the creamery or the collection station in pony (or donkey) and carts. The slow, rhythmic "clip clop" of hooves on the roadway, the clanking of the milk churns rattling in the cart, the steady regularity of the comings and goings, had all given rise to a "timeless", almost surreal quality. It was a reality that provided an image much beloved by Bord Fáilte[19] and those involved in the tourist trade. But this method of delivering milk to the creamery, while quaint and symbolic of the slow-paced image of the "Ireland of the Welcomes" depicted in the tourist materials did little to enhance the economic viability of dairy farming. One could attach some (not inconsiderable) social value to the interactions that this daily jaunt to the creamery engendered. Farmers met, exchanged news and gossip, talked a little treason, plotted and schemed and laughed and generally fought off the loneliness and isolation which can characterise farm existence. For his part, the postman could save long journeys to remote farmsteads by delivering his mail, at the creamery queue, to the assembled farmers.[20] However, it was a relic of a bygone era, an image, frozen in time, poised on the precipice of change. Observing such a scene, the sociologist might praise the creation of so much "social capital" (an academic term denoting the benefits of relationships, trust, familiarity, etc. in community life). The economist, however, might only shake his head at such a breach of the economic laws of supply and demand, efficiency and productivity.

The old farming tradition of "saving the hay" was still alive and well in Kerry at the time. Although silage making began to replace hay making during the 1960s, Kerry farmers only adopted such change slowly and, in many cases, reluctantly. Even by 1970 only 1,000 farmers in the county made silage. Fermented, stored and preserved, silage could provide superior fodder for dairy herds and substantial economic advantages to dairy farmers. Widespread adoption, however, crept along at only a snail's pace.

Dairying in Kerry, and in most of Ireland, was for the most part a seasonal operation. Cows would be put out on grass anywhere from March through the beginning of May, and kept out until October. Yet, even grassland was merely utilised "as given", a gift of Divine Providence rather than an agricultural resource to be managed. A grassland expert from New Zealand, George Holmes, visiting Ireland in 1949 to assess the grass situation, reported that "there is no area of comparable size in the Northern Hemisphere which has such marvellous potentialities for pasture production as Eire undoubtedly has". However, he was amazed that he saw "hundreds of fields which are growing just as little as it is physically possible to grow under an Irish sky".[21] Henry Kennedy, the Chief Executive of the IAOS at the time, was fond of saying that the Irish cows lived, during the winter months, on the most costly food imaginable — beef steak (that is, they were half-starved). They then came into production in the spring in the most haggard state.[22] Peak milk production took place during the period May–August, with very little milk intake at all from November through February. This made for a very uneven flow of income. Farmers often took out short-term loans through the Agricultural Credit Corporation (ACC), co-operative creameries or other sources during the winter and spring, and paid them back during the more lucrative summer months. Of course, Kerry was no different from the rest of Ireland in this regard; milk production was characteristically seasonal nation-wide. One impact of this seasonality was to magnify the importance of having capability to process surplus seasonal milk supplies. The Irish dairy industry was heavily reliant on commodity products like butter, but having the processing capability to manufacture whole or skim milk powder, evaporated milk and other products was critical in making the most economical use of excess milk. In County Kerry, only the Fry-Cadbury plant in Rathmore had the ability to process surplus milk. This lack of processing capability prevented any product diversification for Kerry farmers, who remained almost wholly reliant on the production of butter by their creameries.

Friesian and Hereford cows were gaining predominance in the county, replacing the traditional Kerry and Shorthorn breeds, as farmers tried to improve their milk yields. The Dairy Disposal Company was responsible for most of the breeding and upgrading of stock in the county at the artificial insemination (AI) station it maintained in Castleisland. Still, yields in the county were quite low, averaging less than 500 gallons per year per animal (in 1970). This was less than the average for Ireland, well below European averages, and perhaps even less than half the yields experienced by "best practice" dairy farmers in Denmark and Holland.

One of the primary irritants on the typical Kerry dairy farm of the time was what to do about skim milk. When farmers brought their milk to the creamery, it was first separated into fat (cream) and skim components. The cream was brought into the creamery and churned into butter. As there were no facilities to process the skim milk into useful products, the creameries returned the skim milk to the farmers, who would bring it home with them to feed the few pigs most farmers kept, and to feed to calves. Skim milk is a superior form of protein and an excellent feed for pigs and other livestock. There was, however, far more skim returned to the farms than the farmers could ever use. As often as not, it was poured into ditches, into bogs, along roadsides, or down drains. As the nature of pig farming changed, and large operations that fed hundreds or thousands of pigs at a time became the rule, it was no longer economic to keep a few pigs on the farm, so the problem became even more acute. Skim was treated as pure waste, even though it was, or could be, a useful product if processed.

The Fry-Cadbury processing plant, located in Rathmore in the southern part of the county, used whole milk in the production of chocolate crumb for its parent firm. Of course, by using (and paying for) both the cream and the skim components of the whole milk it purchased, it was able to relieve, to some extent, the surplus supply of skim milk. The problem, however, was that it utilised only a relatively limited amount of the milk available in the county. Two widely variant explanations have been put forward for this. One is that Fry-Cadbury took the milk at their convenience and "as needed", taking advantage of what for them must have been an ideal situation: little or no competition for a huge surplus of its essential raw material input — whole milk. For Kerry farmers, such a situation would have been maddening: one monopsonistic purchaser (only one buyer) for a by-product (skim milk) that they could usually not even give away. This was a far from ideal market. However, a second explanation places more of the onus upon Kerry farmers. This explanation suggests that the *quality* of Kerry milk on offer was simply inadequate, and often did not meet Cadbury's minimum requirements for raw materials used in a good quality chocolate crumb product. Thus, Fry-Cadbury was compelled to source its raw material not only from Kerry, but from the bordering counties of Cork and Limerick as well.[23]

Which of these explanations contains the most truth, however, may be of little importance. The bottom line for Kerry farmers was that their skim milk had value, and farmers in other parts of the country that were blessed with processing plants were able to reap the benefits of it. Why, then, not Kerry?

The Structure of the Dairy Industry in the County

One is immediately struck by the bifurcation of dairy interests in the county between the northern and southern (including West Kerry) regions. Farms in the northern part of the county — an area stretching from the lowlands along the Limerick/Cork border to the north-east, to Kerry Head on the Atlantic Ocean to the lowlands just south of Tralee but north of Killarney — tended to have better

land and larger farms; in fact, in some areas such as Abbeydorney
and Ardfert there was a tradition of tillage and a history of excellence, continuing even today, in ploughing competitions throughout Ireland. The area was generally more compact and farms were
reasonably close to their branch creameries or assembly points.
Climate-wise, some parts of the broad plain and gentle hills of
North Kerry were relatively dry (by Irish standards!).

The southern part of the county presented a different picture. It
was far more mountainous, the quality of the land was poor and, in
parts, the climate was perhaps the wettest in Ireland. Farms were
of smaller size, and were well dispersed over a wide geographical
area. There was virtually no tillage and, in many mountainous areas, the land was unsuitable for anything but the rearing of sheep.
The costs of milk collection from remote locations in West Kerry
like Dingle or Cahirciveen were considerable, and the dairy enterprises in such areas were scarcely viable in the best of times. It
was not unusual to have the two-cow farmer, living out in the back
of beyond, bringing his few gallons of milk to the branch creamery
every day in a churn carried by a donkey and cart. It was a sobering thought to reflect that these few shillings from the milk cheque
were his sole monetary income and his sole participation in the
monetary economy of his society. No matter how inefficient he
may have been, dairying was his only option.

These physical and economic differences were reflected in a
profoundly different structure within the dairy industry in Kerry.
There existed a total of eight co-operative creameries in Kerry, all
of them in the northern part of the county. Abbeydorney, Ballinclemessig, Brosna, Fealesbridge, Newtownsandes, Lee Strand (a
supplier of liquid milk to consumers in Tralee and much of the
county), Lixnaw and Rattoo were all North Kerry co-operatives.
Often grouped with these co-operatives, since they shared the
same milk "catchment area", were two others in Limerick (but on
the Kerry border), those at Mountcollins and Athea. Many of these
co-operatives had been formed at the end of the nineteenth century during the first flush of the co-operative movement when people like Plunkett, R.A. Anderson, and George Russell had spent
time proselytising for co-operative principles and organisation in
the wilds of Kerry, with mixed success.

But where North Kerry farmers had been receptive, farmers in the south had been far less impressed and remained sceptical of co-operatives. The few co-operatives that did form in the west and south of the county were not able to weather the hard times of the 1920s and 1930s and had failed, their assets (and responsibilities to their farmer-shareholders) taken over by the Dairy Disposal Company. Even after 30–40 years, the failure of these co-ops still rankled many who blamed it on poor management and a cynical "beggar thy neighbour" application of co-operative principles. They complained that in these co-operatives, where every share-holder was supposed to be equal, some appeared to have been more equal than others, and benefited far more than others from these enterprises. It is difficult to determine the truth of this con-tention, for even with the best of managers, it would have been very difficult to have maintained a viable, independent enterprise in peripheral areas such as Dingle, Cahirciveen, or Kenmare. Still, whether this cause of failure was real or imagined, many in the west and south of the county looked sceptically on co-operative structures in the light of these failed co-operative experiences.

The Dairy Disposal Company in Kerry

It was not only co-operatives that had failed in the south, but pri-vately owned creameries as well. Before the "Troubles" and inde-pendence, private creameries had dominated the south. With the advent of the Free State, the desire of private creamery owners to exit the business, and the clear need for economic rationalisation, the Dairy Disposal Company (DDC) entered the scene. Notwith-standing the co-operative societies operating in North Kerry, the DDC dominated dairy activities in Kerry. In 1970, the DDC cream-eries accounted for some 74 per cent of the nearly 61 million gal-lons of manufactured milk in the county.[24] The DDC operated eight central creameries in the county, in Ardfert, Castlemaine, Cahir-civeen, Dicksgrove, Dingle, Kenmare, Listowel and Rathmore. Of these, only Listowel and Ardfert could be considered as part of North Kerry.

It should be said at the outset that the DDC had a virtually thankless job. The name of the enterprise itself might give some indication of that, since its ostensible mission was the "disposal" of creameries by selling them to existing or new co-operative enterprises. Of course, the fundamental assumption underlying this logic was that the farmers themselves, the owners of these co-operatives (or potential co-operatives) *wished* to own the assets and run the business. Yet, farmers are not fools, and ownership for its own sake was not sufficiently enticing in cases where the creameries appeared to have no hope of being economically viable. Such was the case throughout Kerry, and the private creameries taken over in the 1920s and 1930s by the DDC remained in the hands of the state. Of course, the word "disposal" could also relate to the "disposal" of the milk that was processed. Unfortunately, "disposal" was precisely the right term. This was long before the time of "market-led" strategies in the dairy industry, before the needs of consumers were studied, understood, and catered to. At this point in time, the milk was brought to the creameries, it was processed into butter, and the butter was passed on to some other entity in the chain to "dispose" of as best they could. Marketing, such as it was, was somebody else's problem . . . not the farmer's and not the creamery manager's. Given this, the typical creamery reflected only the stump of a real business.

Of course, what mattered to farmers fundamentally, and often to the exclusion of almost everything else, was the price they were paid for their milk. The milk prices paid by the DDC in Kerry were lower than those paid by the neighbouring co-ops in Cork and Limerick, as well as those in North Kerry. The DDC creameries in Cahirciveen and Kenmare, for instance, were often held up to criticism on account of their proverbially low milk prices. They were also criticised because each of the DDC creameries in Kerry paid a different price for their milk, based on the cost structure of the individual creamery, and especially the cost of milk assembly. Milk assembly costs were of particular relevance in the more remote western and southwestern parts of the county, where transportation costs into the central creamery could be considerable. There is a famous story told of a DDC creamery manager in Kerry who was ordered by the head office in Dublin to represent the Dairy Disposal Company at a meeting of the County Kerry Committee of Agriculture. The meeting had been called to investigate the price differential between what the co-operatives were paying farmers for their milk, and what the DDC were paying. The creamery manager was a rather shy man, given more to plain speaking than extended eloquence, and he was not looking forward to having to deal with questions from the local politicians. He went into the meeting and, posed with the query as to how this price difference with the co-operatives came about, went up to the rostrum and gave this brief answer:

> First, you've got to go back a little into history, back to the time of Horace Plunkett, the father of the co-operative movement. He put all of his co-operative creameries in the best land and said "to hell with Dingle and Cahirciveen!"

With that, the creamery manager walked out of the council chambers, his explanation complete. The point, of course, was that the DDC was burdened with collecting milk from remote places that were simply uneconomic. Although they had no choice but to service these locations, the cost of collecting milk in those remote locations was high, and thus the payment to the farmers in those locations would, of necessity, be low.

Certainly the low milk prices made the DDC fair game for criticism, and its status as a semi-state body (that is, a self-funding organisation, but controlled by government bureaucrats) served to make it an even more attractive lightening rod for a range of farmer frustrations. One issue was that of control. Farmers in South Kerry, by the mid- to late 1960s, grew increasingly vocal about what they perceived as their lack of control, or even any appreciable influence, upon the creameries that served them. There was a structure of advisory committees in each of the eight DDC areas in Kerry, intended to provide consultation and participation for the farmers, but they were seen to be powerless. Joe Rea, a correspondent for *The Irish Farmer's Journal* (as well as a former national President of Macra na Feirme and a future President of the IFA), was a frequent and strident critic of the DDC. He once wrote that:

> The D.D. acts in the manner of a "Colonial Power", with little regard for the feelings and welfare of the "natives", which in this instance happens to be dairy farmers.[25]

Yet this issue of control is a murky one, for in years past there had been little if any interest in a farmers' take-over of these creameries. But the 1960s brought with them a hint of freedom, and change, or at least the prospects for change, was in the air. Many farmers, however, felt that the DDC, while paying lip service to its pronounced intention to return all its creameries and other interests to farmer (co-operative) control, had scant interest in changing the *status quo*.

One consequence of the DDC's semi-state status was its exposure to political influence. Critics complained that jobs with the DDC creameries were more often awarded to those who were "politically right" than to those who were best equipped for the job at hand. Stories are rife in Kerry, even today, about DDC "fitters" or "mechanics" who would show up at the local creamery to fix a leaky valve or replace a switch, knowing no more about the job than anyone who might have walked in off the street.

Critics of the DDC pointed to its political orientation, its tendency to be autocratic in its decision-making, and the low milk prices that it paid as evidence that it was poorly run and inefficient. It is not within the brief of this short history, however, to pronounce upon this. If so, there may have been other contributing factors as well. First, the DDC was expected to finance its own activities. It had been granted capital upon its formation, but had received relatively little additional funding from the government exchequer. It was expected to support itself. There was not a great deal of funding available for modernisation, and expansion (in order to develop better scale and scope economies) was generally out of the question, as it ran counter to the very mission of the enterprise, which was to pass the business back to the farmers! Nevertheless, as already noted, and with its limited resources, the DDC was involved in the expansion of the industry to many remote areas. Furthermore, its central and branch creamery system had been reasonably well organised and structured.

But by the end of the 1960s, the DDC had, most unexpectedly, survived for over 40 years and memory may have blurred. Any organisation, over time, begins to develop an instinct for ensuring its own survival, and one may certainly have a vested interest in maintaining an organisation that has served as one's home for so long. It is possible that the DDC's commitment to passing enterprises back to farmers, to "dispose" of them in a way that was originally intended, may have waned. It remained for a new administration, a Fine Gael government, to redirect the DDC's efforts towards exiting the dairy business. A further and, perhaps, more effective inducement was the prospect of Ireland soon entering the EEC, which would insist upon the dismantling of such semi-state bodies as a condition of entry. With an eye to the EEC, it became clear in the late 1960s that the tenure of the DDC was soon to end.

Taking pot shots at the DDC is easy, even with the benefit of hindsight. A large, slow-moving bureaucratic organisation that was entwined with the lives of a majority of people in the county makes an irresistible target. Although it is easy to repeat the many criticisms of the DDC activities in Kerry, it is equally important to acknowledge the critical role it played in the very survival of the dairy industry in a large part of the county. The DDC stepped in to take over uneconomic creameries in remote and economically disadvantaged areas; enterprises that no one else wanted. It ensured the survival of these creameries through economic times that were, for the most part, bad. They may not have paid top price for their milk, but they at least paid a price! Its managers may have been criticised for inefficiencies, but they were compelled to do economic battle with both hands tied behind their backs. It was their duty to service farmers from the Dingle and Iveragh peninsulas and other uneconomic areas, as well as the more viable areas, and to do so with staff who were often appointed on the basis of political, rather than technical, competence.

Another contribution of the DDC was its establishment of procedures and methods, its development of an organisation that, while slow-moving and bureaucratic, was at least well-defined and well-organised. There was a structure in place, run by a cadre of managers who were experienced (and almost all trained in Dairy Science at University College Cork, the only such programme in Ireland) and highly competent at what they did. For all the criticism of their performance, and for all the abuse that they took, the farmers of the county may well, after all, owe the DDC a debt of gratitude. Even though it would be Kerry hyperbole to suggest that the DDC was a "heroic" organisation, it is clear that they at least held together dairy farming in Kerry until such time as farmers were ready, willing and able to take back their businesses. Sometimes the greatest success is measured in just keeping things together.

Neighbouring Dairy Co-operatives and the Vision of the IAOS

The situation in Kerry towards the end of the 1960s was also affected by two other important factors. First, the presence of three of the "big five" of Irish dairy co-operatives on the borders of Kerry; and second, the impact of a report issued by the IAOS on the rationalisation of the dairy industry throughout Ireland. Clearly, rationalisation was required, particularly in view of Ireland's imminent accession to the EEC. The IAOS was asked by the government to take the lead in developing such a plan for the rationalisation of the industry.

On the southern border of Kerry were two relatively large and prosperous dairy co-operatives, Ballyclough Co-operative Creamery, and Mitchelstown Co-operative Agricultural Society. Both societies had weathered the economic troubles of the decades before, had shown foresight and courage in purchasing creameries from the DDC back in the 1920s and 1930s, and were now in the process of going further down the road of amalgamation. Their milk prices were consistently higher than the DDC prices available to their neighbours just across the border in Kerry, and farmers in several DDC creamery areas in Kerry had a strong interest in amalgamating with these apparently successful co-operatives. A third major co-operative, Golden Vale, a federation of co-operatives based in Charleville, County Cork and operating in counties Cork, Limerick and Clare in the heart of the prime dairy land of "The Golden Vale", was also by the late 1960s beginning to establish itself as a growth-oriented, forward-looking dairy co-operative and producer of branded dairy products. They had built, in 1967, a new milk processing facility at Charleville. It is not irrelevant that the manager responsible for the construction, start-up and initial operation of the factory was a young Kerryman just out of university, one Denis Brosnan. Brosnan also helped to pioneer Golden Vale's initial foray into animal feeds with the development of an immensely popular calf milk replacer called *Maverick*. Golden Vale provided another point of comparison for Kerry farmers, especially those co-operatives in North Kerry who were clustered around the Kerry-Limerick border.

The IAOS issued its report on a re-organisation of the dairy industry in February 1966, proposing the amalgamation of smaller co-operatives and DDC creameries around the country into 19 larger creamery groups. In this report, Kerry was split into two groups, with the co-operatives in the north, along with Listowel, constituting one group, and the DDC creameries of the south and west another. It seemed any amalgamation of creameries in the county, north and south, into one countywide unit, was so far-fetched that it did not even merit discussion. As the 1960s gave way to the 70s, it was clear that a number of societies in South Kerry had serious interest in amalgamating with either Golden Vale or Ballyclough. To some farmers in Kerry, it seemed that the county was about to be carved up and parcelled out to the neigh-bouring co-ops. It is interesting to note that the IAOS, in their report, stated that plans for a milk processing factory for North Kerry were quite advanced, giving the impression that a factory was imminent. In this, at least, they could not have been more wrong.

Table 1: Co-operative Dairy Statistics 1968 — Milk Supply (million gallons)

Ballyclough (Cork)	23.2	Lough Egish (Monaghan)	9.9
Mitchelstown (Cork)	20.8	Nenagh (Tipperary)	9.7
Killeshandra (Cavan)	14.8	Castlelyons (Cork)	9.3
Drinagh (Cork)	11.0	Thurles (Tipperary)	8.7
Kilnaleck (Cavan)	10.2	Kiltoghert (Leitrim)	8.3
Kerry-based Co-operatives			
Lee Strand	3.1	Rattoo	1.5
Lixnaw	2.4	Brosna	0.8
Abbeydorney	2.1	Ballinclemessig	0.8
Newtownsandes	1.8		

The Importance of a "Milk Processing" Facility

Those unfamiliar with the dairy industry or dairy farming may fail to properly appreciate the importance a milk processing factory had for milk producers. Without a factory capable of processing their milk, farmers had to forego realising the maximum value for it. With no factory at hand, farmers continued to bring their milk to the local creamery. The milk was separated (using a centrifugal separating machine) into the cream (the fat content of the milk which was then churned into butter) and skim (which was returned to them to be used to feed pigs or calves or, just as likely, to be dumped). It was a lamentable waste of a product, skim milk, which was in fact a valuable commodity *if* it could only be processed. Already, in other parts of Ireland, processing plants were manufacturing skim milk powder, casein (a powdered milk protein), and chocolate crumb (both liquid and solid) from skim milk, and condensed milk and butter oil (from whole milk).

Processing the milk (the milk presented to the creameries was called "manufacturing milk" as distinct from the "liquid milk" that is pasteurised, bottled and sold to consumers) thus presented clear benefits. First, it maximised the farmers' return for their milk, since it could now yield its full value. Additionally, it helped to diversify somewhat the dependence of farmers and their enterprises (the co-ops and the DDC) away from complete reliance upon their predominant product, butter. More importantly in the long term, it began to take farmers along the road to more value-added products, with the application of technology to the basic commodities supplied yielding products that were further along the value chain, and had longer shelf lives.

The issue in Kerry was that there was no farmer-controlled processing facility. Strictly speaking, of course, a processing factory did exist, the chocolate crumb factory owned by Fry-Cadbury (Ireland) in Rathmore. Fry-Cadbury had opened the plant on 1st March 1948 to produce chocolate crumb for its confectionery business, and it had made a major contribution to the local economy ever since.[26] As noted earlier in the chapter, however, the Fry-Cadbury plant utilised only a relatively small amount of the milk available in the county. It also appeared unlikely to expand its milk processing activities in the county to an extent that would provide a noticeable benefit to Kerry farmers.

A milk processing facility in Kerry promised at least the beginning of a way out of the economic morass in which Kerry farmers were mired. It could provide an outlet for their milk, and for their hoped-for increases in milk production, and begin to diversify them out of their complete reliance on butter. Butter, produced primarily for export, was a commodity on world exchanges and suffered from static demand. At the time, in fact, it was being sorely pressed by the challenge from "artificial butter" or margarine, which was having a noticeable impact on butter markets.

Notes

[1] Brendan Kennelly (1972), from "My Dark Fathers" in *Selected Poems*, New York: E.P. Dutton & Co, p. 16.

[2] Gabriel Fitzmaurice (1993), Introduction to *Kerry Through Its Writers*, Gabriel Fitzmaurice (ed.), Dublin: New Island Books, p. 7.

[3] John B. Keane has recounted that in a 1793 address to the Irish Parliament, "John Philpot Curran, commented adversely that the magistracy of the county of Kerry were so opposed to the laws of the land that they were a law unto themselves, a Kingdom apart. The name stuck . . ." (John B. Keane (1993), "The Kingdom of God and The Kingdom of Kerry", in Gabriel Fitzmaurice (ed.) (1993), op. cit., p. 13). Richard Hayward wrote that the term dated from the time "a well-fed and well-wined gentleman of Tralee made a post-prandial speech in that sweet town in the year 1787 . . ." (Richard Hayward (1976), *In the Kingdom of Kerry*, Dundalk: W. Tempest Dundalgan Press, p. 1). There are other explanations, but in any case, Kerry has been long known as "the Kingdom County".

[4] John B. Keane (1993), "The Kingdom of God and the Kingdom of Kerry", in Gabriel Fitzmaurice (ed.) (1993), op. cit., p. 1.

[5] Kerry County Committee of Agriculture (1972), *County Kerry Agricultural Resource Survey*, Tralee, Ireland: County Kerry Committee of Agriculture, p. 1.

[6] Gabriel Fitzmaurice (1993), op. cit., p. 7.

[7] Kerry County Committee of Agriculture (1972), op. cit., p. 11.

[8] Kerry County Committee of Agriculture (1972), op. cit., p. 53.

[9] Kerry County Committee of Agriculture (1972), op. cit., p. 8.

[10] Kerry County Committee of Agriculture (1972), op. cit., p. 1.

[11] Kerry County Committee of Agriculture (1972), op. cit., p. 7.

[12] Mary Colum (1928), "Life and the Dream", in Patricia Craig (ed.) (1998), *The Oxford Book of Ireland*, Oxford: Oxford University Press, p. 351.

[13] Kerry County Committee of Agriculture (1972), op. cit., p. 2.

[14] Kerry County Committee of Agriculture (1972), op. cit., p. 63.

[15] Kerry County Committee of Agriculture (1972), op. cit., p. 71.

[16] Kerry County Committee of Agriculture (1972), op. cit., p. 67.

[17] Kerry County Committee of Agriculture (1972), op. cit., p. 164.

[18] Such "carry on", of course, could also occur between creameries and processors like Fry-Cadbury.

[19] Literally, the "Board of Welcomes" or, in the more common but less descriptive English translation, the Irish Tourist Board.

[20] I thank Ned O'Callaghan, who in his early career worked in a bank branch beside a creamery, for this recollection.

[21] G.A. Holmes (1949), *Report on the Present State and Methods for Improvement of Irish Land*, Dublin. This citation was taken from Smith and Healy (1996), *Farm Organisations in Ireland*, Dublin: Four Courts Press, p. 37.

[22] James (Jim) Moloney, personal interview, 8 July 1999.

[23] Bill Sweeney, who began his working career with Fry-Cadbury when the plant first opened in 1948, is a proponent of the later explanation. He notes that Fry-Cadbury paid the "national price" for whole milk to those creameries who agreed to supply a set quota of quality milk during the annual manufacturing period of March through October. Kerry, however, was unable to meet this requirement for quality milk. In point of fact, notes Sweeney, milk supplies came from Kerry (Newtownsandes, Listowel, Fealesbridge, Rattoo, Lixnaw, Abbeydorney, Cahirciveen, Dicksgrove and Rathmore), Cork (Coachford, Terelton, Killunney, Clondrohid, Kilcorney, Dromtariffe, Newmarket, Allensbridge and Boherbue) and Limerick (Bruree, Kilmallock, Effin, Tournafulla, Athea and Mountcollins).

[24] Kerry County Committee of Agriculture (1972), op. cit., p. 160.

[25] Joe Rea (1971), "D.D. Prepares for Europe! — You Must be Joking", *Irish Farmers' Journal*, 3 April 1971, p. 4.

[26] It was Dick Godsil, the creamery manager at the DDC's Rathmore creamery and a native of nearby Cork, who orchestrated the presentation to Fry-Cadbury for locating the processing plant in Rathmore. Listowel was another potential site that Fry-Cadbury had considered, but for various reasons (including the possibility that some important people did not, at the time, apparently want the plant) they were unimpressed. Godsil, on the other hand, pulled out all the stops with his presentation. He had his branch managers dress up in suits and ties after lunch, his office workers clear off the tops of their desks, and other office workers walk around in white lab coats to achieve the desired effect. Rathmore's location at a transportation crossroads also helped his case. Godsil's salesmanship was very effective, and the factory opened in Rathmore.

Chapter 3

The Foundation of Kerry

I have fought the good fight,
I have finished the race,
I have kept the faith.
2 Timothy, 4:7
— Inscription on Eddie Hayes' Mortuary Card

Eddie Hayes' Dream

Despite the continuing host of studies that have tried to identify the "essence" or the "quality" of leadership, it remains a highly elusive concept. Like many other words that are poorly understood, it is also commonly overused. Nevertheless, we can be certain of one element of leadership, that so often in the course of history events are changed by the actions of one person, one leader. Not all these actions need qualify as "heroic". Often, leadership is best expressed as the manifestation of a vision, the practical application of actions to achieve that vision and, most importantly perhaps, the dogged determination and perseverance that allows one to surmount the greatest impediments until, at last, the goal is reached. Another definition suggests that the true measure of any leader may be taken by simply imagining how the course of events may have been different in his or her absence. By that measurement, the shadow of Edmund (Eddie) Hayes would loom large indeed. It is difficult to imagine the creation and development of North Kerry

Milk Products, the forerunner to the Kerry Co-operative, without
his utterly unwavering leadership.

Eddie Hayes was what might have been called in times past a
"strong farmer". Born in October 1917, he was a native of Kilflynn,
a small village in North Kerry not far from Tralee, and educated in
the national school there. Hayes came from a strong co-operative
background. He was the chairman of the local co-operative at Abbeydorney and, from all accounts, was a hands-on chairman who
kept a close rein on the finances and ran a tight ship when this may
not have always been the norm at co-operatives. His father, John
Hayes, had been in the chairman's seat before him, and co-
operation ran in the family. His brother Sean was the chairman of the
co-operative in nearby Lixnaw. The Abbeydorney Co-operative itself was founded in 1895, the first co-operative in Kerry, and had a
reputation for being among the more active and progressive societies. The first Co-operative Agricultural School (commonly called a
"winter farm school") in Ireland, in fact, was established in Abbeydorney in 1965.[1] This farm school was fortunate to have another remarkable Kerryman associated with it, Tim (Tiger) Lyons,
a well-known Kerry footballer and Agricultural Advisor for that
part of the county, who served as the "Schoolmaster".

Eddie Hayes had competed as a hurler for Crotta (a townland
between Lixnaw and Abbeydorney) in his youth, and continued to
compete in and judge ploughing competitions (another local specialty) throughout his life. His pride in Kerry was fierce, and palpable. Like many another Kerryman, he had a burning, intense
pride in his townland, his parish, and his county. But importantly,
his passion was of a remarkably unsentimental sort. His hopes for
his county were absolutely practical, tangible, and in his view at
least, achievable. This, to him, was no cloud-cuckoo land fit only
for itinerant poets, blind harpists and other romantic figures van-
ishing in and out of a Celtic mist. His was a hard-headed idealism
combined with a bias towards action. He was the sort of man to
whom it was always better to light a candle than to curse the darkness. In the Kerry of his time, however, it can be argued that there
was far too much useless cursing of the darkness, and far too little
unity and dedication towards doing anything about it.

Hayes was deeply involved in politics for a good part of his life.
A lifelong member of the Fine Gael party, he served on Kerry

County Council for many years where he also chaired the county's Committee of Agriculture. He also served for many years on the national board of the IAOS. He stood for Dáil Éireann (the Irish Parliament) in North Kerry in 1965 as a Fine Gael candidate, but faced a formidable field and was not elected. John B. Keane, the Kerry writer, remembers that:

> I canvassed with Eddie Hayes, since he was a good friend of mine. He ran a tremendous campaign, and did better than expected, but didn't get elected. He had tremendous energy; he nearly killed me in the campaign.[2]

Hayes also stood for the Seanad (the Irish Senate) the same year, put forward as a candidate by the IAOS for a seat representing agricultural interests, but missed that honour by the narrowest of margins. He was disappointed at this rejection, but it could not have been too surprising, for he had never cultivated a sense of political guile. Diplomacy, in that sense, was alien to him. What he said today, he said tomorrow. He had strong opinions, which he presented forcefully. It was impossible for him to play the political games that all too often seem to be required for political success, or even survival. Still, Hayes' disappointments in politics may have had very welcome effects for Kerry farmers, in that he was able to turn his attention even more fully towards securing a milk processing factory for North Kerry.

Somewhere towards the late 1960s, perhaps not long after he returned from the farmers' march on Dublin in 1966, Hayes became convinced that a milk processing factory was absolutely essential if Kerry farmers were going to have any control over their economic futures. As it was, they had no assured market for their milk. They'd sell some to Fry-Cadbury, some to other neighbouring co-operatives, and most of it was used in the manufacture of butter, for which there was no great, or growing, market at the time. It was an unsettled, uncertain, and economically unrewarding life. A processing factory was the only answer, and Eddie Hayes determined that it was his mission in life to secure such a factory for Kerry. It was a mission from which he never wavered.

At times, it may have seemed to others that he was tilting at windmills. The prevailing wisdom was, to put it mildly, against

him. Farming organisations such as the IAOS generally did not believe that Kerry could sustain their own processing facility, and
instead favoured a plan whereby Kerry farmers would go to
Golden Vale or Ballyclough. The IDA (Industrial Development
Authority) would not back any venture that did not have a ready,
and guaranteed, market for its products. Bord Bainne was not supportive, in that they said they could not sell any more powdered
milk or cheese and were hard pressed to sell what they currently
had. It would be wrong to suggest that any of these organisations
had any outright hostility to Kerry as a region, or acted (or failed to
act) based on any prejudice against the region. Still, certainly in
Dublin, there must have lingered some hint of Kerry as the arche-
typal "backwater", which would not have helped Eddie Hayes as
he was making his case for a processing plant. John O'Flaherty,
another native of Kilflynn who wrote a brief memoir of Eddie
Hayes in 1997, recounts the story of how Hayes, along with Fionan
Harty, Mick Dillon and Stephen Fuller, all from Abbeydorney parish, went to Dublin to meet with officials of the Department of Agriculture. After they had done their presentation on the need for a
processing plant, one of the officials repined:

> What does Kerry want a processing plant for? Sure,
> there's nothing down there but mountains, heather and
> rushes.[3]

To a lesser man, such a reaction might have been crushing, and
the towel would have been thrown in. To Eddie Hayes, clearly the
crusade was only just beginning.

He was a man of many qualities and, like many strong leaders,
was also possessed of great paradoxes. He was a highly intelligent
man, well read and thoughtful, a man of vision, but not always able
to properly articulate that vision. Some acquaintances of his own
vintage, admirers no doubt, have claimed that he was the smartest
pupil ever seen in the Kilflynn national school. Whether this was
true or not, Eddie was the eldest son in his family, and as was cus-
tomary at the time, it was expected that he would take over the
farm, which he did. He was a man who tended to be direct, a serious man with a serious mind, but possessed of a sometimes wick-
edly funny sense of humour. He did not suffer fools gladly, but was

a ready listener to people who had something to say, and said it directly and well. Yet pity the one who drew his wrath in a meeting. A man of little patience, he spent years in a purgatory of delays, and disappointments, and constant waiting for the opportunity to start a processing plant. For a man of his disposition, the wait must have been agonising. Still, he carried on.

He ran a meeting forcefully, and did not tolerate nonsense or straying from the point. One acquaintance remembers him in an car with a number of others, travelling to a meeting in Listowel. One fellow in particular was complaining of this one and that one, of the co-ops that were not doing what they should be doing, of the leaders who had let them down, and he went on and on. Finally, Eddie could take it no longer. "Would you be quiet, you stump of a fool, and let somebody else talk!" he barked. One may assume that the remainder of the journey was quiet indeed.

Eddie Hayes may have been the right man, in the right place, at the right time. In this, perhaps, he was the first of several remarkable men who, either by fate, chance or design, were to found, build and grow the enterprise known first as North Kerry Milk Products, then as the Kerry Co-op, and finally the Kerry Group. His focus in life was to secure that factory for Kerry farmers. His energies for the better part of a decade, at least, were to be directed at this sole aim. And he was not the only one. Elsewhere in North Kerry, farming leaders were beginning to come to the same conclusion, that Kerry needed a factory to process its milk. Eddie Hayes, starting from his position as the Chairman of the Abbeydorney Co-operative Dairy Society, began the long process of organising these people of like mind, and preaching the gospel of a federation of co-operatives as an initial step towards securing first a licence, and secondly the financing, to build the factory. Eddie Hayes, practical idealist, was ready to lead the county's farmers out of decades of stagnation, whether they were ready or not. Years later, Seamus McConville, the former editor of *The Kerryman* newspaper, was to describe Eddie Hayes as "a Moses-like figure, who led the Kerry farmers out of the desert".[4] But it is sobering to realise, extending the analogy further, that Moses in fact wandered in the desert for 40 years before his people were finally delivered.

Early Attempts to Secure a Factory in Listowel

Initial attempts were made in the very early 1960s to begin the process of securing a factory for North Kerry, specifically in Listowel. Listowel was located some 16 miles north of Tralee, and billed itself as the capital of North Kerry. Of course, "capital" may be something of a grandiose title, for it was a market town of approximately 3,500 souls in the early 1960s, completely dependent upon its agricultural trade. It did, however, have a literary reputation, as it was blessed with some of the finest writers in Kerry and indeed in all Ireland. John B. Keane, the writer, playwright, publican, and Kerry raconteur, and Bryan McMahon, writer and schoolmaster, hailed from Listowel. Eamon Kelly, the world famous *seanchaí* (storyteller), was a woodwork teacher in Listowel and well known in the town (although he is a native of the Killarney area). Brendan Kennelly, poet and later a Don at Trinity College, the dramatist George Fitzmaurice, and even the late Maurice Walsh, short story writer and novelist, author of the famous story "The Quiet Man" and serious authority on Scotch whiskey, lived not far away. It also had a reputation as a spirited and social place, with more public houses per capita than perhaps anywhere else in Ireland. It was a consummate provincial town, full of "characters", wit, laughter, spirit, colour, markets and life. But if it had a serious literary heritage, and a rich social life, its economic life left much to be desired. On the commercial side, there was embarrassingly little — and little, apparently, that would serve to encourage industry to locate there. But in Listowel, too, there breathed the desire for a factory, not only for the benefit of the farmers of North Kerry, but also to breathe some life, commercially, into the town itself. Unemployment in the early 1960s was terribly high in the town and probably worse in the neighbouring rural areas, in spite of the emigration of young people to Britain, the United States and elsewhere, and a factory could provide jobs and a badly needed boost to local businesses. A factory could provide an economic ripple effect that would benefit the whole region. As this hope, this dream, began to take hold, the first awkward attempts at gaining a factory were made.

As early as 1960, a local group in Listowel had joined together as the Listowel Industrial Development Association, chaired by prominent local politician D.J. Moloney, TD. This group published a brochure in 1960 entitled "Facilities for Industrialists — What Listowel Has to Offer", which trumpeted the virtues of the town in a manner that may appear naïve and bucolic to our more jaundiced twenty-first century senses. Still, it was one of the very earliest attempts at attracting foreign direct investment into North Kerry. After extolling the virtues of the town, the available tax rebates, its ample pool of labour, its supply of raw materials, its excellent transportation system, and its perfect harmony in employer-employee relations, the brochure goes on to say that:

> the people of Listowel are intelligent, industrious, keen and healthy. They have an Irish sense of humour. They are hospitable and very co-operative.[5]

It was, indeed, a different age.

At about this time as well, deputations of various sorts began to make the long trek across the country from Kerry up to Dublin to attempt to generate government support for a processing factory for Listowel. Bill Sweeney, the Manager of the Rattoo Co-operative Creamery in North Kerry, was deeply involved in these efforts from the very beginning. He recounted a typical such deputation, composed of creamery managers from North Kerry and West Limerick, who went to Dublin in January 1962. It should be remembered that a journey to Dublin (then even more than now!) was a relatively inconvenient affair. If going by rail, one would rise early in the morning, travel to Tralee, take the train to Mallow in Cork, and change for the Dublin-bound train. One would not be in Dublin long before noon. If travelling by automobile, the drive across the width of Ireland was a slow one through towns, villages and hamlets, without benefit of motorways or bypasses. This particular day, the creamery managers had successive meetings with the IAOS, the IDA, the Department of Agriculture, and finally a meeting at the Dairy Disposal Board. At the end of the day, they'd trundle back on to the train for the long trip back down the country to Kerry. This practice was to repeat itself, ritualistically, by a sometimes-changing cast of characters, again, and again, and again, relentlessly, over the next decade. Bill Sweeney, who logged as many miles as anyone, remembers that for many of these men, they travelled on their own time and at their own expense. Most assuredly, there were no fat expense accounts available at the North Kerry co-operatives.

Later, in 1962, this same group, operating under the name of Shannon Valley Milk Development Association, provided information to Foremost Dairies, Inc. from San Francisco, who were contemplating an investment in a milk powder factory in Ireland. Among the areas Foremost had visited was Listowel, and the group had provided them with further information and assurances regarding the available milk supply. The last paragraph of a follow-up letter sent to Foremost Dairies read:

> On these grounds we justly lay claim to the suitability of this area, and we solicit your help, active co-operation and influence in bringing this project to fruition in the interest of the area and the country generally.[6]

Foremost answered that they were considering proposals put forward by various groups in Ireland, and it would be some time before they reached a definite conclusion. That was the last that was ever heard from Foremost Dairies. It was at least a polite and dignified form of rejection.

In 1964, Eddie Hayes convened meetings among all the co-operatives in North Kerry with the intent of jointly pushing for a milk processing plant in Listowel. In connection with this, farmers from these co-ops began to visit other milk processing plants around the country. They visited, by bus, plants at Dungarvan (Waterford Co-op) and at Mitchelstown, both sizeable operations supplied by primarily larger dairy farmers. The general thinking seemed to be that Kerry, with its 8,000 mostly small dairy farmers, was way out of its league in even considering a processing plant. But a subsequent visit to Lough Egish, a small co-operative with a successful processing facility, gave Hayes and the other promoters of the project at least some encouragement.[7] Such encouragement, though in short supply, was vital in combating a general air of defeatism that pervaded the scene in Kerry. It must have been difficult for a "can do" leader like Hayes to have had to listen and respond to an endless litany of reasons why "it can't be done".

Again, in May of 1965, it appeared that the DDC would be establishing a cheese factory in Listowel. A public announcement, in fact, was made by the general manager of An Bord Bainne, A.J.F. (Tony) O'Reilly,[8] at a meeting sponsored by the ICMSA and its North Kerry chairman, Frank Wall. The headline in *The Kerryman* newspaper read "Cheese Factory to be Built in Listowel".[9] This would not be the last such headline that would fail to materialise. This proposed cheese factory would have used about five million gallons of milk a year to be provided by the Listowel Dairy Disposal Board suppliers, producing cheese for export to be marketed through Bord Bainne. There were, however, problems associated with this proposal in that the co-operatives of North Kerry had not been included — only the Listowel DDC stood to benefit. It should be noted that the DDC and the co-operatives in North Kerry rarely sang from the same hymnal, and this incident led to a further cooling of relations for some time to come. In any event, the attempt to build this cheese factory in Listowel went no further.

The year 1968 began with a bang, and offered much promise. Already, in November 1967, the ten North Kerry (and Limerick) co-operative societies had federated into an association by the name of North Kerry Co-operative Creameries, chaired by Eddie Hayes.[10] Subsequently, the federation took a one-third stake in a newly formed enterprise, North Kerry Milk Products (NKMP), in partnership with the Dairy Disposal Company and Fry-Cadbury (Ireland) Ltd. NKMP, at that time, was no more than a "shell company" with no tangible assets, intended to serve as the vehicle for investment in a milk processing factory in Listowel. Frank Wall of Tarbert, who was on the Board of Directors of Bord Bainne and held national elective office with the ICMSA, chaired it. Eddie Hayes, representing the North Kerry co-operatives, Dick Godsil, representing Fry-Cadbury, and Jack Hennigan and Tim Dennehy, representing the Dairy Disposal Company, also sat on the NKMP Board. Although NKMP was not formally registered until May, the enterprise had already "hit the ground running" by January of 1968. In fact, in 1967 the NKMP partners had already proposed a £1.1 million milk powder and cheese processing facility. Additionally, the co-operatives were hoping that a centralised butter churning plant could also be constructed, attached to the processing plant, in order to take advantage of such location efficiencies. Newspaper reports indicated that construction of this plant would start in March 1968,[11] and the Listowel Urban Council placed on record its gratitude to several local people, including Patsy Walsh and creamery manager Tommy O'Sullivan, who played a role in securing the factory. Local support was strong. This is evident in a letter from the branch manager of the Provincial Bank of Ireland, Ltd., in Listowel, to Eddie Hayes in April 1968:

> . . . the Bank is fully prepared to provide financial assistance to assist in the establishment and development of this Project which it is the firm wish of the Bank should meet with full and deserved success.[12]

Then, fate intervened. At the eleventh hour, in another in a series of interminable trade disputes with Ireland, the UK imposed a quota on Irish cheese and Bord Bainne withdrew its support for construction of the factory. With the quota in place, there would be little market for the cheese. Additionally, the EEC was sitting atop huge mountains of butter that had been sold into intervention, which did not augur well for butter exports. Finally, the skim milk powder that was to be produced at the plant was now in huge surplus and was being dumped onto world markets at bargain basement prices. Apparently, Paddy Kelly, the Director General of the IAOS, had also advised against the factory at this time (because of cheese quota restrictions). With Bord Bainne and the IAOS no longer supporting the factory, the expected grant aid from the IDA evaporated. The proposed factory, once again, was in limbo.

Increasingly, the continuing attempts to secure a processing factory for Kerry seemed futile. Perhaps out of frustration, discussions within the co-op federation were growing heated. Eddie Hayes began to push the virtues of amalgamation (as opposed to federation). In his view, if the co-ops were ever going to get this factory they would have to present a single, united and strong front.[13] But it was too soon. The collection of North Kerry (and West Limerick!) co-ops hardly seemed ready for amalgamation. In fact, sentiment seemed quite the contrary.

A survey was circulated to gauge the interest in such an amalgamation, but even getting the survey completed seemed to be a difficult affair. There was a fair amount of dissension in the ranks of the co-ops. Each society, after all, was independent, and most took pride in that independence, displaying it with some regularity. Even with regards to the factory, and in view of the market difficulties of the time, some of the co-ops were weakening. Would it be "madness" to build a factory at the present time, asked one co-op?[14] Was it "too late" to build the factory? Were the North Kerry co-ops "too small" to reap the benefits of this factory? Many of the doubts that had been dealt with before surfaced again. But Eddie Hayes' faith in the project was unshakeable. The minutes of the October meeting quote him saying, as chairman:

> . . . in his view and in spite of the difficulties outlined, the project should go ahead, and that he personally had no reservations because of the dip in the market. On an automated factory we hope to compete. This is the line that must be taken. A modern properly automated factory should be the aim of the Co-op partnership.

Later in the meeting, after more discussion, doubts, and questioning, Hayes summed up his frustration in trying to move the group forward with:

> . . . if decisions which should be taken here are left undone, other people will do the deciding. The Dairy Disposal Company will do it on the ground that the Co-ops have failed . . .

and that:

> What we want is a factory that would be of benefit to the farmers of North Kerry.

The meeting ended with plans for yet another meeting in Dublin, this time with the IAOS, to push for the factory.[15]

These follow-up efforts, desperate as they were, ended in failure. After numerous trips back and forth to Dublin, after the meetings, the applications, the negotiations, the expectations, and even the premature announcements of success, the promoters of the facility had returned empty handed yet again. After all this, one

might expect that even those who were most completely committed to this mission, men like Eddie Hayes and Bill Sweeney, would
be discouraged. And perhaps they were. Still, the efforts continued and were in fact redoubled, and the promoters persevered.
Sheridan once said, "the surest way not to fail is to determine to
succeed".[16] Determination of this intensity was certainly called for
in North Kerry in 1968.

In order for any factory to be constructed, a suitable site had to
be acquired. Luckily, there were others in Kerry willing to support
the promoters' efforts in whatever way they could. Among them
were the Directorss of the Listowel Racecourse Company. The
NKMP Board had identified a field owned by the Racecourse Company, known locally as "The Canon's Field", as being a desirable
site. The Racecourse Company had bought the field in the early
1960s from Canon Peter O'Sullivan of St. Mary's Catholic Church
for use as a car park. The 22-acre field was adjacent to the racecourse and located on the River Feale, which would provide the
water needed in a facility of that sort. It was reasonably well situated on the outskirts of Listowel and located on the N69 national
road between Listowel and Tralee. The land was flat and buildable, if not particularly dry, and had adjacent vacant land that
could be available for future expansion. Bill Sweeney remembers
being in a meeting room at the IAOS headquarters on Merrion
Square in Dublin when the call was made to ask the Racecourse
Company about selling NKMP the field. Speaking on behalf of the
company was Louis O'Connell, a local solicitor:

> We asked him to put a figure on it . . . and I think the figure
> was something on the order of £6,500. It was a very low
> figure. O'Connell said, "It has been given to me to state
> that if ever a factory comes to Listowel, we really don't
> want the field, we don't need the field, but we will give it
> to whoever gives us that factory for the same price that we
> paid for it ourselves. We don't want any gains, we want a
> factory for Listowel".[17]

So, the Racecourse Company sold the field in November 1968 for
roughly what they had paid for it themselves a few years previously.[18]

So despite the aborted plans for the factory, efforts continued through the end of 1968. There were various meetings in Dublin and in Kerry. The actual purchase of the "Canon's Field" was completed. Paddy Kelly, Director General of the IAOS, visited to explain his concerns with the proposed factory once again, describing the marketing difficulties of the time, and urging caution in setting up a milk processing facility as "monuments to nothing, maybe".[19] The IAOS position seemed to be that the co-operatives should first amalgamate, and only then embark on plans for rationalisation, a milk processing plant, and a central churning capability. It was on this note of further consideration, further study, and further delay that 1968 came to a close. Not with the bang that had attended its beginning, but with a whimper.

At the beginning of 1969, amidst continuing discussions of amalgamation throughout the county and in the midst of a generally bad year for dairy farmers, a new possibility appeared on the horizon. A French firm, Sapiem Ltd., had arrived in Kerry searching for a site to build a sweetened condensed milk plant. They toured the Canon's Field in Listowel in February and followed-up with meetings with the federation of North Kerry Co-operatives, North Kerry Milk Products Ltd., the IDA, and Bord Bainne. The attraction for Sapiem was clear. There was a more than adequate milk supply and there would be generous government grants and incentives available. The North Kerry Co-ops could hardly negotiate from a position of strength. Bill Sweeney, Secretary of NKMP, was quoted at the time saying:

> Things have not been going so well for North Kerry Milk Products' proposal for a factory to manufacture cheese and powdered milk. . . . This offers hope for North Kerry milk processing and we would welcome it.[20]

Eddie Hayes was quoted saying that:

> I would have preferred if we had been successful in promoting our own plant — the co-operatives have a one third share in North Kerry Milk Products, Ltd. — but since that has not been successful I think that we must welcome these people.[21]

Sapiem seemed to offer the one thing that the Kerry Co-ops lacked, that is, a ready market for their output. Without a "guarantee" of such a market, it appeared that the Kerry factory would remain no more than a pipe dream.

But, besides some questions as to the extent of Sapiem's market claims, there were two more emotional and ultimately intractable issues. The first was Sapiem's insistence on a majority 51 per cent stake in any factory, and the second was the actual extent of Sapiem's investment. They apparently wished to transfer from France a considerable amount of used equipment from a processing plant in Normandy, and use this as their tangible investment. This would have meant that the North Kerry Co-ops would contribute something in the region of £300,000, the IDA would have provided a £1 million grant, and Sapiem would have contributed primarily used equipment, technical know-how, and its market outlets. Despite a visit to France by representatives from IAOS and Bord Bainne, and a return trip to Kerry by Sapiem, these differences were never resolved. The French were absolutely adamant about retaining their 51 per cent share, rather than the one-third proposed by NKMP. Kerry farmers were equally adamant. No matter how desperate they may have been for a factory, they were unwilling to relinquish their own control over such an enterprise. On the second issue, some in Kerry were convinced that what Sapiem were doing was dismantling an old factory in Normandy for reassembly in Ireland, and that the equipment itself was "fit for no more than the scrap heap". Such suspicion of the "quality" of Sapiem's investment was widespread. Nevertheless, discussions had continued through the middle of 1970. They abruptly ended with a letter dated 15 July 1970, from Mr R. Green, a Dublin solicitor to the Dairy Disposal Company and the Co-ops, who had been active in the attempts to broker an agreement with Sapiem. He advised that Sapiem (now Preval) were to "terminate their interest in North Kerry without outlining any reason".[22] Clearly, however, the issue of control had been pivotal, as Sapiem had stuck to their insistence for majority ownership, a point which the federation of co-operatives were unwilling to concede. It was yet one more disappointment, one more false start on the long road to construction of the factory. Yet the promoters persevered, and seemed in fact to focus their energies with an even greater sense of urgency. Eddie

Hayes exhorted his colleagues to such efforts, saying, "It was little use being green. Graft [in the sense of hard work] . . . was now an essential element of success."[23]

Almost immediately upon the heels of Sapiem's withdrawal, Hayes proposed that the co-operatives, along with the Dairy Disposal Company, should approach Golden Vale as an alternative partner in the "diversification factory". Golden Vale at the time was considering construction of a skim powder plant at Newcastlewest in County Limerick, not far from the Kerry border. But there was little enthusiasm among the co-ops for participating in the construction of a facility that was not located in Listowel, and the comment of Board member Tom Sheehan was fairly typical, "All of us would be happier in Listowel."[24] It was decided that they would still seek to have discussions with Golden Vale, along with the Dairy Disposal Company, but on the condition that any such factory sponsored by the partnership would be located at Listowel. The good offices of the IAOS were to be used, as so often before, to arrange for these meetings.

At this juncture, in late August 1970, an old familiar pattern had been played out again. There had been the promise of a processing factory for Listowel, endless negotiations, complications and disappointment as nothing came to fruition. At around the same time, however, at least one "Listowel Factory" was proceeding at a very rapid pace. It seems that a local donkey christened "Listowel Factory" in comic recognition of the factory that never arrived had made a name for itself by winning the Donkey Derby at a Kerry Festival held in Listowel. It had then gone on to win a similar donkey derby in Tralee. Perhaps this was a sign, for unbeknownst to the promoters of the real Listowel factory, their luck, too, was finally about to change, and from a most unexpected source.

The Arrival of the Erie Casein Company

Bill Sweeney remembers his first inkling of this:

> One morning about 10:30 I had a call from Dick Godsil. After exchanging pleasantries, Dick mentioned something about a "casein factory" for Listowel. I said, "Jaysus, not casein." My sense of casein was that it was a raw material for buttons and combs, not even classified as a dairy

product at all. Dick said, "No, there is edible casein too.
And there is no edible casein factory in Ireland." Dick
said that he had got it through the grapevine that these
people had been to the Department of Agriculture and
wanted to put up a casein factory. They were looking for a
good milk supply that was not being used and where they
wouldn't be stepping on the toes of other people. He
didn't know who these people were, or any of the details,
except that it looked pretty good.[25]

"Those people" were, it turned out, a pair of representatives — in
fact a husband and wife team — from the Erie Casein Company in
Erie, Illinois. Bob and Sylvia (Reisenbigler) Siewert had been rov-
ing Europe like "a pair of gypsies" in a reconditioned VW mini-
bus, searching for a potential supply of casein for the family business.[26] Arden F. Reisenbigler, who bought six casein manufacturing plants from his former employer, Hercules Industries when
they decided to exit the business, had started the firm in 1938. At
the time, all such casein was used in industrial applications such as
paint, billiard balls and buttons. With a halt in domestic manufacture in the late 1940s (due to the lack of sufficient supply of skim
milk), Erie had shifted their manufacturing efforts to Australia,
where they established a joint processing venture with a local
dairy co-operative.

Casein itself is no more than the principal protein component in
milk. It is extracted from the milk by a process of precipitation
triggered by the addition of either hydrochloric acid or rennet (a
coagulating enzyme), which has the effect of clotting the casein
into curds which are almost all protein, leaving the remaining liquid whey as a by-product. The casein curds are then washed,
dried to a powder and packaged. Acid casein is used in many
products, including coffee creamers, cream liquors, gravies, and
soups; rennet casein is used primarily in cheese products. The
technology for casein manufacture was straightforward and relatively unsophisticated. Of more importance to the efficient manufacture of casein was the availability of a sufficient supply of milk
so that the equipment's capacity could be fully utilised.

The use of casein had begun to change considerably in the
1950s, as the United States Department of Agriculture published

new standards for the edible casein and milk proteins which were increasingly used in a wide range of formulations for bakery, dairy and meat products.[27] Erie, with a supply of casein provided by its Australian joint venture partner, had been able to supply much of the demand for the product in North America. In the late 1960s, however, Australia implemented a plan to reduce their production of milk by nearly 40 per cent, and Erie was compelled to seek out alternative sources of supply. In June 1970, newlyweds Bob Siewert and his wife Sylvia, the daughter of the founder, were planning a honeymoon trip to Europe. Since they were going to the continent, they were also given the job of making a few calls on potential casein suppliers. They eventually spent nearly six months scouring Europe for alternative suppliers who could reliably deliver high quality casein to Erie. The idea, however, was to do this via a marketing arrangement with a producer; Erie had little interest in taking any equity interest in a manufacturing facility itself.

The Siewerts started in Germany, then continued on to Denmark, France and eventually west to Ireland. When they arrived in Dublin, Sylvia recounts:

> We heard of a co-op that was dumping a lot of its milk on the ground because they didn't have any way to process it. That whetted our appetite.[28]

They found their way to the offices of Bord Bainne and met with Joe McGough, the chairman, who arranged for them to meet with representatives of North Kerry Milk Products. Of course, the story that has made the rounds in Kerry ever since, and has become part of the mythology of the company, is somewhat more embellished. According to this story, Bob and Sylvia turned up on Bord Bainne's doorstep in Dublin, both young people in their 20s who appeared more like they were trekking through Europe on an extended holiday than conducting business, and Bord Bainne hadn't a clue what to do with them. So they sent them down the country to Kerry to get rid of them. When Sylvia was asked about this, she replied:

> That's probably exactly what happened. I mean, we were in our twenties for Pete's sake. We went to a lot of meetings, and people would poke their heads in the door and

say, "Excuse me, I was looking for Mr and Mrs Siewert."
They couldn't believe that was us![29]

In any event, the connection was made and it was surprising how
well the two groups seemed to hit it off from the beginning. There
would clearly be no repetition of the negotiations with Sapiem. In
September 1970, the Siewerts rang Erie Casein's Illinois headquarters from Dublin to announce that they had found an area, in
Ireland, which might serve the firm's needs, but unfortunately
there was not yet a factory there. Discussions then began among
the Dairy Disposal Company, the Federation of North Kerry Co-
operative Creameries, and Erie Casein Company about the construction of a factory.

And so Erie Casein Company from America wound up in North
Kerry, sometime in the late summer/early autumn of 1970, on the
doorstep of North Kerry Milk Products. Eddie Hayes and the other
promoters of the Listowel factory grabbed at this opportunity as a
drowning man would grab on to a life preserver. Up to this point, it
had been years of sheer frustration. Clearly they were not about to
let this one get away, but there was still a long road ahead . . . negotiations with many diverse parties and many conflicting interests, set within the always contentious and unpredictable context
of Irish farming politics.

One of the first issues to sort out was the extent of Erie's participation in the manufacturing facility. Erie had proposed a simple
marketing arrangement, with no equity in the plant, but the promoters insisted on some form of equity participation as a "show of
goodwill". It was put to the Reisenbiglers that, if they did not take
an equity interest, the plant would never go up. Arden G. Reisenbigler, the founder's son who was by now involved in the negotiations, asked if a 1 per cent stake would be a sufficient show of
"good faith".[30] It wasn't, and Erie eventually agreed to pick up a 15
per cent participation in North Kerry Milk Products (Fry-Cadbury
would pull out of NKMP, and its share was reallocated). Other issues that dominated discussions at that time were the total cost of
the project and, importantly, the amount of grant aid that would be
provided by the IDA. By the end of 1970, tangible efforts were well
under way. Bill Ebrill, chief engineer at the IAOS, and his assistant
Pat O'Neill, along with the consulting engineers Pettits of Cork,

had begun to design the layout and structure of the plant and develop cost estimates for submission of the grant application. Indeed, the prevailing sentiment at a meeting of the co-ops in January 1971 was that it was "now or never" to make a start on this Listowel factory.[31]

By April 1971, the proposal to erect a casein factory in Listowel was approved at a meeting of the Federation of North Kerry Co-operatives, and the formal application was submitted to the IDA. Chairman Eddie Hayes complimented the co-operative societies on their decision, stating that he "was sure it would be momentous in the expansion of the dairy industry in Kerry in the future". He also quoted a potential profit figure of £133,000 for the first year.[32] At the same meeting, representatives of Erie Casein were introduced to representatives of the co-operatives, and spoke with enthusiasm about the partnership.

It would have been most uncharacteristic if things had proceeded smoothly, and indeed they did not. It remained on the shoulders of Eddie Hayes to keep the farmers together on this project as internal disputes broke out during the next few months. There were concerns about co-operatives that had not paid up the first call on capital for the plant, the decision of one co-operative to withdraw from participation in the project, and general disappointment at the "niggardly" grant likely to be awarded by the IDA.[33] There was also the element of time. On one level, it was clear that if the Kerry farmers were not able to bring this plant to fruition, someone else, outside of Kerry, would shortly be making decisions about the future of the dairy industry in Kerry. On a second level, time was of the essence in that the plant had to be up and running by May/June of 1972 if it were to take advantage of the peak milk production months. That the chairman was able to keep this "bag of cats" together and on course is a testament to his considerable skills as a leader, to his single-minded commitment to the project, and to his seemingly inexhaustible reservoir of perseverance. He had not known how to quit in even the darkest times; it was hardly likely that he'd do so now with the prize within reach.

Yet, this casein plant was not the "be-all and end-all" to Eddie Hayes. To him and some of the other promoters of the facility, it was only a beginning, for they had bigger plans for the farmers of North Kerry. Still, as the first step that had taken so long, it was

clearly the most important one. Bill Sweeney remembers Eddie
Hayes saying at the time, "It is a start, and it is a start with good
people [the Reisenbiglers], family people."[34] The relationship
between the Kerry farmers and the Reisenbiglers from Illinois
seemed comfortable from the start, as both saw a real mutual opportunity. But still, to Eddie Hayes, casein was only the first step.
As recorded in the minutes of a meeting of North Kerry Co-
operative Creameries Ltd. later in 1971, he stated that:

> . . . the Casein Factory is only Stage I of a huge develop-
> ment in processing and diversification. The plant may be
> late, looking at what is done in the other parts of the
> country, and it may be dear, but we live in a time of great
> change.[35]

By April 1971, the estimated cost and financing plan for the factory
was finalised, and the grant request was submitted to the IDA by
Joe Madden, an economist with the IAOS who had done a considerable amount of work in connection with the financial side of the
grant request. The initial cost estimate for the plant was £575,000,
of which it was hoped the IDA would provide the maximum grant it
was allowed, nearly 50 per cent or £283,000. The IDA, however,
approved only £145,000, based on a formula of £5,000 per job created. Based on this, the promoters planned to finance the construction as follows:

£81,000	Share capital, North Kerry Co-operatives Creameries, Ltd.
£81,000	Share capital, Dairy Disposal Company, Ltd.
£28,000	Share capital, Erie Casein Company, AG
£145,000	IDA grant
£95,000	ACC Loan (Agricultural Credit Corporation, Ltd.)
£145,000	Taisce Stait (a seven-year, non-interest-bearing government loan)[36]
£575,000	Total

At this point in July 1971, however, there was very little of this
money on hand: approximately £16,000 that had been provided by
six of the co-operatives who had answered the first call on capital
for the initial, abortive venture in 1968. On the financing side,

things were not going to get better quickly. Additionally, the IDA had attached several qualifications to its grant. One qualification was that "satisfactory market arrangements are entered into between the promoters and North Kerry Co-operative Creameries Ltd". Essentially, the IDA wanted written assurance that there would be a sufficient milk supply provided to the factory. The federation of co-operatives provided this in short order. In addition, the IDA wanted further assurances that there was a more or less "guaranteed" market for the casein. This was more difficult to deliver. In order to satisfy this IDA qualification, Erie Casein Company signed a letter of "good intent" setting forth its willingness to participate in NKMP and to provide a North American market for the casein to be produced. It also included a clause that specified that NKMP would not sell to anyone else in the US without Erie Casein's permission. It should be emphasised, however, that it was a letter of "good intent" rather than a binding contract. Erie intended, but did not acknowledge a contractual obligation to, market all of Kerry's production of casein. Kerry, for its part, did not acknowledge a contractual obligation to sell its casein to Erie, exclusively. In any event, the "letter of good intent" was objected to quite strongly by some in Kerry (particularly Denis Brosnan when he arrived on the scene in January 1972). However, it was quite essential in order to placate the IDA and receive the grant. Many years later, this document would again prove to be problematic for a, by then, very different organisation.

By December 1971, the planning was complete and the builders, Jeremiah Galvin & Sons Ltd. of Killarney, were overseeing the work necessary to prepare the site for construction. The target date for commencement of production was the second week of May 1972, a period of less than five months from the clearing of the site to the start-up of the factory.[37] Remarkably, there was little comment at the time about the aggressiveness of this schedule. Perhaps it was due to the fact that it was absolutely *unthinkable* that the plant would go into production much later than May. Certainly it would be even more difficult to obtain the necessary finance for a plant that would be completed only later, to sit largely idle through the winter months. The peak milk season could not be missed.

Certainly, the groundbreaking in the Canon's Field was a culminating event in the long years of tribulation endured by North
Kerry farmers and their leaders, especially Eddie Hayes, who laboured to bring the Listowel factory to reality. What had been a
dream was now on the verge of being a reality. Little did they
know that this was only the beginning. Indeed, a far more important event in the short life of North Kerry Co-operative Creameries
was unfolding. The Directorss at NKMP had decided, in early
autumn 1971, that it was time to appoint a General Manager.

Assembling the Management Team

In early September 1971, advertisements for the position of "Production Manager" at North Kerry Milk Products were placed in
newspapers throughout Ireland. The reasons why the initial recruiting was for a "Production" rather than a "General" Manager
seem to be lost in the mists of time. Despite the title, however, the
job description and the search were clearly for the "number one"
executive at NKMP. Application letters and materials were sent to
a recruiting committee organised under the aegis of the IAOS,
comprised of Jim Moloney, Assistant Secretary of IAOS, Eddie
Hayes, Chairman of North Kerry Co-operative Creameries, Ltd.,
Tim Dennehy from the Dairy Disposal Company, and Bob Siewert,
representing Erie Casein Co.

The newspaper ads drew a good response and generated a
pool of highly qualified candidates with impressive credentials.
On 27 September 1971, Jim Moloney drew up a list of candidates
who were "probable" for interviews.[38] Ideally, the committee
sought an Irish national with some broader experience. Most of the
individuals on that "short list" seemed to fit these criteria, among
them one Denis Brosnan, a young Kerryman working as the foreign
sales manager for Golden Vale in London. Although only 27, Brosnan had already had an extraordinary track record with Golden
Vale, then one of the country's largest processors.

In a formal sense, Brosnan was applying as any other candidate,
but in a very real sense, he was being actively recruited. Hayes
knew the Brosnan family well. First, Denis was a neighbour of Eddie
Hayes in Kilflynn, and in fact a distant relation. Hayes, a perceptive
man who made it his business to examine what was going on about
him with a critical eye, would most certainly have known something

about the qualifications and potential of his young neighbour. Indeed, Hayes served on the Board of the Abbeydorney Co-operative Dairy Society along with Denis' brother James, who ran the family farm in Kilflynn. An uncle, Tom Brosnan, had been the manager of Abbeydorney Creamery for many years. It was Eddie Hayes who called James Brosnan one day, and asked him to ring his brother in London and ask him to apply for the position in Listowel. Was it a pure hunch on Eddie Hayes' part that Brosnan had the right mix of skill, experience, and energy to build, and run, the Listowel factory? Was it the fact that Brosnan was a Kerryman, one of their own, whom Kerry farmers could trust to bring their dream of a milk processing plant to a successful culmination? Whatever it was, Eddie's eldest son Mundy maintains that his father had long had Brosnan earmarked for this job. Mundy remembers

> . . . the Sunday morning, just after Mass, when James rang my father to say that "Yes, Denis would be interested in the position", as being a moment of great personal satisfaction for him, almost as great as getting the approval for the factory itself![39]

What is clear is that Brosnan was Hayes' chosen candidate from the very beginning. Still, it would take some convincing! Denis Brosnan was young, newly married, on a "fast track" at Golden Vale, and enjoying life in cosmopolitan London to the hilt. Friends have maintained that Brosnan was anxious to return home, but Brosnan himself maintains that he was in no particular rush to get back to Kerry. According to his recollection, it was Eddie Hayes who pressured him to at least come in and have an interview. On the other side, the hiring decision would ultimately be made by the Board of North Kerry Milk Products, and quite a few well-qualified, experienced, senior managers had already thrown their hats in the ring. If Hayes showed favouritism to Brosnan in this choice, it would have to be because he really *was* the man for the job, and that would have to be patently clear to everyone.

Interestingly, this was not the first time Jim Moloney had heard of Brosnan. Some years earlier, after the death of Dave O'Loughlin, GM of Golden Vale, Moloney asked Michael Herlihy, who was on the Board of Directors there, how the search for a new GM was going.

> Well, Michael Herlihy paused and I knew immediately
> that he had somebody in mind. So I said, come on, tell me.
> He said, "If I had my way I'd give it to a Kerryman called
> Brosnan, but he's too young. They wouldn't agree to it."
> Who was this Kerryman? I asked. "His name is Brosnan.
> Dave O'Loughlin told me that he had put him in charge of
> the building of the factory and then in charge of running
> the factory and he told me that that young fellow is a
> humdinger who will get places."[40]

Jim Moloney had filed that conversation in the back of his mind, only to recall it on the eve of the interview. The interviews took place during the first week of November 1971, at the Plunkett House in Dublin. The interviewing committee consisted of Jim Moloney, Eddie Hayes, and Tim Dennehy.[41] On 4 November, the final day of interviewing, some six or seven candidates were interviewed, with Denis Brosnan the final candidate of the day.[42] As he had to travel in from London, the committee had accommodated him. It would be wrong to suggest that the interviews were a formality, for Jim Moloney remembers that the calibre of the other applicants was extremely high, but Brosnan was the best. It was an easy choice. As there was a meeting of the Board of Directors of North Kerry Milk Products the next day, the committee decided to recommend Brosnan for the job. There were, however, a few problems to be ironed out. First, Brosnan was not interested in a position as "Production Manager"; it was "General Manager" or nothing. Secondly, there was the small matter of the company car.

The first matter was cleared up rather easily, and in a manner that appealed to the Board of NKMP. Tim Dennehy of the Dairy Disposal Company, a very shrewd man, said:

> Look, we recommend that he be appointed General Man-
> ager and not Production Manager, because if we appoint
> him Production Manager now, and then in a few months
> promote him to General Manager, he'll be looking for
> more money. If we appoint him General Manager now,
> we'll get him at the same salary![43]

Some members of the board were uncomfortable that they had advertised for one job title and were appointing someone to another, but this objection was overcome and Dennehy's logic won the day. It was agreed that a General Manager would be hired. But even though the matter of the title and the amount of salary had been agreed, the seemingly small matter of the company car had still to be negotiated, and Jim Moloney was not sure how well this would fly. Brosnan was, and is, fond of sporty, high performance automobiles, and his company car in the UK was a Rover 3000. He wanted the same in Ireland, but the NKMP Board was thinking more of a small Ford! In particular, Jack Hennigan, the Chairman of the NKMP Board and a career civil servant, was partial to a more modest vehicle. Jim Moloney remembers the discussion:

> I said, "You can't have a man as General Manager for the factory in Listowel, responsible for high quality products, and needing to visit the various milk dairies and customers, without providing him with a company car. Now, the only car for a man like that would be a Rover. Isn't that right, Tim?" And Tim Dennehy said, "That's right, Jim." And I could see some assurance on Jack's face that his colleague of 30 years was agreeing with this.[44]

They got the car for Brosnan, although a slightly more modest Rover 2000, and North Kerry Milk Products got its first and only General Manager.[45]

The following is an excerpt from the minutes of the NKMP Board meeting on 4–5 November 1971:

> Mr Moloney reported that they were very gratified at the very high standard of all the people interviewed. However, despite this Mr Denis Brosnan was considered to be by far ahead of anyone else. It was felt that Mr Brosnan should be offered the position of General Manager and that because of his experience previously in organising in industry, from the building stage up, he would be a very desirable person to have as General Manager. Mr Hayes then proposed that Mr Brosnan be offered the appointment.[46]

The offer was made that same day, 5 November 1971, and it took Brosnan the better part of a week to accept. Why did he return home to a huge challenge and a very uncertain future? Brosnan says:

> I'm not sure. It was probably one of the most difficult decisions I've ever made. Perhaps it was a bit of the persuasive powers of Eddie Hayes, who said, "You have to apply; you have to come back!" Of course, he was aided and abetted in this by his great friend, Jim Moloney. I suppose at the end of the day it was, "Let's do something for the local farmer; let's do it."[47]

Other observers speculate that Brosnan was simply anxious to run his own operation, and the opportunity to do so in his own county won the day. After all, this was a man who rumour had it would have been chosen as the chief executive at Golden Vale after the untimely death of Dave O'Loughlin, but for the discomfort some there had felt about giving the position to someone so young. That is not to say that there was not similar discomfort felt by many farmers in Kerry, but Eddie Hayes and others on the Board of NKMP prevailed. Denis Brosnan was the new General Manager of North Kerry Milk Products and, officially, employee #0001. He was 27 years of age.

Brosnan was born in 1944 on a dairy farm in Kilflynn. He attended St Brendan's, a boarding school in Killarney, and then moved on to University College Cork for a degree in Dairy Science, and followed that up with a Master's degree. Why had he chosen this path? It is not a question that he can answer, even now, except to suggest that it might have been because his uncle had been a creamery manager. He got his first job after college selling industrial detergents for a Scottish company, a position he found attractive because it paid £1,100 a year and included the use of a company car.[48] It was a position he seemed to enjoy enormously, but he spent no longer than six months there. It seems that he had made a sales call on a Golden Vale creamery one day, in the course of which he had a conversation with Paddy Mullane, the creamery manager, who asked him, "Why are you wasting your time driving around the roads of Ireland selling detergents? We are building a new factory at Charleville, in County Cork." Mullane arranged the interview for him, and Brosnan was hired by Golden Vale, responsible for getting the new factory built and commissioned.[49]

Brosnan's career with Golden Vale was, in point of fact, "golden". He successfully oversaw the construction and commissioning of the Charleville facility, on time and on budget. The challenge had been similar to the challenge that would be facing the new head of North Kerry Milk Products: that the facility had to be up and running by the time the peak milk supply became available in June. So, there was an enormous amount of pressure. After successfully accomplishing this, he was appointed the Production Manager. Shortly thereafter, he became involved with research and development activities, and along with some others, pioneered the development of a new brand of calf milk replacer, named *Maverick*. This product proved to be a hugely successful brand for the co-operative. Golden Vale, under the able and dynamic leadership of Dave O'Loughlin, was one of the more successful co-operatives in Ireland at the time (although it was going through its own traumas, not the least of which were financial) and Brosnan was an acknowledged "wunderkind" in whom O'Loughlin took a special interest. Michael Drummey, later to become a pivotal player in the Kerry story, but at the time working for Bord Bainne, remembers going into Stack's pub in Charleville one night to have a pint with a few people from Golden Vale. He saw

> this guy in the background, dark hair, young, close set eyes. They told me, "That's Denis Brosnan, the man most likely to succeed. He is Dave O'Loughlin's protégé." Now, what was interesting was that this guy said nothing. He was just there, observing. A part of the thing without being part of the thing.[50]

While at Golden Vale, however, Brosnan began to grow restless. He and his fiancée Joan were planning on getting married in September 1970, and then moving to Canada. They had all the forms and were making plans when the GM of Golden Vale, who had got wind of this, suggested that if they wanted to go abroad, Denis should take a job in London as Golden Vale's Foreign Sales Man-

ager. They went to London later that year. In that post Brosnan
travelled extensively in Europe and North Africa, and made quite a
number of trips to the United States. The trips to the States, especially, were to make a dramatic impression upon him and supplied
him with contacts and acquaintances on whom he would call again,
to great effect, in the future.

Brosnan faced an exciting challenge, and a daunting prospect
in North Kerry. Some wag in London had said, upon learning of his
departure, "Young Brosnan, I can't understand why you want to go
back to the backside of the empire!" Maybe Brosnan himself could
not have explained it properly. But they came back, and that was
that. There were some rumblings in Kerry about the youth of this
new general manager. A number of experienced, highly qualified
creamery managers had been passed over for the position, and
some feathers had been ruffled. It was up to Eddie Hayes and the
other NKMP Directorss to absorb or deflect this criticism and allow
the new manager the necessary space to get on with the job. In this
matter, too, Eddie Hayes showed an unusually enlightened approach to management. His philosophy was quite simple. Hire the
best people, pay them well enough so that they need only worry
about the business (and not how much money they are or are not
being paid!), and get out of their way. In his support of management, he was a tower of strength, but he was no meddler. In some
ways, too, it was a passing of the torch that Hayes had carried for
so long. It was now up to Brosnan. Hayes had given him, as they
say, enough rope to hang himself.

The First Months

For a process that had moved at a seemingly glacial pace for
years, the momentum now picked up tremendously. Time was absolutely of the essence if the facility were to begin processing milk
in time for the peak milk season. It was hoped, at this point, that
the factory would be open by 8 or 9 May 1972. Everything de-
pended upon it. Things began to happen in stunning progression.

Having accepted the position, Brosnan tidied up his affairs at
Golden Vale and he and Joan returned home for Christmas 1971.
He also found time to attend a Board meeting of NKMP on 3 December, where he was officially confirmed as General Manager,
and attended other meetings the following week in Listowel. The

minutes of the 3 December meeting indicate that Brosnan, though he had to leave early to catch a flight back to the UK, had sufficient time to make a bold declaration: "Let it be known that the new factory would be commencing on 10 May."[51] Indeed, Brosnan was not lacking in confidence, but when he officially arrived for work on Monday, 3 January 1972, he was clearly facing a huge challenge.

At this point, site work had begun and contracts for construction had been awarded, but construction details were not to be Brosnan's first concern. Of more immediate concern was how to pay for it. The original budget for the plant was £575,000, but this figure would shortly be increased to £668,000 due to inflation and a very sensible increase in processing capacity. (It would be far less expensive to add capacity as part of the initial construction and installation, than to wait for a separate expansion later.) Not only was the cost going to be higher, but the finance (even for the original, lower cost) was not yet in place. In fact, some elements of the financing plan were already unravelling. Only about half of the promised share capital of £190,000 had been collected. Some of the co-operatives were not so eager to turn over their money too quickly, and Erie Casein would not turn over its share money until things were ironed-out with the "statement of intent". Additionally, the IDA grant, while it had received tentative approval, was still very much "in process", and the "final" grant application (having attended to the IDA's several qualifications) would not even be submitted until late February. Furthermore, there was a "Catch 22" at play. The banks were reluctant to provide the funding for the project until the IDA grant money was actually provided; similarly, the IDA preferred that the banks provide their funds before releasing the grant aid. It was a recipe for paralysis. These were some of the financial Gordian knots that remained for Brosnan to untie. Meanwhile, concrete for the building foundations was being poured.

Getting the money was to occupy some good portion of the first quarter of 1972. For these first three months, Brosnan, who as yet had no staff of his own, worked largely with the IAOS engineers who were heavily involved with the project, Bill Ebrill and Pat O'Neill. Ebrill, the Chief Dairy Engineer of the IAOS, had joined the staff nearly 40 years earlier in 1932. He had been educated in

Germany in the latest dairy techniques, was equally at home with theory as with practice, and was a devoted employee and a convinced co-operator. He had already been involved with the planning for a milk processing facility in North Kerry for many years, and was responsible for much of the grant application for the factory. He was ably assisted by Pat O'Neill, the assistant dairy engineer for IAOS, who was later himself to join the Kerry organisation. It was in fact the IAOS engineering staff who designed the facility and the process at Listowel, and although they remained based in Dublin, the time they devoted to the Listowel project was considerable. Additionally, in the first few months of 1972, when Brosnan was still without a staff of his own, they were pressed into service to help with the project management and co-ordinate with the consulting engineers.

Not only had Brosnan no staff of his own yet, but when he arrived he had no office, and no telephone. There was only a muddy field and a construction caravan for the builders. For the most part during the first weeks, he worked from home, where at least he had a phone. At the beginning of February, Brosnan confirmed the rental of a 22-foot caravan from Barrett's Garage on Bridge Street in Listowel, at £4 per week, payable in advance. It was provisional on Barrett removing the bunks, and clearing the caravan to offer maximum floor space. Granted, this was by no means the most important transaction made by North Kerry Milk Products. Still, the placement of the caravan in the parking lot of this muddy construction site was to create a vivid image that has become a genuine component of the Kerry mythology. This cramped, unpretentious caravan that was to house the first Kerry employees became, in many ways, symbolic of the very genesis of the organisation. Although we will return to this later, there was clearly no romanticism involved with the caravan at the time! It was a cheap and practical means of housing people and getting the job done. By all means, it was the production side of the facility that would be given the absolute priority, not the office accommodations. They were an afterthought. All eyes were to be utterly focused on the prize, which was the opening of the plant on schedule. The priorities were clear.

It was a maelstrom of activity, and for Brosnan probably the worst time. He was literally a "one man shop". A brief review of his correspondence is indicative of the pace of activity. There were reams of memos on the pricing and ordering of equipment, changes in equipment specifications, and requests for price quotes on raw materials like hydrochloric acid. There were quick notes written to maintain contact with brokers in the US with whom Brosnan had dealt while at Golden Vale, requests for information on casein pricing, and inquiries about shipping costs and insurance coverage. There were numerous responses to the many queries about employment at the new plant; many of them written, not by the applicants, but by local politicians writing on their behalf. Old habits die hard, and these requests had to be handled with great sensitivity. In addition to gathering up the loose strings of the finance, Brosnan also was travelling out to all ten of the co-operative partners to have a look at their facilities and equipment, and more importantly, meet his new constituents. He also began to come to grips with operational issues such as delivery of skim milk to the factory, plans for milk separation at the factory, quality standards and penalties for low quality milk. Knowing that whey disposal would be at least somewhat problematic, he was searching for contracts for the disposal of the whey that would be generated as a by-product of casein production. Most importantly, however, he began the process of recruiting the core staff of NKMP — the group that would need to complete the construction, effect the start-up, and actually run the factory and the business. Advertisements for a number of key positions including Production Manager, Assistant Production Manager, Chief Accountant and Chief of Quality Control were placed in the national press at a fast and furious pace early in the first quarter of 1972.

The Gang of Eleven

The target was to have the first wave of employees on Board by the beginning of April. On Monday, 3 April, Brosnan was joined by ten new employees:

- Hugh Friel (Chief Accountant)
- Denis Cregan (Production Manager)
- Michael Leahy (Assistant Production Manager)
- Brian Milton (Chemist)

- Eddie Moylan (Laboratory Supervisor)

- Pat Hartnett (Casein Supervisor)

- Noel Mahony (Casein Supervisor)

- Martin O'Grady (Fitter)

- Tom O'Connor (Electrician)

- Shirley Walsh (Secretary)

Although Brosnan's initial team was later nicknamed the "twelve disciples" by local wags, there were, in fact, only ten of them. To contemplate the scene through their eyes may offer a window on the reality, and the enormity, of the challenge.

Michael Leahy remembers that day.

> There was a fence up, the foundation walls were in place, and there was mud everywhere. Denis Brosnan greeted me and said, looking about the caravan, "You have a space from here to there." My first job that morning was to run a telephone wire from one office to the next, for the one black telephone that we all shared for almost a year. My next job was to go up to Mrs Carroll's hardware shop in town to get a bottle of gas to heat the office. When I got there Mrs Carroll said, "Where is your bottle?" I'd never bought a bottle of gas in my life! I was, at the time, just 22 years of age.[52]

Denis Cregan, another one of the new recruits who reported for work that day, remembers:

> I found a building site, but I couldn't quite tell what it was all supposed to mean. There were ad hoc buildings, some in various stages of development, some of it on the ground, some in foundations with no roofs. It really wasn't the shape of a factory, as I would understand it. I was coming from a food industry background, where when you went to commission a factory they were nearly finished. Here we were laying concrete, so . . . we were really in the deep end.[53]

Construction was well underway. The first of the staff, and certainly the nucleus of the key staff, had now arrived, and the work of getting the facility built, and commissioned, continued at breakneck pace. Luckily, the weather during the first few months of the year had been good. The target date for start-up (which had been May) was now 1 June. To say that this target date was ambitious would have been a wild understatement; it was an enormous stretch. Michael Leahy remembers sometime later on that first day beginning to look at some of the drawings of the process and thinking:

> Jeez, this is very easy, we'll have this thing whacked by year-end. So I said to Denis, "When are you going to start production?" He said, "Oh, the first of June." I said, "No way."[54]

But all resources were fully committed to one job and one job only: to get the factory up and running to process milk in early June.

There was no "give" in that date, no "wriggle room", no room for deviation and no allowance for slippage. It had to happen. To even speak of not making that date was heresy. That two-month period of time, from April to June 1972, was to become one of the more critical stretches in the history of the Kerry organisation. It was the first commitment that Kerry, as an organisation, was to make. Whether they delivered on this promise or not, they would be setting a precedent. To Brosnan, it was critical that the fledgling organisation developed a reputation for meeting, rather than missing, its commitments. A more immediate motivator, however, may have been simply fear. County Kerry was sitting atop a large and growing milk pool in 1972, and the milk had to go somewhere to be processed. The NKMP facility had to be up and running and processing as much of that milk pool as possible; as it was, the plant capacity would have been insufficient in any event to process all of it. (Brosnan, however, had already promised that he would take all the milk from the federation of North Kerry Co-operatives, and made arrangements for any milk that could not be processed in 1972 to be sold, through NKMP, to Golden Vale.) From NKMP's perspective, this was a less than desirable situation, since it left an opening for this milk to go elsewhere, and there was a great fear that Golden Vale could ultimately take a good part of the Kerry milk pool. In any event, Brosnan was determined that as little of this milk pool would "leak" as possible.

For the newly recruited staff, there was no "honeymoon" period while they "transitioned" to their new jobs. As Hugh Friel, newly hired as the Chief Accountant, recalls, "We arrived, and we were off like a shot . . . just like that. They were exciting times!"[55] With Cregan and Leahy on site, most of the responsibility for the construction, installation, and commissioning of the plant fell upon them. Friel, for his part, dove immediately into the crisis over the financing of the plant. Brosnan was at the centre, co-ordinating it all and attending to the "political problems". One must also examine the nature of the challenge facing this management. First, they were charged with implementing a strategy that they themselves had had no hand in crafting, manufacturing a product with which they were unfamiliar. Secondly, they were building a plant that they had not designed. Not to say that there were major flaws with either, but the fact is that they took the ball that was handed to them, ran with it and never looked back. Thirdly, they were owned by a disparate coalition consisting of a semi-government agency, a family-owned American corporation, and an often-fractious federation of fiercely independent North Kerry Co-operatives. Finally, the entire enterprise was woefully undercapitalised, financed by a patchwork of government grants, loans, and equity from each partner. So the "gang of thirteen", working in close quarters in the caravan, tried to keep the shaky edifice together, going about their mission to get the factory built. For his part, Eddie Hayes, having hired Denis Brosnan and seen the subsequent hiring of a management team, stepped back and gave this new team his absolute, unwavering support. But this didn't mean that he was idle. The "political issues" were sufficient to keep him and Brosnan busy for quite some time.

The first of these issues was the necessity of keeping the ten federated North Kerry co-operatives together and singing from the same hymnal. This was not an easy task. Small dairy co-operatives in Ireland had always jealously guarded their independence. There was also apparently a movement afoot within some of the West Limerick co-operatives to amalgamate with Golden Vale, deserting the NKMP enterprise. In fact, Golden Vale was aggressively canvassing for support in Mountcollins (the co-operative located the furthest from Listowel) and elsewhere. It should be remembered that the members of the co-operative federation had essentially "guaranteed" that their milk supplies would be made available to NKMP. Any erosion of this milk pool could have had serious consequences for NKMP at this critical time, sending the worst conceivable message to lenders and other supporters. Golden Vale's active canvassing of NKMP suppliers, at a time when the new venture was scarcely off the ground and clearly at its most vulnerable, was clearly not appreciated by the factory's promoters. Also, at this point the IAOS was finalising a major revision of its 1966 proposals for rationalisation of the dairy industry. It had already met with representatives of the "big five" dairy co-operatives in Ireland (Avonmore, Ballyclough, Golden Vale, Mitchelstown, and Waterford), the Minister of Agriculture, James Gibbons, TD, and other senior members of the Department of Agriculture on 19 April. Representatives of Kerry were not invited; a separate meeting was held with representatives of NKMP in June 1972, a meeting that some in Kerry considered to be an afterthought at best. This was to be a "political problem" of the first degree.

For Brosnan, Friel and Cregan, the months of April–June 1972 were marked by frequent trips to Dublin for meetings at the IAOS and, increasingly, to meet with lenders. In fact, even as construction proceeded, the planned finance was eroding. Fortunately, the total share capital of £190,000 had, by April, been paid and the IDA grant of £145,000 at long last approved (although it would actually be paid out in instalments). Also, the long-term loan for £95,000 from ACC was expected to receive final approval shortly. However, a major blow was dealt when the long-term loan of around £200,000 expected from Taisce Stait failed to materialise. Compounding the shortfall was the fact that the estimated project cost had increased to £668,000 by this time. This left a gaping hole of £238,000 in the finance for the project. In the Ireland of 1972, for a fledgling dairy co-operative with no track record and a young management, this was a major sum. Even before production had started, it seemed that NKMP might not be able to meet its financial obligations. They say that when one knows he is going to be hung in the morning, it concentrates the mind wonderfully. Brosnan and

Friel urgently needed to plug this gap, or the entire enterprise could collapse like a house of cards.

Initially, they attempted to negotiate bridging loans with a major Irish bank, but the bank ultimately declined to provide such finance. Other financial institutions showed an equal lack of interest in taking Friel's phone calls. As the plant began to near partial completion in May, and the beginning of production was close at hand, things looked rather bleak. Bills were coming due and the money to pay them was simply not there. At just that moment, however, NKMP were to be the recipients of another twist of fate, or luck!

Joe Madden, the IAOS economist who had laboured so diligently on the preparation, revisions, and various submissions of the grant proposal for the processing plant, had decided to leave IAOS to take a position elsewhere. This was, at first, bad news for Hugh Friel, since no one knew the ins and outs of the project better than Madden. However, when he learned that Madden would be taking a position with the Northern Bank Finance Corporation, Friel was less aggrieved. In fact, the day that Madden took up his new position he was contacted by Friel to discuss funding prospects. When they met later to discuss the possibilities, Madden was taken aback when Hugh Friel handed him his own report, the IDA grant proposal, as the basic project information. Not only did no one know the details of the project better than Madden but, importantly, he also knew the people behind the numbers, believed strongly in the project, and had every confidence that it would succeed. Madden was able to overcome a certain amount of scepticism within the bank, which although it was Irish had a UK parent, and allayed the various fears about the youth of the management, the priorities of co-operatives, the impact of the EEC Common Agricultural policy in 1973, and similar issues. Still, it was by no means an "easy sell" to the Bank's Board of Directors.

By the end of May, Northern Bank Finance Corporation had approved £200,000 in Redeemable Cumulative Preference Shares to be invested in NKMP. These shares would be redeemed over a period of seven years, at a rate of 3.5–4 per cent, and were guaranteed by the various partners in NKMP. For the bank, they also had the benefit of offering certain tax advantages because of NKMP's status as an export company. This loan facility was the "missing link" that finally tied together the finance for the project; it had literally come in the nick of time. Madden remembers that "the day that the loan was approved, they were so desperate for it, they picked up the cheque that night in Dublin".[56]

Even today, Madden is amazed at how close they had come to having the entire scheme unravel.

> The finance was not arranged! There was a huge hole. I don't know how they did it. They had an underfunded company, with a doubtful milk supply and doubtful finance, no money and no staff. I honestly don't know how Denis and Hugh got it going!

But while the finance was being dealt with behind the scenes, construction of the plant continued apace. The weather had been relatively forgiving. Galvin, the builder, was co-operative and efficient, and the work crews had shown a superb work ethic. There had been no slowdowns or disputes of a kind that were not uncommon in Ireland. By the end of May, the factory was far from finished, but Denis Brosnan was not going to let that stand in the way of the start of production.

The Opening of the Factory and "Teething Problems"

Although production officially began on Monday, 12 June 1972 (it had actually begun operations on 2 June), the factory itself was not nearly finished. There was no roof on part of the building (tarps were being used to keep out the elements), the Quality Assurance lab was not finished, there was no office block, and the equipment itself had only been started up less than two weeks before. Nevertheless, milk deliveries began and the process was kicked into motion, ready or not; Kerry was well into its milk season, and there was literally no time left. Getting production started in a half-finished plant was no small achievement. It was also important that production got going on the 12th because Brosnan had scheduled a luncheon for all the principals in the enterprise, followed by a press conference, at the Ambassador Hotel in the nearby holiday resort of Ballybunion. The Reisenbiglers came in from the States, Jack Hennigan of the Dairy Disposal Board came in from Dublin, and many leaders of the North Kerry Co-ops and local dignitaries were in attendance. Everyone said a few words. At the press conference, Brosnan spoke of NKMP becoming one of the "big six" companies in the dairy industry, and made particular note of the new plant's effluent treatment plant that was "probably the most elaborate" in the country.[57] Reisenbigler said he was "delighted we were given the opportunity to share in a small way in your operations, and it is projects such as this which will keep Irish youth in the country".[58] Hennigan paid tribute to North Kerry farmers:

> We couldn't have it at all without the farmers who have been patient and borne with disappointments in the past in regard to getting a factory here in Listowel. Manufacturing isn't going to finish at casein. I can see Listowel becoming one of the big centres in the country for milk products.[59]

But even as the speakers concluded their brief remarks, there were problems brewing at the plant. The start of production was premature (as was clear from the lack of a roof!), but Brosnan felt he had no choice. There was literally no tomorrow, and the plant had to get going. If it had been sheer force of will that had got the project started in the first place, it was a similar force of will that powered the plant start-up. Unfortunately, the "teething problems" of the new facility manifested themselves almost immediately and, as we might say today, in "real time".

As production commenced, the manufacturing process for casein worked reasonably well. It was the disposal of the liquid whey that presented immediate and dramatic problems. When the plans for the Listowel factory had been initially presented, it was assumed that the whey generated by casein manufacture could be disposed of through its sale as a raw material to a lactose factory. Specifically in mind was another proposed factory that would be a joint venture of North Kerry Milk Products and majority owned by Unigate. This factory was never built. A second alternative for whey disposal was to sell it to pig farmers, for whey was an excellent feed for pigs. However, there was too much whey, and too few takers had been lined up. Part of the reluctance on the part of pig farmers to take the whey was because, first of all, many of them were accustomed to feeding only skim milk. If they used whey at all, it was something called "sweet whey", made from the rennet from milk. But since Listowel's whey had been generated using a more corrosive process, farmers were sceptical. A third alternative would have been to actually process the whey in-house. This would be the longer-term solution, but there was simply no capital available at the time. For the moment, whey was simply stored in the effluent tank (which created its own problems) or simply hauled away and dumped.

NKMP began to dump whey wherever it could find an appropriate disposal site, in old bogs, in sandpits and in the ocean where it would be quickly diluted. The plan was that:

> . . . it would be disposed of by spraying over waste land or
> bog, storing in lagoons until oxidation took place . . . and . . .
> discharging into tidal waters at rapid outflow.[60]

The community reaction was quick and emotional, and a few unfortunate accidents fanned the flames. The first incident occurred on June 14 when a lorry loaded with whey was en route to an old bog owned by Eddie Hayes in Kilflynn. The lorry got stuck in the mud on the way up the hill, and in the process of trying to dislodge itself dumped the entire load of whey into the road where it spilled into a local stream, which in turn, drained into the local reservoir. The reservoir caretaker, one Michael Fitzgerald, discovered a two-foot high head of froth and foam in the 120,000 gallon storage tank, and cut off the water supply to the surrounding community. The water remained cut off for a day, until the tank could be scoured and the reservoir cleaned. It became front page news, a local cause célèbre, and a very messy public affairs issue for the infant company. At the same time, there were protests at public meetings in the seacoast resorts of Ballybunion and Ballylongford concerning the dumping of whey from local piers.[61]

Although whey itself is a food, and not a dangerous chemical pollutant, NKMP was on the defensive. Eddie Hayes, in reply to questions from the local media, said that:

> People can be assured that whey in the water is not a
> health hazard. If the disposal problem does nothing more
> than highlight the need for processing the whey into
> powder then I'm happy.[62]

Bill Sweeney, also a member of the NKMP Board, attended the
public meeting in Ballylongford and reiterated that "no one associated with the Listowel project would dare do something that was
hurtful to the livelihood of the people in the area".[63] The key to
dumping whey was to make certain it was in water with a rapid
flow to ensure quick dispersion. Ironically, having pressed so hard
to meet the production timetable, and having been blessed with
strong community support, NKMP was now, in its first week of production, on the defensive in that same community.

The effluent treatment plant was also problematic. It was a new
and, in Ireland in 1972, untested technology and the process of
effluent treatment was largely one of trial and error. By the middle
of June, the effluent tanks were full, the weather was warm, and a
terrible odour developed. What had happened was that protein in
the effluent had accumulated in the tank and begun to degrade,
oxidising in the summer heat. The resulting odour was not pleasant. From July through September 1972, this terrible odour ema-
nated from the plant, causing considerable problems with the
community in Listowel. As Denis Cregan remembers:

> The factory was, in actual fact, shipshape, considering
> where we'd come from. After all, the guys had worked
> hard. But this is where we probably alienated a lot of peo-
> ple in the town who had supported us. They said, "Yes,
> guys, I can accept this, that and the other thing, but I can't
> sleep at night for the smell. We can't tolerate this." And
> we couldn't solve the bloody problem. [64]

There was no other effluent plant like it in Ireland. There was little
or no research available on it. Other factories producing casein, in
Australia and New Zealand, had no effluent treatment at all to
worry about. Here NKMP was, in reality, light years ahead of others, but this was in relative terms only. The local reality was that
effluent treatment, and the odour, was a festering sore for the entire summer of 1972.

Certainly, the first few weeks of the plant operation were critical, and the first five to six months remained extremely difficult.
Indeed, this would have been true under probably the best of circumstances. Conditions at NKMP, however, were far from ideal,

and the pressures on the management were intense. There were only a few managers with experience who knew how to run a processing plant, and they had to keep the operation going, and train a cadre of spirited but inexperienced operators at the same time. This was a 24-hour-a-day, seven-day-a-week process. A solution had to be found to the whey problem, which was casting a pall over the entire enterprise. The effluent tanks were full, the weather was warming up, an awful smell was emanating from the plant, milk was streaming in to be processed, and the factory was not only expected to be operational, but also supposed to be profitable in its first year. The plant's performance during the first few months of operation would set the precedent for the years to follow, and for the very future of the enterprise.

The problem was, quite simply, that they had started too soon. The clock had run out, and rather than wait until the facility had been fully started-up, the processes de-bugged, and production gradually scaled-up, Brosnan had had to make a difficult decision. Should they begin production and catch the milk season, or wait until everything was in order, and miss a good part of it? He chose the former. Now, after perhaps a month of production, it was decision time again. A meeting was held in late June to discuss the numerous start-up issues, and to decide whether to stop production until the problems could be solved. Brosnan, Cregan and Friel all agreed that it would be suicidal to shut down production. If they stopped, they were doomed. The milk season would have been missed, farmers would have had to scramble for some other way to dispose of their skim, and the entire enterprise would have been in jeopardy. It would also amount to a broken promise to the farmers in Kerry who had funded the project, and to an admission of failure. For that matter, if the plant had shut down to get its house in order, would it ever have reopened? This was not a rhetorical question, but a real possibility. Taking this kind of risk was simply unacceptable. Rightly or wrongly, production was maintained, and the management continued to grapple with the whey disposal problem on an *ad hoc* basis. They would also have to continue to deal with negative public reactions.

Another problem, which beset the factory from almost the very beginning, was the absence of adequate storage facilities. Although the silos used for incoming milk had already been sized-up from the original plant specifications, they were still insufficient to handle the massive amount of milk that was being delivered to the factory. Things were so tight that silos were filled almost immediately once they were emptied of the previous day's milk that was sent into production. All the production steps were tightly, tightly coupled, and if there were any delays in processing (as in typical start-up situations associated with any production process) everything backed up. Having additional storage tanks would have provided a larger buffer for such problems, but they didn't have them. What did happen was that tanker trucks (lorries) would be lined up outside the gates of the factory and all the way down the road towards Listowel, waiting for their opportunity to offload their milk. This, too, was a difficult and, by its nature, a very public problem. It was not unusual at the time for lorries to wait four, five or six hours to be unloaded.

It is very important to note here that these sorts of issues are absolutely typical of the start-up and commissioning phase of a new factory, and are experienced by manufacturing and process engineers around the world. What is unusual about the case of NKMP, however, is that there simply was no time to go through a "normal" commissioning process. To meet their commitments regarding opening the factory, and processing as much of the milk pool as possible, it was necessary to "take off" at a gallop from ground zero. There was to be no leisurely commissioning process, no "dotting of i's and crossing of t's", no gradual ramping up of processing over an extended time period. At a meeting of the Listowel Urban Council in late June, the Listowel town surveyor commented upon this:

> I was told that the plant was going to start slowly; that they were only going to take in so much milk at a time and that this would be built up over a number of months, thus giving the plant a chance of properly forming. In fact, what happened is that they seemed to have taken quite a large quantity in from the beginning with the result that the plant wouldn't be capable, in my opinion, of dealing with the quantities involved.[65]

It was into the deep end from the beginning. Problems were addressed as they were happening; whatever had to be done was done at the time. The important thing was to take in as much milk as possible, and process it. That was "Job Number 1", and all efforts were focused upon it.

The pace of the plant activities was dizzying, the problems daunting, and the stakes were clear — it was a matter of survival. Contemporary public accounts of the opening of the factory and its first six months of operation promote the image of a factory opening, its staff working hard, yielding a highly successful first year of operations — as was planned. One might have formed the impression that it was a seamless progression of planning, execution, and results. True, the plant was successful, but the road it travelled to get there was bumpy, messy and not without cost. It is not fully appreciated, outside of the principals involved, how close the project came to failure. Throughout 1972, the operation was very much day-to-day, as the milk came in, the process was debugged, people were trained, disposal issues were managed, plans were made for the future, and not incidentally, a profit had to be made!

How did the management keep the "house of cards" from collapsing? The answer to this question represents perhaps the cornerstone of Kerry's vaunted organisational culture, the essential foundation upon which its successes of later years were built. Quite simply, the survival and success of the factory was a clear testament to the will, the efforts, the determination, the energy, the cohesion, and the spirit of its people. They simply refused to even acknowledge the possibility of failure; the word was not even in the vocabulary. Failure was inconceivable.

The core staff was young, energetic, fully committed and relatively inexperienced. Even the more senior people like Brosnan, Friel and Cregan had only four to five years of industrial experience. Brosnan was 27, Cregan 26, Friel 27, and Michael Leahy was the youngest at 22. There was in Kerry at the time, and indeed probably throughout Ireland, a lack of experienced, trained skilled workers to operate in highly technical food, beverage and pharmaceutical operations. Many of the new recruits for the factory, in fact, had never been on a factory floor before, and were far better acquainted with the farmyard than an industrial operation. The skills available were limited and basic, but the new people were good physical workers, highly intelligent, with a serious work ethic and a massive amount of energy. But it was more difficult to recruit people in the trades — electricians and fitters, for example — who, after the first few months of plant operation, were needed to maintain the equipment. In fact, in Kerry it was almost impossible. Advertisements were placed in the papers, but the results were disastrous, and maintenance staff could not be recruited. There were some, however, who came to work on a contract basis and kept the operation afloat.

These problems were overcome, in large measure, by a developing work culture that emphasised joint responsibility for the accomplishment of the goal. It was never articulated, never committed to policy, but clearly implicit in everything that was done. Although people had job titles, these did not imply limits to job responsibilities. Everyone, regardless of rank, did various bits and pieces as needed. If a truck came in to deliver milk and there was no one at the weigh station, Hugh Friel or whoever was around would go out and do it. If some material had to be moved, Denis Cregan would hop on a forklift. If they were short of staff one day and the floor of the casein plant had to be washed, Denis Brosnan would grab a hose and wash it down. Workers still tell stories of being on a production line on the third shift in the middle of the night, bagging casein, when a member of the management staff would walk in to check on things. If they were falling behind, the manager would grab a white coat and pitch in bagging until the pressure was lessened. These were common occurrences. There was no such phrase as "but that's not my job".

The management team was "on" nearly 24 hours a day. Indeed, for the first five to six months, the managers ran on a "semi-shift" basis, with somebody always around, and with managers coming in just to "check" on things in the middle of the night or three o'clock in the morning. It was not at all uncommon, say, for Denis Cregan to appear in the middle of the night and make his rounds of the factory, checking out the operation. Now, in the early days, many of the workers were quite new and unfamiliar with the procedures holding sway in the operation of a very hygienic, food-processing operation. As such, it was often hard to get them to keep on their white lab coats and white hats while they were working. They had a tendency to leave them off, especially as the weather warmed. The story is told about the time that Denis Cregan turned up in the middle of the night, and word of his appearance began to spread. One young man, a new fellow, was duly warned and dutifully passed the word on to another guy who was standing around without his white coat. "For Christ's sake", he said, "put your white coat and hat on, Cregan's around!" He didn't know it was Cregan himself to whom he was giving the friendly warning!

On the marketing side, things had gone relatively well. Erie Casein had been able to move virtually all of the casein that was produced, and was in fact introducing the Kerry product under a new brand name in the United States. Some of the casein had been shipped out of the small Atlantic port of Fenit, about five miles from Tralee, but this had to be scrapped for less direct but more conventional shipping points.

There was no magic wand waved to solve all the problems of the start-up of the plant. They were solved, over time, and through a series of trial and error. With the cooler weather, the odour problem began to resolve itself, and the necessary bacteria had begun to build up in the system enough to ensure that the problem would never reach such severity again. The effluent plant began to operate at a higher level of efficiency. Additional storage was added. More pig farmers were taking the whey by-product, and better sites for dumping any surplus had been located. They began to pull away from the crises that had threatened to shut down the plant in June/July.

So, one may tally the successes and failures of those first six months. Among the bumps and bruises was the unfortunate public fallout associated with the whey disposal, effluent and odour problems. Transportation and unloading problems also persisted, and a fair amount of protein was lost in that first year, as processes were debugged. But ultimately, the critical goals had been achieved. The milk had been processed, the farmers had been paid, the plant had finally been completed, the factory had survived and even a profit had been delivered. And, importantly, plans for the future were being laid, for activities at NKMP proceeded in parallel, and not sequentially! While the staff were fighting the day to day fires and dealing with urgent crises, Brosnan was already dreaming, planning years out. Although there may have been no formal, written strategic plan, there was a clear vision of the organisation's future already taking shape in Brosnan's head.

It is interesting and telling to note that while others may have looked for a breather towards the end of 1972, a chance to slow down the pace, take stock, and consolidate, Brosnan and his staff would have none of it. The pace did not slacken. Even before the casein plant was wholly complete, they had already embarked on a further expansion of processing capabilities at Listowel, specifically the construction of a milk powder processing plant. They had secured the necessary financing from another call on capital, the IDA (by way of an additional grant), and the banks, and had the equipment ordered by September so that the new plant would be online for the milk processing season of 1973. Time, as always, was of the essence.

Profit for 1972 would total just under £100,000, on sales revenue of approximately £1,000,000. It was a remarkable achievement, but there was little time to celebrate. Enormous changes were about to occur in Irish agriculture, particularly in Kerry, and the managers and promoters of the factory were going to be centre stage. Nineteen seventy-three was going to be a very busy year.

Notes

[1] "Farm Schools" were established after the Knapp Commission Report on co-operative activities in Ireland, which recommended to the IAOS that education and training activities be given priority and focus. These schools commonly offered courses in practical farming skills and new techniques that farmers could take two days a week during the winter months, when work on the farm was less pressing. Also of interest is the fact that the General Manager of the Abbeydorney Co-operative at the time the farm school started was Tom Brosnan, uncle of Denis Brosnan.

[2] John B. Keane, personal interview, 29 March 2000.

[3] John O'Flaherty (1997), "A Tribute to Eddie Hayes, a Man of Vision and Persistence", hand-written memoir.

[4] Seamus McConville, personal interview, 27 May 1999.

[5] Listowel Industrial Development Association (1960), "Facilities for Industrialists – What Listowel has to Offer", p. 1.

[6] Letter written by Bill Sweeney, Secretary of Shannon Valley Milk Development Association, undated; reply from Foremost received 12 March 1962.

[7] "Eddie Hayes Saw his Dream Come True", *Kerry's Eye*, 13 February 1997. This obituary of Eddie Hayes appeared in *Kerry's Eye*, a weekly newspaper in County Kerry. It provides a good sequential summary of Hayes' efforts to secure a milk processing factory for Kerry.

[8] As already noted, O'Reilly was the first general manager of Bord Bainne, and has been credited with much of its initial success. He went on to become a well-known businessman in both the United States and Ireland, as CEO of Heinz, Inc., as the Chairman of Independent Newspapers Group, and as an active board member of other firms.

[9] *The Kerryman* (1965), "Cheese Factory to be Built in Listowel", *The Kerryman*, 15 May 1965, p. 1.

[10] A *federation* of co-operatives should not be confused with an *amalgamation* of co-operatives. A *federation* is a loose association of co-operatives, operating in league together in matters of joint interest. In a federation, each co-operative maintains its own identity and independence. An *amalgamation*, on the other hand, is a full-scale merger of two or more co-operatives into a larger, singular entity. The co-operatives involved in this federation were Abbeydorney, Ballinclemessig, Fealesbridge, Lee Strand, Lixnaw, Newtownsandes, Brosna and Ratoo in County Kerry and Athea and Mountcollins in County Limerick.

[11] *The Kerryman* (1968), "Want Butter Making Plant at Listowel", *The Kerryman*, 27 January 1968.

[12] Letter from John O'Donnell, Manager of the Listowel branch of the Provincial Bank of Ireland, Ltd., to Eddie Hayes, 25 April 1968.

[13] See, for example, the Minutes of North Kerry Co-operative Creameries committee meeting, 25 October 1968.

[14] Minutes of the North Kerry Co-operative Creameries committee meeting, op. cit.

[15] Minutes of the North Kerry Co-operative Creameries committee meeting, op. cit.

[16] Clyde Francis Lytle (ed.) (1964), *Leaves of Gold*, Williamsport, PA: Coslett Publishing Co. (Sheridan's quotation is found on the unnumbered second page of the Table of Contents).

[17] Bill Sweeney, personal interview, 16 July 1999.

[18] Both Bill Sweeney (from the NKMP side) and Johnny Moriarty from the Listowel Racecourse Company related this story to me.

[19] Minutes of the North Kerry Co-operative Creameries committee meeting, 8 November 1968.

[20] *The Kerryman* (1969), "French Hope for Listowel", 29 November 1969, p. 1.

[21] *The Kerryman* (1969), "French Hope for Listowel", 29 November 1969, p. 1.

[22] Minutes of a Special Committee Meeting of North Kerry Co-operative Creameries Ltd., 4 August 1970.

[23] Minutes of a Special Committee Meeting of North Kerry Co-operative Creameries Ltd., 18 August 1970.

[24] Minutes of a Special Committee Meeting of North Kerry Co-operative Creameries Ltd., 18 August 1970.

[25] Bill Sweeney, personal interview, 16 July 1999.

[26] Arden G. Reisenbigler, personal interview, 9 February 2000.

[27] Erie Foods International, web page, www.eriefoods.com.

[28] Sylvia Reisenbigler, personal interview, 6 March 2000.

[29] Sylvia Reisenbigler, op. cit.

[30] Arden G. Reisenbigler, personal interview, 9 February 2000.

[31] Minutes of a Special Committee Meeting of North Kerry Co-operative Creameries Ltd., 26 January 1971.

[32] Minutes of a Special Committee Meeting of North Kerry Co-operative Creameries Ltd., 26 April 1971.

[33] Comment from T. Sheehan (Newtownsandes), as quoted in the Minutes of a Special Committee Meeting of North Kerry Co-operative Creameries Ltd., 26 January 1971.

[34] Bill Sweeney, personal interview, 16 July 1999.

[35] Minutes of a Special Meeting of North Kerry Co-operative Creameries Ltd., 17 December 1971.

[36] Taisce Stait was something of a government "reserve bank". It loaned funds at no interest, most typically to either "bail out" failing firms, or to provide "start-up" funding to new ventures. In 1971, however, this programme was in the process of being eliminated. It was thought that the funding provided to NKMP would be the last grant made by Taisce Stait. Unfortunately, however, the programme was eliminated before the NKMP grant was made.

[37] Minutes of a Special Meeting of North Kerry Co-operative Creameries Ltd., 17 December 1971.

[38] Memo from Jim Moloney to Jack Hennigan, 27 September 1971.

[39] Mundy Hayes, personal interview, 12 October 1999.

[40] Jim Moloney, personal interview, 8 July 1999.

[41] Bob Siewert from Erie Casein did not participate in any of the interviews, as he spent only a week or so a month in Ireland during this time. He did, however, review resumes and offer comments, and later he and his wife Sylvia met with Brosnan in London.

[42] Michael Dowling, former Secretary of the Department of Agriculture and a current Board member of Kerry Group, went to school with Brosnan at St. Brendan's, Killarney. He tells the story, perhaps apocryphal, of a fellow classmate sitting in a room waiting to be interviewed for a job. When he saw Denis Brosnan walk in to the waiting room, he got up and left. With Brosnan among the candidates, he knew already that he wasn't going to get the job. So, even to people who were only at university with him — they knew.

[43] Jim Moloney, personal interview, 8 July 1999.

[44] I draw largely on Jim Moloney's recollections of the process of hiring the General Manager.

[45] Memo from Jim Moloney to Denis Brosnan, 5 November 1971, offering him the position of General Manager of North Kerry Milk Products.

[46] Minutes of a Meeting of the Board of Directors of North Kerry Milk Products, 4–5 November 1971.

[47] Denis Brosnan, personal interview, 7 October 1999.

[48] Aileen O'Toole (1987), *The Pace Setters*, Dublin: Gill and Macmillan, p. 95.

[49] Denis Brosnan, personal interview, 7 October 1999.

[50] Michael Drummey, personal interview, 6 January 2000.

[51] Minutes of a Meeting of the Board of Directors of North Kerry Milk Products, 3 December 1971.

[52] Michael Leahy, personal interview, 6 December 1999.

[53] Denis Cregan, personal interview, 12 October 1999.

[54] Michael Leahy, personal interview, 6 December 1999.

[55] Hugh Friel, personal interview, 31 May 1999.

[56] Joe Madden, personal interview, 31 March 1999.

[57] *The Kerryman*, 17 June 1972, p. 17.

[58] *The Kerryman*, 17 June 1972, p. 17.

[59] *The Kerryman*, 17 June 1972, p. 17.

[60] *The Kerryman*, 1 July 1972.

[61] *The Kerryman*, 17 June 1972, p. 1.

[62] *The Kerryman*, 17 June 1972, p. 1.

[63] *The Kerryman*, 17 June 1972, p. 1.

[64] Denis Cregan, personal interview, 27 March 2000.

[65] A.N. Dillon, quoted in *The Kerryman*, 1 July 1972.

Chapter 4

The Formation of Kerry Co-operative Creameries, Ltd.

Many dedicated Kerry farmers had fought hard over the years for such a farmer owned Group to control and influence the incomes of the Kerry farming community. Few would have believed it possible to achieve so much in such a short space of time. We owe much to the dedication of those farmers who have kept the flag flying. — Eddie Hayes[1]

The IAOS Proposals for Rationalising the Dairy Industry

By 1972, it was clear that the IAOS proposals for the rationalisation of the dairy industry in Ireland, originally presented in 1966, were "seriously out of date".[2] For the most part, they had never been acted upon. Now, with the advent of Ireland's accession to membership in the EEC, it was more critical than ever that Ireland's small co-operatives, as well as the Dairy Disposal Company, take steps towards amalgamating and rationalising their activities. Without the advantages to be gained from scale and scope economies in the production of milk and the processing of milk products, the industry would be seriously disadvantaged in competition with other producers in the Common Market. As noted earlier, the IAOS and the Minister for Agriculture, James Gibbons, had met with representatives of the "Big Five" of Irish Dairy Co-operatives in April. Later, Paddy Kelly, the Director General of the

IAOS, had a one-on-one meeting with the representatives of NKMP who were, at the time, just starting up their processing plant in Listowel.

At this meeting on 16 June at the Listowel Arms Hotel, Denis Brosnan presented to Kelly and his colleagues from IAOS his vision and plan for the amalgamation of all the creameries in Kerry into a countywide co-operative organisation. Hugh Friel, who along with several NKMP Board members accompanied Brosnan to the meeting, remembers that although Brosnan's presentation was not a formal, sophisticated one, the representatives from IAOS took notes furiously. He obviously had their attention. Clearly, Brosnan's intent was to get to the IAOS before they issued their final report. He wanted to make the IAOS aware that there was a plan for the amalgamation of all of Kerry into one co-op, that the start-up of the milk processing factory was only the beginning, and that he was personally committed to pushing the amalgamation plan forward. Brosnan had a very, very clear picture of what he wanted to do. That he was able to do this at a time when he and his staff were contending with serious start-up issues at the Listowel factory is a testament to his vision and ability to balance pragmatic operational issues with longer-term goals. One is reminded of the popular adage often found posted on office walls. It goes like this: "When you're up to your neck in alligators, it's hard to remember that your original intention was to drain the swamp!" Brosnan and his colleagues, however, had a remarkable ability to keep their eyes on the larger issues, while successfully managing the day-to-day ones. Although it may not always have existed on paper, or in detail, Brosnan always had a plan; he saw the big picture, the long run. He saw what he calls the "jigsaw puzzle", and was focused upon fitting the pieces to the puzzle, one by one. If the construction of the factory had been the first piece of the jigsaw, then the amalgamation of Kerry creameries was the logical next step.

But Brosnan was negotiating from a position of weakness. The NKMP management was young, with energy, ambition and plans but no track record. Their manufacturing facility at Listowel was only now getting off the ground, and in any event, did not yet have the necessary capacity to process all of the county's milk, unless they expanded. The problem with expansion was that they had no money. It had been a huge challenge to raise the finance for the construction of the casein plant, let alone an immediate *expansion* of processing capabilities. Despite the fact that NKMP's management was already planning just such an expansion, most outside observers would not have shared such confidence.

Eddie Hayes had a good friend at IAOS, Jim Moloney, who was the Assistant Secretary working directly for Paddy Kelly, the Director General. Although Moloney was a strong supporter of the idea of an all-county co-operative in Kerry, it was a view that most in IAOS did not share. Indeed, the predominant view at IAOS was that the formation of a countywide co-operative in Kerry was an unrealistic possibility. Since approximately two-thirds of the milk in the county was handled by the DDC, it was expected to be extremely difficult under those circumstances to finance the purchase of the DDC assets, especially by the farmer-shareholders of a new co-operative. Looking at the neighbouring co-operatives, the IAOS could see that Golden Vale, Mitchelstown and Ballyclough already had purchased, or were about to purchase, their local DDC creameries. But, in the view of IAOS, there was no such strong co-operative in Kerry to fill that same role.

The IAOS published their "Proposals for Creamery Rationalisation 1972" in July, and the response to Brosnan's proposals was more in what was not said than in what was. Effectively, Kerry had been written out of the plan. Although the IAOS did recognise a "North Kerry Group" of co-operatives and the Ardfert, Listowel and Dingle DDC creameries, it suggested that Golden Vale and Ballyclough had the "inside track" with regard to the large DDC creameries in South Kerry — creameries handling nearly 26 million gallons of milk. Thus, although the official proposal did not read as such, people in Kerry read between the lines, and what they read was unsettling. The county's milk supply would be carved up, with some going to Listowel, some to Golden Vale, and some to Ballyclough. Effectively, this meant that NKMP would remain a small, amalgamated co-operative with a processing factory, with no opportunities to grow beyond its current size. Ultimately, it would have to amalgamate itself with one of the larger societies. So, the issue of this report was a body blow to the hopes of the NKMP managers. Indeed, it did not even mention the plan for a countywide co-operative presented by Brosnan at the June meeting. It was as if the proposal had never been made.

Unlike the 1966 proposal, the 1972 IAOS plan did have an immediate and lasting effect. Although events did not proceed in a way that the IAOS may have anticipated, the result it ultimately yielded must have been very satisfying to those, like the IAOS, who were supporters of the co-operative movement in Ireland. In effect, the proposal became something of a rallying cry for those in Kerry seeking to amalgamate the co-operatives, buy out the Dairy Disposal Company creameries, and create a countywide co-operative.

Keeping the Co-ops Together — Mountcollins and Brosna

Even while the impact of the IAOS proposal was still being absorbed, a second disturbing event had occurred. Mountcollins, one of the ten federated co-operatives in North Kerry Co-operative Creameries, Ltd., had decided by the end of 1972 to abandon the federation and amalgamate instead with Golden Vale, the giant co-operative to the east. This could have been a serious blow to NKMP and to the plans then afoot to amalgamate into a countywide co-operative organisation. After all, the factory had not yet even been completed, and here was Mountcollins, a shareholder that had already paid its first call on capital, abandoning the ship.

NKMP was heading into a second programme of expansion, and they were now short one shareholder. It was as if one of the boards in the boat had a crack and sprung a leak. Of itself, it was not critical, but if it got larger, the ship could go down. The analogy probably held true for NKMP. If other co-operatives followed Mountcollins out, the entire enterprise could unravel. The loss of Mountcollins was also critical because NKMP had received grants from the IDA for both the casein plant, and for the milk powder plant coming on line in 1973, based on written assurances of a dependable and certain milk supply being provided to the plant. Mountcollins, like the other co-operatives, had provided such assurances. Milk supply was the lifeblood of the factory, and the factory could only produce efficiently if the supply of milk was available to make full use of its capacity. The loss of Mountcollins cast a pall over things generally, and led to the fear that support from other co-ops could erode as well. Would there be a "domino effect"?

What led Mountcollins to leave in the middle of the project? First, there was the matter of geography. Mountcollins was almost squarely at the intersection of the borders of counties Kerry, Limerick and Cork, and well within the area serviced by Golden Vale. Indeed, the distance to Golden Vale's plant in Charleville was not much more than the distance to Listowel. Secondly, Golden Vale was canvassing the Mountcollins farmers very aggressively, and NKMP simply did not have the resources at the time to effectively contest them. Indeed, the Kerry managers had their hands full in Listowel, and one might suggest that the fledgling North Kerry enterprise was at its weakest as Golden Vale took Mountcollins. Of course, the fact that Mick Lenihan (who had recently been named General Manager of Golden Vale) was from that area may also not have been irrelevant. He had many friends and family members there. Terminology is also important here. Some in Kerry might suggest that Mountcollins was "poached", that is, lured away from Kerry with incentives or promises. Golden Vale might reply, rightly, that what it did was clearly legal; co-operatives have a perfect right to sell their milk to whomever they wish, and amalgamate with whomever they wish. Nevertheless, Golden Vale's refusal to play by the "unwritten rules" of the co-operative movement angered the managers at Kerry. The "defection" of Mountcollins rankled, and would not be easily or soon forgotten. In fact, when the "milk wars" between Kerry and Golden Vale developed in the early 1980s, some of the bad blood that characterised that dispute could be traced back to events in Mountcollins in 1972–73.

Later in 1973, the battlefield moved to Brosna, a small co-operative only a few miles from Mountcollins. Golden Vale again canvassed aggressively, but this time Kerry reciprocated in kind. NKMP had to stop the erosion of its milk supply. If Brosna were lost, and amalgamated with Golden Vale, there was a very real fear that other co-ops or DDC creameries would follow. Golden Vale, after all, was already holding meetings in Dicksgrove, Castlemaine, and even Dingle. Brosnan, in any event, was determined that Brosna would not be the next "domino" to fall.

Luckily, although Golden Vale had considerable support in Brosna, there was also a camp of strong Kerry supporters. Among the leaders of this group were Michael Murphy, Leo O'Connor, and importantly, the chairman of the Brosna co-operative, Pat Moriarty. Brosnan, accompanied by Moriarty, Murphy and O'Connor, spent the better part of a month canvassing every supplier to the Brosna co-operative door-to-door. They met with varying reactions. At some farms they would be offered a cup of tea or a glass of whiskey, at others only a cold shoulder. The three men who accompanied Brosnan on his rounds knew the suppliers well, and were able to read the signs and develop an accurate vote count. It was cold comfort, for the vote was literally too close to call. The membership was nearly evenly split.

The rules of the co-operative called for two votes, to be scheduled two weeks apart, with a simple majority required for the resolution to pass. The resolution itself called for Brosna to amalgamate with a number of North Kerry co-operatives who had themselves recently amalgamated to form Kerrykreem (shortly to join the Kerry Co-operative — see below). If the resolution did not pass, however, it was clear that Brosna would then amalgamate with Golden Vale.

At the first meeting, the resolution passed by one vote. Two weeks later, however, the vote was evenly split. The chairman, Pat Moriarty, then cast his own deciding vote, as permitted by the rules of the co-operative, in favour of the resolution. By this one slim vote, Brosna had elected to stay with Kerry. The Golden Vale supporters questioned the legality of the chairman's vote, and contested the vote in the High Court, where the case dragged on for years. Eventually, a settlement was reached by which Brosna amalgamated with the Kerry Co-operative, and those suppliers who wished could transfer to Golden Vale. About 20 of them did so.

Although, with the benefit of hindsight, the vote at Brosna may not seem like a major event in the history of the Kerry organisation, in the context of its times it was crucial. If Brosna had left, it is quite possible that other co-operatives, not to mention the DDC creameries, may have followed. The milk supply required to keep the Listowel factory viable would have been jeopardised, and subsequent efforts to create a countywide co-operative may have been compromised. Denis Brosnan called the vote in Brosna a virtual "Custer's Last Stand". Luckily for Brosnan, the outcome for him, close as it was, was far better than the one that awaited Custer! Keeping Brosna within the fold stanched any erosion of support within the co-operatives in North Kerry and sent a clear message that the Kerry organisation would vigorously contest attempts to woo its suppliers and cut into its milk pool.

At this time, from the middle of 1972 through to 1974, all of the major dairy co-operatives in Ireland were grabbing for territory. These large co-operatives were canvassing the smaller co-operatives as well as the DDC creameries, and not only those in their own "territory". There were plenty of disputes between the major co-operatives, and no lack of accusations of "poaching". Mitchelstown, for example, had taken several co-operatives that had been Golden Vale suppliers. Golden Vale, in its turn, went after Mountcollins, Brosna, and several of the DDC creameries in Kerry. If nothing else, the IAOS document on creamery rationalisation had made it "open season" on Kerry's milk supply. As the document had implicitly suggested that the county be carved up between Ballyclough and Golden Vale (with provisions to cater to the needs of the Listowel and Fry-Cadbury plants), the neighbouring co-ops were only too happy to oblige. But it is said, "what goes around, comes around!" Although the Kerry managers were clearly on the defensive against Golden Vale in 1972-73, this would not be the case in the future. Kerry's executives had, perhaps, learned their lessons well. Ironically, from now on it would more often be Kerry that would be accused of using aggressive and unsporting tactics and not playing by the unwritten rules of the co-operative movement, and Golden Vale and Ballyclough crying "foul".

Pressures for Amalgamation and Rationalisation, and the Formation of "Kerrykreem"

The IAOS Report did spur co-operatives to begin the process of amalgamation, but this was in recognition of far larger forces at play. The most important of these was Ireland's accession to the European Economic Community on 1 January 1973, along with the United Kingdom and Denmark. Ireland now had access to a huge internal market, along with the various price supports and incentives supplied by the Common Agricultural Policy. On the other hand, its businesses would now have to compete within the mar-

ket, particularly in the UK, which was long Ireland's primary market. In Irish agriculture, it was clear that farmers would have to become more productive, and processors would have to rationalise,
modernise and consolidate to succeed in this new economic arena.

Accession to the EEC had one other far more practical implica-
tion. The Dairy Disposal Company, by now entering its fifth decade as a "semi-state body", stood in clear contravention of EEC
regulations concerning state participation in agriculture. Simply
put, it would have to go, and its constituent units finally "disposed"
of, sold back to local co-operatives as had been originally envis-
aged in 1927. But through the 1960s, with the EEC on the horizon
and with the government showing an increasing willingness to encourage this process, transfers of DDC assets to co-operatives had
still been relatively few. With a change of administration in the
elections of 1973, however, Mark Clinton had assumed the Minis-
terial post at the Department of Agriculture. Clinton, a Fine Gael
TD, was fully prepared to move with dispatch in facilitating the
sale of DDC creameries and other assets in County Kerry. One way
of encouraging this was by pricing the sale of assets reasonably.

Throughout 1972 and into 1973, amalgamation was in the air, in
Ireland generally and in Kerry particularly. But even while amalgamation efforts got underway, additional projects and rationalisation activities were taking place at the factory. In the autumn of
1972, Denis Cregan, Michael Leahy, and the other managers began to take stock of the first six months of operations in the plant,
and put the finishing touches on completion of the casein plant.
Additionally, they were wrestling with two more projects. The first
was a proposal to the IDA for a planned expansion into skim milk
powder for the 1973 milk season. This would involve the purchase
and installation of a spray dryer. The IDA provided an additional
grant, bank financing was obtained, and profits from the first year
of NKMP's operations were ploughed back into the new milk powder plant. A second project was the installation of milk separation
equipment, so that whole milk might be received into the factory,
rather than going to a creamery first for separation, and the skim
then being transported to Listowel. Cregan kept an eye on the
home front, while Brosnan and Friel devoted their attentions to
meeting with members of the committees of the co-operatives in
the federation. The idea was to amalgamate the North Kerry Co-

operatives as a first step in the eventual amalgamation of all milk activities in the county. Actually, two of the co-operatives, Abbeydorney and Ballinclemmsig, had already amalgamated by that time. This started the ball rolling.

For this purpose, a "shell" co-operative had been registered, christened "Kerrykreem". Since it was possible that all ten North Kerry Co-operative societies would not decide to amalgamate, Kerrykreem would serve as the amalgamated co-operative for those that did. On 1 April 1973, five of the original ten North Kerry Co-operatives (Abbeydorney and Ballinclemmsig, Lixnaw, Athea and Rattoo) amalgamated and began trading as Kerrykreem Creameries Ltd. The other five North Kerry co-operatives, however, resisted amalgamation for varying reasons. Brosna, for instance, was on the fence and, as already detailed, was being aggressively courted by Golden Vale. Lee Strand, for its part, was a profitable liquid (consumer) milk business based in Tralee and had never shown any interest, let alone eagerness, to amalgamate with other societies. Fealesbridge and Newtownsandes (Moyvane) simply preferred to maintain their independence. Mountcollins was already lost to Golden Vale. At this point, on the cusp of the 1973 milk season, amalgamation was at best a partial success. The major test was still to come.

At the time of the formation of Kerrykreem, NKMP took some rapid steps to bring about a measure of rationalisation. It was not an all-encompassing, carefully choreographed series of steps by any means; rather, it was an attempt to achieve some economies immediately. Like so much in the early years of Kerry, it had to happen fast. Butter churning was halted at some of the individual creameries and centralised in Abbeydorney, which had a more modern continuous butter-making process. Administration was centralised in Listowel and, by the middle of 1973, the new milk powder plant was on-line. The stage was now set for the next stage of the drama: the proposal of a far-reaching plan for the amalgamation of *all* of the co-operatives *and* Dairy Disposal Creameries in Kerry into a single, countywide co-operative organisation.

The Plan for the Formation of Kerry Co-operative Creameries, Ltd.

By the middle of 1973, the county was awash with activity, but it was fragmented and disjointed as farmers in various areas looked to their own best interests and evaluated their options. In the Listowel DDC area, there was considerable talk of buying the DDC assets and forming an independent co-operative. There were also moves afoot further south in the county (in the Dicksgrove, Castlemaine and Cahirciveen DDC areas) to buy out the DDC assets and form their own co-operative. This group was also pushing vigorously for consideration of construction of another milk processing plant to be located in mid-Kerry. John Roche, a spokesman for the group, said that:

> We are not satisfied that Rathmore and Listowel are enough for the county and we are adamant that there should be a third processing factory. We have more than one-third of the county's milk . . .[3]

The Dingle DDC group was also interested in forming an independent co-operative, again, with talk of a processing plant for west Kerry. Yet, it was clear that any independent co-operatives that were formed would need to affiliate in some manner with the larger processors. Nor were Golden Vale and Ballyclough on the sidelines; each was actively canvassing for support in the Kerry DDC areas. There were many discussions at countless meetings, agreements in principle one way or the other, but no concrete action. There was also growing discussion of a forthcoming proposal, prepared by the managers of NKMP, to buy out the DDC and form an all-county co-operative organisation. But there was as yet no action, for there were a number of critical questions that needed to be answered. First, what kind of deal would the government be willing to accept for the purchase of the DDC? How much would it cost, to whom would they be willing to sell, and finally, would the farmers in Kerry support it?

It is at this point that the vital contribution of Frank Wall must be recognised. As noted already, Wall was a leader of the ICMSA at the national level and the head of the ICMSA in Kerry. A leading-supporter of the Fianna Fáil party, Wall was well connected politically, and well respected within the agricultural community throughout Kerry. He was a powerful figure within the dairy industry, not only in Kerry, but nationally. Wall was a consummate politician, in the best sense of the term. He was well able to work with people behind the scenes, capable of persuading them and influencing them, but also able to hear them. In his quiet way, Wall was seriously capable of getting things done. Given the weight of his influence in Kerry, Wall's support would be essential to the formation of a countywide co-operative.

Of course, Eddie Hayes' support for amalgamation could be counted upon. Hayes had been preaching just such a step for years. But Hayes could deliver only the North Kerry co-operatives that had already amalgamated as Kerrykreem; he had little influence in the DDC areas elsewhere in the county. This is where Frank Wall entered the picture. Indeed, Wall and Hayes were, in many ways, a study in contrasts. Eddie Hayes was a member of the IFA (the farming organisation that predominated in the Kerry co-operatives), where Wall was a member of ICMSA (the dominant organisation in most of the DDC areas). Hayes, active with the IAOS, was the co-op leader in Kerry where Wall, the ICMSA's nominee on Bord Bainne, was no doubt the "milk" leader. Hayes was Fine Gael, while Wall was seen as a Fianna Fáil supporter. Hayes always "led from the front"; once he had set a direction, he would doggedly, relentlessly follow it through. This may have been done, at times, with a certain lack of sensitivity. Over time, Hayes acquired as many enemies as friends. Frank Wall, on the other hand, used a very different leadership style. He exercised his influence quietly and effectively, but in the background. Eddie Hayes could be more direct, challenging the established system to secure his goals. Wall, a prudent man, would search for ways to work within the system. Observed one friend of Wall's, "Frank would want to know that the horse was a winner before he backed it!" For his part, Frank Wall had apparently few enemies. Given the tenor of farm politics in County Kerry, this was no mean feat!

Brosnan knew that to "sell" his plan for the creation of an all-county, Kerry Co-operative, he would need the support of Frank Wall. Wall had not been involved in any major way with the construction of the Listowel factory, which had been driven by Eddie Hayes. Although he had no direct role, Wall watched with more than a casual interest as NKMP was established and sorted itself out during its first year of production. But now, Brosnan would need Wall to use his huge influence with the suppliers to the eight DDC areas in Kerry (the majority of whom were members of the ICMSA) to support the plan. In a very real sense, Frank Wall was the key to a successful campaign to buy out the DDC and form the countywide co-operative.

Brosnan was quite confident that, if the proposal appeared to be in the best interest of the dairy farmers in the county, Frank Wall would support it. Brosnan, with Eddie Hayes' blessing, approached Wall, who agreed to come on board in support of the effort. Clearly, Wall must have sensed that in this proposal, and in Brosnan's management team, Kerry farmers finally had a horse (and a jockey!) on whom they could confidently place their money. The proposal to take over the Dairy Disposal Company assets in Kerry, and amalgamate into a countywide co-operative, was given instant legitimacy with the support of Wall and the ICMSA.

If Eddie Hayes had been the driving force in the construction of the Listowel factory and the creation of NKMP, then Frank Wall should be given equal pride of place for his support of the creation of the Kerry Co-operative. Denis Brosnan has gone so far as to say that "without the support of Frank Wall there would have been no Kerry Co-operative".[4]

Already, by June, Kerry Co-operative Creameries Ltd. had been registered, intended to serve as a "shell" society with which other societies or DDC groups could amalgamate (similar to the vehicle used in the Kerrykreem amalgamation).[5] Further, a negotiating committee had been formed that included one representative from each of the eight Dairy Disposal Area Advisory Committees, with the brief to negotiate with the Department of Agriculture for the transfer of DDC assets in County Kerry to the Kerry Co-operative. This negotiating committee, with the addition of Eddie Hayes representing Kerrykreem (the North Kerry co-ops), formed both the initial membership of the Co-op, as well as the first board of directors. Their contribution of £1 each totalled up to the Co-op's initial capital of £9. Frank Wall from Tarbert represented the Listowel DDC, and served as the first chairman of the Kerry Co-operative as well as the chair of the negotiating committee. Other founding members of the Kerry Co-op included Thomas

O'Connor, Michael Barry, Patrick (Patsy) O'Connell, Alexander (Sonny) O'Donnell, Thomas O'Sullivan, Patrick Golden and James O'Shea. With the co-operative "shell" formed, the negotiating committee in place, and the critical support of Frank Wall and the ICMSA, it was time for the effort to begin in earnest.

Jim Moloney of the IAOS played a major role in laying the groundwork for the negotiations. On 11 June, Moloney had a private meeting with Mark Clinton, the Minister for Agriculture, and asked him if he would be prepared to meet with this group of farmers (the negotiating committee) in Kerry who were interested in buying the Dairy Disposal interests in the county. The Minister agreed to meet with the delegation on 21 June. Now, it should be noted that Moloney had always offered strong support for the idea of a countywide dairy co-operative. Years later, he recollected that:

> I always took the view there should be an opportunity created for Kerry to form, if possible, a county co-operative. That would be a better way of dealing with the application of rationalisation, rather than trying to split the various co-operatives and the DDC. I always felt that there was a pride in Kerry, there was a determination there to succeed in the business and that rather than have them go to Golden Vale or Ballyclough, it would be better at least to try this first. However, in IAOS at the time, there was a strong feeling that the possibility of having a county co-operative in Kerry was unlikely to happen. But this was a view I didn't share, so once I got the opportunity to help [those in Kerry] develop the possibility, I did.[6]

The 21 June meeting was a good one. The Minister agreed in principle that he would be prepared to transfer all the DDC interests in Kerry *if* they were going into *one*, all-county co-operative, and *if* an acceptable transfer price could be agreed upon. It was precisely the signal that the negotiating committee needed. There was no more discussion of individual DDC areas buying the assets and forming independent co-operatives. The focus was now on a countywide co-operative. An opening offer of £750,000 had already been decided upon by Kerry (for assets, excluding transport equipment and the AI Station in Castleisland), and was conveyed to the Minister the following day, 22 June. The negotiations were on, and the response of the government was surprisingly swift. On 6 July, Clinton replied that the offer was too low, but in order to effect a "speedy transfer" he proposed a figure of £1,000,000, a figure described as "non-negotiable" and a "final offer". Clearly, the negotiating committee was not going to walk away from such an offer; after all, the value of DDC assets in Kerry was probably considerably higher, the most common estimate being £3,000,000. A further meeting between the negotiating committee and the Department of Agriculture was arranged on 13 July to deal with other outstanding assets, and a conditional agreement was reached. The Department was prepared to transfer all the assets of the Dairy Disposal Company creameries and branches, all the transport currently being used in the county (lorries, vans, etc.), its 42.5 per cent interest in North Kerry Milk Products (the Listowel factory), its pig farms at Cahirciveen and Kenmare, and its AI Station in Castleisland, for a total consideration of £1,150,000.

The deal was to be conditional on three critical points:

- The agreement would be subject to acceptance by the farmer-suppliers to the Dairy Disposal Creameries. So, even though their representative negotiating committee had accepted the deal, it would have to go to a vote of the full membership in each area. This was an absolute requirement of the Minister. At the several meetings that he had held with the negotiating committee, Clinton had often posed that question "but would they (the suppliers to the DDC creameries) support it?" The IAOS was to supervise elections in each of the eight areas to answer, conclusively, just this question.

- A continuing and adequate milk supply to Fry-Cadbury's chocolate crumb factory in Rathmore would be *guaranteed*. This had been a continuing concern, for the Rathmore factory was totally dependent on milk from the DDC suppliers. As the plant was a major employer in Kerry, it was essential that this milk supply be maintained. This was a particular concern for the Rathmore suppliers, many of whom had relatives, or even worked themselves, in the Fry-Cadbury plant.

- All the staff of the DDC Creameries would be taken on by Kerry Co-operative Creameries Ltd. There would be no re-dundancies or forced retirements.

The buy-out was to be financed by a bank loan (to be arranged by the Kerry Co-op) and paid to the Department in two equal instalments on 1 January 1974 and 1975. The suppliers of the Dairy Disposal Company in Kerry were to be encouraged to join the new co-operative. These farmers would subscribe for shares in the co-op on the basis of one 1 £1 share for every 41 gallons of milk supplied (at a minimum), with a maximum permitted shareholding of 1,000 shares. Milk suppliers had the option of paying cash for these shares, at a discount of 4%, or having the amount deducted from their milk cheques at the rate of 0.4p/gallon until paid in full. This was the plan that was accepted by the negotiating committees from the DDC creameries at a meeting in Tralee on 23 July. The announcement of this put an end to all the speculation in the county concerning the negotiations with the Minister, what would be included, and how much it would cost. The stage was now set to take the proposal to the farmers.

Selling the Proposal

The new co-operative would handle approximately 70,000,000 gallons of milk annually with a turnover of £25,000,000, putting it in the same league with the existing "Big Five" of Irish Dairy Co-operatives. A series of informational meetings was arranged throughout the county in each of the DDC areas, where the Kerry Co-operative promoters explained the plan, addressed questions, and laid out the benefits. Certainly Brian O'Shea, the IAOS Field Representative for Kerry, was the key man in this effort, organising the meetings, setting the procedures, and handling all of the important details and arrangements. An informational brochure outlining the proposal was distributed to every DDC supplier. Denis Brosnan attended each of the meetings, made a presentation, and answered questions. Hugh Friel attended most of the meetings, and Jim Moloney attended a few of the larger, and more contentious, ones. The members of the negotiating committee were also deeply involved, attending the meetings, answering questions, and forcefully arguing the benefits of the proposed amalgamation. In addition, the two primary farming organisations in the county, the IFA and the ICMSA, whatever their differences, offered their strong support, and urged their members to vote "yes".

As Kerry farmers considered the proposal and prepared to vote, the perceived opportunities and risks were widely discussed, in public and in private. In public houses, outside of church after Mass on Sunday, at the sporting matches, in any and every public forum, Kerry was abuzz with discussion of the buy-out and formation of the "giant" Kerry co-operative. In fact, one could go so far as to suggest that discussion of the proposal itself had taken on the proportions of a major football match. Everyone had an opinion. It provided a substantial diversion to Kerry farmers, and all connected with them, for a good many months in 1973. Certainly, the necessity to consolidate, amalgamate and rationalise was well recognised; Ireland had been in the EEC for nearly a year, and the benefits of membership were already widely recognised and in fact realised. However, membership in the EEC also provided the impetus for the big strides that the dairy industry in Kerry would have to make to continue to reap the benefits of membership. Milk quality would have to be improved, milk assembly and collection would need to make significant advances in efficiency, Kerry farmers themselves would have to update and upgrade their facilities and equipment, and the use of fertiliser, silage and other feeds would have to be expanded. All of this could only be facilitated through a dairy organisation of sufficient size and scope. A Kerry-wide dairy co-operative made economic sense. Still, as the Speaker of the US House of Representatives, Thomas (Tip) O'Neal, said many years ago, "All politics is local". And nowhere more so than in the county of Kerry. Whatever the global merits of consolidation might be, the many local concerns somehow had to be addressed.

One such issue centred on the plight of the creamery employees, and particularly the creamery managers employed by the DDC. Unions represented both groups, and both were concerned over their prospects with the new co-operative. To properly understand the workers' concerns, one must recognise that employment by the DDC, a semi-state body, represented generally a "job for life" at a time in Ireland when secure jobs were in relatively short supply. Further, the DDC was an organisation not immune from political interference. Many an individual was placed in a creamery job through a good word from the local politician. The removal of such political "protection" from the field could also cause some unease.

The case of the creamery managers was more complex, but no less personal. These were men who, by and large, had been qualified in Dairy Science at University College Cork, and represented a cadre of well-trained and educated technical men. They were people of no little importance in their communities, and in their creameries their word was law. They were powerful men in the small worlds of their areas. The advent of the countywide co-operative could only bring about some diminution of this status, for clearly many of the creameries would be closed and activities consolidated. Additionally, many of these were senior employees who had worked within the context of the Dairy Disposal Company for their entire professional lives. By all accounts, what they did, they did well, but the environment had changed and was still changing rapidly. The commercial environment of the new co-operative would be very different from the stable, albeit stagnant, environment faced by the DDC for the better part of 45 years. It would be a highly charged commercial environment in which the bureaucratic approach of the DDC would become largely irrelevant. Such considerations had to have affected the perspective of the DDC managers on the new proposal. Importantly, as men in leadership positions in the creameries, the opinions of the DDC managers were important to the farmers. Although clearly this was a decision for farmers to make, alone, the opinions of the DDC managers would be given a full and fair hearing, and offered full consideration. That, despite such concerns, most of the creamery managers supported the proposal, is a testament to their professional integrity, their commitment to the success of the dairy industry in Kerry, and indeed to their courage in confronting significant change. Bill Sweeney, the former Manager of the Rattoo Creamery (by now a part of Kerrykreem), had recently accepted a position at North Kerry Milk Products as group transport manager. He was one of several who sought to allay the concerns of creamery managers, saying that the new co-operative would help to create entirely new structures that would provide even "more challenging and interesting careers" to those in the profession.[7] To his mind, redundancy would not be an issue and, in fact, opportunities

for "job satisfaction" were sure to increase. This sort of enlightened view, combined with the "guarantees" provided by the
Kerry Co-op promoters who promised no redundancies or forced
early retirements, went a long way towards defusing this issue.

Another subtext in the debate derived from the "North Kerry"
versus "South Kerry" divide. There was a fear in South Kerry that
they would be "taken over" by the North Kerry co-operatives.
South Kerry had no strong tradition of co-operation, and tended
towards a strong allegiance to the ICMSA. North Kerry, of course,
was composed largely of co-operatives, with a strong allegiance to
the IFA. Some in the south, seeing the prominent roles played by
Hayes, Brosnan, and even Frank Wall (who were all from North
Kerry) feared that the South Kerry farmers would be in the same
position as when they were in the DDC. This concern, however,
was easily allayed by recourse to the rules for representation on
the new Kerry Co-operative. Generally, representation on the representative committee of the co-operative was to be on the basis of
one representative for every million gallons of milk. This committee would elect a board of directors of at least ten members, with
representation on the board assured in the rules for each area.
Under these rules, the farmers from the former DDC creameries
(mostly from South Kerry) would constitute a substantial majority
of the board of directors of the co-operative, since they produced
approximately 70 per cent of the milk in the county. If anything,
farmers in the North Kerry co-operatives (at least, in the Kerrykreem co-operative) would have had more grounds for concern.

But the north versus south divide was not really worthy to be
called an "issue". It was not. It was a source of diversion not unlike
the arguments over which part of the county gets the most assistance from Dublin for road repairs or infrastructure improvements
today. More noteworthy, perhaps, is the way in which some element of overall Kerry pride seemed to manifest itself as farmers
contemplated this countywide co-operative. There was the notion
that, in the wake of the IAOS report on consolidation in the dairy
industry, failing development of a countywide co-operative, the
county would be carved up under them with parts given to Golden
Vale and others to Ballyclough. Combined with this was the sentiment, or at least the perceived sentiment, on the part of many
pundits that Kerry would not be able to put its own house in order,

put aside its various internal differences and internecine squabbles, and combine into one cohesive entity. The reaction on the part of Kerry farmers, north and south, was almost tangible. County pride came to the fore, and sentiment for the county co-operative seemed to gather strength. It was not the first, or last, time a Kerry team came together as the end of the match neared to salvage victory from the jaws of defeat. The momentum seemed palpable everywhere but Rathmore. Rathmore remained, to put it mildly, problematic.

Rathmore is located on the border with County Cork, about 14 miles east of Killarney. One of the larger DDC creameries, it handled 8,000,000 gallons of milk annually, and supplied much of it to the Fry-Cadbury plant, adjacent to the creamery. A number of its suppliers were from County Cork, and availed themselves of branch creameries at Millstreet and Ballydaly, both actually located in County Cork. For many years, suppliers in Millstreet and Ballydaly had been agitating to be allowed to join the giant Ballyclough Co-operative, but the government had not permitted them to break off from the DDC area. The suppliers at Millstreet and Ballydaly were still committed to joining Ballyclough, and this appeared at long last to be their opportunity to do so. They had scant interest in joining a countywide *Kerry* co-operative. Other suppliers to Rathmore also took a position that amalgamation with Ballyclough would be better for them economically. Ballyclough was larger and had a track record of paying relatively high milk prices and providing top quality farm services. There were further complications in Rathmore by virtue of the Fry-Cadbury factory there. Although Fry-Cadbury did not campaign actively against the formation of an all-county co-operative, it was hardly enthusiastic. The new co-operative would effectively control the entire milk pool in the county, and remove from Fry-Cadbury the highly advantaged position they had had to date in sourcing milk in the county. They would now be dependent on the new co-operative. Since many Rathmore suppliers had family members, or were themselves, working in the factory, this created difficult complications. Given a relatively contentious history, the Rathmore situation was a powder keg.

The Vote

The voting began at the end of August in Castlemaine, and finished on 12 September in Dingle. Rathmore's vote had been scheduled to take place on 7 September, the next to the last of the DDC creameries to vote. The order of the voting did not appear to be coincidental. Tactically, it seemed sensible to begin the voting on a positive note in an area that seemed to strongly favour the proposal. Clearly, as Rathmore was the least likely area to vote "yes" on the proposal to join the co-operative, it seemed that tactically it made sense to have them vote near the end of the process. After all, the Minister was looking for a strong majority in the county to support the measure — he had not said that each and every creamery area had to support it. Also, if the first few areas started off by voting "yes", a momentum would be built that would be difficult to derail. Although each DDC area's farmers would make up their own minds, they were not impervious or immune to what was being done elsewhere, and they watched the activity in other areas throughout the county intently. One could only imagine what would have happened if Rathmore had voted early! Voting procedures were handled by the IAOS, and Brian O'Shea, the Killarney IAOS field officer, again handled almost all the details of the elections.

Procedural details were worked out between the IAOS and the representative committees of each of the creameries. The vote was to be decided by a show of hands, unless five or more suppliers demanded a secret ballot. Castlemaine, with its over 1,200 suppliers, voted first on 25 August, in favour of the DDC buy-out. Listowel, a strong supporter with the processing factory located in its backyard (and with Frank Wall as its representative on the negotiating committee), voted on 27–28 August, Dicksgrove on 29–30 August, and Ardfert, another North Kerry location, on 31 August, all in favour of the proposal. When Caherciveen voted in favour on 4 September, the all important majority vote had already been achieved. Kenmare then voted in favour on 6 September to add some icing to the cake before the scheduled vote at Rathmore on 7 September. To this point, approximately 2,612 suppliers out of a total of 4,900 had attended the meetings to vote, and of this number some 2,472, or 95 per cent, had voted "yes" to the buy-out.[8]

The vote in Rathmore, however, was described in the press as "confusing", and by participants as "contentious".[9] The Millstreet and Ballydaly "dissidents" did not participate in the meeting; they had already put forward a separate proposal to the Minister to purchase the assets of their branches. In the words of their spokesman John O'Regan:

> We would not participate in the vote because we do not want to be part of the Listowel set-up and we did not wish to make a decision for the rest of the Rathmore group.[10]

Other suppliers in Rathmore complained about a lack of information concerning the proposed takeover and, after three hours, the meeting ended in a stalemate with Rathmore refusing to actually take a vote at all.

Nevertheless, despite the complications at Rathmore, the countywide vote was decisive — out of approximately 3,000 suppliers who had voted (including Dingle which had voted shortly after Rathmore) only 140 objectors were recorded. The situation at Rathmore would continue to simmer, and occasionally explode, over the next few years, but the buy-out of the DDC and the formation of the county co-operative were now a "go". The farmers of County Kerry had indicated their support for the proposal at a level sufficient for the Department of Agriculture to begin to move on the transfer of assets.

On 12 October 1973, Mark Clinton, TD gave a speech to the Institute of Bankers in Tralee, in which he announced that the various legal and other arrangements were being settled and the transfer of DDC assets to the new Kerry Co-operative Creameries would take place on 1 January 1974. He congratulated the farmers of Kerry on their decision and provided a bit of a toast to them as they sailed off into relatively uncharted waters:

> I am very glad that as a result of these arrangements Kerry milk producers will shortly be in full control of their own creameries and artificial insemination station. I have a feeling that I was soft about the price and that the Kerry farmers made a good bargain, but I have no regrets. Far from it, I wish them well and I hope they will now use the strength that unity can give them to advance in every

sphere of agricultural activity. While these negotiations
were going on, there were some pessimists who thought
Kerry couldn't unite, but I, too, was a footballer and I have
long since known what a Kerry team could do in the last
quarter. The dairy farmers of this county are now playing
a new kind of game and it's on a county basis. So long as
the people of Kerry can think in terms of county rather
than parish I have no fears for their future.[11]

Jim Moloney of ICOS remembers having a strong feeling of relief
after the meetings and the voting were over. So often in the past,
attempts had been made to "co-operatise" the DDC in Kerry, and
these had all resulted in bitter rows, and no co-operative. This time
was different. Moloney remembers meeting with Denis Brosnan
shortly after the voting was over, and congratulating him, saying,
"Now, there you have it. There is the opportunity you wanted."
Moloney was also pleased that now, after several weeks spent almost entirely in Kerry for the farmers' meetings, he'd be returning
to Dublin. To Moloney's surprise, Brosnan turned and said:

> We haven't it yet. Would you come down for another week
> or two, because we have to get the money to pay for it.[12]

Brosnan was absolutely determined that the Kerry Co-operative
would avoid the plague of under-capitalisation that had afflicted
other co-operatives and had proven their Achilles Heel. He was
determined that the group would start off well financed, and that a
substantial portion of the total cost would be subscribed with share
capital taken out by the farmer-suppliers. Only then would he consider this portion of the job done. There was to be no rest for the
weary.

Preparing for the Takeover

Events moved along quickly. Operational plans had to be made for
the takeover of DDC assets on January 1. Rationalisation would
have to commence almost immediately. On the financing side,
planning for the co-operative share drive was already well underway. On the more political front, the situation in Rathmore, as expected, remained fairly chaotic. Finally, and surprisingly to many,

five (of the original ten) North Kerry co-operatives had not yet chosen to amalgamate.

The government had agreed to sell and the farmers had agreed to buy, but there would be no contributions from farmers until the share drive took place midway through 1974. Even then, the success of that effort could by no means be assured. It was well known that historically, co-operatives in Ireland had been undercapitalised, and dairy farmers had generally been unenthusiastic about investing in their own enterprises. Kerry's goal, of course, was to raise as much of the £1,150,000 price as possible by way of subscriptions to shares. But payment to the government could not wait until the results of the share drive were in; the first of two instalments of £575,000 was due to be paid on 1 January 1974. Additionally, with the expansion of its trading activities on that date, Kerry Co-operative would need to secure significantly larger loan facilities to meet its larger working capital needs. Clearly, other financing in the form of a banking (loan) facility would need to be arranged to get the co-operative off the ground as scheduled on 1 January 1974.

Since the Bank of Ireland were already the bankers for NKMP, it was decided to approach AIB, the Allied Irish Bank (which had been formed through a merger of the Munster & Leinster Bank, the Provincial Bank and the Royal Bank) for a loan facility. In November 1973, Brosnan and Friel met with representatives of AIB in their recently completed offices at the Listowel factory. Ted Sheehan, the AIB manager for Listowel, was anxious to develop a banking relationship with Kerry Co-operative. He was accompanied that day by P.J. (Paddy) McGrath, an experienced bank veteran who was the regional general manager of AIB for the Limerick region, which included North Kerry. He was also the bank's resident expert on the dairy industry, and regularly reviewed the accounts of the larger Irish dairy co-operatives for the bank.

Friel had put the meeting back until such time as he could prepare a very detailed document for the bank. As the chief financial officer of the enterprise, Friel was determined that the document and presentation would be detailed, intelligent, cohesive, impressive and above all, persuasive. He put considerable effort into its preparation, and geared himself up for this important presentation. In his view, a lot was riding on this, and Friel for one did not want the new co-op's "numbers" to be found wanting. But P.J. McGrath had a somewhat different agenda in mind. Friel remembers that:

> He didn't read the document at all. He had a couple of questions, but only to make it look like . . . to not put me away completely. The meeting was devoted to discussion, and we had a long chat, wandering in and out of subjects with great ease.[13]

As the meeting went on, Friel and Brosnan wondered what McGrath thought about the document, but he did not deal with it at all. For McGrath, the meeting was apparently more about the two young fellows he had in front of him, as he tried to take their measure. At one point, Friel pointed out that "I think we're going to need about a million and a half to carry us through", but McGrath did not deal with that at all. The conversation continued, discursively, wending its way through people, and places, and events, and experiences. The extent of Friel's work that had been discussed could have fit on a stamp! Still, McGrath left feeling very comfortable with, and very confident in the abilities of, the two young managers of the new co-operative. He wrote a very supportive note to his superiors at the bank, and a loan facility of £2.85 million was approved for Kerry Co-op.

Although there was a widespread feeling that the performance of the DDC could be improved substantially, the money put up by farmers to buy shares in 1974 was done largely on blind faith. The only return on co-op shares, after all, would be a dividend if the enterprise had a good year, and perhaps a bonused-up number of shares from time to time. One paid £1 for a share upon joining a co-operative, and received £1 per share upon leaving. There was no return on capital — and indeed, none was expected. To Kerry farmers, putting up the money for the co-operative was more of an expense, a cost of doing business, than an investment (despite the brochures about investing in the business). It was simply the entry fee to play the game.

The Structure and Management of Kerry Co-operative Creameries Ltd.

Prior to the meetings and the voting in late summer 1973, Brosnan, Friel, and the members of the negotiating committee had created the "shell" of Kerry Co-operative Creameries Ltd. They used an off-the-shelf rulebook provided by the IAOS, and customised it based on their own reasoning. The fact that it was completely *de novo* was, in fact, a distinct advantage. Although they couldn't necessarily draw on their own experiences, they could look around them at other co-operatives and, with a sense of their own vision of how they wished to run a business, create a structure that avoided mistakes that were made elsewhere. Although this would clearly be a co-operative in form, controlled and owned by the farmer-shareholder-suppliers, the framers were also determined that it would permit the enterprise to be *run as a business.* Interestingly, the structure set up so quickly in the summer of 1973 endures, basically intact, to the present day.

The bedrock of the organisation began with the farmer/shareholders in the co-operative. All suppliers were encouraged to be shareholders. Although anyone connected with or interested in the success of the co-operative was also welcome to take out shares (in or out of farming), the co-operative was designed to be controlled by, and run for the benefit of, the dairy farmers who availed of its services. Importantly, however, the co-operative principle of "one man, one vote" held sway. Each and every participant in the co-operative, whether he had the maximum 1,000 shares or only one share, had the same vote. In Kerry, with its many smaller farmers, this was a distinction of no little importance. Beyond the shareholders themselves was a three-tier system of governance. Each shareholder voted for representatives on a local committee known as the advisory committee. There was one local committee in place for each of the eight Dairy Disposal Creamery areas, and one local committee for the former Kerrykreem co-operatives. The local committees, in turn, elected a representative committee of approximately 60 members, based on one member for every million gallons of milk supplied. The representative committee, for its part, elected a board of directors of at least ten members. Since representation at board level was assured in the rules for each of the nine areas, there was also opportunity for additional members to be "co-opted" onto the board. In this, a member would be selected (by the representative board) to sit on the board of directors as a representative of a particular area, even though not originally elected. Importantly, the board of directors would remain relatively small, unlike many other co-operatives.

The responsibility of each tier was to elect the next tier, and the responsibility of the board of directors was to select a chief executive officer. All authority, ultimately, rested with the board of directors and the management that they had selected. Unlike many other co-operatives, authority for major business decisions, capital investments, acquisitions, and other decisions was not "pushed down" to the lowest possible level. For example, in many other co-operatives, capital investment expenditure approvals would have to be voted on by the local advisory councils! Although certainly in the true democratic spirit, it was not an efficient or effective method for running a business, was a very difficult way to preserve confidentiality, and made it almost impossible to surprise one's competitors. To the leadership of the Kerry Co-op, it was essential that lines of authority and responsibility be clear, unambiguous, and practical. In the structure of the new Kerry Co-op, they were. The board of directors had the ultimate authority. The management worked for the board of directors. The shareholders, and their area advisory and representative committees, made the decisions as to the composition of the board of directors. 100 per cent of the business decisions rested with the board, in a manner not inconsistent with the board of a public company. This "business orientation" of the Kerry Co-operative began even with the development of this co-operative structure. It was perhaps the first "commercial co-operative". Even at the beginning of Kerry's history as an organisation, the mantra was being drilled into people, the idea that "this is a business", and it would have to be run as a business in order to survive and thrive.

As 1973 came to a close, the finance had been arranged and the organisational structure was in place. Denis Brosnan, with the strong support of both Eddie Hayes and Frank Wall, was selected to be the co-op's first general manager. To their credit, both Hayes and Wall were prepared to step back from the day-to-day operations and let Brosnan and his management team face up to the challenge. There was little doubt that 1974 was likely to be a momentous year for the dairy industry in Kerry.

Notes

[1] Eddie Hayes (1975), "Chairman's Statement", *Kerry Co-operative Creameries Annual Report and Accounts 1974*, p. 4.

[2] Irish Agricultural Organisation Society Ltd. (1972), *Proposals for Creamery Rationalisation, 1972*.

[3] *The Kerryman*, "Milk Suppliers Get Together in Co-op", 20 January 1973, p. 1.

[4] Denis Brosnan, personal interview, 16 August 2000.

[5] *The Kerryman*, "Milk Co-op On — But at What Cost?", 7 July 1973, p. 1.

[6] Jim Moloney, personal interview, 8 July 1999.

[7] Minutes of a Meeting of North Kerry Co-operative Creameries, Ltd., 17 October 1973.

[8] Calculated from the election results reported in a memo from Denis Brosnan to Minister of Agriculture Mark Clinton, on 15 September 1973.

[9] *The Kerryman*, "Rathmore Would Not Support Co-op Deal", 15 September 1973.

[10] Ibid.

[11] Mark Clinton (1973), Press Release from the Department of Agriculture and Fisheries, 12 October 1973.

[12] Jim Moloney, personal interview, 9 July 1999.

[13] Hugh Friel, personal interview, 31 May 1999.

Chapter 5

Kerry Co-operative Creameries: The Early Years, 1974–1980

We took what help we could from Dublin, from Brussels, and from God! — Denis Brosnan

Kerry Co-operative Creameries Ltd. began trading on 1 January 1974, when the assets of the Dairy Disposal Company were formally transferred to Kerry Co-op control. Frank Wall continued to serve as the Co-op's first chairman, since the elections for the various levels of co-op leadership (area advisory committees, representative committee, and ultimately the co-op Board of Directors) would not be completed until nearly the end of the year. At this time, there was only £9 of paid-up share capital (contributed by the members of the negotiating team and Eddie Hayes as the Kerrykreem representative), and nearly £2.75 million in borrowings. It was a sobering beginning to what would prove to be a most challenging year. To Brosnan, "It seemed everything was against us — God, the weather, and the economy!"[1] It was a bad year for farmers, one of the worst in memory. The weather was wet, as bad as 1939–1940. There was a worldwide recession, the oil crisis was driving the inflation level higher, and interest rates were reaching into the high teens. This was not good news for an enterprise that was exclusively dependent upon milk, and was leveraged to the hilt. (Among the bright spots, however, were the positive impacts of Ireland's entry into the EEC in 1973, including rising milk prices and other incentives for expanding milk production.)

Under such generally inauspicious circumstances the Kerry Co-operative began trading. The critical tasks for the year were to 1) mount a successful share campaign, 2) begin the important process of consolidation and rationalisation, 3) complete the third phase of the Listowel factory expansion, that of the whey powder plant, and, importantly, 4) generate the forecasted profit for the year. The importance of mounting a successful share drive to fund the £1,150,000 due to the Dairy Disposal Company should not be underestimated. This was not only to help reduce the mass of debt that the new enterprise was carrying, but also to obtain the necessary "buy in" from the new co-op's approximately 4,500 former Dairy Disposal Company suppliers. Certainly, this was the primary task facing the leadership of the co-op throughout 1974. During the spring, brochures were prepared and information meetings held throughout the county. The share drive commenced on 1 July and was slated to end on 1 October, although it was in fact extended for several weeks beyond that time.

Brian O'Shea, the ICOS field representative in Killarney who had played a key role in the meetings and voting of the previous summer and autumn, was again pressed into service to organise meetings to "sell" the share scheme. The members of the negotiating committee, the top executives of the Kerry Co-op, Jim Moloney, and others also figured prominently in this effort. By July, informational letters had been sent to all suppliers of the Kerry Co-op and meetings were scheduled throughout the county. The leaders of almost every major farm organisation in the county also threw their considerable support behind the share scheme. T.J. Maher, the President of the IFA, James O'Keeffe, the President of the ICMSA, and Tom Sheehan, the President of Macra na Feirme, all encouraged Kerry farmers to participate fully in the share scheme. This was at a time when the leaders of these organisations could agree on very little else! Another voice that carried significant weight in Kerry was that of M.G. Moyles, the county CAO (Chief Agricultural Officer). His encouragement of Kerry farmers lent a further imprimatur to the share drive.

Frank Wall, as the Co-op's chairman, kicked off the share drive with an appeal to all suppliers:

> Profits from Kerry milk are now being kept in Kerry for
> the people of Kerry. You are invited to take shares in a
> brighter future for yourself, your family and your commu-
> nity. It is only right that all suppliers should benefit from
> the build up of Kerry Co-op Creameries. A unique op-
> portunity now exists for all to become shareholders at the
> very beginning. . . . This is a milestone in Kerry farming.[2]

Jim Moloney noted that, "it is essential that it be well financed and
well supported by farmer members if it is to overcome the challenges of the market place".[3] Tom Sheehan from Macra Na Feirme
was more blunt:

> As farmers we could be fairly accused of callous disre-
> gard for the co-op movement through our small commit-
> ment to it. I look to the farmers of Kerry with confidence
> that they will give a lead to the rest of the country. Buy the
> shares so that you may own what is yours. Give commit-
> ment so that you may consolidate and strengthen farming
> in Kerry.[4]

If the message had something of the tone of a Redemptorist mission, it was perhaps appropriate. Kerry farmers now had to "put
their money where their mouth is", dig down into their pockets,
and invest in the fledgling co-operative.

The share register was formally opened in late July, and by the
time the drive was closed on 1 October, £865,000 had been subscribed, about 75 per cent of the total issued share capital of
£1,150,000. About one-quarter of this was via cash payments, while
the remainder was to be collected via a deduction from farmers'
milk cheques over the next six years, a popular option for a "pain-
less" contribution on the part of most farmers. Although the share
drive did not net the full targeted amount of £1,150,000, it did represent an almost unheard of contribution on the part of farmers to a
co-operative organisation, providing some indication of the support and enthusiasm that greeted the share drive. Stories are still
told of the old banknotes that some farmers had pulled out from
under the mattress or the floorboards, and brought in to purchase
their shares. Some of the notes were of such age that they had to be
sent to the Central Bank for identification! That having a share in

the Kerry Co-op was considered worthy of prying up those floor-boards was high praise indeed.

There are many apocryphal stories in the banking industry about co-op share drives, and they provide a flavour of the times. Ned O'Callaghan tells one in which an investing farmer arrived into the local bank and emptied a small churn containing a mixture of coins, notes and out of date cheques on the counter saying, "I want to put £500 into the new Co-op". The sweating teller eventually separated the coins, notes and cheques into three bundles and after much counting and recounting announced to the farmer, "you have only £499 there". To which the unmoved farmer responded, "Oh, Jaysus, I brought down the wrong churn".[5] Certainly, for many farmers in Kerry, investing such a sum was a relatively novel experience. Few could foresee, at that time, how their level of financial sophistication would grow so dramatically over the next few decades.

It should be noted, in fairness, that despite all the glowing recommendations and exhortations for Kerry farmers to invest in their new co-operative, these farmers were, in fact, taking a chance. The track record for co-operative organisations in Kerry was chequered at best, and more than a few farmers remembered co-operatives that had gone bust or never got off the ground. Some remembered co-ops that, while they were around, appeared to exist to the advantage of a few well-connected members rather than for the many. Kerry farmers, however, were able to get past such fears and were willing to take the risk. It is fair to suggest that none had any notion of the extent to which that risk-taking would be handsomely repaid over the years.

Disturbances in Rathmore

Although the share drive may have been the most crucial issue facing the managers of the new co-operative, there were other "sideshows" that required attention. One of the more unsettled issues was the situation at Rathmore in the south of the county. There had been no improvement in the climate since the abortive meeting on the DDC buyout the prior September, in which Rathmore suppliers had refused to vote "yes" or "no". If anything, concerns had festered and the mood was increasingly ugly. Already, some 300 farmers in the Millstreet and Ballydaly districts of

Rathmore had received approval in principle from the Minister for Agriculture to switch their allegiance, as well as their milk supply, to Ballyclough Co-operative in County Cork, a move for which they had been agitating for years. Said Pat Cashman, a long time Rathmore supplier from Millstreet:

> For 36 years we in this part of the country have been sending milk into Kerry whether we liked it or not. We never want to do it again. We have made our choice and nobody can reverse it.[6]

Other suppliers to the Rathmore creamery were similarly disposed and wished to follow their Millstreet and Ballydaly colleagues to Ballyclough, but it is difficult to know to what extent most Rathmore suppliers supported this rebellion. It appears that farmers who supported the Kerry Co-op found this an opportune time to keep their heads down. Supporters of the move to Ballyclough, however, claimed upwards of 90 per cent support. The fact that many of the Rathmore suppliers actually lived in County Cork may not have been irrelevant. Cork suppliers at Rathmore had little confidence that their interests would be properly looked after by what they saw as a North Kerry dominated co-operative, and county pride was no less important in Cork than in Kerry. Said one of the dissident farmers at the time:

> We are Corkmen. We want to stay here. We would only be a small minority behind in Kerry. We will spill milk down the drains rather than supply it to Kerry.[7]

Rathmore suppliers began 1974 with a five-day strike commencing on 4 January, in which they blockaded the entrances to the creamery, effectively preventing lorries from collecting milk from the branch creameries. This was followed, over the next three months, by a milk strike on the part of the Millstreet and Ballydaly branch suppliers, who withheld their milk from Kerry Co-op to protest delays in transferring them to Ballyclough. These delays were related to objections of union workers at the Rathmore (Fry-Cadbury) milk processing plant to the transfer. Workers at the plant were concerned that the movement of milk supplies to Ballyclough would reduce employment opportunities at Fry-Cadbury. A clause in the original agreement on the purchase of DDC assets by Kerry Co-op stated that no transfer of the Millstreet and Ballydaly branches would take place "until all parties are agreed", and the trade unionists were very reluctant to signal such agreement. Ballyclough, for its part, was willing to accept the Millstreet and Ballydaly branches into the fold, but had held no talks with other Rathmore suppliers. One reason for this lack of eagerness on their part was that almost all of the milk that they would "gain" would, in turn, probably have to be guaranteed to the Rathmore facility (the same assurances that Kerry had given).

It was a messy, complex situation. Milk suppliers temporarily occupied the Millstreet and Ballydaly branch creameries in February. They continued to pour their milk down drains rather than supply it to Kerry Co-op. As 1974 moved along, however, the situation began to sort itself out, although it was not until a court ruling years later that Millstreet and Ballydaly suppliers finally moved to Ballyclough. Until that time, an uneasy peace prevailed. The remainder of the Rathmore assets and suppliers remained, per the terms of the original agreement with the DDC, with the Kerry Co-operative. Some individual farmers who felt strongly about the matter exercised their individual freedom to sell their milk to whomever they pleased and, after giving notice, joined the Ballyclough Co-operative.

Consolidation, Rationalisation and Expansion

Despite the distractions of the Rathmore situation, however, Kerry's management began quickly to take steps to consolidate the operations of the DDC creameries with the North Kerry Co-ops. To forge a new and efficient dairy organisation, a significant and rapid rationalisation of activities would have to take place. This could have been a cathartic experience. After all, the dairy industry in Kerry had scarcely changed for decades, and such change as there was had happened at a glacial pace. Now, agriculture in Kerry was about to undergo a revolution, at a pace utterly unknown until then, and Kerry Co-op was to be a prime agent of this transformation.

The Co-op, however, was fortunate in several respects, and had been dealt some cards that, if used judiciously, could help facilitate this effort. First, and despite the unfortunate weather and the economic recession, the EEC was full of promise for Irish dairy farmers. Milk prices were guaranteed to rise to the higher European levels over a transition period, and milk production would invariably increase with it. Entry into the EEC opened a door to Irish farmers and ushered in a new time of comparative plenty. Kerry farmers, for their part, were anxious to take all the necessary steps to improve their milk quality, increase their herd sizes, upgrade their facilities and increase their production. Knowing that they could sell all their milk, and for a reasonable Common Market price, injected new life into this process. A second factor that helped the rationalisation effort was the continued expansion of the factory in Listowel. With a whey processing plant scheduled to go on line in 1974, the already heavy recruiting of personnel for the factory was only going to increase. Any workers whose jobs were affected by rationalisation would not have to confront redundancy, but could transfer into the Listowel factory if they chose. If they chose not, other job opportunities were beginning to surface such as the ESB (Electricity Supply Board) station being constructed in Tarbert. Finally, for all of its shortcomings, the Dairy Disposal Company did provide a well organised administrative and manufacturing structure and much of the apparatus for rationalising activities was in place. It may not have exhibited the height of efficiency, but it was very disciplined. As Denis Cregan says:

> They had systems. They had controls. Their people were
> of high quality, at least in terms of what they did. They had
> a high level of ethics, the civil service ethic.[8]

The fact that some amount of rationalisation had already been undertaken by the DDC was a bonus.

One of the first rationalisation efforts was the centralisation of butter churning. In early 1974, as an interim step, churning was consolidated at the existing creameries at Abbeydorney, Listowel and Rathmore. Later, all butter churning was centralised at the former DDC creamery in Listowel (not the Listowel factory), using equipment transferred from various creameries throughout the county. Annual output at the time was approximately 8,000 tons.[9] Yet this itself was only an interim solution, an opportunity to gain some rationalisation efficiencies without expending much in the way of capital. At the time, all available capital was being spent on the protein side of the milk business. Ultimately, a new butter churning plant was developed inside the Listowel manufacturing facility, centralising all butter churning in the Co-op in a new, highly efficient facility that came on line in 1979.

Another somewhat controversial activity was the elimination of many branch creameries and their replacement with metered lorries that picked up the milk at specific intake points. Implementation of this plan began in Ardfert, and was expanded to Dingle and Listowel later in 1974. In late 1975 it was further expanded to the Castlemaine, Dicksgrove, Rathmore and Caherciveen branches. At the time, Eddie Hayes, speaking to *The Kerryman* newspaper, said:

> The supplier will continue to bring his milk to the branches but it will be transferred to the trucks rather than processed on site. This will mean a saving in power and fuel costs and, in some places, manpower. People may be transferred to specialised jobs but we expect that we will be able to continue our policy of forcing no redundancies.[10]

Rationalisation of branch creameries continued through 1976 and into 1977, but it was never an easy process. When the new collection system was introduced to the Cratloe and Athea creameries in West Limerick in 1977, farmers picketed the plant in Listowel, as well as three branch creameries, disrupting work in the process. A spokesman for the protest was quoted in *The Kerryman* saying:

> The workers, shareholders and suppliers want to keep the creamery open. We were able to pay for managers there during bad times but now the Co-op don't want any manager there at all. When we were taken by the Co-op we were promised there would be no change for fourteen years but there are plans to change now after four years.[11]

No one at Kerry Co-op knew where the promise of 14 years of "no change" had come from, but it would have been most uncharacteristic of the Kerry management to agree to anything of the sort!

This matter of closing the branch (and main) creameries and moving to collection by bulk tanker lorries was a difficult one, and only a first step on the road to bulk storage and collection of milk at the farm. In many ways, it was the collision of economic reality with tradition, custom, and social intercourse, a wrenching change from a way of life that had long endured. The creamery had been called "the symbol of Ireland in the 1950s".[12] There was a social dimension to the farmers' daily trips to the creamery to offload their milk, the waiting, the conversation, the gossip, the debates, and the lies told. The creamery was the centre of far more than just milk collection. It was, for many farmers, the social highlight of the day. For some, it was nearly impossible to conceive of life without this interaction. There were other local interests as well who promoted the retention of the local creamery. The shopkeepers, publicans, and the local petrol station all lobbied for retention. Having come into town, the farmers rarely left for home empty-handed. These interests were arrayed against the rationalisation schemes that inevitably sounded the death knell for the local village creameries. Yet, it was a dimension of an older Ireland, the Ireland that was an economic backwater, provincial, protected, impoverished, stagnant, and quite out of touch. Bulk collection was the only economic way to collect and transport milk in the new Common Market Ireland and it finally came to Kerry in the decade of the 1970s.

Throughout the late 1970s, rationalisation of milk assembly continued. Each year, a greater percentage of the co-op's milk pool was collected by bulk tankers and brought to Listowel for separation and further processing into butter, and into casein, caseinates, whey and other protein-based powders. Although many farm stores still remained at the branch creameries, their numbers were likewise reduced. Kerry Co-op's emphasis on efficiency was relentless. Additional steps, of course, were taken in succeeding years as bulk storage and collection took place on the farm. This meant that farmers would have to install bulk refrigerated storage tanks, and the tanker would call only every other day. The Farm Modernisation Scheme (EEC) provided grants to help in the purchase of bulk tanks, and Kerry Co-op itself offered funding incentives for its farmers to make the necessary investments. But this did not happen overnight; the expansion of bulk collection at the farm occurred gradually. By the end of the decade, in fact, less than 10 per cent of co-op suppliers had such bulk collection. For the co-op's many small suppliers, bulk collection was in many cases more than a decade away.

Tim Lyons and Farm Development Activities

While rationalisation efforts were critical in building an efficient dairy industry in Kerry, a second leg of Kerry's focus on quality and efficiency, that of development of its milk production capacity was equally important. This effort did not take place at the creamery or at the manufacturing facility, but at the farmyard gate. If Kerry Co-op were to be successful, and indeed even competitive on world markets, it would need to upgrade the facilities and productive capacity of its farmer-suppliers very quickly. To head up this effort, it was fortunate to secure the services of an extraordinarily talented, well-known, and highly respected Kerryman, Tim (Tiger) Lyons. If Eddie Hayes, Frank Wall and Denis Brosnan were to be classified as the "right men at the right time" in the history of Kerry Group, then it would seem appropriate to include Tim Lyons in that company. Kerry had got an exceptional man to lead this all-important effort.

It would be fair to say that for Tim Lyons, the effort to help Kerry farmers improve their yields, improve the quality of their milk, adopt better methods, use new technologies, and generally become efficient producers of a high quality product, was not merely a job. It was a crusade, and one on which he had embarked even before joining Kerry. He had first made a name for himself on the football pitch, playing on the Kerry teams that won All-Irelands in 1959 and 1962. His nickname "Tiger" was (in addition to a play on "Tadhg", the Gaelic for "Tim") a tribute to his ferocious style of play, as a tough cornerback who gave absolutely nothing away. After graduating from University College Dublin with a degree in Agricultural Science, he had returned to Kerry as an instructor with the County Committee on Agriculture. He was the agricultural instructor for the Abbeydorney area at the time he was recruited to Kerry Co-op, and had been instrumental in setting up the pioneering farm school there. It was here, in fact, that Denis Brosnan first met him. Tim Lyons was a determined, committed man who was passionate about bringing modern and efficient farming methods to the farmers of Kerry, and had actually pioneered silage-making in Kerry in the early 1960s. If there was one man who was seriously respected in the dairy industry in Kerry, it was Tim Lyons.

Certainly, agriculture in the county was changing, with the help of government funds, Common Market schemes, and the critical role of the County Agricultural Advisors who covered the entire county, pushing modern methods, explaining programs, educating and cajoling farmers into making necessary changes. But to Denis Brosnan and others, it was clear that the Co-op itself would have to play a very active role in facilitating and speeding up such change. Even before the DDC buyout, it was decided to set up a Farm Services Department to provide assistance and advice in upgrading farm facilities, improving milk quality and increasing productivity. This may also have been done with an eye to the amalgamation that was to come, and to the need and the promise to provide an outstanding level of farm service to suppliers. Almost all activities within the farmyard gate would come under the purview of this new function.

Brosnan and Friel stayed over in Dublin after the All-Ireland Final in 1972 to meet with Lyons and ask him to take the position. It took a bit of convincing. He had a secure, pensionable, civil service position, and was a man of no small stature in the county. He was being asked to take a significant risk in joining this group of young managers at North Kerry Milk Products, an enterprise on which the jury was still out. Still, the opportunity to have an even greater impact on farm development within the county must have been very attractive to him. Lyons eventually accepted the position, but, as a prudent man, did so only on secondment. There was an understanding in place that if things did not work out, he could return to the corps of County Agricultural Advisors. Nevertheless, on 1 January 1973, at the age of 37, he joined the "caravan brigade" in the Canon's Field. He was, at that point, the most senior man on the staff, considerably older than the rest of the Kerry managers who were still in their twenties. With the hiring of Tim Lyons, Kerry's senior executive team of Brosnan, Friel and Cregan had recruited not just a respected technical man. Perhaps more importantly, they had acquired in the person of Tim Lyons no small measure of respectability and legitimacy in the eyes of farmers, and a vehicle through which they could communicate with Kerry farmers, north and south.

Denis Cregan remembers:

> He was a gentleman, a great purist. He wasn't strictly
> commercial, but a seriously respected guy in the agri-
> business in Kerry. He was a very high quality individual in
> every sense of that word. That this guy would come and
> join us ... this was significant![13]

From the beginning, Tim Lyons became something of a "father figure" of the Kerry management group. Amidst the whirlwind of activity, controversy, and crises, he was an ocean of calm, impossible to ruffle. On every level, he dealt with Kerry farmers in the
most sincere, effective, easy manner.

In the technical sphere, he pioneered a construction service at
Kerry that helped farmers lay out and build new milking parlours,
storage sheds, barns and other facilities, improve their silage
making, and make more effective use of their feed and fertiliser.
But importantly, he was not a distant, impersonal "name" on a
memo, making pronouncements from a remote office. He was a
"hands-on" manager, invariably out in the field, visiting farmers on
their own sites, and not averse to taking off his jacket and pitching
in to help or demonstrate something. People recollect even today
his Saturday morning rounds of the AI Station in Castleisland and
the other farms owned by the Co-op; he was always in motion, always on the move. Although to many in Kerry, he remained always
the football hero, he was a hero with the true common touch. In
every sense, to Kerry farmers, he was one of their own. A native of
Kerry, a football hero, an ardent proponent of better farming, a
convinced co-operator, Tim Lyons brought balance to the equation.
Where Brosnan, Friel and Cregan may have been seen as young,
aggressive and overtly commercial, Lyons anchored a different and
perhaps "softer" side. He had the utter and complete trust of Kerry
farmers, a trust that it would take Brosnan and his team, as yet un-
proven, some years to earn. Denis Cregan remembers that Lyons
had joined Kerry on the heels of their first very hard year. Although
it had turned a profit, the management team had been through the
mill with the plant start-up, whey disposal problems, the odour
problem, and then the bombshell from IAOS. Was Kerry going to
make it? Was Kerry going to be partitioned? With Tim Lyons on

board, farmers saw an anchor — tangible proof that this enterprise was going to be around for the long term. Certainly, it would have to be, if Tim Lyons were willing to take a chance on it.

If Tim Lyons had been hired with an eye to enhancing the reputation of NKMP, and later Kerry Co-operative, it was a stroke of genius. If not, it was a stroke of luck, for Tim Lyons brought yet another serious asset to the organisation that was particularly important at this point in its development. He was "good at a meeting, good on a platform, good to get a message across",[14] truly someone with whom farmers could identify. Once a strategy for dealing with an issue had been decided upon, Tim Lyons was the man to take it to the farmers and win their support. The legendary support that the Kerry Co-op and Group were to gain, and hold, from their farmers over the years goes back, in great measure, to Tim Lyons on the platform.

And the issues were many. There were new standards on the quality of milk and new testing procedures that would have to be conducted. There was the implementation of bulk milk collection at the farm and the leasing of bulk tanks to farmers, and an all-out effort to heighten awareness of the need for increased hygiene on the farm. All this was done with the sometimes (apparently) competing aims of improving quality, increasing quantity and reducing cost. Approximately 70,000,000 gallons of milk were produced in County Kerry in 1972; the goal for 1980 was 100,000,000. That Ireland entered the Common Market on the same day as Tim Lyons began as Farm Services Manager may have been mere coincidence, but it did define the economic context in which his work would be done. It would be one of more, and better, and more profitable production of milk, and his crusade was to ensure that this happened.

Lyons, in speaking to the County Committee on Agriculture in early 1973, shortly after joining NKMP, offered this assessment of farming, and farmers, in the county:

> More farmers do not get the full fruits of their efforts because of high labour management systems — tie up cow byres, hay and root-crop feeding, hand-and-bucket milking, badly designed farmyards and farms, etc. If [they] are to increase milk production, then this can only be possible

by a wider adoption of self-feeding of silage, loose housing, parlour milking, bulk handling of milk and improved
farm layout, which will enable farmers to manage bigger
cowherds. Farm development on these lines, which has already been achieved on many Kerry farms, will stream-
line dairy farming, giving better working conditions and
better incomes to farmers.[15]

Yet there was a wide range of reactions to the changes that would
need to be made. Some of the older, smaller farmers were very,
very resistant to change and loathe to abandon the farming methods of a lifetime. With them, Lyons took a very gradual approach,
helping them implement incremental change in small measures,
leading them slowly along so that change was almost impercepti-
ble. Still, the motion was forward. For the younger, and the larger
farmers who were ready to move quickly and forcefully, Lyons
took a more dynamic approach, pushing them farther and faster,
sensing how far they were prepared to go in implementing improvements. This often produced revolutionary change and remarkable improvements in quality and productivity. Nor did Lyons
ignore those farmers who were in-between; each farmer had his
own pace, and Tim Lyons was sensitive enough to discern what
that pace was, and lead change in a way that the farmer was always with him, always "with the program". It was a remarkable
ability, because the process was not easy, and there were casualties along the way. Inevitably, the numbers of farmers would
shrink as the more marginal producers exited the industry. Clearly
the penalty system for sub-par milk would hurt, and clearly the
farmer investment in bulk storage and handling equipment and
refrigeration would be sizeable. Hugh Friel remembers the unique
talent Tim Lyons had in bringing the message to the farmers, saying something like:

> "OK, lads, this is what we have to do. I'm sorry to say that
> there are new regulations coming down, and this is what
> they are" . . . and the reaction would be "no, not again",
> but Tim would stay working at it and get it done. Change
> occurred, and he was a great part of that change.[16]

Over the next decade, Tim Lyons and the staff of the Farm Services Department relentlessly pursued improvements in and expansion of dairy farming in Kerry. Larger herd sizes, better cattle breeding, improved feed and other farm inputs, more grass, and better farm facilities — all were targeted, along with the overarching issue of better farm management. Kerry farmers availed of funds available through the Farm Modernisation Scheme — an EEC program designed to keep farmers on the land by improving the economic efficiency of their holdings — and other credit facilities organised by the Kerry Co-op. At the initiation of the Farm Development Service in 1973, the following profile of the average dairy farmer existed:

- 16 cows

- 50 per cent hand milked

- 75 per cent don't make silage

- 40 per cent have bucket plants

- 10 per cent have milking parlours.

This profile, indicative of a fairly primitive and undeveloped milk industry, was to undergo a radical transformation over the next decade. It would be a remarkable accomplishment for the county and its advisory service, for its farmers, and for the efforts of the Kerry Co-operative's Farm Service. It remains even today a testament to and a legacy from Tim (Tiger) Lyons.

Continued Expansion at the Listowel Factory

Although the factory had got through perhaps the darkest moments of its somewhat premature start-up in 1972, the pace had not slackened. No sooner was the casein plant running in 1972 than equipment for the next phase, a milk powder plant (a spray dryer), had to be ordered in September for installation by spring 1973. The milk powder plant had been running for only a few months when the equipment for another spray dryer, this one to process whey, was to be ordered. The whey processing plant was due to come on stream in time for the 1974 milk season. (This, however, would not be the final solution to the whey disposal problem, but did serve to concentrate the whey to make it easier to transport.)

Also, it should not be forgotten that the butter churning operation that had been centralised at the old Listowel creamery was also expected to be centralised in-house at the Listowel factory as soon as practicable. For the staff involved in manufacturing production and other operations functions, there was little time to pause for rest and reflection. The only imperative was continuing expansion, and the only speed was "fast". This factory, which had commenced production long before it was actually finished, was a continuing "work in progress", unfinished still.

This continuing flux fostered a mix of excitement and uncertainty, stress and more than a little anarchy on the factory floor. These were conditions that could have had widely differing impacts. One impact could have been that the entire enterprise would unravel as the demands, the complications, and the high expectations overwhelmed the staff. The other could have been that a culture of "can-do" determination, a culture of pure stubbornness and refusal to give in, could have been fostered. It appears, with the benefit of hindsight, that the latter was the case. Michael Leahy, who at 22 years of age was the Assistant Production Manager and one of the few who understood the process and the equipment well, remembers that:

> There was a broader enthusiasm there. For example, Eddie Hayes would come to the factory and he would be praising us managers, telling us what a great job we were doing. Even the workers had it, even though they may have been undisciplined in some ways. There was a shared belief in what we were doing. I'd meet people on the street and they would compliment you and say "you guys are doing a great job down there".[17]

In many ways, the plant was powered simply by hard drive and energy, for the level of sophistication, technical knowledge, and experience was relatively low. Leahy remembers that:

> We were running by the seat of our pants for many years. All these projects happened on time, but we were running so close to the wind it was unbelievable. You'd just stay with it, never give up, and keep it together. The word "failure" simply didn't exist.[18]

In addition to the lack of experience of the plant workers, there was also the issue of a shortage of people in the crafts. Electricians, fitters, and mechanics were in very short supply; this required the managers themselves to know the equipment inside out, and how to fix it. This was another impetus to the "hands-on" orientation of Kerry management at the time. A further complication in the equation was the influx of workers into Listowel from the former DDC and Kerrykreem creameries. Since the agreement with the government over the purchase of the DDC had guaranteed there would be no forced redundancies, all jobs in the plant were offered first to these displaced workers. For some of them, it was difficult to adapt to a process factory like the one in Listowel, a 24-hour-a-day, seven-day-a-week operation. Many were unprepared for the shift work that was demanded and the pace of work in the factory. It was a difficult time as staffing issues sorted themselves out, as some workers got up to speed and adapted to work in such a setting, and others gradually fell out. It would appear that, at the time, training was also probably not given a high priority. In the pressured atmosphere of the plant in these "go-go" years, there was simply no time. It was, in many ways, a matter of "sink or swim" in learning to operate the equipment.

At this point in 1975, Kerry Co-op also began to expand and diversify the product line in the Listowel factory, commencing production of a new calf milk replacer called *Bloom*, and other fatfilled milk products. Already, there was an emerging emphasis on developing and producing value-added, as opposed to commodity, products. This emphasis would become a distinctive characteristic of the enterprise in the years to come.

To summarise activities in the Listowel factory, the casein plant came on line in 1972, the milk powder plant in 1973, and the whey processing plant in 1974. Storage capabilities had been substantially expanded. Milk separation facilities were in place, and the co-op was now capable of processing substantially all of the county's milk supply. Butter churning would, within a few years, be centralised in a new facility within the plant. Further extensions to the Listowel plant, providing additional cold storage and warehousing facilities, were slated to be in place by the end of 1977. Despite the continuing expansion, and with the countywide production of milk projected (and targeted) to be 100,000,000 gallons (or higher) by 1980, still further processing capability would be required. Towards the end of the 1970s, a new and ambitious expansion to the Listowel factory was being planned. In 1977, a four-year plan for expansion and diversification at Listowel was unveiled, that eventually totalled £14 million. This expansion, which would include facilities for the production of demineralised whey, lactose, whey protein, coffee whitener, butter oil and other fat-filled milk products, would probably signal the end of major expansion work at Listowel, since the 25-acre site at the Canon's Field would be largely filled. Completion of the work would clearly represent the end of a decade of enormous change and, indeed, the end of an era.

Expansion activity within Kerry Co-op, however, was not limited to the Listowel factory alone, as two other major projects were announced and completed before the end of the decade. Both the new animal feed mill at Farranfore and the new headquarters offices in Tralee were perhaps as important symbolically as they were operationally.

The Feed Mill at Farranfore

Animal feed in County Kerry had most typically been manufactured and marketed by the local farmers' co-operatives, which were typically very small affairs, or was sold at the local feed store. With the consolidation of co-operatives and purchase of the DDC, Kerry Co-operative had decided to shut down the small co-op mills as part of the overall rationalisation effort. Small mills at Athea, Ballinclemmisig, Lixnaw, Rattoo, and Abbeydorney were shut down, and most mixing and packaging activities were assigned by Kerry Co-op to contract suppliers. But as milk production grew, and the Farm Service relentlessly pushed improved feeding practices, there existed a clear need for a convenient source of high quality, reasonably priced animal feeds. As one of the promises made upon the creation of Kerry Co-op was the provision of superior farm services, the decision to build an animal feed mill was a relatively easy one. However, it was only after the first great burst of construction at Listowel slowed somewhat in 1975 that Kerry management was able to make serious plans for a feed mill.

Kenmare Travelling Creamery, May 1938.

Delivery of milk to Rattoo creamery in 1960.

"Farming between the rocks" at Cahirdaniel, Co. Kerry.

Tim "Tiger" Lyons, Agricultural Advisor addressing the Abbeydorney farm school in January 1966. Photo courtesy of Mr. P. Kennelly, *Kerry's Eye*.

Canon's Field, Listowel, site of the North Kerry Milk Products plant, January 1972.

Federation of North Kerry Co-operatives meeting, Brandon Hotel, Tralee, January 1972.

Addressing the first ever NKMP Press Conference held in the Ambassador Hotel, Ballybunion, Co. Kerry on 12th June 1972, Denis Brosnan (General Manager – centre); to his left, David Reisenbigler (Erie Casein Co.) and on the right, Mr Bill Sweeney (Director NKMP).

At the NKMP Press Conference 12th June 1972, left to right: Arden Reisenbigler (President Erie Casein Co.) John Hennigan (Chairman NKMP Ltd.), Sylvia Reisenbigler-Siewert and Bob Siewert (Erie Casein and Director of NKMP).

Aerial shot showing progress at the North Kerry Milk Products site in late 1972.

Kerry Co-op Creamery Managers meeting, January 1974. Front left to right: T. Lyons,
T. Condon (Kenmare), P. Daly (Castlemaine), B. Walsh (Rathmore), D. Houlihan (Dicksgrove),
T. O'Brien (Listowel), D. Brosnan. Back left to right: N. O'Mahony (Cahirciveen), H. Friel,
J. Kelleher (Ardfert), J. Dineen (Kerrykreem), M. Droney (Dingle).

Kerry Co-op Creameries Ltd. Board of Directors 1974. Back left to right: T. O'Connor,
A. O'Donnell, T. O'Sullivan, P. Golden, P. O'Connell and D. Brosnan. Front left to right: H. Friel,
E. Hayes, F. Wall (Chairman), J. O'Shea and M. Barry. Photograph courtesy of K. Coleman.

At a Kerry Co-op Creameries shareholders meeting in Tralee, 1975. Left to right: M. Barry, E. Hayes, T. O'Sullivan, T. Carroll, A. O'Donnell, F. Wall, P. O'Connell, J. Moloney (IAOS), J. O'Shea, D. Brosnan and P. Golden.

Launch of *Kerry Co-op Creameries News*, May 1974. Left to right: Mr Eddie Hayes, Mr Denis Brosnan, Mr Gerry Moyles (Chief Agricultural Officer, Co. Kerry Committee of Agriculture), Mr Frank Wall (Chairman).

Denis Cregan, Production Manager, North Kerry Milk Products, pictured in 1974 (now Deputy Managing Director of Kerry Group plc.)

Milk intake at North Kerry Milk Products, Listowel in 1974.

Launch of Winter Feeds, December 1974. Left to right: E. Hayes, J. Barrett, T. Carroll, D. Brosnan, F. O'Driscoll, D. O'Connor.

Dairy Farming near Castleisland in 1978.
Mr Charlie Horan and his herd.

"The move to milk refrigeration"

Launch of *Bloom Feeds* in Co. Monaghan. Photograph includes Mick O'Connell, the legendary
Kerry footballer (far right) and Finbarr O'Driscoll (second from left).

"Moving in" employees transferring to Kerry Co-op's new headquarters in Tralee in 1978. Left to right: K. Dillon, K. Ryan, K. Moran and D. Walsh.

Milk bottling at Killarney Dairies in 1978.

Production of *Kingdom County* butter at the Listowel plant in the mid 1970s.

Shareholders at the Kerry Co-op AGM in the Ashe Hall, Tralee, August 1978.

Bloom 550 final in 1978, Tralee. Left to right: Tom and Lena O'Connor, Eddie and Betty Hayes and Denis Brosnan.

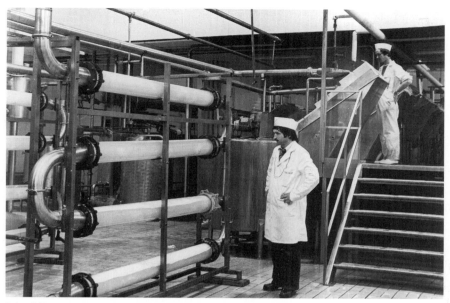

John O'Brien overseeing casein production at the Listowel plant in 1979.

Offical opening of Farranfore Feed Mill in June 1978. Front left to right: D. Brosnan, M. O'Regan (Chairman of Kerry County Council), Senator K. Ahern, J. Gibbons TD (Minister for Agriculture), M. Egan, T. Collins (County Manager), Back row: E. Hayes, J. O'Leary TD, C. O'Connor TD and T. McEllistrim TD.

Photographed at the presentation of the Published Accounts Award 1979 to Kerry Co-operative Creameries Ltd., Denis Brosnan, An tUasal Aonroí O'Beollain (Haughey Boland & Co. Auditors) and Eddie Hayes.

Following the expansion of the Listowel factory, official opening by Minister for Agriculture Mr. Ray McSharry TD on 11th May 1981. Left to right: Denis Brosnan, Archdeacon Doherty, Bishop McNamara, Fr. Dermot Clifford, Minister McSharry and Eddie Hayes.

Kerry's executive team in 1984. Denis Cregan, Denis Brosnan and Hugh Friel.

At the signing of the agreement to acquire Henry Denny & Sons (Ireland) Ltd., in 1982. Pictured (seated): M. Hanrahan (Chairman of Kerry Co-op), J. Denny (Chairman of E.M. Denny (Holdings) Ltd., Denis Brosnan (Chief Executive of Kerry Co-op); (standing): A. Denny (Chairman Henry Denny & Sons (Ireland) Ltd.), D.J. McCarthy (Henry Denny & Sons (Ireland) Ltd.).

Sausage packing at the Denny plant in Portadown, Co. Armagh in the late 1930s.

Photographed at the opening of Messrs Henry Denny & Sons Ltd., bacon factory in Portadown in April 1935, Sir Basil Brooke, Minister for Agriculture, Lord Craigavon, Mr. Fred Denny .

Photographed at the inaugural Tim Lyons Golf Classic at Tralee Golf Club on 18th May 1985.
Left to right: Tommy O'Toole, Denis Burns, Sis Lyons (widow of the late Tim Lyons),
Denis Brosnan and Eddie Moylan.

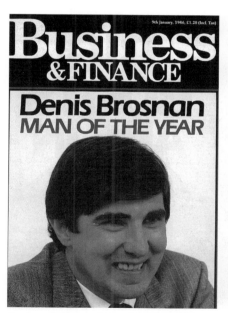

Business & Finance Man of the Year 1985,
Denis Brosnan.

Production of *Dawn Light Butter* in Listowel,
October 1986.

The launch of Kerry Group plc on the Irish Stock Exchange on 9th October 1986. Photographed from left to right: Angus McDonald (President of the Irish Stock Exchange), Denis Brosnan (Managing Director of Kerry Group) and Hugh Friel (Deputy Managing Director of Kerry Group).

The Board of Directors of Kerry Group plc in 1986. Front left to right: M. O'Donoghue, D. Fleming, M. O'Riordan, M. Hanrahan (Chairman), D. Fitzgerald, D. Counihan, A. O'Donnell. Back left to right: D. Lynch, D. Brosnan, T. Carroll, D. Buckley, J.J. O'Neill, H. Friel, E. Hayes, P. O'Connell, P. Healy and M. McCarthy.

Although the investment was sizeable enough (approximately £2 million) and the mixing and blending activities were to be computerised, the technology was not particularly complex and the production process was relatively straightforward. The major decision to be made concerned the new mill's location. A number of sites were considered, of which Abbeydorney in North Kerry, and Farranfore, located centrally in the county roughly midway between Tralee and Killarney, were the prime candidates. Farranfore, in addition to its central location, was also on a main railroad line and was well placed for shipping and receiving. Importantly, Farranfore was also *not* in North Kerry, and an investment there would be taken as a demonstration that the young co-operative organisation was fully committed to making investments throughout the county, and not only in Listowel. Farranfore was announced as the chosen location in the summer of 1975. There were a few delays when objections were lodged with the planning authority, but these were later withdrawn. There were further complaints that the builders of the facility were from the UK (the complaints were from competing local firms). But these were all overcome and Minister for Agriculture James Gibbons formally opened the feed mill on Monday, 29 May 1978.

The opening of the feed mill was certainly of importance in the operational sense, in that it filled a pressing need for the co-operative's milk suppliers. It was also important symbolically in being an investment in the southern part of the county, in an area where local farmers had been agitating for some type of manufacturing facility since long before the arrival of Kerry Co-op on the scene. However, what is also of great interest is not just the fact that the mill was opened, but importantly, the *way* in which it was opened. Kerry had never seen this before, and indeed, may have seen nothing of the sort since!

The event itself was crafted by Michael Drummey, and represented perhaps one of the first examples of corporate image management in Ireland, reflecting a marketing approach that was far ahead of its time. The grand opening was staged over four days, to accommodate everyone who had been invited to attend (which was virtually everyone in Kerry!). Michael Drummey remembers that:

> I'm not saying we were looking for an excuse for a party, but we wanted to increase our profile, not just for the purpose of amplifying what we were doing for our farmers, but we wanted it to be very much a "Kerry thing". In Kerry, there was always this North Kerry-South Kerry divide, with a lot of strands of disharmony. We saw it as an opportunity for people to see what was theirs.[19]

Local and national politicians, the clergy, farm leaders, bankers, local merchants, employees, the local people from the surrounding communities, the Garda Siochána, the Fire Brigade, suppliers, customers, school children, and most of the approximately 7,300 milk suppliers to the Kerry Co-op (and their families) descended on the facility on the various days set aside for them. Now a feed mill would not normally be considered the most attractive venue for a social event of this sort, but in this case it was perfect. The event was catered by the Earl of Desmond Hotel, and there was ample food and drink. Everything was "first class". Kerry farmers viewed the first screening of a documentary film, "Another Ring to Kerry", sponsored by Kerry Co-op and narrated by the well-known actor Niall Toibin, which depicted the co-operative's activities. It was an opportunity for visitors to see what Kerry was all about. They then donned white coats and hats (Drummey claims that even this small touch suggested to the farmers that "these boys mean business") and were taken on a tour of *their* facility. Indeed, at every stage of the proceedings they were reminded that the enterprise, and this facility, were owned by *them* and were operated for *their* benefit. It was a carefully crafted event, a public relations coup, and in a sense a party that announced "we have arrived". The festivities accompanying this event have still not been forgotten by many in Kerry. Drummey remembers:

> We said, look, this is Kerry, come and see us! It was top class. Some complained that, God, what did this cost? Well, it cost a hell of a lot! But in terms of the value that it added to the stature of this fledgling organisation, it was really incalculable. . . . We put 11,000 people through Farranfore over the course of a week. Now it nearly killed me, but apart from that, it was very successful.[20]

The event, as choreographed by Kerry, was intended to send a strong and unmistakable message. First, that it was a first-rate enterprise that would do things the right way. Second, that the owners of the enterprise — that is, the farming community in Kerry, north and south, former co-operators and former Dairy Disposal Company people — could be justly proud of *their* co-operative. It was a sign that the Kerry Co-op was not going to be a "typical" co-operative organisation. Already, they were breaking the rules.

There is an ironic postscript. At the opening of the mill, James Gibbons, the Minister for Agriculture, announced the start of a government campaign involving compulsory measures for the elimination of bovine brucellosis in the county. It seemed a sensible plan, necessary and worthy of support, as far as Kerry's managers were concerned. But they could have had little idea, as they stood on the dais and applauded the announcement politely, of the cathartic effect that this announcement would have on them, the organisation, and farming in Kerry.

The New Headquarters in Tralee

With the rapid expansion of the business, it was clear by the middle of 1975 that additional space for administrative and support functions would be required. In January 1976, Pettits of Cork, the engineering firm that had overseen construction of the original factory at Listowel, was engaged to evaluate potential sites for a new administrative headquarters for the Co-operative. The sites evaluated were essentially limited to Listowel and Tralee, and both towns lobbied hard to gain the headquarters. Listowel's UDC (Urban District Council) was particularly aggressive, resorting to passionate entreaties and reminders of the many ways in which the town of Listowel had helped Kerry Co-op along in its development. Their arguments were, in many ways, predicated upon an assumption that Kerry Co-op "owed it" to Listowel. Yet, Tralee was the county town, and a far more central location. That there also existed a need to re-emphasise that this was a countywide (and not a North Kerry) co-operative, could also not have been far from the minds of management. With the major investment in plant facility already made in Listowel, it seemed to many that Tralee would be the logical location. But this did not make the external debate any less acrimonious. Listowel supporters sarcastically noted that most

of the Kerry managers already commuted to their current offices in
Listowel from Tralee. The hyperbole was excessive even by North
Kerry standards. One Listowel UDC member was quoted, in Janu-
ary 1976, as saying:

> ... the Urban Council helped in every way towards the
> construction of the factory and the local Race Company
> had sold the site for £6,250 which was exactly the same
> amount for which they had purchased the land, which
> could have been sold by the Race Company for £18,000-
> 20,000 because it amounted to about twenty acres. The
> Urban Council turned cartwheels in order to facilitate
> them with the original site.[21]

At a similar meeting the following week, another UDC councillor
stated that "they would be building the offices in enemy territory if
they built them in Tralee!"[22]

Despite the objections from Listowel, Tralee was chosen as the
site for the new headquarters. As expected, there was a great hue
and cry from many in the Listowel local government. One counsel-
lor said, "It appears the co-op has failed to honour their promise.
... This news is very bad for the town of Listowel."[23] But the Chairman of the Listowel Area Co-op Advisory Committee evaluated the
decision more even-handedly:

> A majority of the [board of] directors voted for Tralee and
> it was a democratic decision. There is not really much that
> can be done about it....[24]

The fact that the 11 to 4 vote of the Co-op's board of directors was
leaked to the media points to the politically contentious nature of
the decision. It is very rare for votes of the board to be given such
a public airing, but perhaps it was important in this case to provide
"cover" for the board representatives from North Kerry. In any
event, the rhetoric faded fairly quickly as Kerry Co-op made massive investments into the Listowel factory over the next few years,
providing far more jobs than would have been provided with the
group headquarters. The controversy over the location of the
headquarters became largely moot, and construction of the new

facility proceeded. The administrative staff began moving into the new facility on Prince's Street in Tralee in February 1978.

Marketing Activities —Casein, *Bloom*, and Butter

Marketing activities at Kerry Co-op can be said to have begun with two important hirings that were made, within a month of each other, in late 1974. Michael Drummey, the marketing executive at Bord Bainne responsible for all casein exports, was hired as the new Marketing Manager, and Finbarr O'Driscoll, a sales manager at IAWS (Irish Agricultural Wholesale Society), responsible for animal feed sales, was hired as a nutritionist. They were each to leave their imprint upon the activities of the Kerry Group over the next quarter century.

Michael Drummey, a native of Dublin, had held a number of jobs since university, but most recently had spent five years with An Bord Bainne (The Irish Dairy Board). One of his primary responsibilities there, in addition to marketing cheese and the *Kerrygold* butter brand in the UK, was marketing Irish casein, primarily in North America. Of course, this represented practically all the casein being produced in Ireland at the time, with the exception of Kerry's, since it had a marketing arrangement with Erie Casein as one of the partners in the Listowel factory. During those early years of the 1970s, the protein market was "bubbling" and casein was something of a buzz product. There were a number of producers of casein in Ireland at the time, some relatively serious and others less so. Miloko in Carrick-on-Suir, North Cork Farmers Co-op in Kanturk, Mitchelstown and Avonmore were perhaps the most prominent. Drummey remembers being severely hampered in marketing this casein in the US market, since the quality of the product was inconsistent and not always up to a high edible standard. At the time, industrial casein was almost impossible to market. Amidst all the challenges involved in selling Irish casein, however, Drummey was gaining substantial knowledge of the casein market. It was this knowledge which probably led Brosnan to invite him to consider coming down to Kerry and joining the fledgling co-operative.

The relationship between Erie and Kerry was, from the beginning, one of mutual respect as they pursued a business arrangement of logical, joint interest. It could be described as going even beyond respect, into one of genuine fondness and friendship. But this did not mean that there was any charity involved; nothing was *given*, on either side of the relationship! Already, in the mid-1970s, Kerry Co-op was allowing no grass to grow under its feet. It was moving quickly, and seeking to expand aggressively on any number of fronts. Everything was fair game, including casein. Kerry was clearly itching to move considerably faster than Erie was prepared to go. Erie, for its part, was deriving some significant advantages from its supply of high quality casein from Kerry and, fearing the likelihood that Kerry would at some point begin marketing casein in the States themselves, played its cards very close to the vest. Erie jealously guarded its lists of customers, and Kerry had great difficulty in getting Erie to allow them to visit customers. A "go slow" approach was perhaps more suitable to Erie's interests at the time. This combination of joint and cross-purposes on the part of both organisations made for some element of confusion, suspicion and conflict. This was not by any means a major issue . . . but just as in human relationships, it was enough to keep things interesting!

One of Drummey's first assignments at Kerry in 1975 was to spend time in the States and learn the current and future prospects of the casein market. He knew that Kerry's casein operation was technically very strong and the product was excellent and able to command a premium over other casein sourced from Ireland or New Zealand. However, Kerry was not "plugged-in" to the end user at all. Drummey's brief was to fix this. With that end in mind, he would travel to the States without telling Erie, which led to certain complications. Drummey remembers getting phone calls like:

> We heard you were in Pillsbury two weeks ago, and you met so and so, or you were in Chicago, or New York. I was running ahead of my shadow the whole time, almost cloak and dagger stuff. It was fascinating.[25]

At the time, Bord Bainne was selling all the Irish casein on the North American market with the exception of Kerry's, which Erie was marketing. Drummey found himself in the middle, almost as a minister without portfolio, calling on customers with a line somewhat like:

> Well, of course, Erie are working for us, but still let us
> build up a relationship. If you want a safe, secure supply
> from Ireland, should you not be hitching your horse to our
> wagon rather than Bord Bainne, where you won't know
> whose casein you are going to get? So, we built up some
> positive relationships.[26]

Casein sales still went through Erie Casein, but Kerry was beginning to cultivate relationships for the future and, in a small way,
making its presence known in North America. At the same time,
Denis Brosnan continued to cultivate his contacts with other
agents, customers and suppliers whom he had met originally
through his work with Golden Vale. The entire process was one of
an ever-expanding web of information-gathering on casein, its
customers and uses, and the likely trajectory of future requirements. Brosnan and Drummey began to see very clearly the possibilities for various milk proteins that were beginning to reveal
themselves in the North American markets, and were determined
to squeeze out any bit of intelligence they could. Their travels in
North America in the mid-1970s were to set the stage for Kerry's
ultimate movement into the ingredients business in a major way a
decade later.

Casein also represented a minor irritant in the evolving relationship between Bord Bainne and Kerry Co-op. The fact that Kerry
was selling its casein through Erie Casein and not through the
Dairy Board — as did every other Irish co-operative — fuelled
some suspicion that Kerry was less than interested in utilising the
good services of the Board. Even so, at the time, it was clear
enough that Erie as a partner in the factory had a right to market
the product in competition with the Dairy Board.

Even while the Co-op began to prospect half a world away in
North America, it simultaneously was expanding its activities
within the more "traditional" co-operative sphere at home in
County Kerry. Kerry had by now added Tim Lyons to the staff,
moved John Dineen, former manager of the Abbeydorney Co-
operative, to a new position as Stores Manager, and added Finbarr
O'Driscoll to the staff in November, 1974. It was now poised for significant activity in the area of its farm inputs business. The "bottom
line", of course, was to foster the production of more milk, the life-

blood of the casein and skim powder plants at Listowel. Feeding more feed to cows, and more calf milk replacer to calves, would help accomplish this. Kerry Co-op involved itself in the farm inputs business, bringing with it its own distinctive marketing touch.

Calf milk replacer was a relatively new product in Ireland. Basically, it represented a combination of whey (the protein-rich leftovers after the casein had been extracted from skim milk), combined with vegetable fats and minerals. On the farmer-supplier side, it was seen by experts to be the direction in which Kerry farmers needed to move if they were going to increase their productivity. Produced as a powder, it was combined with tap water to provide an instant liquid feed for calves. Its efficacy related to the fact that the whole milk produced by the cow, which could be (and often was) used to feed the young calves, was more valuable to the farmer if it was processed. Not only was it cheaper to feed calves on milk replacer, but better animals would be produced as well. With the emphasis on improving milk yields and increasing milk production throughout Ireland in the 1970s, calf milk replacer was finding a receptive market among dairy farmers. Unfortunately for Kerry Co-operative, the clear market leader in both the UK and Ireland was a Golden Vale product, *Maverick*, which, ironically, had been developed by Denis Brosnan during his tenure there in the late 1960s. The key to *Maverick* was the utilisation of new technology that would spray-dry the milk replacer in a manner that would make it soluble in tap water. Prior to that, calf milk replacers had had to be mixed with warm or hot water that was not always easily available on a farm. *Maverick* had become "the" calf milk replacer to use in Ireland; it would be a hard sell to convince even Kerry farmers to abandon it.

The first moves on this front were taken with the development of *Bloom*, the branded Kerry entry into the calf milk replacer business. The advertising claim for *Bloom* was that it would dissolve in water in 28 seconds, a rate faster than *Maverick*, and deliver the same nutritional content. To a farmer who is feeding a lot of calves, the time saving was not trivial. The product was manufactured starting in late 1974, when the new whey-processing centre was commissioned in Listowel. Once the product was available, "seminars" were organised throughout Ireland to introduce farmers to this new product, usually at public houses in the evening once the day's work was done. These were highly social affairs, where the Kerry team touted the benefits of calf milk replacers in general, and *Bloom* in particular. It was a huge task, for the smaller co-operatives and the agricultural traders and merchants in the bigger towns were fairly rigid in their thinking. The fact that *Bloom* was not the "first mover" in this market was a real impediment, since coming as a "me too" product into a small market represents a huge challenge. Certainly, as farmers gathered together at these meetings up and down the country and were presented with a massive sales pitch, some movement to *Bloom* could be discerned. Local merchants were aggressively enlisted to get them excited about the product. This sort of roadshow went on week after week, year after year, up and down the country for the better part of the mid- to late 1970s. Yet, Kerry was characteristically in a hurry to grow the business, and Michael Drummey and Finbarr O'Driscoll were called on to work some marketing and sales magic in this area. It appeared that more extreme marketing measures were in order.

One initiative Drummey took was associating the *Bloom* name with the sponsorship of sporting events. In Kerry, there are two sporting passions — Gaelic football, and greyhound racing. Quite a number of farmers in Kerry would keep a few dogs, and Kerry was known (at least in Kerry!) as the breeding ground of some of the best dogs that were ever raced in Ireland, the UK or America. It seemed that since *Bloom* was targeting farmers throughout Ireland, it would be sensible to sponsor a major greyhound race at the Tralee greyhound track. Drummey approached Brosnan with the idea, and he agreed, but with the usual proviso: "If we are going to do it, we are going to do it right!" The event Kerry sponsored was christened the "Bloom 550". It didn't have the biggest purse, but because of the hype supplied by Kerry — the formal invitations, the reception before the semi-finals, the attempt to make as many people as possible a part of the event — it became a major event. The first final of the "Bloom 550" brought in the largest crowd ever to the Tralee park. As the race developed over the years, the purse grew larger and it became both a very prestigious event and an effective promotional tool for the marketing of *Bloom*. Michael Drummey remembers that:

> We used to bring in some of our people from up the country. People would nearly pay to be on the invitation list! As part of the promotional package, we would bring in some of our stockists from around the country, husbands and wives, and give them a weekend in Kerry. You know, nobody else was doing this, it was totally alien to everybody else. Some of our competitors said, "they are bribing their stockists", but it was our way of saying "thanks". Let them see us for what we were. We might have a hundred couples and put them up in a hotel in Killarney, lay on the entertainment and tours, speakers, and general activities. It was meant to be an "event". This was totally new for Irish agri-industry. But it worked![27]

Having harnessed Kerry farmers' fondness for greyhounds to the cause, Drummey next moved on to enlist Kerry's other passion — football. He did this through engaging the services of Mick O'Connell to serve as something of a spokesman for *Bloom*. O'Connell was a genuine Kerry legend, a team-mate of Tim Lyons on Kerry's All-Ireland football teams, and one of the giants of Irish football. Indeed, some would still regard him as the greatest footballer of them all. One wag said, "Mick O'Connell was to Irish football what Michael Jordan was to basketball". Through Tim Lyons, Drummey was able to get in touch with O'Connell, who replied that he'd be "half interested". However, O'Connell wouldn't promote the product unless he was satisfied that it worked. Says Drummey:

> So he went out and started to buy calves. I said to Tim Lyons, "You'd better buy the calves with him, and we'll get the photographers going around, and we'll monitor the progress of the calves." He went along buying calves in Tralee and various places, and word would spread at the marts that "Hey, O'Connell is here today buying calves!" This gave *Bloom* a huge profile.[28]

Then O'Connell, usually joined by Ned Fitzgerald (a fullback himself and the father of current Kerry football star, Maurice), began to accompany the Kerry sales and marketing team as they conducted their seminars "up country", in Longford, Monaghan or

Cavan. Throughout rural Ireland (and not only Kerry), Gaelic football is a passion, and having O'Connell as part of the team swelled the attendance at the seminars.

> We used to get farmers in there who had little interest in buying anything, but the fact they could get in there and rub shoulders with Mick O'Connell was something they couldn't do every night of the week, and they were prepared to put on a shirt and a tie and go into town.[29]

O'Connell was never asked to say anything formally in this setting, but would usually be there at the back of the hall with perhaps 150–200 farmers in attendance. Drummey remembers being up at the front, talking about the properties of *Bloom*, when:

> Mick would just out of the blue come out with "I'd agree with that. I bought some calves and I must say that the calves have done very well. Now I wouldn't say that unless I was sure; I wouldn't be telling you lies, my calves are really 'blooming' on *Bloom*!"[30]

The first time Kerry ever placed an advertisement on television was a piece with Mick O'Connell at Croke Park, in a track suit, kicking a goal and singing the praises of *Bloom*.

Certainly the Kerry team in this effort had complementary skills. O'Driscoll was an aggressive seller, familiar with most of the co-operatives in Ireland because of his experience calling on customers for IAWS. Tim Lyons provided a "marquee attraction" due to his Kerry footballing fame, and added his undoubted credibility, genuineness, and technical competence to the effort. People would come and listen to "Tiger". Michael Drummey put his marketing genius to work in developing various packages and promotions, and spearheading Kerry's entry into "branded" products. It must be remembered that such promotion was not by any means common in the Ireland of the time, and certainly not by a co-operative. The general view of co-operatives was that they were relatively slow to change and generally unimaginative. Kerry, spurred by its marketing group, began to change this way of thinking about co-ops in Ireland. It also began to build a reputation for being a growth-oriented, commercially hard-nosed and market-focused organisation. It was not afraid to "rock the boat", take risks, and push well beyond the more "traditional" ways of doing business. It was setting the trend for what would follow, again and again, in the next 20 years of its history.

Bloom, as Kerry's first foray into a branded product, was ultimately a tremendous success. But it did not happen overnight; it took time and prodigious effort. The business gradually began to grow, to a point where by 1979, it could truly be said that the market was fairly well shared by *Maverick* and *Bloom*.

Meanwhile, production of butter continued, centralised in the old Listowel creamery and later in the Listowel factory. Production had totalled approximately 8,100 tons in 1974, rising to 10,800 tons in 1977, following the continuing increase in the supply of milk. Most of the butter was sold through An Bord Bainne, under the Bord's export label of *Kerrygold* (or exported as butter oil). The remainder was sold domestically under the *Kingdom County* label. During the decade of the 1970s, in fact, Kerry was probably the largest exporter of butter through the Dairy Board.

The Cheese-Tek Joint Venture

Toward the end of the 1970s, even as Kerry Co-op's core businesses in milk processing, animal feeds, and liquid milk continued to grow amidst the general prosperity in Irish agriculture, Brosnan and his management team decided to make investments in two ventures that were considerably further afield. Neither investment was destined to last long.

In early 1978, Kerry made an investment of $500,000 for a 25 per cent interest in the Cheese-Tek Corporation, headquartered in Illinois. The American company also was granted a 25 per cent share in a subsidiary set up by the Co-op, Kerry Cheese Tek Ltd. Interestingly, this was an investment that had its genesis about ten years earlier, in 1968–69, when Denis Brosnan was travelling around the US calling on potential customers for Golden Vale. In his travels, Brosnan met Dimitri Vakalleris, the founder of Cheese-Tek, who at the time worked for a company called Fisher Cheese. Vakalleris was a researcher and professor, and had developed the technical capability to manufacture an imitation cheese. In imitation cheese, or cheese analogues, vegetable oil replaced the butterfat (a substantial cost savings), casein provided the protein, and whey provided the carbohydrate. These formulated cheese-type products were easy to use in many food manufacturing processes, were adaptable and inexpensive, and had a long shelf-life. This made them particularly useful in numerous popular fast food applications. Of course, the use of casein and caseinates in the formula was of particular interest. In 1968, the product was still in the laboratory and far from commercial. Brosnan made a mental note, and filed away this interesting information along with other insights from his travels in the States. He maintained contact with Vacalleris over the years, and waited until such time as it might bear fruit. Ten years later, it did.

In the minds of the Kerry management, as always, was how to go beyond casein as a commodity and into more value-added products. How would they derive more value from the sale of casein? Of course, Kerry had already been exporting casein to the States, primarily through Erie Casein Co., since 1972, but the Cheese-Tek opportunity was different. Until this point, the final customer for its casein had been hidden from it, and Kerry had to labour mightily to even learn who the customers of their casein were. This opportunity provided a direct outlet for Kerry's casein. For once, Kerry would be able to sell directly to an end-user, and to a venture in an industry that was then in its infancy.

In addition to its initial investment, Kerry also provided considerable technical expertise, and was given the rights to manufacture and market the imitation cheese outside the United States through its 75 per cent stake in Kerry Cheese Tek Ltd. Plans were made to develop the business in Dingle, the remote peninsula in the western extremity of Kerry, utilising the existing creamery building. If the business prospered, a new factory would be planned. Just as Kerry had the Listowel plant in the north of the county, Tralee in the middle, and Farranfore in the south, now it was planning to invest in the west. Denis Brosnan said that this "continues our policy of spreading the activities of the co-operative around the county". Eddie Hayes, in his remarks, gave perhaps a hint of things to come, suggesting that the Kerry Co-op would have to look outside the traditional milk businesses. "We have to go into more diversified food lines if we are to get a proper return for farmers. And I am very pleased with this development."[31]

The investment, however, never had the chance to mature. By March, 1979, the food giant Bordens came in and bought Cheese-Tek, effectively putting an end to Kerry's venture. Kerry did, however, reap considerably more than their initial $500,000 investment on the way out. It also played an important role in Kerry's thinking for the future. They saw, in this incipient industry that was to become known as "food ingredients", the place where the rich pickings would be. They noted the hefty cheque that Bordens had been willing to put on the table to buy their way into this infant industry. It helped Kerry to understand that casein exports from Ireland or anywhere else were no more than commodities, and that the real action was in providing specialised ingredients to the end users. While the financial return on the Cheese-Tek investment had been excellent, the less obvious return — the insights provided into the food ingredients industry in general and the American consumer food industry in particular — would be enormous. Kerry had every intention of revisiting this scene as soon as possible.

Union Camp Joint Venture

In September 1979, Kerry made its first foray outside the milk and food industry with the purchase of a one-third stake in Union Camp Ireland for £1.2 million. The new company, located outside of Dublin, planned to erect a manufacturing facility to make corrugated boxes exclusively for the Irish market. Union Camp had been attempting for years to enter the Irish corrugated market, but would not do so without an Irish partner. Pat O'Hara, a New York lawyer who had been engaged by Union Camp to find an Irish partner, led them to Kerry and Denis Brosnan.

At the time, there were certainly questions about the wisdom of investing in a venture so far afield from their core business, and with a non-controlling interest to boot. Brosnan's response to such criticism was that it was a long-term investment and "the Kerry Co-op will invest in any sector of industry which will give its shareholders a good return".[32] While perhaps indicative of Kerry's future willingness to expand aggressively, the investment at the time was not generally seen as a good fit with the organisation.

But to Brosnan, there was a serious logic behind the investment. In fact, to Brosnan it seemed that they couldn't lose. At the time, there was a virtual cartel in Ireland, with the corrugated box market dominated by four companies (the Smurfit Group was by far the largest).[33] On one hand, Brosnan recalls, "there was an exorbitant price for corrugated in Ireland. If one were involved in the production of those boxes, one could live handsomely off the profits."[34] On the other hand, Kerry itself was a big user of corrugated boxes, and if competitors dropped their prices to compete with the new entry, Kerry would benefit from a significant cost saving. Either way, figured Brosnan, they would win.

Factory construction commenced in June 1980, and the plant was completed by the end of 1981. Union Camp remained responsible for all operations, with Kerry as a passive partner. By 1982, the venture had captured over 15 per cent of the Irish corrugated market, and had begun a second phase of expansion. Although the venture was performing well, Kerry decided not to participate in the further calls on capital required by the expansion; it had other, more pressing, capital needs of its own. Over time, Kerry's investment was reduced to a 17 per cent stake. Finally, in 1986, Kerry exited the business, selling its stake back to Union Camp at approximately its book value of £1.4 million. Looking back, was the investment worthwhile? Says Brosnan:

> It certainly helped us to lower our own costs, but we may have taken a lot of profitability out of corrugated boxes. I suppose, less importantly for us but more importantly for Ireland, that we lowered the price of corrugated for everybody else.[35]

This investment was antithetical to what Kerry was fast becoming — an organisation that preferred to be in full control of all its enterprises, with its managers fully engaged in various operational details and with an almost obsessive need to get deeply into the "guts" of their businesses. This would be the last time that Kerry would make an investment as a minority shareholder. Ultimately, the "box factory" investment had little strategic relevance for Kerry.

Expansion into Liquid Milk

Even as Kerry's managers were energetically raising the necessary finance for the buyout of the DDC, expanding the shareholder

base, and managing the tempest at Millstreet and Ballydaly, negotiations were underway for the firm's first acquisition, the purchase
of Killarney Milk Suppliers Ltd. Killarney was a small, privately
owned, and profitable dairy, owned by a number of local farmers
and businessmen, the major shareholder of whom was Mackie
O'Shea, a well-known Killarney businessman. They had made it
clear that they were interested in getting out of the business, and
there may have been some fear on the part of Kerry's management, well-grounded or not, that they might sell out to Ballyclough,
the neighbouring co-operative in County Cork. Ballyclough, of
course, was the beneficiary of the defecting milk suppliers in Millstreet and Ballydaly. There was also, perhaps, an element of
county pride at play. There was no way that the management of
Kerry would let this enterprise be taken over, from under their
noses, by someone outside the county. They had worked too long
and hard to unify the county, and still had their hands full trying to
keep it unified in these trying days of 1974.

Certainly, as liquid milk suppliers go, Killarney was a small operation with a throughput of approximately 2,500 gallons per day
collected from some 50 milk suppliers, about half of whom were
themselves shareholders. It distributed a quite narrow range of
milk products in the local Killarney area. It had been started in
1959, at a time when the milk business was just converting from the
delivery of raw unpasteurised milk to towns by individual farmers
to a system of private dairies. These private dairies would take in
the milk, pasteurise and homogenise it, and deliver it to the farmers' old "runs". But, pasteurising milk involved some investment of
capital, and required a licence granted by the government. Such
expenditures were well beyond the means of most individual farmers, so private dairies began to spring up, often owned by combinations of local farmers and merchants who saw an opportunity in
supplying pasteurised milk.

The negotiations were concluded at the end of 1974, and the
takeover effected on 1 March 1975. The purchase was agreed for
£144,000 plus 12,000 £1 shares in Kerry Co-op Creameries. Despite the reputation for strategic planning that Kerry earned in
later years, this first acquisition was not part of any grand corporate plan. It was opportunistic and perhaps even defensive in na-

ture. It may have been more a matter of what Denis Cregan called "protecting the territory".

> What was happening was that we were being attacked . . .
> there was an offensive on, resulting from the Ballydaly/
> Millstreet situation, and [the fear] that a neighbouring co-
> op, Ballyclough, would move into Killarney. We thought to
> ourselves, we've got to keep this in Kerry! Really, aside
> from the economics of it, it was really a kind of warfare.[36]

Additionally, it could also have been related to the fact that Lee Strand was putting pressure on the milk price. The liquid milk business was relatively lucrative, and Lee Strand had the county sewn up, with no competition except for Killarney who up to then had only serviced the immediate Killarney area. There was no competition for them, and they were able to pay their farmers a top price for milk. A few Kerry Co-op farmers had even deserted for Lee Strand. At this point, when holding the Kerry Co-op together in its first year was all-important, this type of pressure was not helpful. So, in a way, Kerry decided to take Lee Strand on.

It is important to distinguish between what is called the "liquid milk" business and the "processed milk" business that was conducted by Kerry Co-op at its Listowel factory. The primary difference is that supplying liquid milk is a year-round rather than a seasonal operation, reflecting the year-round market demand for this perishable product. Standards tended to be more meticulous, and refrigeration was a must in order to retain the integrity of the product. Unlike processed milk products like casein, whey, and lactose, milk derivatives in powdered form, liquid milk for the retail trade was a highly perishable product. Quality was key. It was also a business with which Kerry was totally unfamiliar, not only in terms of the operations side of it, but also the fact that it was a consumer business. Luckily, along with the business, Kerry acquired the services of a fine manager by the name of Liam Chute who was the general manager of Killarney Dairies and went on to play an important role in the growth and development of the Dairies Division of the Kerry Co-op afterwards.

Although Kerry would have been unconcerned in any event, reaction to the acquisition was generally positive, as Killarney was

clearly within Kerry's "territory" and fitted in well with the predominant view of the major farming organisations that it was generally good for the co-operatives to take over the private dairies.
Lee Strand, however, was less than enthusiastic about the entry of
Kerry into the market. It was, after all, the only other liquid milk
operation in the county, and concentrated on supplying Tralee and
most of North Kerry. It was also a shareholder in the milk processing facility in Listowel, but had declined to join Kerry Co-op. Over
the years, however, Lee Strand and Killarney Dairies had rarely
crossed swords, with each focusing upon its own "territory". Of
course, the fact that Liam Chute's father was the chairman of Lee
Strand for some time may have also contributed to the relative
peace that prevailed. The entry of Kerry into the equation was
bound to shake things up. In later years, Denis Brosnan was quoted
as calling the purchase "part of a process [of continuing to] mop
up Kerry".[37]

Then began the serious matter of learning the liquid milk business. Performance during the first few years was mediocre at best.
Competing with Lee Strand was a significant challenge, particularly in terms of the quality of the milk. Many of Killarney's milk
suppliers were small, and did not yet have refrigeration on the
farm. Raw milk quality, in the beginning, was somewhat questionable. Lee Strand, on the other hand, had a well-established, high
quality milk pool. Kerry quickly set about investing in the refur-
bishment of the business, trying to get the basics in place, at the
same time as they had to keep the business going and generate
some sort of return. Filling and packaging equipment and cooling
and pasteurising equipment were modernised, and Kerry made
urgent efforts to make Killarney an operation "as modern as anybody in the world".[38] Gradually, the corner was turned and it became clear that, as Denis Cregan put it:

> Looking at unit contributions and relative contributions
> between liquid milk and manufactured milk, we saw that
> this thing looked alright, it makes money. We should do
> more of it![39]

In addition to the operational issues, Killarney also began to expand their product line and, importantly, their geographic scope

of activities. They decided to go head to head with Lee Strand in Tralee. Michael Drummey remembers that Tralee was Lee Strand's market, and that:

> People said we'd never sell milk in Tralee. I remember Liam Chute and I walking into every store in Tralee, introducing ourselves, and asking if the Killarney milk van could call on the merchant. "No! Take your milk out of here!" So, the rejections, the refusals, you wouldn't want to have a thin skin in a situation like that! At this stage, we had moved our offices to Tralee. There were four to five shops in Tralee where my wife Ann used to give her custom on a regular basis, and four to five of my colleagues had the same thing. So, all of our wives and us acted as salespeople. My wife would say to the shopkeeper, "James, I'm spending £15 a week here; would you mind taking a crate of Killarney milk?" And a little bit more of that. Once you have a crate here, and a crate there, and maybe stick a fridge in there and then "by the way, we have a new butter, Kingdom County". Our vans were coming refrigerated. This helped the sales pitch. We had a much more broadly spaced form of packaging; we had a two-pint package. We were the first with low-fat milk, with vitamins added. We were bringing a lot of those to the market. We were taking the dullness out of the market. And it worked. Ultimately, it got to the stage where no matter what product Kerry brought along, it would be tried.[40]

By 1977–78, Killarney Dairies was beginning to come into its own. However, it became clear that the purchase of the private dairy in Killarney was only the first salvo in a series of acquisitions of private dairies, leading to the contentious dispute that would be called by the media, and popularly known as, the "milk wars".

Limerick Dairies and the Beginning of the "Milk Wars"

The purchase of Limerick Dairies in May 1978 represented Kerry's first take-over of a business outside Kerry. It also caused a massive ripple in Irish agricultural circles, since Limerick was well within the "catchment area" of Golden Vale, Ireland's largest dairy co-operative at the time. In short, all hell broke loose. Golden Vale took extreme umbrage at this purchase, and at Kerry who had dared to break the unwritten rule of "thou shalt not move out of thine own patch". In many ways, this breakout beyond the borders of County Kerry was to be more difficult than Kerry's ultimate expansion out of Ireland, and out of its core dairy and agricultural businesses! It was also the first serious shot in the "milk wars" that were to prove something of a distraction to the activities of the organisation for the ensuing seven to eight years.

On the surface, the transaction was relatively straightforward. Limerick Dairies was a privately owned dairy, with about a dozen shareholders, one of whom was Senator Ted Russell, a former Mayor of Limerick. Discussions on the purchase had spanned roughly a three-month period, and the eventual price agreed upon was £320,000. It had been reported that Golden Vale had been offered the opportunity to buy it but, after a look at the books, had declined.[41] Says Hugh Friel:

> These businesses [the privately owned dairies] were there for the taking. But [Limerick Dairies] was seen as a run down business, and who'd be interested? Golden Vale had a look at the Limerick guys a year earlier, took away the books, and wouldn't buy it. We bought it.[42]

There were a number of reasons, however, that made the acquisition attractive to Kerry. First, Kerry by now knew something about the liquid milk business, and recognised that there was profit potential in an efficient, well-run liquid milk business. Secondly, it also represented an additional source of milk supply for its factory, since private dairies, especially during the summer months, tended to have lot of excess milk that was not needed for the consumer business. As Denis Brosnan put it, "the private dairies always had lots of surplus milk. The surplus milk was something you needed in your factories, like at NKMP or Golden Vale."[43]

Interestingly, at almost the same time that the purchase of Limerick Dairies was being finalised, the new feed mill at Farranfore was being commissioned, and the announcement of the start of a brucellosis eradication scheme was made. Certainly, Kerry Co-op was in support of brucellosis eradication, although it was probably not fully aware of just how significant, indeed catastrophic, the reduction in the herd size would be. This reduction in productive capacity would have a dire impact on the amount of milk processed in the county that is felt up to the present day. Indeed, milk production figures for 1978 have never been matched. Given such an environment, and even though it is highly unlikely that Kerry management foresaw the extreme nature of the consequences, the acquisition of additional supplies of milk for processing was to become even more critically important than was suspected at the time of the purchase of Limerick.

Regardless, however, of the commercial logic of the acquisition, and the fact that Limerick Dairies had been available for purchase to anyone who wished to bid on it, neighbouring dairy co-operatives were angered. Says Brosnan:

> There was a viewpoint around that you dare not go anywhere else to take milk from your co-op neighbours and from farmers. We thought it would be reasonably within the rules to buy privately owned milk plants which weren't affecting other co-ops, which were doing their own business and which were stable, in as much as the liquid milk business is stable.[44]

The reaction in co-operative circles, though muted, was unmistakable. To most of them, this was scarcely the "gentlemanly" way to go about business, certainly not in keeping with the most fundamental principles of "co-operation" in Ireland. Golden Vale, in particular, was incensed at Kerry's move into Limerick, in the heart of its territory. But Brosnan was unapologetic.

> Limerick Dairies was a dairy where the shareholders would tell you that they had offered it on many occasions to Golden Vale. It was a dairy that wasn't making any money and nobody wanted it. We had learned the liquid milk business because we had Killarney Dairies and we took the view that we could buy Limerick Dairies and make money out of it.[45]

Remembers Michael Griffin:

Kerry were doing their own thing and not complying with
the ICOS vision of what was best for Kerry in terms of
splitting the milk pool. It was seen as a bit of a rebel, and
now it had the audacity to move outside of what was destined to be its natural, geographic territory to acquire a
milk enterprise, albeit not a very prestigious one. Kerry
was seen as clearly moving outside its territory.[46]

Beyond the political issues raised by the purchase, however, substantial operational challenges existed. One may assume that there were some reasonable bases for Golden Vale's refusal to buy the business. Certainly, Kerry was already aware that it had not made any money for years. But the full scale of the challenge was only to reveal itself once Kerry took control of the business. On Kerry's first day of ownership, Michael Griffin, who had been the General Manager of Killarney Dairies for only the previous six months, was quickly summoned to run the Limerick operation. He thus became the first employee of Kerry to be permanently stationed outside the county. He had arrived home from Killarney one evening to find a note under his door from Denis Cregan.

It said, "You'd better go to Limerick in the morning. Mick
Casey, the manager there, was taken ill with shingles and
we are taking over the place." So that was my negotiation
about relocation. There was nobody else to send, I sup-
pose, so I got sent there. At the time, I was the only person
at Limerick Dairies from the Kerry Co-op.[47]

Griffin was concerned by what he found. It was a singularly unattractive facility that had seen little investment for many years. It was also, unfortunately, located on a main thoroughfare out of Limerick City, on display for all to see. Nor was it particularly profitable. Kerry's attitude was fairly straightforward; they simply could not be seen to fail in Limerick. They tried for a while to get the existing facility in shape, but it became clear that a new dairy facility would be the only solution. At the time, however, capital was scarce, particularly to fund investment in a business that had relatively poor to modest prospects of providing a sufficient return on that investment. Until they could see a return, Kerry would have to do the best it could with the existing plant.

Limerick Dairies did have a competitor within the Limerick City market, Shannon Dairies, owned by the Madden family. Golden Vale may have held talks with Jimmy Madden, but apparently declined to make a purchase. So, during the first 12 months that Kerry was in the Limerick market, Golden Vale did not react in any tangible way. However, that was soon to change after Kerry's next major private dairy purchase.

Ballinahina and Deel Dairies

In March 1979, less than a year after its takeover of Limerick Dairies and while it was still struggling to digest that purchase, Kerry made what became its most provocative purchase to date. With the acquisition of Ballinahina Dairies near the city of Cork, Ireland's second most populous city, Kerry had gone deep into the lion's den, the territory of the giant Mitchelstown and Ballyclough co-operatives. Owned by the Buckley family, Ballinahina Dairies was founded in 1963, and had a milk intake of roughly 3.5 million gallons annually, supplying about half of Cork City's liquid milk requirement as well as other sales in County Cork. Kerry paid £1,100,000 for it, widely regarded as a premium amount at the time. Ballinahina was one of two dairies supplying Cork City; the other was Cork Milk Producers Ltd., a part of the Mitchelstown Co-op Creameries Group.

Michael Buckley, the owner, was a dairy farmer himself (although some maintained he was a cattle man at heart). He was also a particular fan of Kerry and a well-known critic of his local co-ops, Ballyclough and Mitchelstown. Buckley welcomed Kerry with open arms, but he would be one of the very few outside Kerry to applaud the venture. The evolving strategy for Kerry was to build up a liquid milk enterprise in the south and west of Ireland, and with the purchase of dairies in Limerick, Cork and Killarney, it was well on its way to achieving that objective. The large Dublin market, itself served by two dairies at the time, was also a conceivable target in the longer term. Indeed, many observers saw the commercial logic of the acquisition. But the reaction to the purchase from co-operative and farming organisation circles had nothing to do with commercial logic. It had everything to do with the perceived "rules of the game" for co-operatives.

To say there was a negative reaction would be a considerable understatement. The reaction, in fact, was deafening, and it seemed to come from all sides. The most immediate, and scathing, reaction came from the leadership of the IAOS, Ireland's umbrella organisation for co-operative farm organisations. T.J. Maher, the president of IAOS, and John McCarrick, its Director General, were vocal, and public, in their criticism. Upon hearing the news of the acquisition on 9 March, Maher sent the following telex to Eddie Hayes, Denis Brosnan and Hugh Friel:

> The IAOS views with concern your recent moves to diversify into liquid milk outside your own area and away from your own shareholders. Repeated attempts to contact by phone have failed. Before serious damage is done to the relationship between co-ops we urgently request a meeting with your committee.[48]

The *Irish Independent* reported that Maher also:

> Doubted whether the move was in the best interests of Kerry's own members. He also warned it might lead to confrontation between co-ops. It seemed to his organisation that the incursion into Cork — a tiny "island" in the middle of another co-op area — was not conducive to harmony among co-ops. Both men [Maher and McCarrick] said that it completely contravened co-op principles as outlined in the recent "Framework for Co-Operative Development" and they sought urgent discussions with Kerry Co-op to see what could be done. Mr. Maher said that he recognised the fact that the IAOS had no mandatory powers in the matter, but he added, "If a co-op steps out of line, it is our business to take that matter up in the overall interest of the co-operative movement."[49]

Kerry was quick to respond to the assault. Eddie Hayes, who had spent his lifetime in the co-operative movement, and was the IAOS' strongest supporter in Kerry at a time when friends and supporters were few and far between, was the first to counter with a statement that was anything but equivocal:

We may be a co-op but we run a business. We are work-ing as best we can in the interests of our 8,000 sharehold-ers. There must be freedom in this country to do business in the same way as there is political freedom. Within the scope of that freedom we bought Ballinahina and we haven't the slightest intention of standing down. The board members may differ from time to time but they were never more solid about anything as they are about this issue.[50]

An editorial in the March 16 issue of the *The Kerryman* newspaper was even more direct, if not biting, in its reaction:

It's not so many years ago since the IAOS . . . was carving up Kerry between Ballyclough and Golden Vale Co-ops. That was in 1972 when most of the existing co-ops in North Kerry had come together in a single grouping, after much encouragement from Eddie Hayes, of Kilflynn, the current chairman of Kerry Co-op. Seven years later, all but three creamery co-ops are under the Kerry Co-op um-brella. And they have had to compete with the Cork co-ops to get what they now have. The farmers of Kerry have created in seven years something that the IAOS never en-visaged. Perhaps, the growth of the Kerry Co-op has taken others by surprise. Maybe it is being looked on as the cheeky youngster of the Co-operative movement. It seems that way. And it may be a surprise to some to hear that the man who raps them on the knuckles, Mr. Maher, comes from a county which hasn't got a major co-op of its own.[51]

For his part, Denis Brosnan's reaction was unusually emotional. He threatened to withdraw the Kerry Co-op's affiliation with the IAOS, suggesting that, "instead of trying to run the IAOS from a textbook up in Merrion Square that they (IAOS) might spend a bit more time down the country".[52] The threat to leave the IAOS was not an idle one. Said Brosnan:

The next move is up to the IAOS; they have made com-ments interfering with the right of an individual in Cork to sell his property, and interfering in the internal affairs of a

co-operative, and saying we cannot manage our own affairs or that we are not in a right mind to do what we do.[53]

Brosnan repeatedly stated that Ballyclough had already had
chances to buy Ballinahina, but had not been able to come to terms
with Buckley. This time, they claimed that they had been given no
opportunity to buy the firm, and further claimed that if they had
had the chance, they would have paid more than Kerry.[54] One
wonders, however, if their offers in the past had been nearly as
generous. Probably not. With no competition to buy the business,
there was little incentive to bid high. Now that Kerry had inserted
itself into the equation, however, the calculus had changed. For
Ballyclough, though, it was too late. Kerry was not going to back
down from the purchase. Clearly, Mitchelstown was also not
pleased with Kerry's presence in Cork, nor happy to now have
Kerry as a competitor with its liquid milk business. But whatever
the matter of bruised feelings, the contest between the two was no
more than a skirmish. There were no "milk wars" with Mitchelstown.

The same could not be said for relations with Golden Vale,
which had gone from bad to worse. Still bruised from Kerry's purchase of Limerick Dairies, bad relations were further exacerbated
when Kerry purchased Deel Dairies in Rathkeale, County Limerick
in June 1979, scarcely three months after the purchase of Ballinahina. Deel was another privately held liquid milk company located
some 15 miles out of Limerick City, again deep in the heart of
Golden Vale "territory". Owned by the Roche family, Deel Dairies
was a small operation, handling around 1,000,000 gallons annually.
Kerry purchased it for a reported £650,000, more than double what
it had paid for Limerick Dairies less than a year before. The *Limerick Leader* newspaper reported that Golden Vale had bid on the
property to a total of £700,000 but had withdrawn because of certain "special terms" in the contract.[55] Kerry actually closed down
Deel Dairies before the end of 1980, and transferred the business
to Limerick Dairies. In point of fact, they had no use for the physical
plant anyway.

In any event, Golden Vale (which had not responded immediately when Kerry bought Limerick Dairies in 1978) had now decided to counter Kerry's incursion by a different means. This may

have been something of a delayed reaction brought about by the hue and cry surrounding the Balinahina purchase, as critics called on Golden Vale to respond. It had decided to enter the liquid milk business, and to counter Kerry head to head in the Limerick City market. This would mean building, or acquiring, a liquid milk facility and distribution capability. It also meant that there would now be three dairies competing in the Limerick market, and strongly suggested that now none of them could expect to make any money. In the words of one Kerry manager:

> They (Golden Vale) invested, and suddenly we had three dairies in Limerick, and the whole market went south. It went absolutely right down. The tit for tat then started, because we started delivering milk all over County Limerick, distributing flyers, etc. Of course, Mitchelstown and Ballyclough, the two giant Cork co-operatives, were watching, enjoying the fun.[56]

At that time, around June of 1979, both Kerry and Golden Vale were courting Clare Dairies, a private dairy based in Ennis, County Clare, within reach of the Limerick market. Bidding at that point was reported to be up to £1,000,000.[57] *The Farming Independent* reported that Golden Vale was:

> . . . seriously concerned over the latest move by Kerry to acquire the dairies at Ennis. Kerry has already been rebuked by the IAOS over their movements on the purchase of the dairies outside their own area, but they are now determined, it appears, to acquire a monopoly in the south west.[58]

This bidding came to a close by October 1979, when Golden Vale announced that it had purchased a 50 per cent interest in Clare Dairies. It also announced plans to install a bottling plant at the former Landsdowne factory at Limerick.[59] Clare Dairies gave Golden Vale a facility with which they could attack the market with pack milk until such time as they had a new facility of their own up and running in Limerick. With this, a new phase of the "milk wars" began.

Golden Vale was coming into the fray with a clean image, with good quality milk, and they were doing extremely well. They were also seen, in the Limerick market, as being the "local" supplier. Kerry was seen as an external intruder. Even the Bishop of Limerick reportedly denounced the foreign influences coming in to disrupt the status of the farming enterprise in Limerick. Although Kerry was not mentioned by name, there seemed little doubt concerning the identity of the greedy, commercial interlopers he had in mind.

The "poaching" of milk suppliers then commenced in a serious way on both sides. Kerry was trying to upgrade its liquid milk supply, and Golden Vale extended the battle by sending teams to canvass Kerry milk suppliers. The promises were flying thick and heavy. Michael Griffin remembers:

> I was out there in my car, knocking on farmers' doors, calling in to them, telling them what we could do, along with Tim Lyons, although I'm not sure that Tim ever really believed this was the right way of going about it.[60]

A large part of the "pitch" to farmers was that Kerry was offering them the status of liquid milk suppliers, which was more lucrative than producing milk for processing. Of course, it did have additional requirements, like producing milk all year round. Not all of the milk suppliers who promised to become year round producers, however, actually did.

The "milk war" between Golden Vale and Kerry Co-op was to continue, interrupted by the occasional truce, for the next five years. Countless meetings were held between Golden Vale and Kerry, usually under the auspices of Jim Moloney and the ICOS, with the aim of bringing order to the Limerick milk market. They also aimed to put a stop to the unseemly competition for each other's milk suppliers by the two neighbouring societies and the public name calling and recriminations on both sides that many farm leaders felt gave a black eye to the entire co-operative movement. The meetings were generally unsuccessful, and the best that could often be hoped for would be that the parties remained on speaking terms. Certainly the milk wars took a toll on the management of both organisations, as they became a serious distraction from the operational and strategic aspects of the business. Says one dairy manager at Kerry at the time:

> The business was on automatic pilot. It took all of us out there to fight the war, it took all of our days and nights, out there talking to farmers. Eventually it took us down to County Clare as well, talking to groups of farmers wherever we could.[61]

In summary, by the end of 1979 Kerry had bought four private dairies in the south-west of Ireland. Its first purchase in Killarney, naturally, caused little reaction. The second purchase in Limerick set off alarm bells, even though Golden Vale didn't react for nearly a year. The purchases of Ballinahina in Cork and Deel Dairies in Rathkeale, County Limerick, precipitated an open break with ICOS and a destructive "milk war" with Golden Vale. Kerry, once again, and not for the last time, had rocked the boat in a fairly major way. The gauntlet had been thrown down. Not only were there economic business issues at stake, but serious and deep philosophical issues as well. What *was* the prime obligation of a co-operative organisation? What *were* the uses of competition, and should co-operative organisations compete just as other business organisations do? *Should* co-operatives be limited to certain geographic territories, and to certain businesses? Kerry's actions had thrown these questions into very sharp relief, and the debate would rage on for years. In the meantime, Kerry's relations with other co-operatives were very chilly at best — it was in a state of war with Golden Vale and it had withdrawn from ICOS.

As the decade of the 1970s came to a close, Kerry could look back on a solid record of profitable growth and development. Table 2 provides summary financials for the first five years of the co-op, and Table 3 shows some operating statistics. Kerry had also earned a reputation, for better or worse, as the combative "bad boy" of the co-operative movement. Clearly, it was an organisation that made things happen. But, beginning in 1979, Kerry's resilience and adaptability would be put to the test; it would be compelled more than ever before to look itself in the mirror and decide what type of organisation it was, where it wanted to go, and how it wanted to get there.

Table 2: Summary Financial Results through 1978 (£ '000s)

	1974	1975	1976	1977	1978
Turnover	20,748	31,139	36,941	48,809	62,429
Operating Surplus	673	1,542	1,986	2,645	3,604
Net Profit to Shareholders	388	1,219	1,657	2,327	2,987

Table 3: Miscellaneous Operating Statistics through 1978

	1974	1975	1976	1977	1978
Total Milk Intake (million gallons)	64.5	69.9	77.4	86.0	98.0
% Bulk Collection (ex-farm)	4.6%	6.3%	7.3%	7.3%	7.5%
Number of Milk Suppliers	7,711	7,625	7,654	7,420	7,294
Average Milk Supply per Supplier (gallons)	7,502	8,110	8,987	10,296	11,941
Total Dairy Cows	116,270	114,940	121,054	125,467	133,363
Milk Price Per Gallon (to Suppliers)	24.32p	31.51p	36.03p	49.05p	53.53p
Annual Milk Yield per Cow (gallons)	497	538	568	609	653

Notes

[1] Denis Brosnan, personal interview, 28 May 1999.

[2] *Kerry Co-op Creameries News* (1974), "Kerry Shares Drive to weld a Golden Future", July 1974, p. 1.

[3] Jim Moloney (1974), "Why Co-op Needs Capital", *Kerry Co-op Creameries News*, July 1974, p. 2

[4] Tom Sheehan (1974), "The Complete Co-op", *Kerry Co-op Creameries News*, July 1974, p. 2.

[5] Ned O'Callaghan, private correspondence, 21 June 2000.

[6] Dick Cross (1974), "Cork producers won't send milk to Kerry", *Irish Independent*, 23 February 1974.

[7] Donal Musgrave (1974), "Cork, Kerry Farmers Pour Milk Away in Creameries Dispute", *Irish Times*, 7 February 1974.

[8] Denis Cregan, personal interview, 12 October 1999.

[9] Des Maguire (1975), "Kerry Co-op, an Interesting Case History in Co-operative development", *Irish Farmers Journal*, 29 November 1975, p. 18.

[10] *The Kerryman*, "Streamlining £30 million Co-op", 24 October 1975, p. 1.

[11] Jimmy Woulfe (1977), "David and Goliath Crux at Creamery", *The Limerick Leader*, 12 March 1977.

[12] Daniel Dixon (1996), "Essay" in *Dorothea Lange's Ireland* (Photographs by Dorothea Lange, Text by Gerry Mullins), Montgomery, Alabama: Elliott & Clark Publishing, p. 8.

[13] Denis Cregan, op. cit..

[14] Hugh Friel, personal interview, 12 October 1999.

[15] *The Kerryman*, "Kerry's £11 million Worth of Milk Last Year", 3 February 1973.

[16] Hugh Friel, op. cit.

[17] Michael Leahy, personal interview, 6 December 1999.

[18] Ibid.

[19] Michael Drummey, personal Interview, 6 January 2000.

[20] Ibid

[21] *The Kerryman*, "Listowel Plugs for Co-op HQ", 23 January 1976.

[22] *The Kerryman*, "Listowel puts Pressure on Co-op", 30 January 1976, p. 1.

[23] *The Kerryman*, "Co-op HQ is Going to Tralee", 19 March 1976, p. 1

[24] *The Kerryman*, "Co-op HQ is Going to Tralee", 19 March 1976.

[25] Michael Drummey, personal interview, 6 January 2000.

[26] Ibid.

[27] Ibid.

[28] Ibid.

[29] Ibid.

[30] Ibid.

[31] *The Kerryman*, "Kerry Co-op Factory for Dingle", 3 February 1978.

[32] *Irish Business*, "Brosnan: The Maverick Empire Builder", November 1979, p. 7.

[33] Ibid.

[34] Denis Brosnan, personal interview, 1 June 1999.

[35] Ibid.

[36] Denis Cregan, op. cit.

[37] Aileen O'Toole (1987), *The Pace Setters*, Dublin: Gill and Macmillan, p. 100.

[38] Noel O'Mara (1978), "Killarney Milk — Big Growth Years", in *The Kerryman*.

[39] Denis Cregan, op. cit.

[40] Michael Drummey, personal interview, 6 January 2000.

[41] *Irish Business* (1979), "Brosnan: The Maverick Empire Builder," November 1979, p. 11.

[42] Hugh Friel, op. cit.

[43] Denis Brosnan, personal interview, 1 June 1999.

[44] Aileen O'Toole (1987), op. cit., p. 102.

[45] Ibid.

[46] Michael Griffin, personal interview, 5 January 2000.

[47] Ibid.

[48] Archives of the Irish Co-operative Organisation Society.

[49] Aengus Fanning (1979), "Stage Set for 'Milk War' after Dairy Take-over", *Irish Independent*, 10 March 1979, p. 3.

[50] *The Kerryman* (1979), "Co-op Won't Step Down", undated.

[51] *The Kerryman*, "Room for Competition", 16 March 1979, p. 8.

[52] *The Irish Press* (1979), "Kerry Co-op's Cork Buy Leads to Threat to Withdraw from IAOS", 13 March 1979.

[53] Ibid.

[54] Ibid.

[55] *Limerick Leader*, "Rathkeale Dairies Purchased by Kerry Co-op Society", 31 March 1979.

[56] Hugh Friel, op. cit.

[57] *Farming Independent*, "Co-ops Battle for Milk Trade", 16 June 1979.

[58] Ibid.

[59] *Farming Independent*, "No Benefit from Milk Price War", 6 October 1979.

[60] Michael Griffin, personal interview, 5 January 2000.

[61] Ibid.

Chapter 6

The Milk that Never Came: A Shrinking Milk Supply and the Move to Diversify, 1979–1985

God doesn't close one door but He opens another!

The End of the Honeymoon

Entering into 1979, the business was running smoothly, almost as if Kerry Co-op would never again have a bad day. As shown in Figure 2, milk production in 1978 was up to 98 million gallons (an increase of over 40 per cent in just three years), farmers were steadily increasing their herds and expanding their facilities, and milk quality was steadily improving. The Farranfore Feed Mill was officially opened on Monday, 29 May 1978 by the then Minister for Agriculture, James Gibbons. It was a day of great celebration, and great promise. Kerry Co-op was in its fifth year of existence, increasingly profitable and continually expanding. The milk supply throughout the 1970s had been steadily increasing, and EC subsidies and common market prices had made these good times for dairy farmers throughout Ireland. Yet there was a cloud on the horizon, and it ironically announced itself at this most propitious of events. As he opened the mill amid hoopla and congratulations, Gibbons announced that a national campaign to eliminate bovine brucellosis and tuberculosis would commence in County Kerry in the autumn of 1978. This eradication would be compulsory, and Kerry would act as a test case for the rest of the country.

Bovine brucellosis was a bacterial infection that could cause spontaneous abortions in cows, and undulant fever in humans. It was also highly contagious. Nearly 13 per cent of the cows in Kerry in 1978 (reduced from nearly 17 per cent in 1975) had tested positive on the "ring test" for brucellosis in 1978. It was a serious problem and worthy of significant attention if the milk supply was to attain higher levels of quality. Of course, Kerry Co-op supported such a campaign. They, after all, traded on the basis of a quality product that could be sold anywhere in the world, and for a premium price. To have the taint of brucellosis in their supply chain would be unthinkable. They could not be exporting dairy products to the United States, while taking any chances of having milk tainted by bovine brucellosis. Ireland still faced restrictions on exports of its cattle, meat and livestock products, and needed to achieve what the EEC termed "officially free status" to compete fully with its EEC trading partners. Said Gibbons:

> The majority of our EEC partners have already reached this status and are fully determined to remain so. If we want our export trade to flourish in the years ahead — and it is vital to the national economy that it should — we must succeed in eradicating brucellosis and TB from our national herd.[1]

The campaign would involve mandatory blood testing of all dairy herds in Kerry, and the marking, isolation, and slaughter of all "reactors" (those animals who appear to carry the disease) within 30 days. Herds in whom "reactor" cattle were found would also be restricted (that is, no movement of cattle into and out of the herd) until they were cleared. Said Gibbons, "Kerry will be the bridgehead" of this campaign. Since it tended to have an "outward" as opposed to an "inward" movement of cattle, and since it was bordered on three sides by the sea, making it relatively remote and easy to control and monitor inbound and outbound movement, Kerry was the chosen "pilot area" for the project. One might suggest it was "Kerryman's luck".

Although Kerry Co-op management supported this campaign, the immediate effect of it was certainly not foreseen. No one accurately predicted the devastation that would occur in Kerry. At a meeting of the County Committee of Agriculture in October 1978, farmers themselves began to react. "Farmers are having herds cut in two and the loss is something terrible," said one farmer.[2] Through October, roughly 20 per cent of the countywide herd indicated brucellosis, resulting in a "wholesale slaughter of cattle" in the county. The government compensated farmers on the basis of £140/cow, but this was claimed to be poor compensation for farmers who would be paying the price of smaller herds for the next several years.[3]

The impact clearly was more severe than anyone had foreseen. All in all, the Kerry milk herd and milk supplies were reduced by approximately 15 per cent by 1981 (or up to 20 per cent, if one considers the growth in the milk supply that could otherwise have been anticipated). The lessons learned in Kerry by the Department of Agriculture were transferred to other counties as they entered into eradication programs, and their herd culling was far less severe than in Kerry. Further exacerbating the situation in Kerry was the fact that it would take several years to build up the county herd again. There would be no quick relief in sight. Additionally, with the setting of EEC quotas on milk production looming on the horizon, things looked even worse. With Kerry's reduced production, any quotas introduced would likely be based upon this reduced production. It was bad timing all around. At this time, Kerry Co-op was solely dependent upon its milk supply, both for manufactured milk products like casein, milk powder, caseinates, whey powder and other products, as well as for serving its growing liquid milk businesses in Killarney, Limerick, and (in 1979) Cork and (in 1982) Galway. All of Kerry's eggs were clearly in the one basket. They were completely and utterly dependent upon their available milk supply. Such exposure to the vagaries of one primary raw material must have been very disconcerting.

Although clearly a factor, the brucellosis eradication campaign cannot be singled out as the sole cause of Kerry Co-op's troubles. It was only one, albeit the most important, of several factors which combined to reduce Kerry's milk supply. They all converged, coincidentally, during the 1979–1980 milk seasons, combining to put to an abrupt end the hitherto continually escalating production of milk in Kerry that had characterised the good times of the second half of the 1970s. It was a "war on three fronts". First, of course, was the impact of brucellosis eradication. Second was the weather. It was perhaps the most severe weather that had been experienced in many years. Third was the construction of a large new aluminium plant at Aughinish in nearby County Limerick on the Shannon Estuary. The construction of this massive project attracted a number of farmers out of farming and into the more lucrative construction trades. Other farmers were tempted by industrial jobs in the factory itself. All these factors combined to reduce the number of farmer suppliers by nearly 20 per cent, from 7,400 in 1977 to 5,900 in 1981.

Compounding the problem was the fact that a massive capital development program at Listowel was nearly completed, increasing milk-processing capacity by approximately 50 per cent. Instead, there was now a 20 per cent *decrease* in the milk being supplied. It was an expansion in expectation of "the milk that never came". The good times at Kerry Co-op were abruptly over, and there were more than a few satisfied smiles on the faces of Kerry's detractors as they watched for Kerry, the upstart co-op, brash and acquisitive, to receive at long last its comeuppance. Had the Kerry Co-op, and its "whiz kid" managers, finally met their Waterloo? The sense at Kerry was, as Denis Brosnan remembers it, that "we were totally surrounded by the sea".[4]

As Brosnan, Friel and Cregan contemplated their shrinking milk supply (it did begin to stabilise in 1982) and their now excess processing capacity, it was clear to them that the organisation had now reached a crossroads. There were perhaps three major options, all with their risks:

- Tighten up on expenses and ride out the crisis

- Aggressively pursue additional milk supplies

- Diversify out of complete reliance upon milk.

Michael Drummey remembers that:

> . . . we used to have these meetings in the Mt. Brandon Hotel in Tralee, and I can remember that one night dis-

tinctly. There were a bunch of us around the table, and I don't remember who said it, but we all agreed that there would have to be a diversification away from milk. We would not abandon milk, but there would have to be other strands to our business.[5]

Members of the board of directors at the time also remember Brosnan clearly and forcefully making the point that "we will never again be totally dependent on manufacturing milk".[6] Yet, in true Kerry fashion, the organisation moved aggressively on all three fronts.

First, there was aggressive belt-tightening at all levels of the organisation. Extraordinary measures were taken to reduce expenses and tighten up on working capital, such as placing strict limits on stores inventories and closely monitoring all purchases. This was particularly important given the weakness in the currency, high interest rates and massive inflation that prevailed at the time. Second, the organisation's expansion into the liquid milk market continued with the purchase of Ballinahina Dairies in Cork, and in 1982, the acquisition of Galway Dairies. These acquisitions precipitated the "milk wars" that reached their nadir in 1983, and eventually ended, not with a bang but a whimper, around 1985. Importantly, milk not needed for the consumer liquid milk business could be diverted for use as manufacturing milk, so the liquid milk businesses represented a reasonable instrument for gaining additional milk.

But it was the decision to diversify out of milk that would represent a critical turning point in the history of the organisation — a decision that even today has left its impact upon Kerry Group. More accurately, though, it was less the decision to diversify than the decision to formally *plan* their way out of the challenges they faced in 1979 that has left a lasting imprint upon the Kerry organisation. A formal corporate planning process emerged from the crucible that was 1979. Never again would Kerry have to contend in an *ad hoc* manner with business circumstances that had not been anticipated. The planning process was expected to supply the map that they needed to take them out of their dependence upon milk, and towards a more diversified array of activities. Without the spur of the disappointing 1979 results, and the realisation of the fragility

of their milk business, corporate planning may not have been implemented for some time to come. Certainly it would not have
been embraced with the same level of seriousness, conviction and
urgency as it was at Kerry.

The Beginning of the Formal Planning Process

There was a meeting off-site with the board of directors and top
company executives to kick-off the formal planning process. Hugh
Friel, who had been evaluating various planning models, had returned from the States with the Kami and Kami Corporate Planning
Model, a detailed process that took an organisation through a step-
by-step development of the annual and long-range plans. Certainly, Kerry had done five-year plans in the past, but the idea of
formalising a "process" was quite different. This process was to be
formal, structured and inclusive. One of the key ideas, emphasised
Friel, was to induce *clarity* into the process, to develop a keen and
clear sense of the organisation's goals, and the knowledge of and
commitment to the means to accomplish those goals. Friel remembers:

> They had a very detailed model for corporate planning,
> and I was quite taken with it. The process went through a
> variety of stages to arrive at a corporate plan. It dealt with
> the whole organisation, how it was going to get from point
> "A" to point "B", the type of organisation it was going to
> be. It was quite detailed.[7]

Implementation of this planning process was not as difficult as
might be surmised, since Kerry at the time was a highly centralised organisation, with most key people concentrated in Tralee.
This started the formal planning process at Kerry. If nothing else, a
clearer picture of the environment and circumstances of the Kerry
Co-op quickly began to emerge. The process began with what is
known as a SWOT analysis, that is, an appraisal first of the organisation's *internal* capabilities (its strengths and weaknesses), as
well as an evaluation of the *external factors* (the opportunities and
threats in the external environments) that may affect its performance. Importantly, the review of the external factors called for a
review of *multiple* environments: macroeconomic policy (at both

national and European levels), competitors, supply factors, political, social, legal and regulatory environments, demographics, and marketing and distribution channels. The corporate planning process, if approached with commitment and discipline, fostered an intense, objective and dispassionate analysis of all these factors. With the initial analysis serving as a shared foundation, various levels of medium and long-term planning could proceed.

At the time, Kerry could point to a number of strengths. First, the fact that it was selling casein in North America was not an insignificant point. Its presence, modest though it was, in the largest market in the world provided them with a window from which to watch, learn, and plan. It also differentiated them from other Irish dairy co-operatives at the time. Kerry's expansion into liquid milk was also providing it with a base in the consumer foods business, from which it could further expand. Kerry's "can-do" organisational culture of commitment, hard work, and informality was still developing, but was already an obvious strength. Its charismatic leader and cadre of highly talented and committed executives brought drive, vision and cohesion to the organisation. The extraordinary support provided by its shareholders and board of directors provided the confidence needed to make difficult decisions. Kerry's track record from 1974–78 was extraordinarily consistent. All of these could be considered important strengths as Kerry began the necessary self-evaluation. Of course, many of these strengths are relatively intangible; they are not to be found on the balance sheet. Weaknesses, on the other hand, were far more explicit. The primary weakness, already discussed, was the firm's total dependence upon the milk pool. This was an exposure that could only be remedied by diversification. A second weakness was Kerry's relatively undercapitalised state; investments were being funded through retained earnings and borrowings. Farmers could not be expected to supply large amounts of capital. Funding concerns provided constraints that would certainly limit the enterprise's freedom of action in the future. A third weakness was the flip side of a strength; although Kerry had a presence in the US, it did not have *direct* exposure there. Additionally, although sales of casein had provided Kerry with excellent profits since its inception, Kerry's sole reliance on those profits represented another area of exposure.

Kerry used the Kami and Kami process through the 1989 planning process, and then moved on to the more compact Argenti
model, which it has used since 1990. The Argenti Model is a ten-
stage process, and stage one is "start"! But less important than the
model used by the organisation is the deep-seated commitment to
the *idea* and the *process* of planning. Says Friel:

> It is a process and people understand the process. It is
> diffused throughout the organisation. It has introduced
> clarity, a lot of clarity. By that I mean, if you were to ask
> twenty different people, at different levels throughout the
> organisation, about the organisation and where it's going
> and why it does particular things, that the answers you'd
> get should be pretty similar to those you'd get from the
> top executives in the company.[8]

With the advent of the formal planning process for 1980, Kerry began to look more systematically for acquisitions that would allow it
to diversify out of its total reliance upon milk. It also began to focus
upon higher value-added sectors of the food industry, and particularly on the possibility of getting into businesses that had
strong consumer brands. They were also beginning to evaluate the
desirability of combining their various liquid milk businesses under one brand (what would eventually become the *Dawn Dairies*
brand).

At this point in the history of Kerry, it had already made several
opportunistic ventures into diversifying its reliance on milk. Its investment in Cheese-Tek, the manufacturer of cheese analogues or
artificial cheese, was an excellent move, but had been snuffed out
by Borden's purchase of Kerry's American partner. Kerry's joint
venture with Union Camp never really demonstrated any strategic
"fit" with the organisation, and in any event was highly inconsistent
with Kerry's increasingly demonstrated strategy of having "hands-
on" control of its enterprises. Kerry was still selling casein in the
United States through Erie Casein, and playing a cat-and-mouse
game trying to get nearer to their end customers. They were intently studying where the "value-added" was in the industry. They
were engaged in the "milk wars" at home, expanding and consolidating their liquid milk business in Ireland. They were beginning

to search for another food firm that would take them out of the dairy business, but not so far away from the agricultural heritage that they had as an agricultural co-operative. Specifically, Kerry was interested in consumer branded foods as a way out of its milk dependence. Ironically, Kerry had not to look far. An opportunity existed in their back yard.

The internal debate at the time concerned whether or not Kerry *could* transfer its skills outside of the milk business. Conventional wisdom might suggest that Kerry should have stuck to its knitting, focusing upon businesses in which it had a proven expertise. Denis Brosnan had a starkly different view. They had learned the casein business almost from scratch; they had learned the liquid milk business the same way. Brosnan was confident that Kerry's capabilities could be successfully applied outside of its familiar core businesses, and equally sure that it was critical that the portfolio of Kerry's businesses be broadened. Denis Cregan, the Deputy Managing Director, has summed it up this way:

> What was evolving among us at the time was a theme — that through our ability, energy and application, we could get things done, faster and more effectively than our peers.[9]

But Kerry's first major acquisition outside the milk business would put this self-confidence, and Kerry's reputation for getting things done, seriously to the test.

Diversification through Denny and Duffy Meats

The Denny Story

Perhaps the most prominent name in Tralee was that of Denny. A Sir Anthony Denny had done remarkably well as the Executor for King Henry VIII. Later, during the reign of Elizabeth I, his son Sir Edward Denny had been sent to Ireland to help suppress the Desmond Rebellion, and subsequently, to assist with the plantation of Munster. In recompense for his service to the crown, he was granted substantial lands in Kerry, as well as in England after the dissolution of the monasteries. Although most of the merchant adventurers who went to Ireland on behalf of the crown and did the dirty work of subduing the population did not stay, the Denny family remained. Even today, the main street in Tralee is Denny Street, and the Town Park is on the lands of the Denny demesne. At some point, a branch of the family had established itself in Waterford, where, in 1820, one Henry Denny, the son of a shoemaker and prominent citizen of the town, established a provisioning business. Waterford at the time was the centre of the bacon industry in Ireland, so it was only natural that Denny's soon began to sell bacon into the domestic market, as well as for export to Britain, where demand was burgeoning. The business grew, an office was maintained in Hibernia Chambers on London Bridge, and additional plants were added in Limerick and Cork. Later, plants in Tralee and Sligo, and a head office in Dublin, were added. Denny's was the leading brand in Ireland, where its bacon and ham had a stronghold on the domestic market. At some point, Denny's began to supply bacon and lard to provision wholesalers and the great chain stores. At the time, Irish bacon was the world market leader and commanded a price premium. Denny's later expanded into Northern Ireland, with facilities in Portadown and, later, a modern plant in Newry. The Waterford branch of the family ran the Denny's operation, but for many years the family had had no residence in Ireland, nor had they any further contact with the Tralee branch of the family. James Denny, who along with his brother Tony represented the last of the Denny family actively engaged in the business, remembers that, "We were always regarded as Anglo-Irish landlords".[10] The location of a Denny's plant in Tralee, the original stronghold of the family, was mere coincidence.

By the end of the 1970s, however, Henry Denny & Sons (Ireland) Ltd. was in trouble. Although the Denny's brand was one of the best known in Ireland, sales were declining. If anything, it was a "sleeping brand". "Everyone knew it, but no one bought it."[11] By this time the Denny's range of products encompassed ham, bacon and, most importantly, sausage, as well as other cooked and fresh meat products. Denny's Gold Medal brand of sausages, in fact, remained the single best-selling sausage brand in Ireland. The production facilities, however, were starved of capital investment and quality standards were dropping. Although the firm was still owned by the Denny family, there were internal conflicts among them. After the death of a cousin (Edward Denny) who had owned 51 per cent of the enterprise, James and A.M. (Tony) Denny had had to purchase equity from other family members to gain sufficient control. The problem, however, is that they were to pay for the shares from the profits of the business, and, as it transpired, they were hard pressed to make such payments. Most available funds were utilised for paying down the debt, and little remained to plough back into the business. In the words of James Denny, "Sadly, the operation was running out of steam. We were in a corner."[12] By the late 1970s, rumours already abounded that Denny's was going to fail. This did not escape the notice of Denis Brosnan and the Kerry management.

It may be a stretch to suggest that Kerry's targeting of Denny's was a calculated, deliberate outcome of a detailed strategic planning process, for the formal planning process was only beginning to get underway in the very early 1980s. More likely, it was an opportunistic move, a chance to make profit, and in a manner not inconsistent with the general strategic consensus that was only then beginning to emerge. Denny's was an attractive target for Kerry for any number of reasons. First, it was in the co-op's backyard, with a slaughterhouse and meat packing facility a stone's throw from the Tralee headquarters. As in the case of Killarney Dairies in 1974, it may also have been unthinkable that an "outside" entity would come in and take Denny's from under Kerry's very nose. Denny's was important to the people of County Kerry, and Kerry Co-op was by now the strongest economic force in the county. Some feelings of responsibility and stewardship may have provided some further context for Kerry's interest in Denny's. Michael Drummey, at the time Kerry Co-op's Director of Marketing, remarked on this social side:

> Denny's was to the town of Tralee what Wedgewood is to Staffordshire. The factory was based right in the centre of town. God only knows how many generations of Tralee people have been educated through the existence of the Denny factory. But it was literally falling asunder. It was inevitable that it was going to go under, and Denis was obviously aware of it. It was an opportunity to do something in a new agri-activity, and at the same time, and I don't know to what extent his feeling would have leaned

towards the social cause, but it would have been a very serious blow to Tralee if Denny's had disappeared.[13]

However, Kerry Co-op was already connected to Denny's in a far more tangible and down-to-earth manner, for both enterprises had a practical interest in pigs and pig meat. Denny's had the value-added and retailing arm, and Kerry was a major provider of the livestock. Kerry had originally become involved with pigs as a supplier of whey to the pig industry. After all, the creation and development of a large pig-raising industry that used whey for feed had helped solve (or at least mitigate) the whey disposal problems that had so bedevilled the enterprise in its first years. Kerry's existing involvement in pig breeding and pig raising provided a direct connection to Denny's. Additionally, it could not have been far from their minds that if Denny's had, in fact, closed down and suffered liquidation, the market for their pigs would disappear. If the market for the pigs disappeared, there would be complications, again, in disposing profitably of their whey. The strategic logic came full circle. As Denis Cregan put it years later:

> We found ourselves in a very curious quirk of supply-side circuitry: as part of the whey disposal solution, we got involved in pigs. Suddenly we were supplying maybe one-third of the total number of pigs to Denny's, and what do we do with all this whey if Denny's closes?[14]

An acquisition of Denny's would provide, at the very least, a modicum of vertical integration.

Denny's was a business with a substantial "upside" potential, a solid heritage, and the sort of operational challenges that Kerry seemed to relish. Kerry had commissioned a research survey on the response of consumers and retailers to Denny's, and it had yielded some important and unusually conclusive findings. It found that consumers' awareness of the Denny's brand was surprisingly high, particularly in view of the fact that sales of the product were static. Or, as it was put far more poetically by Michael Drummey, the survey:

> . . . showed that Denny's had an enormous body, a body that was ailing and falling asunder and decrepit, but it had

> a very, very magical soul. I thought at the time that if one
> side of the house can get the body in order, let me try to
> get the soul and the heart stirring again. Once we get
> those two right, we'll have a business![15]

The survey clearly delineated the dual challenge that Kerry would face: the operational challenge and the marketing challenge, and by all indications it would be the operational challenge that would predominate.

Strategically, the purchase of Denny's would present a dramatic shift out of the dairy sector and into the branded consumer foods business in Ireland, entirely consistent with the designs Kerry had set out for themselves through their corporate planning process. Secondly, it was a business that was neither making nor losing money, and that would represent not just a substantial investment of capital but also a massive commitment of people, talent and effort. Thirdly, Kerry was going into uncharted territory. Although they had done their homework, it was a business that, operationally, they did not know. They would have to learn it from the ground up. They would need to place a massive gamble on the belief that they could turn the operation around, and quickly, and that the talents and capabilities they had been honing for the past ten years on the dairy side could be applied effectively in the consumer meats business. In purchasing Denny's, Kerry was upping the ante, betting that through strategic vision, energy, commitment, and an ability to learn quickly, it could become a major player in consumer foods in its domestic market. Clearly, Kerry's success, or failure, would be watched closely by industry analysts, its farmer-shareholders, the financial community and, importantly, the other co-operatives in Ireland (of the Big Six). And not everyone would want them to succeed. Brosnan remembers:

> It wasn't the first time that the dairy industry in Ireland
> looked at us and said "they'll really come a cropper this
> time, because they don't know what they're doing".

Armed with some figures provided by their consultants, Price Waterhouse, Brosnan and Friel approached the Denny's management at the beginning of 1982. During these discussions, James

Denny pushed for a more palatable price for the business, and Hugh Friel remembered that:

> As we evaluated the Denny business and a brand aware-
> ness survey that scored the brand highly (albeit this was
> not reflected in its sales), James Denny argued that we
> were not properly valuing the brand. It was a brand that
> he understood to be a first-class brand. He was subse-
> quently proven to be right.[16]

These negotiations ultimately led to the purchase of Denny's (Ireland) for £1.7 million on a phased payment basis, effective 1
August 1982. At that point, Denny's "was probably on its last
legs".[17] For James Denny, it was:

> . . . a very sad moment for the family. But at least by going
> back to Kerry, it was going back to its origins, and the ori-
> gins of the family.[18]

At the same time that Kerry was negotiating for the purchase of
Henry Denny & Sons (Ireland) Ltd., another piece of the strategic
puzzle had surfaced. Duffy Meats Ltd. was a small meat processor
that specialised in cooked specialty and delicatessen meats. It
produced a wide array of cooked meats, many for export to continental Europe, from its plant in Hacketstown, County Carlow. To
demonstrate its product range, it is interesting to note that one of
its more successful products was an "Irish Whiskey Sausage" that
was exported to Germany. Duffy's problem was that it had over-
extended itself, and had simply run out of money. It was already in
receivership. Duffy Meats was particularly attractive, however, in
that its product line almost exactly complemented that of Denny's.
Duffy's had everything Denny's didn't have. It had value-added
meats, good products, and a modern plant, but no distribution and
no money; Denny's had a brand, primary processing and distribution, but an old plant. Putting the two together was a logical strategic move. As Brosnan put it:

> We went after Denny's because it was the biggest brand
> on the Irish market. We thought it had potential and it was
> in our hometown of Tralee. We took the view that the pig

meat industry was in absolute chaos with nobody making any money out of it. At the time we were in processed milk, animal feeds and liquid milk and we proved to ourselves that we could do it better than anybody else.... We took the view that if everybody was so bad in the pig meat sector then it probably gave us the greatest opportunities. It gave us the most heartaches as well.[19]

After negotiations with the firm's receivers, Duffy's was purchased for approximately £300,000 in September 1982, one month after Denny's. Both enterprises were purchased for less than £2 million in total.[20] With manufacturing plants in Tralee (Denny's) and Hacketstown, County Carlow (Duffy's), along with Denny's (Ireland) head office in Dublin, Kerry was now in the meat business.

Kerry took over Denny's on 1 August 1982. Despite the new focus on branded consumer products, it may be fair to suggest that many in the Kerry organisation still had not a real appreciation for the power of a strong brand. Certainly, not everyone would have been in favour of buying Denny's. It was a major leap, for Kerry did not have the in-house skills on the manufacturing side to transfer in to the Denny's operation. During the negotiations, Kerry had not even been permitted to go into the plant. When they arrived at the beginning of August, it was easy to see why. The annual report for 1982, in noting the purchase (and referring to Duffy's as well), soberly suggested that:

> Both traded profitably but have a long way to go to meet our criteria of return and profit. Substantial re-organisation and capital expenditure will have to take place and this is now being worked on.[21]

The reality, however, was far grimmer, for the situation operationally was far worse than Kerry had imagined. As Kerry got deeper into the operation in 1983, the full extent of the challenge began to reveal itself. The turnaround of Denny's would take considerably more time than originally thought, and would demand an enormous commitment of organisational resources. But no one knew *how* much time it would take. The business, after all, was a new one to Kerry. They would have to learn before they could teach, and that learning would be done by the seat of the pants rather than from a textbook. Kerry would also have to throw everything, and almost everybody, into the effort. Brosnan remembers that:

> We had to pull out all of the resources, and the resources were basically people who had come up through the milk industry, in factory management or sales management, or accounting. These were all people who trained only in the dairy industry, and who were put in to see if they could actually run a consumer branded food business in pig meat.[22]

It was a situation in some ways analogous to that of a decade previously, when people worked around the clock to get the Listowel plant up and running. Here, too, the crunch was on in the race to get the Denny's and Duffy's operations operating profitably.

One of the first realisations was that Kerry would have to recruit and import experts in the pig meat industry. At the product level, Kerry's in-house expertise in milk processing did not transfer well to the pig meat sector. Said Denis Brosnan:

> We thought we would get them into profit within two years but we didn't realise the level of capital and technology we would have to inject. We had to bring management in from Denmark to run Denny's and we sent our supervisors to be trained in a Danish butchery school for six months. We also brought a good technologist in from Austria and he came up with new products that have since been launched, such as pineapple and maple flavoured rashers, a high meat content sausage and gammon steaks.[23]

These new products provided Kerry's marketing group with ammunition with which they could trumpet the "re-emergence" of the Denny's brand. On the manufacturing side, however, it should be acknowledged that there was a considerable amount of skill that had built up in the Denny's plant that could not be easily sourced outside. The challenge for the new Kerry managers was to harness these skills in an effective and efficient manner. This challenge was complicated by the relatively poor relationship with the rank and file workers that had built up over time in the Tralee plant.

To put it far too mildly, industrial relations at the Tralee facility were less than ideal. This was of particular concern because major changes in work practices would be needed to improve the productivity and efficiency of the plant. The industrial relations culture at the Tralee plant was a town-based, industrial culture — something with which Kerry had not had to contend before. It tended to be adversarial in nature, nearly the opposite of the "all for one and one for all" attitudes that continued to prevail, for instance, in Kerry's Listowel factory. Workplace discipline was very slack. The joke making the rounds of Tralee at the time that Kerry bought Denny's was that they should have bought the public house across the street from the plant as well, since more employees were often in the pub than in the plant! Kerry ran into this culture head-on. There were major strikes during the first few years after Kerry bought Denny's, and relations were generally messy. It was, after all, a profound shock for the workforce. They had been accustomed over the years to dealing with a largely absentee upper management that had devolved many responsibilities to the local level. In this decentralised structure, local management had had considerable autonomy of action. With the entry of Kerry Co-op into the picture, this scenario changed overnight. Kerry was nothing if not a "hands-on", "get involved", "make it happen" organisation. The plant went from a remote owner to a local direct presence, from passive to highly active management, from a *"laissez faire"* approach to a hard-nosed focus on production, efficiency and profit. It was a stunning change, and the work force at first did not respond well. The complication, of course, was that the existing workforce and management knew something about the pig meat business, while the new managers from Kerry had to learn. One Kerry manager remembers a colleague walking through the plant, and seeing a production worker trimming a shank made some sort of a critical comment. The worker shrugged, handed over his knife to the manager, and said, "here, you show me how it's done", knowing the manager did not know how to trim meat. This was characteristic of interactions at the time. This manager later went to school in Denmark to learn how to cut and trim meat; the next time it happened, he was ready to take up the challenge and demonstrate to the employees on the shop floor how it was to be done. But this took time.

In recounting this time, it is probably fair to say that Kerry was shocked by the full extent of the problems at Denny's. If anything, they were taken aback that a long-established company like Denny's, with excellent brands and a fine tradition, had fallen so far. The work standards and practices were far below the level to which Kerry was accustomed. The physical plant was little better. Because of the long period when there had been no investment in the plant, it was in a deplorable shape, with much of it woefully out of date. Denis Cregan was stunned when he got his first good look at the Denny's trucks that plied the enterprise's trade throughout Ireland. They were almost literally held together by bits of string and elastic band, in bad repair, and dirty. This was precisely the condition that the retailers had noted in the 1982 survey. Cregan had to get rid of almost all of them and buy a completely new fleet.

On the marketing side, the going was perhaps less difficult. It was quickly apparent that it was a very good brand, and that for all the woes on the operations side, the sales prospects were outstanding. Drummey began aggressively to promote the Denny brand, trying to re-alert both retailers and consumers that the Denny brand was not only still alive, but it was a fresh, new Denny brand that was coming back. The addition of the Duffy range of cold meats provided an ideal complement to Denny's product offerings. The variety and range of the products was improved, operational changes began to reap benefits in better product quality, and the Kerry marketers were preaching a strong message of upgraded quality, higher meat content, better value, and a range of products that were going to "walk off the shelves". Enormous efforts were expended in communicating this message, in a very straightforward way, to both retailers and consumers. Drummey also pulled a page from his past efforts with *Bloom*, and initiated the sponsorship of an annual horse race at Leopardstown (outside Dublin) on St Stephen's Day, 26 December. The major stakes race of the day was "The Denny Gold Medal Novice Steeplechase", with the huge trophy presented by the managing director of Denny's. This race meeting attracted large crowds and a very substantial television audience. Very quickly, the Denny's name was in the public eye again, communicating to consumers that Denny's was back. Even today, more than 20 years later, it remains a prominent event on the Irish racing calendar.

Nineteen eighty-two was only a partial year, but the Denny's operation was marginal. The necessary capital infusion, for an organisation of Kerry's size and for a co-operative in particular, was massive. The following year, 1983, was, in the words of another Kerry manager, "crucifying", with the strikes and a continuing haemorrhage of cash out of the operation. In 1984, it was expected that the operation would hit the black, but, in the first part of the year, the losses continued. The business was beginning to turn around, the situation was under control, and there was no panic, but nevertheless, there was a rising level of impatience. It was not unlike watching and waiting for a kettle to boil. Michael Griffin, although he remained with the dairy side of the operation, commented upon the stubbornness of the Kerry managers in making the Denny's operation work:

> Call it the "Kerry Way", the belief that if we got involved in the enterprise we weren't going to *not* succeed, we weren't going to walk away. The fundamentals of the business were right, and we were going to stay with it. It may have taken a lot of blood, sweat and tears, but we were going to make it work.[24]

Finally, the elusive corner was turned in November of 1984, when the operation made money for the first time. Said one Kerry manager involved with the Denny operation at the time, "we never looked back".

It is difficult to say who suffered the most in the Denny's turnaround. Was it the front line managers who, having come up in the dairy industry, had to learn a new business while in the middle of a major effort to turn that business around? Was it the more senior executives who watched anxiously from the Tralee headquarters, hoping to see their risky gamble vindicated? Or was it the labour force at Denny's itself, as it moved from the old comfortable relationship with the factory into a different, more competitive and perhaps more cold-hearted relationship with a large organisation? With the benefit of hindsight, some Kerry managers have suggested that perhaps they should have waited for Denny's to go into liquidation before buying it. That way, the workers in the plant, who did not at all realise that the operation was in trouble, would have

got a true picture of the state of the business. Revamping, improving, and reshaping the business may have been made that much
easier. Regardless, the turnaround of Denny's was itself a turning
point for the Kerry organisation. First, it ultimately "delivered"
what it was supposed to in the strategic sense. Kerry now had a viable, branded, non-dairy consumer business that would help it to
balance out the vagaries of its dairy business. However, there were
other outcomes that were less tangible, but perhaps ultimately
even more important for the organisation as it went forward. Michael Drummey put it well:

> It was an expensive learning program. A lot of people, in-
> cluding myself, said, "I hope we don't have to do this
> again!" It did take a long time. But, because of the meas-
> ure of the results that we got, I think a lot of people
> learned an awful lot, to the extent that maybe they thought
> "hell, give us any mountain now and we could move it".
> We always had to get into the nuts and bolts of an opera-
> tion, so we learned an awful lot about the fundamentals of
> the business literally from the factory floor right up to
> where it really mattered.[25]

This organisational self-confidence, formed in the early years with
the commissioning of the Listowel plant and the formation of the
Kerry Co-operative, had now been further hardened in the crucible of Denny's. In addition to the nearly £6 million in capital that
Kerry spent in the end, this investment had given Kerry a beach-
head in consumer foods. It had also given it the further self-
confidence to begin to look at businesses that were even further
afield. In every way, it was a milestone for the organisation.

The "Milk Wars" Continue: Further Expansion in Liquid Milk and the Development of Dawn Dairies

Through 1980 and into 1981, the "milk war" with Golden Vale continued unabated, and "poaching" of each other's milk suppliers
ebbed and flowed with every new campaign. Kerry has claimed
that they got the better of the exchange, pointing to the additional
milk supply they were able to build after the debacle of brucellosis eradication in 1979–1980. Many, but not all, would agree with
this assertion, and it is difficult to independently confirm. It may

well be that most of the additional milk came by virtue of the acquisition of the private dairies. Jim Moloney, however, as one who watched with interest probably every milk "war" or "skirmish" during nearly four decades of involvement with the co-operative movement, evaluates it differently. He surmises that both Kerry and Golden Vale were successful in culling, for the most part, each other's dissidents, and for the most part did each other a favour!

By the end of 1979, Kerry was deeply enmeshed in sorting out affairs at its three dairies (Killarney, Limerick, and Ballinahina), and Golden Vale was making plans to install a new bottling plant at the Landsdowne factory in Limerick. In the meantime, it was supplying customers from Clare Dairies, which it had bought in September. Additionally, both co-operatives were investing heavily. Moloney and his colleagues at the ICOS stepped in repeatedly to attempt to 1) keep the two co-operatives, at a minimum, on speaking terms; and 2) broker an agreement that would represent a reasonable compromise for both sides and provide for an orderly market that would return at least a modest profit to the co-operatives. This was no small task: mediating between the two would try the patience of a saint.

A number of compromises were, in fact, seriously considered and very nearly implemented. One agreement would have provided for a 50-50 joint venture whereby the two liquid milk businesses would be merged and operated to maximise the return from the liquid market. Coupled with this was the proposed cessation of all poaching of suppliers, and withdrawal of all special offers and promotions to shopkeepers. While agreed in principle, this agreement never made it past the finer details. The canvassing and poaching continued, not only in County Limerick but also in County Kerry where Golden Vale had reportedly sent some 20 employees to canvass. Meanwhile, the major farming organisations kept up the heat on Kerry. The following is a press release from a meeting of the IFA Munster chapter in January 1981:

> The meeting regretted the action of co-ops in undercutting each other in selling dairy products and offering incentives to other farmers over and above the price paid to their existing suppliers. All suppliers, big or small, should be paid a similar price, otherwise the smaller farmer

would be subsidising the bigger farmer. Mr Fitzgerald
[the IFÁ Munster Vice-President] said that some co-ops
are tending to stray away from the principle of central
marketing. The boards of management should get them
back on the right course and also must ensure that the
principle and spirit of co-operation which many farmers
are relying on for a better future must be upheld between
the co-ops themselves.[26]

There is little doubt which co-operative was the prime target of
that message. Surprisingly, however, Kerry was quite willing to
get out of Limerick. In February 1981, an agreement in principle
had already been arrived at to sell Limerick Dairies to Golden
Vale. It was the only sensible economic decision. But once again,
the devil was in the details. Negotiations broke down, and the
"milk war" in Limerick continued with no end to the hostilities in
sight. Not only that, but within a year the entire nasty business
would expand to a "two-front war".

Trouble in Connacht — The Acquisition of Galway Dairies

Kerry continued on the acquisition trail in liquid milk, turning its
attention to Counties Clare and Galway in the west of Ireland, not
far from Limerick. After lengthy negotiations, Kerry agreed to buy
Galway Dairies for £2.6 million on 27 January 1982. With sales of
about £4 million and profits in the range of £300,000 annually,
Galway Dairies was an attractive target. Some suggested, however, and not for the last time, that Brosnan had paid too much.
This purchase, not surprisingly, generated renewed outrage on
the part of Kerry's critics in general, and vociferous objections
from a number of west Ireland co-operatives.

During February and March 1982, there were a number of
meetings between representatives from Kerry Co-op, the Mid-West
Farmers Co-op, and the Shannonside Milk Products Co-op (a processing plant partially owned by Mid-West). Mid-West's basic position was that it wished to buy out Kerry's recently purchased inte r-
est in Galway Milk Company at cost plus expenses, while Kerry
preferred some sort of a joint venture. After more meetings, including the Kiltoghert Co-op which also owned a piece of the
Shannonside venture, Kerry agreed in principle to sell Galway Milk

Products, but no price was put upon it. Subsequent to that meeting, in March Mid-West purchased Oranmore Dairies, the only other private dairy supply in Galway, for a reported £2.1 million. At this point, Kerry claimed that it had not yet received a formal offer for Galway Dairies, and Brosnan stressed, as reported in an ICOS summary of a meeting on 30 March, that:

> The Oranmore purchase by Midwest had changed the position about the sale of the Galway Milk Co. In that regard he also pointed out that the decision of his Board on March 2nd was to consider an offer from Midwest and he felt that this was not forthcoming to date. Brosnan thought it unlikely that the Minister would allow two dairies in Galway to combine because of monopolies concern. "He [Brosnan] pointed out that it would be a very bad business decision for Kerry to be known to be selling the Galway Milk Co., if at the end of a period of negotiations the sale was held up by the Monopolies Act. He said that in that situation the development and expansion of their business in Galway would suffer seriously and they were not prepared to run that risk." Mr Dodd still wants to buy, at cost plus expenses. Shannonside and its three member co-operatives "was a cohesive and comprehensive grouping . . . that the Kerry involvement in Galway was cutting across". He was not prepared to accept Mr Brosnan's interpretation of the Monopolies Act as he felt that any problems in this regard could be overcome. He emphasised that there was very bad feeling in the West towards Kerry and he felt that the matter could not be taken any further in discussions between the parties.[27]

With that, there was no further need of meetings. With the exception of very vocal and public condemnations of Kerry on the part of the co-operatives in Galway, however, the issue eventually quietened down considerably. But the condemnations were very telling, and present even today a sense of the emotional outrage generated by, or some would say provoked by, Kerry on the part of some co-operatives. A few examples, below, are typical:

***Extracts from a Brochure Put Together by Shannonside
Milk Products Co-op (NCF, Mid-West and Kiltoghert)***

The Kerry Threat to You

*The new enemy, however, is a much cuter proposition and it oper-
ates under the mantle of the co-operative movement. It is called
Kerry Co-op and its policy is one of commercial domination and ex-
ploitation of opportunities in order to finance their empire building
outside of agriculture. They are at present engaged in a calculated
plan to undermine the co-operative movement in Connacht and so
far in their dealings with the Connacht co-ops have shown themselves to be totally dishonest, devious and dangerous. They moved
into Connacht against the strong objections of the co-operatives in
the area and in the process undermined the plans of our Shannonside Partner, Mid-West Farmers Co-op, to buy Galway Milk Co. at a
reasonable price. Kerry Co-op had previously informed the ICOS
that they were not interested in purchasing Galway Milk Co.*

This dispute continued to fester well into 1983. The following is an
extract from an "Open Letter" to Kerry milk suppliers that was run
in *The Kerryman* on 22 July 1983, and signed by the chairmen of
the three Connacht co-operatives:

An Open Letter to Kerry Milk Suppliers

*We must defend ourselves against Kerry Co-op in order to preserve
our multi-purpose Co-ops in Connacht, whose services are vital to
farmers working in the most disadvantaged areas of Ireland and, indeed, of Europe. From their public statements it seems to be the
policy of Kerry Co-op to use the profits obtained from dealing with
farmers to fund investment outside agriculture and outside of the
country. The Chief Executive of Kerry Co-op, speaking and acting
for that organisation, believes that the principles of the Co-operative
movement are no longer relevant. We have a totally different concept of business ethics and we still hold to the Co-operative principles espoused by Plunkett which have not become any less relevant
in the 1980s. We would like to think that Kerry farmers will respect
and accept our need to be different and to develop in a way which
suits the circumstances of a region considerably more disadvantaged, climatically and agriculturally, than your own.*

There was little doubt that Kerry was breaking the unwritten rules of co-operation in Ireland. It was rocking the boat, stepping on toes and making enemies. It had also become the most successful co-operative in Ireland.

Dawn Dairies

When Kerry first entered the consumer (liquid) milk business in 1974 with its purchase of Killarney Dairies, and through its subsequent acquisitions of Limerick, Deel, Ballinahina and Galway, it was almost an article of faith that each dairy would retain its unique identity and brand. This approach, however, was anathema to Michael Drummey, who complained at the time that in marketing the co-op's liquid milk, his marketing team literally had nothing with which to do battle. To Drummey, there was simply no way to effectively market the individual products of four separate dairies (Deel Dairies had already been combined with Limerick Dairies). Kerry would have to *brand* its milk business. Branding the entire business would provide Kerry's marketing arm with the ammunition it needed to promote the product throughout Ireland. It would also provide a point of departure, and a mark of difference, for carrying themes of high quality, consistency, and flexibility to a new level of consumer recognition.

Reflecting one more aspect of "the Kerry Way", the *Dawn* brand itself was developed internally at Kerry. As with many of the more important efforts at Kerry, the preference was that they would "hoe their own row" in the marketing and promotion areas as much as in operations. It was important, in order to sell the idea internally, and especially to convince the farmers who supplied the liquid milk business that this was the right path to follow, that those most intimately acquainted with the operation play a major role in the development and implementation of the brand. The new brand was initially introduced in Limerick, coincident with the opening of a new, ultramodern dairy facility in 1983. It was later agreed that the brand would be expanded to the other three dairies in Killarney, Cork and Galway in 1984. The challenge was that the roll-out would all have to occur simultaneously in each dairy. Within the course of one week in 1984, farmers and stockists had to be sold on the idea of the new brand, new packaging had to be integrated into the operation, an advertising campaign had to be launched, and the new

Dawn product had to appear in all locations on the same day. The day before the big change stockists were invited to hotels (throughout Ireland) and fully briefed on the change to happen on the next day. Drummey remembers that:

> When we decided to brand our milk as *Dawn*, it was a very important commercial milestone for us. We were kicking over a lot of old traces, and we needed the goodwill of farmers in Galway, and Cork, and Limerick and Kerry. When we branded our milk we were embarking on a very serious mission to combine everything we were doing in the milk area, from a consumer perspective. It was important in convincing our farmers that it wasn't we who were determining their future, it was the consumer! The message was that we are not doing this just because this guy Drummey likes to spend a lot of money on advertising, but because we want your milk to have the flexibility to be identified the same way in Galway as in Limerick. This was totally different.[28]

By 1985, the *Dawn* label served as the umbrella brand for the full range of liquid milk and fresh consumer dairy products sold in Ireland. Kerry had grown to become the second largest supplier of liquid milk in the Irish market. It pioneered the introduction of low-fat milk to supermarkets and other retail outlets, and later the introduction of low-fat spreads and other dairy products that were finely tuned to the changing desires of a health-conscious market. *Dawn* products were supplied out of the four dairies and out of a number of processing areas within the Listowel facility.

Aside from the acquisition of Snowcream (Midlands) Ltd., located in Moate, County Westmeath, in October 1986 (an acquisition that caused barely a ripple), Kerry made no more dairy purchases. Although it had at one time seriously considered attacking the Dublin market (the largest in Ireland, by far), discussions with Drogheda and Dundalk Dairies had not gone far. With Premier Dairies dominating the market, and Drogheda and Dundalk having only an insignificant share, there seemed little sense in waging a bruising, uphill battle. For that matter, as well, there were very few other private dairies that were even available to purchase in Ireland. There was simply no more room for expansion. The *Dawn*

business had, of course, become a profitable one, and would remain so. But it was a very hard-won victory. The "milk wars" had
been a serious drain on energy, and all those who participated in
them, on both sides and at all levels, had the scars to show for it. By
this time too, the resident visionaries and planners at Kerry had
their sights set well beyond the purview of the liquid milk market
of a small island nation. There were far more attractive businesses,
far further afield, where Kerry's relatively scarce capital could be
better applied.

There is a coda to this story. In the context of the liquid milk
business, as well as milk processing, there was of course another
way to expand. That would be by a merger of Kerry with another
co-operative — specifically, Golden Vale. Ballyclough and Mitchelstown, the two Cork co-operatives, were already discussing a similar merger (although it took until 1990 to bring such talks to fruition). Jim Moloney of ICOS was a great believer in the efficacy of
such an arrangement, and lobbied both groups to at least consider
the idea. In September 1983, ICOS recommended to both societies
that a study on the advantages and disadvantages of amalgamation
be undertaken. At a day-long discussion attended by Denis Brosnan, Tony Curtin (the chief executive of Golden Vale), Jim Moloney,
and others, the parties agreed to put the ICOS request for a study
to their respective boards. The proposal to the boards read as follows:

> Both sides, conscious of the basic need for good co-
> operative and commercial relationships between them,
> are agreed to recommend to their respective Boards at
> meetings to be held in the coming week, to commence
> immediately a study of the advantages and disadvantages
> of an amalgamation. The study is to be based on an ex-
> amination of the financial, commercial and structural im-
> plications of such an amalgamation.[29]

Brosnan, in a newsletter to shareholders, commented upon a certain "hysteria" that had been created by rumours that Kerry was
going to amalgamate with Golden Vale. He re-emphasised that
what had been agreed to was merely a *study* of advantages and
disadvantages, and nothing more. Accordingly, Kerry advised

ICOS that it would be prepared to "go along with the idea of the proposed study".[30] Golden Vale, for its part, rejected participation in the study. This represented the death knell for any further discussions of amalgamation. Brosnan was deeply aggrieved that the study had been agreed to at the meeting, and then later rejected by Golden Vale, and relations between the two societies were even chillier than usual during 1984. In 1985, the "war" flared up again, and a considerable number of smaller Golden Vale suppliers in County Clare decided to move to Kerry. By this time, however, the trajectories of the two competing co-operatives could not have been more different. It was increasingly clear that the future of Kerry Co-op was not to be solely in milk, and the depredations of the "milk wars" would soon be behind them for good.

Kerry in North America

Although Kerry Co-op had been dependent since the very beginning of its existence on the profits supplied by casein exports to North America, these sales had been handled for the most part by Erie Casein. Effectively, Erie acted as Kerry's agent in the United States. Erie's stake in the Listowel factory, originally 15 per cent, had by 1983 dwindled to approximately 2 per cent (since it had not participated in further calls on capital to expand the facility beyond its original casein plant). Some small amount of business had also been done with several brokers in the United States, including M.E. Franks, whom Brosnan had met long ago travelling to the States for Golden Vale. These brokers usually sold casein that was surplus to what Erie could market. Erie, however, remained fiercely protective of its business, and resented Kerry's attempts to forge direct relationships with its casein customers. The type of information-gathering that Michael Drummey and others had engaged in during their visits to the States in the mid-1970s continued, at this time with people like Finbarr O'Driscoll and Michael Leahy. By the early 1980s, they were criss-crossing the United States on extended trips over from Ireland, working to a very busy agenda. They were visiting customers, "trolling" for new products, prospecting for potential acquisition candidates (that might provide Kerry with an entrée into the emerging food ingredients business), and sucking up as much information about the industry as they could. In Kerry fashion, it was learn, learn, and learn. And the more they learned from customers, agents, suppliers, or even from examining supermarket shelves, the clearer it was that Kerry should enter this market.

For Erie, on the other hand, the original "gentleman's agreement" with Kerry still stood, that is, that Erie would do *all* the marketing of casein and Kerry would be solely a producer. This "understanding" was a bone of contention. Brosnan, for his part, had never been comfortable with it; the rather nebulous "understanding of intent" had been brokered before his arrival in January 1972, and only under the direst circumstances. (It was necessary to get the IDA grant for the construction of the factory.) For Kerry, particularly at this point in its growth as a business enterprise, such a separation from the end customer was simply untenable. Kerry, after all, was increasingly modelling itself as a customer- and market-driven enterprise. It was also an organisation that had uncompromisingly set its sights beyond the borders of its own small domestic market. To Kerry, the relationship with Erie was increasingly a straightjacket that limited its freedom of action in North America — and clearly the North American market was where the action was. It was not only the primary location for future market opportunities, but also a leading indicator of the trends that would eventually migrate to Europe and the rest of the world as well. Inevitably, the intrinsic conflicts in the Erie–Kerry relationship would have to be brought to a head.

As early as 1968, when he had made his first trip to the United States as a young manager with Golden Vale, Brosnan had been dazzled by the size, scope, diversity and dynamism of the food markets in the US. He was particularly struck by an incipient market, an infant industry in fact, that was only beginning to emerge — that of the "food ingredients industry". The fast food industry in the States was in a period of rapid growth, as McDonald's, Burger King and Pizza Hut became household names. Convenience foods of all descriptions were burgeoning as the American market for fast and convenient prepared foods took off. What was particularly interesting to Brosnan was the type of ingredients used in these foods — highly specialised, engineered, and product- and customer-specific ones that offered high margins with large, quality customers in rapidly growing markets. Formulated cheese was one of the early products in this category. Although many, but not all, of the ingredients were based upon primary foods like dairy products, it was categorically *not* a dairy industry. The products developed were the result of significant research and development efforts and were targeted at specific applications of specific customers. In this way, it was possible to "lock-in" particular specialised ingredients into product formulations. Given the high costs to customers of switching suppliers, this made for very stable demand and long-term supplier–customer relationships. It was nearly a mirror opposite of a commodity industry — a substantial and growing, highly technical, value-added industry. This was where Kerry wanted to be.

Despite the "cat and mouse" game at play in North America over the years, the relationship between Kerry and Erie, for the better part of more than a decade since Erie had come to Ireland, had been a good one. From the very first, the Reisenbiglers and the management and leadership of Kerry had got along well, on a personal as well as on a purely professional basis. And clearly both sides had benefited from the relationship, precisely as had been hoped for at the start. Erie had found a reliable source of high quality, fairly priced casein, and Kerry had found a steady market for its product. Without Erie's participation at the very beginning, in fact, there would not likely have been any Kerry Co-operative at all. But after more than a decade of association, the relationship was showing signs of wear. Kerry was straining at the bit, aggressively expanding, eager to participate in the market as more than just a supplier. Erie was more content with the status quo, happy to continue its relationship with Kerry under the terms negotiated in 1971, and less inclined to take aggressive risks in this new market. The differences were becoming too profound to paper over.

It was decided in June 1983 that Kerry would establish its own presence in America, and Finbarr O'Driscoll, who had been travelling in the States studying the protein business, had told Brosnan that he'd like to be the first one over. "You're too old", he remembers Brosnan telling him at the time. He was, in fact, 36 years of age. In the end, Brosnan relented, and O'Driscoll began to make preparations for opening an office in the States and beginning to sell directly to Kerry's casein customers.

The marketing arrangement with Erie, however, was by now beginning to unravel. Ardie Reisenbigler recounts that Denis Brosnan came to him and said, "our future lies in utilising the ingredients manufactured in Ireland in more value-added products in the States". Brosnan apparently made some informal overtures to feel out any potential interest on the part of Erie in being bought out by, or somehow merging with, Kerry. At the time, Erie was constructing a new $25 million facility in Rochelle, Illinois. But, said Reisenbigler:

> Being a second generation company, we didn't look beyond somebody apparently rejecting us, which I don't think was the case. It was Denis looking beyond.[31]

Reisenbigler remembers the feeling at Erie at the time:

> To us, it was like, you served the purpose, you arrived here in 1970, and we don't have much need for you any more. That was the initial reaction. But as I told Denis years later . . . he was just further ahead of us in terms of where he was going. We should have talked more extensively about how we could have worked together.[32]

Now, with Kerry on the cusp of a direct entry into the North American market, the lawyers were attempting to delineate more explicitly the agreement and to judge the extent to which it represented a valid legal contract. It was ambiguous — something more than the vague general agreement in principle that a "gentleman's agreement" would be, but something far less than an ironclad contractual agreement. The optimal course of action seemed to be a negotiated "buy-out" of Erie's interest in NKMP.

Over a period of perhaps six months (from mid- through late 1983) there was a fair amount of tension, as the value of Erie's shareholding was negotiated. Denis Brosnan, in looking back at those negotiations, has said that:

> I would have a lot of respect for Ardie and David Reisenbigler, the two sons. They saw Kerry growing, and saw Kerry with a lot of ambition to expand in the US, and they didn't stand in the way. We obviously argued for a while over what their shareholding was worth, but at the end of the day, they didn't stand in the way, and a settlement was

agreed. Kerry was able to get on with developing an ingredients business in the USA, so I couldn't compliment
the two brothers highly enough for that. We knew we had
to expand, and we couldn't just be confined back in
County Kerry; they would have felt that they got Kerry
established there in the first instance, but both parties, I
think, recognised the needs of the other.[33]

Kerry bought out Erie's interest with effect from January 1984. Finbarr O'Driscoll, who had already been spending a great deal of
time in the States, had been searching during the later part of 1983
for a suitable office location in Chicago. He remembers his charge:
"The boss always said to go for a decent office, to find the right
place."[34] Along with Michael Ryan (the Group Financial Controller
from Tralee) and a few others, he settled on a small, 1,600 square
foot, three-room office on the thirtieth floor of the prestigious John
Hancock Tower in the centre of Chicago. It was a decision and a
choice that was as much symbolic as functional, for if the truth be
told the operational aspects of the business could as well be run
far more economically out of offices in a perhaps less impressive
part of Chicago. But an office in the John Hancock Building made a
statement: Kerry was serious about its business in North America,
and serious about doing it "the right way". It had long been a pre-
cept at Kerry that if something was to be done, it would be done
"right". That logic, imprinted on the Kerry culture, had now been
transplanted to North America. Although Kerry was far from being
a serious player in the North American market, it was not going to
ensconce itself in a cheap office. The new office, at least, would
convey some element of size, strength and presence to its potential customers. The first of the Kerry "pioneers" moved into the
Hancock Tower in January 1984, just as negotiations with Erie were
heading towards a conclusion. Kerry, however, was not waiting for
the agreement to get started.

A Learning Experience: Finding their Way in the States, 1984–1985

Having "arrived" in the States, Kerry's business had to proceed on
several levels simultaneously. On the most basic level, the stock of
casein produced at Listowel had to be "moved" at the best possi-

ble price. At this point, in 1984, the Co-op was still dependent upon casein for the majority of its profits. On another level, it was a learning experience — learning what the ingredients market was, learning the needs of the customers (indeed, even *who* the customers and potential customers were), and learning how to do business in the United States. At the topmost level was the more strategic question: precisely *where* did Kerry want to locate itself in this ingredients market in the States and, in view of the specific vagaries of this market, *how* could it make that entry? It is important to note that, in early 1984 in North America, the Kerry operation was barely a blip on the radar screen. It was tiny compared to the important players in the industry. It was, in fact, not yet a player at all. Although they had a brand name, *Kerrynor*, for their casein, Kerry was an unknown commodity with few customer relationships to build upon. That would have to come in time. But Kerry did not have a great deal of time, for even in the short term, profits had to be maintained.

A key point to note is that, in early 1984, there was a worldwide oversupply of casein, and consequently, falling prices. Kerry Co-operative's dependence on the casein business made this a trying time. The challenge was significant: to move the casein, and at a profitable price, while beginning to take control of the customer for the first time! As Kerry moved away from Erie Casein, it had begun to use other agents in the States, notably M.E. Franks. This was to be a "temporary fix" until Kerry was able to take control of customer relationships itself. In the interim, agents were a necessity. M.E. Franks was very helpful to Kerry insofar as they were willing to work with Kerry on a short-term basis, and even provide Kerry with some of its first real leads to customers. It was Franks, in fact, who first led Kerry to Beloit, Wisconsin, to a casein user by the name of Beatreme Specialty Products.

The leader of the management team in the States, at that time, was Finbarr O'Driscoll, the Vice-President of Kerry Foods, Inc. Stan McCarthy, a native of Kerry and a young accountant in the Tralee office, had arrived at the beginning of 1984. He was followed a few months later by Brian Lynch, another recruit from Tralee. O'Driscoll took the lead in dealing with the brokers and finding and forming relationships with customers, and later, in severing the relationships with brokers and focusing directly upon customers. Lynch took responsibility for the caseinate business, which was smaller in volume but higher in margin. McCarthy handled the administration of the office, that is, he "watched the house" while the sales force of two was on the road, as they were constantly, spending time trying to get near the buyers. Stan McCarthy remembers the feeling of those days:

> It was a very close knit group . . . it was the nucleus of a group of people. It was a great education more than any-thing else, because it was our first step into learning about the food ingredients business in the United States. It was quite an educational time, because every page you turned and every article you read was something new and exciting, because we knew very little about the food in-dustry at the time. Being "green", or at least less experi-enced, made for quite a challenge. We learned to become streetwise, to learn about business the hard way very quickly. We were in a new business environment, we were unfamiliar with the legislation and the ways of doing business, and we were essentially starting from scratch without any help from anybody. I would say it was quite competitive, quite tough. From the learning perspective, we did learn a lot, because we just went in at the deep end.[35]

Learning was a constant, inquisition was the order of the day, scavenging for information was the rule. The Kerry managers tried to see the range of varied applications of the finished casein that they had been shipping to the States. They learned about the ex-tent of price tolerance within the various markets, as not all mar-kets for casein were the same. For example, a nutraceutical or nu-tritional company might be in a better position to accept a higher price, since raw materials supplied to them were high quality and very specific to their end needs. Casein for use in imitation cheese, however, would not command such premiums, since buying was done almost entirely on price in a far more commod-ity-like marketplace. Developing an understanding of costs all along the supply chain, from Irish farmers to the end customer in North America, was also important. To justify higher prices you had to know your costs, and your cost "drivers". All costs are not the same, and savvy buyers would exploit any gaps in the knowledge of those salesmen unfamiliar with their own product costs.

Significant changes were also occurring with customers at this time. Beatrice, Bordens and other giant food companies were getting ever larger, acquiring other companies and increasingly becoming targets themselves. The era of the leveraged buy-out, the tool of choice in the mergers and acquisitions craze of the 1980s, was about to hit the food industry full force. In any event, it was essential that Kerry find a way to get to some of the larger food accounts, but it was proving difficult. Supplier relationships with the majors had been developed over many, many years, and change of suppliers did not come easily. This was particularly the case if the new prospective supplier was an almost complete unknown, with no track record, and from Ireland to boot. One of Kerry's large accounts at the time, however, was Fisher Cheese, which was subsequently acquired by Borden's. At one point in 1985–1986, Kerry was supplying a container-load a week of casein into four individual plants — a godsend to Kerry at the time. This was a high point. The overall reality, however, was that it was proving enormously difficult, and slow, to break into the American market. By the end of 1985 and into 1986, the pressure was beginning to mount: what would Kerry have to do to break into this ingredients business? This question, and the various approaches to answering it, was to be the prime strategic issue faced by Kerry over the next several years. It was clear to Kerry's management that decisions made in this arena would be pivotal for the future of the enterprise at large.

Summary and Commentary

During the period of 1979–1985, Kerry turned a profound challenge into a sterling opportunity and came out of the brucellosis crisis stronger and more strategically focused than ever. Its formal corporate planning process began to take root, becoming more and more deeply ingrained in the fabric of the organisation. Yet even as it began to develop strategic "clarity", it retained its opportunistic tendencies, acting quickly and decisively as profitable opportunities presented themselves. It proved in convincing fashion that it was prepared to endure whatever was necessary to turn around an ailing business, to learn that business from the ground up, and to train in the crucible of that challenge a cadre of highly committed, capable and mobile managers. It successfully mastered the challenge of its first significant foray into consumer branded goods with its revival and expansion of the Denny's brand. It went through the challenges of the "milk wars" and earned a reputation as a tough, "commercially-minded" co-operative that was not prone to shrink from criticism. In the face of such criticism and animosity from some (not all) of the other "Big Six" dairy co-operatives and from leaders of many farming organisations, Kerry Co-op continued to strengthen its foundation of support from its farmer-shareholders in County Kerry — a source of unwavering and unconditional loyalty. The distinctive organisational culture of Kerry, born in the early challenges of the plant in Listowel, was further honed and developed in the significant challenges of this period. The increasingly self-confident organisation began to act on Denis Brosnan's charge — "Look beyond the shores of this little island; it's a big world out there!" — by opening its first offices outside of Ireland. With its foray into North America, it now had a foothold — or perhaps more appropriately, a "toehold" — in the most important, lucrative and dynamic market in the world.

It was a period of proving its mettle, surmounting challenges, diversifying and growing. It was also a mere prelude to the period of significant activity and growth that was to follow.

Table 4: Summary Financial Results, 1979–1985 (£ '000s)

	1979	1980	1981	1982	1983	1984	1985
Turnover	78,350	79,860	95,658	129,259	158,079	180,470	211,239
Operating Surplus	3,975	3,021	1,462	4,213	4,307	4,756	5,113
Net Profit to Shareholders	3,061	1,865	1,856	3,622	3,774	4,299	4,527

Notes

[1] *The Kerryman*, "Kerry in Fight Against Brucellosis", 2 June 1978, pp. 2 and 9.

[2] *The Kerryman*, "Brucellosis: Farmers React", 13 October 1978, p. 11.

[3] Ibid.

[4] Denis Brosnan, personal interview, 28 May 2000.

[5] Michael Drummey, personal interview, 6 January 2000.

[6] Denis Brosnan, personal interview, 28 May 2000.

[7] Hugh Friel, personal interview, 31 May 1999.

[8] Ibid.

[9] Denis Cregan, personal interview, 12 October 1999.

[10] James Denny, personal interview, 6 January 2000.

[11] Hugh Friel, personal interview, 31 May 1999.

[12] James Denny, op. cit.

[13] Michael Drummey, op. cit.

[14] Denis Cregan, op. cit.

[15] Michael Drummey, op. cit.

[16] Hugh Friel, personal communication, 26 October 2000.

[17] Denis Brosnan, quoted in *Business & Finance*, "As Kerry Co-op Prepares to go Public, We Salute Denis Brosnan, Man of the Year", 9 January 1986, p. 17.

[18] James Denny, op. cit.

[19] Aileen O'Toole (1987), *The Pace Setters*, Dublin: Gill and Macmillan, p. 104-105.

[20] *Business & Finance*, "As Kerry Co-op Prepares to go Public, We Salute Denis Brosnan, Man of the Year", 9 January 1986, p. 17.

[21] Kerry Co-operative Creameries Ltd., Annual Report, 1982, p. 4.

[22] Denis Brosnan, personal interview, 11 October 1999.

[23] *Business & Finance*, "As Kerry Co-op Prepares to go Public, We Salute Denis Brosnan, Man of the Year", 9 January 1986, p. 17.

[24] Michael Griffin, personal interview, January 2000.

[25] Michael Drummey, op. cit.

[26] Teletype copy of press release from the IFA, 21 January 1981.

[27] ICOS Memo, 1 April 1982. From the ICOS Archives.

[28] Michael Drummey, op. cit.

[29] Quoted in the *Kerry Co-op News*, 3 October 1983.

[30] Ibid.

[31] Arden Reisenbigler, personal interview, 9 February 2000.

[32] Ibid.

[33] Denis Brosnan, personal interview, 7 October 1999.

[34] Finbarr O'Driscoll, personal interview, 14 July 1999.

[35] Stan McCarthy, personal interview, 6 December 1999.

Chapter 7

A Defining Moment — The Launch of Kerry Group plc, 1986

It is with a certain amount of admiration for his courage, tinged with some scepticism, that we watch the current guru of the co-operative movement, Denis Brosnan of Kerry Co-op, try to drag his society into the 1980s and onto the stock market.[1]

I would not rule out the possibility that this will be Denis Brosnan's Waterloo.[2]

The Strategic Context

If Kerry's decision to begin to diversify out of the milk business in the early 1980s represented a strategic turning point for the enterprise, then its decision to convert to a public limited company (plc) structure in 1986 was an even more profound decision. The decision to "go public" did not occur in a vacuum, but was the product of a carefully thought-out evaluation of the enterprise's mission, objectives, and strategies. It represented the logical culmination of a series of decisions intended to answer the most basic of strategic questions: who are we as an organisation, what are our fundamental goals and objectives, and how do we achieve them? It was in a very real sense one of the early fruits of Kerry's corporate long-range planning process, first initiated in 1979–80.

But one may legitimately wonder why, given its track record of success, Kerry management felt the need for such a revolutionary step. Indeed, converting from a co-operative to a plc structure was unprecedented, and not without risk. There were no templates to follow and no exemplars to emulate. In the twelve years since its formation, Kerry Co-op had already, by 1985, compiled an enviable record. The smallest of the "Big Six" dairy co-operatives in Ireland when it was formed in 1974, it had grown to be, in the eyes of many, the most successful.

Table 5: Growth in Sales for Multi-Purpose Co-operatives, 1974–1984

Co-operative	1974 Sales (£m)	1984 Sales (£m)	Compound Annual Growth Rate %
Avonmore	33	233	21.6%
Waterford	31	195	20.2%
Mitchelstown	49	189	14.5%
Kerry	21	180	24%
Ballyclough	29	156	18.3%
Golden Vale	26	142	18.5%

Source: Paul O. Mohn, John Butler and Leon Garoyan (1985),"Sources and Uses of Funds by Selected Irish Dairy Co-operatives", Bank of Ireland Centre for Co-operative Studies, University College Cork, Working Paper Series, No. 7. Table 9 in this work provides sales data for the "Big Six" co-operatives in 1974.

Table 6: The "Big Six" Dairy Co-operatives, 1984 Results (£ Millions)

Co-operative	Sales	Net Profit	NP % of Sales	Cash Flow	Cap. Ex.
Avonmore	233	.06	.03	5.8	7.7
Waterford	195	(.26)*	(.10)*	4.2	6.9
Mitchelstown	189	.67	.40	4.3	3.3
Kerry	180	4.30	2.39	8.7	9.6
Ballyclough	156	1.30	.83	4.7	2.3
Golden Vale	142	(.50)*	(.35)*	2.3	3.4

Source: *Aspect* (1986), "Milk Co-operatives Walk Financial Tightrope", March 1986, p. 14–16. * *Note*: Figures in brackets represent losses.

It had expanded and diversified its product and geographic markets. It was eager to build upon and expand its relatively minute market presence in North America and the UK. Indeed, its management and Board had explicitly adopted as a corporate objective the goal of building "a profitable and growing business in food and agricultural activities thus providing our farmer shareholders with continually improving returns".[3] Despite its co-operative structure, the Kerry Co-op had almost from the beginning operated with a distinctly "commercial" orientation; it was "market-driven" and "bottom line"-focused long before such terms were in vogue. It had, in the years 1982–1984, apparently overcome the trauma of the 1980–81 downturn and was moving rapidly to reduce its exposure to the vagaries of the milk business. With a management team that was (oftentimes grudgingly) acknowledged to be among the best in Ireland, a proven track record of success and achievement, and an aggressive, hard-nosed, commercially focused organisational culture, it seemed to be going from strength to strength. If success breeds success, one might ask, what was the problem? Put another way, one might fall back on an American adage, "If it ain't broke, don't fix it!"

But there were good reasons to avoid just "standing pat". Strategy guru Danny Miller, in his book *The Icarus Paradox*, examined many highly successful companies that had paradoxically been trapped by their own success.[4] Having employed particular techniques, skills and strategies to good effect in the past, they continually sought to further develop and refine them. The better they seemed to work, the more they used them. But in the process, they failed to look to the future to discern what skills and strategies would be necessary for success then. By focusing on their past and current successes, they failed to adapt to the changing circumstances of the future. They assumed that their skills and capabilities, the approaches that had worked so long and so well for them, would always work. They behaved in a manner not unlike Icarus, who, given wings of wax that enabled him to fly, flew higher and higher until he flew too close to the sun. Organisations are prone to similar failures of judgement, but to its credit Kerry did not fall into this trap.

Perhaps it is Kerry's corporate planning process and the disciplined vision of its top executives that deserves some fair amount of the credit for this. By 1983–84, it did not appear likely to them that long-term results would reach the ambitious targets that Kerry had established for itself — that is, real growth of 5 per cent annually, a return on capital employed of 20 per cent, and a debt/equity ratio of no more than 60 per cent. Given the structure of their business, and the prevailing and anticipated competitive climate, Kerry's planners saw very real danger signals. Such *anticipation* is the very essence of the planning process. In examining Kerry Co-op's internal strengths and weaknesses, and reviewing the opportunities and threats in the external environments (the typical SWOT analysis), multiple areas of concern were pinpointed. Paraphrased below are a number of concerns documented by Hugh Friel in materials prepared for a Board of Directors meeting in December 1985.

- Milk volumes, with the imposition of a quota system by the EEC that took effect from 1984 (based on 1983 volumes), were now significantly restricted. The days of continually increasing milk volumes were over for good. Nevertheless, overhead costs associated with the processing of milk were likely to increase. Opportunities to pass on these increased costs would be dependent on marketplace conditions. Furthermore, Kerry's attempts during the "milk wars" to garner additional milk volumes had met with only limited success.

- In connection with the quota system, many current farmer-suppliers to Kerry Co-op were likely to give up production of milk altogether and rent or sell their quota allotment to more efficient neighbours. Thus, many of the farmers who had played such a large role in starting up the co-op in 1974 would increasingly be "dry" shareholders in Kerry Co-op, that is, not active milk suppliers. The ratio of non-supplier shareholders in Kerry Co-op, by the end of 1985, was approximately 30 per cent.

- The Co-op had a "dangerous" exposure to the casein market in the US. As a commodity product, casein was subject to the usual uncertainties of supply and demand. Kerry had also terminated its marketing agreement with Erie Casein Co. and was beginning to market its product directly, and through brokers, in America. However, there had been noises coming out of

Washington concerning a quota on the importation of casein into the States. In any event, given Kerry's level of dependence on profits from casein exports to America, it was uncomfortably reliant on a commodity market over which it could exert little influence.

- Kerry had expanded successfully into the consumer (liquid) milk business in Ireland with the purchase of private dairies. But there were few such dairies still available for acquisition in Ireland.

- It was taking longer than expected to turn a profit in the meat business (Denny's and Duffy's) and generally to bring the meat processing operations up to world standards. Capital requirements in this area were still high.

- The availability of capital had to some extent restricted management's ability to further grow the business, both internally and externally.

In the face of these issues, and in order to provide its farmer-shareholders with "continually improving returns", Kerry would have to reorient itself in one of the following overarching strategic directions:

1. It could attempt to merge or take over one of the other large dairy co-operatives in Ireland, building the necessary economies of scale and scope to absorb increased costs in the future. This would have been very consistent with the hopes of the IAOS and Department of Agriculture who were pushing for amalgamation of co-operatives and rationalisation of the dairy industry.

2. It could invest internally or via external acquisitions in other markets and regions that would counterbalance dependency on North American casein sales.

3. It could "change course" by cutting overheads, marketing and related costs and retreat into more of a traditional dairy co-operative like others of the "Big Six".

The idea of merging with another large co-operative was not at all outrageous. In fact, as already noted, Kerry had agreed at one time to discussions with Golden Vale, under the auspices of the IAOS, to explore if there were sufficient grounds to enter into more substantive discussions of an amalgamation. Jim Moloney, the Director General of ICOS at the time, saw great merit in such a combination. Said Moloney:

> I remember posing the idea one day at a meeting in Limerick and I could see the Kerry people could see possibilities, but some of the Golden Vale staff were very much opposed to it. It would have been the sensible thing to do, and perhaps a bit ahead of its time. They were contiguous. There could have been a lot of rationalisation. They would have had approximately 20 per cent of the milk in the country. It would have been a logical development.[5]

Although initial discussions were held, the idea went nowhere, perhaps more a reflection of the politics of co-operative organisations than of economic realities. Given such political problems, this was an unlikely strategic alternative for Kerry.

Conversely, the notion of retreating into more of a "typical" dairy co-operative, cutting costs, and hunkering down to ride out the storm was all but unthinkable, and not worthy of any serious consideration. It was surely included as more of a rhetorical device, a straw man to react against, than an option worthy of serious discussion. Emphatically, this option was a non-starter.

The decision made by the Board was to adopt a revised corporate objective: "To build a profitable and growing *international* food organisation thus providing farmers, suppliers and shareholders with continually improving returns." In other words, Kerry would pursue substantial growth in the international arena, and not exclusively in the severely limited marketplace of its home nation. It may appear that the logic of such a decision was clear and compelling, and that the Directors ought not to have agonised over it too long. But it would be wrong to underestimate its importance. It was, as Hugh Friel put it in his memo:

> . . . a crossroads [that is] not an easy one to cross. . . . Going forward within this objective almost certainly means

> bringing in outside money and obviously some loss of
> freedom in the areas where we now have total control.[6]

It was well understood that this would mean pursuit of an aggressive external acquisition agenda. It would mean development of more advanced technical capabilities, more capital expenditure, upgrading of quality to international standards, and importantly, a further reduction in Kerry's already declining use of Bord Bainne for the marketing of its products abroad. It was a significant decision in that it also meant, to some extent, leaving the milk business behind. As Kerry grew in size and scope in other food areas, it was inevitable that the milk production of its existing farmer-shareholders would constitute a smaller percentage of its total activities. It meant a virtual crossing of the Rubicon — with no option to turn back.

With the decision to wade into the international food business now made, there was only one certainty: substantial amounts of capital would be required. The Board, having voted in favour of aggressive international expansion, now had to struggle with the question of how to pay for it. In the area of corporate finance there are two very distinct but interrelated decisions. The first is the investment decision — where do you want to invest and what kind of return does the investment provide? The second distinct but connected decision is, after you have chosen your investment strategy, how do you fund it? It was with the latter decision that Kerry management and Directors now had to struggle.

Options for Raising Capital

Even before the formal "reorientation" of Kerry's objectives, the idea of going public had been "floated", in characteristic fashion, by the Kerry management. As early as April 1983 it had been discussed at the Board level. An extract from the Board minutes is telling:

> . . . it is true that the sale value of the shareholder's investment [in the co-operative] is always limited to the original investment. It is desirable, therefore, that there be an alternative means of providing the investor/shareholder with means of sale etc. Also, there is the possibility

that in order to achieve our growth objectives, we must go public. On the other hand, going public even on a sectoral or division basis means a substantial loss of control by Kerry Co-op. It was decided that in the absence of any more compelling reasons to go public and because of the associated loss of control that we should remain a fully private concern.[7]

If it was too soon, in 1983, to press the case for going public it was clear that within the next several years the "compelling reasons" examined earlier in this chapter presented themselves. But the point is that the discussion over going public was active from at least early 1983 onwards. There were already media reports in early 1984 about the possibility of Kerry seeking funding in the unlisted securities market. At the annual general meeting of the co-operative on 15 May 1984:

> . . . a speaker from the floor referred to an article in the *Farming Independent* which referred to Kerry Co-op's need for cash and the possibility of its seeking additional capital on the unlisted securities market. The speaker was opposed to the Co-op raising additional capital in this way.[8]

Denis Brosnan, in reply, merely pointed to Chairman Michael Hanrahan's statement that appeared in the 1983 annual report:

> However, the ongoing requirement for both fixed and working capital is such that we must aim for either a higher level of retained earnings, further capital from our existing shareholders or outside capital. Your Board and management will be addressing this issue in the months ahead.[9]

During the following months, Kerry's management, and particularly Hugh Friel and the corporate finance staff, investigated a total of seven options that were to be considered by the Board as potential solutions to the "financing problem". Among the options considered were:

- The "flotation" (the offering for sale to private investors) of various parts of the existing Kerry Co-operative, singly or in various combinations (usually excluding agricultural activities that would remain in co-operative hands);

- Direct investment in Kerry Co-op by a financial institution;

- Raising of non-equity finance (also known as "off-balance sheet financing");

- Raising of additional funds from existing shareholders;

- The flotation of 20 per cent of the total Kerry Co-op enterprise.

Only the last option was thought worthy of serious consideration. Partial flotation options were considered to be generally unattractive to investors, and generally disliked by Kerry's management. As Hugh Friel put it:

> It never really appealed, certainly not to me. We always felt that, in a matter like this, we'd keep all our kittens in the basket. You cannot confuse yourself, the public at large, and shareholders in particular with questions of "Is it in or is it out?" "What are the charges?" and "Who is the management working for?" type questions. Put it all in; if it works, it works, and if it doesn't it doesn't, but you can't have side-shows in the organisation.[10]

The option of seeking a direct investment from a financial institution was discounted after a major bank proved unwilling (or unable) to invest, at least in terms acceptable to Kerry management. Off-balance sheet opportunities such as leases, sale and leaseback arrangements, and other funding sources that would not have to be reported on the balance sheet, were lacking. In fact, using off-balance sheet financing could be very risky, particularly since it was more often associated in the minds of investors with troubled enterprises than with healthy ones. Finally, the possibility of raising necessary capital from existing shareholders was thought to be unlikely. The amount of capital necessary would be substantial and perhaps beyond the resources of farmers who either a) didn't have the money, or b) would prefer to keep it in more liquid form (particularly since co-operative shares did not trade and were difficult to transfer). The option to float 20 per cent of the entire enterprise appeared to offer the best range of opportunities with the fewest disadvantages. At its September 1984 meeting, the Board of Directors decided that this option should be investigated in more detail.

Advantages and Disadvantages of a Public Flotation

The successful execution of the flotation proposal was expected to yield a number of substantial benefits. First, it was expected to raise the largest amount of money of all of the financing options. The exact amount, however, was uncertain, and would ultimately be decided by the investors (both institutions and the public). Naturally, the amount that could be raised as equity capital (for an offering of 20 per cent of the proposed Kerry Group plc) would be dependent on investors' assessment of the value of the entire enterprise. In the case of Kerry's initial public offering, however, there were a number of factors that made valuation problematic. We will return to these factors in a moment.

An additional, and critical, advantage was that an offering of shares in the Kerry Group or an offering of shares plus cash, could pay for future acquisitions by the company. The fact that Kerry shares would be quoted (that is, would have an objectively determined market value), would make such offerings far more straightforward. Presuming the initial public offering of Kerry Group shares went well, and the record of successful growth in earnings continued, raising capital in the future would be expected to present few difficulties. Kerry could then avoid the pitfalls of being too highly geared (having a high debt/equity ratio), by having the ability to access capital from equity markets instead. Furthermore, dividend payments on shares were expected to start at around 4 per cent, and would not exceed 6 per cent (assuming 10 per cent annual increases) for the first five years. Thus equity capital, at a time of high interest rates, would be significantly cheaper than debt. Additionally, with the phasing out of preference share schemes and other tax-advantaged borrowings, the cost of long-term debt was expected to increase by a not insubstantial 50–60 per cent. A further important distinction between equity and debt is that dividends on shares do not *have* to be paid, nor does equity itself have to be *repaid*. Interest and principal on debt, however, must be repaid regardless of economic conditions.

This is a distinction that every farmer-shareholder in Kerry Co-operative (regardless of their level of financial sophistication) could readily appreciate! Of all the occupations, perhaps farmers most readily appreciate the burdens that can be imposed upon a business by excessive debt. Thus, the opportunity to fund the firm's aggressive expansion plans with equity rather than debt was viewed as a very significant advantage.

Of more direct importance to farmers at the time was the fact that, as the 20 per cent flotation was crafted, Kerry Co-operative (with an 80 per cent shareholding in the plc) would effectively retain control of the plc. The existing electoral structure of the co-operative would also continue to operate, and the Board of Directors of the Co-op would also serve as a Board of Directors for the plc. The bottom line: farmers would retain control of the enterprise. The Kerry Co-op management, a management team that knew its shareholders and their concerns, fears and interests intimately, crafted this structure very, very deliberately. The issues of farmer control of the enterprise and, more generally, whether the enterprise would (or should) retain the philosophy, ethos and principles characteristic of co-operative organisations were both emotionally charged. Like valuation, the issue of farmer control will be addressed separately below.

Valuation Issues

The amount of equity capital raised by any share offering would reflect investors' own *valuation* of the company and, more importantly, their *evaluation* of the company's future prospects. In a very real sense, the valuation exercise is both art and science. As a "scientific" and primarily technical exercise, analysts evaluate the financial statements and position of the firm, develop various financial ratios, compare them with relevant industry averages, make judgements as to future industry and market trends, and then assign an estimated valuation to the firm. On a more intangible level, however, analysts also evaluate firms based on implicit, "gut feel" factors, such as management capability and leadership, strategic direction, ethos and track record. Combining these factors, analysts try to predict future performance and value the company and its shares accordingly. However, other intangible factors were also "in play" in attempting to determine the underlying value of a proposed Kerry Group share. Most importantly, the firm's heritage as a co-operative organisation and the novelty of a co-operative to plc conversion were factors that would have to be considered. The combination of tangible and intangible factors made the initial valuation of Kerry shares, and hence the price of the initial issue, a somewhat uncertain exercise.

Hugh Friel and his staff had valued the Co-op at approximately £75 million, based on a P/E (price to earnings ratio) of 12 and projected 1986 earnings of £6.2 million. This was based on the prevailing P/Es of about 12 then current for the major UK food companies. Friel was also hopeful that Kerry's successful track record would serve to bolster that P/E ratio by a further one or two points. On the other hand, J. & E. Davy, the stockbrokers chosen to float the issue, took a more cautious approach, counselling a lower P/E and consequent valuation at a more conservative £60 million. Of course, the market itself would ultimately value the shares. Although the Kerry management continued to believe the higher valuation was more appropriate, they used the more conservative valuation for planning purposes. Finally, based on the lowest end of the P/E range for UK food companies, Kerry's minimum valuation was expected to be around £40 million. In assessing the 20 per cent flotation option, then, the Board of Directors recognised a range of anywhere from £40 million to £75 million in potential valuation for the enterprise. A 20 per cent public offering, then, could be valued at anywhere from £8 million to £15 million.

A large unknown in the valuation process was the impact of the novelty of the co-operative to plc conversion. Quite simply, it had never been done before, there was no template to follow, and no rules-of-thumb that could conveniently be pressed into service. Kerry's track record as an enterprise would have been a net positive in any evaluation, but the fact that it was a co-operative, and retained a strong, majority co-operative ownership, could be perceived very negatively by potential investors. In some financial circles, there was a fear that agricultural co-operatives would "pay the farmers first" and everyone else only later. In the case of Kerry, there was a very real possibility of a conflict of interest (or even merely a *perceived* conflict of interest) between the interests of the milk suppliers on the one hand and outside ownership on the other. This conflict could manifest itself regularly as the enterprise decided the appropriate price to pay its suppliers for milk. Indeed, Kerry co-operative had an explicit policy of compensating its suppliers/shareholders largely through the milk price. How would outside shareholders, and distinctly minority shareholders at that, react to this? To what extent would this represent a concern? The market would provide the answer to this question. The greater the level of concern, the more outside investors would discount Kerry's "multiple" (P/E ratio) and therefore the amount that Kerry could realise from any stock issue.

Issues of Farmer Control

It is difficult to conceive of a more emotional issue than that of farmer control of the Kerry Group. Founded by dairy farmers against all odds and only after years of disappointment and struggle, and already successful beyond the imaginations of most, the feeling that the Kerry Group/Co-operative was "theirs" was utterly absolute. For them, the idea of "control" went well beyond the bland definitions of financial control or mere majority ownership. It was deeply heartfelt, emotional, philosophical, and inextricably tied up with the history of the organisation. If ever an organisation, its shareholders, and its geographic home were truly "one", Kerry Co-op was it. The relationship between the enterprise and its shareholders was deep, complex and often overlapping. Milk suppliers were also shareholders. Shareholders might also be non-farmer community members. Many milk suppliers had family members who were employees. The shareholders were concentrated in County Kerry, with a shared fierce sense, and pride, of place. The concept of ownership went well beyond the words written upon a share certificate; it was fundamental, genuine, and almost visceral. It was inevitable that having outside shareholders involved at any level would fundamentally affect the structure of the Kerry organisation.

Another concern was that additional future issues of equity shares could further dilute Kerry Co-operative's control of the enterprise. But, as management was quick to point out, dilution of shareholding is not the only way to lose control of an organisation. Control can perhaps be even more easily lost to financial and lending institutions because of excess borrowing. Given Kerry's aggressive growth plans, and the fact that farmers were unlikely to be willing and/or able to fund any substantial part of the capital requirements for it, it was clear that some level of control would need to be relinquished one way or the other.

Yet the issue of farmer control was still more complicated than that, and directly linked to the issue of "dry" or inactive shareholders. "Dry" shareholders were any shareholders who were not also milk suppliers. At Kerry, most of them were former suppliers who had retired or had left dairy farming, but still retained their shares in the co-operative. At the founding of the co-operative in 1974, approximately 5,600 of the total of 7,700 milk suppliers in Kerry had become shareholders and a further 300 non-milk suppliers had also bought shares. Thus, at the time, only 5 per cent of the co-op's shareholders were not suppliers. By 1983, however, the situation had changed appreciably. Some 30 per cent of the co-operative's shareholders were not milk suppliers, and with the advent of quotas (and the EEC superlevy) on milk production, it was likely that more and more shareholders would be leaving the ranks of active milk suppliers in the very near future.[11] Strictly speaking, normal co-operative policies would suggest that dry shareholders should have their shares in the co-operative redeemed, since one element of the co-operative philosophy is that ownership should be confined to "patrons" (in this case, milk suppliers). Furthermore, these shares would theoretically be redeemed at a rate of £1 per share (the price originally paid for a share), since members presumably received benefits during their years as suppliers, and through an annual dividend. Such redemption would be without regard to the underlying value of the co-operative share; in the case of Kerry Co-op at the time, it was approximately £5/share. One must remember that capital appreciation of a co-operative share would be complete anathema to the co-op philosophy. To the leadership of Kerry Co-operative, this was simply and patently unfair. Taken to its ultimate, it would arguably lead to a very unfortunate conclusion. Simply, the underlying value of the co-operative would gradually be concentrated in the remaining fewer and fewer active suppliers, while those who had been the very founders of the co-operative would be left out in the cold. Hugh Friel addressed it in this way:

> I have a very, very simple view on something like this: that
> a co-op is not there in perpetuity for some great common
> good. Because it's fine for you if you survive as a milk
> producer, but what about those who, through no fault of
> their own, were wiped out by a government decision that
> in my view went wrong [the brucellosis eradication cam-
> paign in Kerry in 1979]? There were several thousand
> milk producers here in County Kerry who had put up hard
> cash in 1974 to give us what we had. And we were not go-
> ing to kick them while they were down! We couldn't do
> that. So, they stayed in the co-operative.[12]

In order to attend to this perceived inequity, Kerry made plans to
offer some 5.3 million "A" ordinary shares in the new plc to existing co-operative shareholders, milk suppliers and employees at a
very attractive "placing" price of 35p per share. Although the
overall co-operative shareholding in the new plc was to be diluted, existing shareholders would have the opportunity to own
liquid, marketable shares in the new plc. In a sense, this represented a partial "unlocking" of the shareholders' investment in the
co-operative. Importantly, it was a way of ensuring that those who
had been there at the founding of the co-operative were able to
receive some recompense for their investment; such a "payback"
would have been impossible under the prevailing co-operative
structure. So, balanced against a reduction in complete farmer
control of the enterprise was the *de facto* creation of farmer "capitalists" in County Kerry.

Years later, Denis Brosnan, in his pragmatic way, would argue
forcefully against the emotion-laden content of discussions of
farmer control:

> Control is too emotional a term. I have always said that
> having the organisation functioning well is much more
> important than who has 50, 40 or 30 per cent.[13]

The Conversion Plan

The Board of Directors of the Kerry Co-operative gathered for a
special meeting on Monday, 9 December 1985, at Ballyseedy Cas-
tle outside Tralee. It was clear to all gathered there that it repre-

sented a truly pivotal event in the history of the organisation. The sole item on the agenda was to decide "whether or not Kerry Co-op should bring in outside share capital for the purpose of funding its future plans and development."[14] In addition to the 15-member Board, Brosnan and Friel, Michael Ryan, Margaret Davin and Brendan Dinneen from Kerry's Finance Group, Denis Bergin, the firm's solicitor from Arthur Cox & Co., and Ronan Nolan, the firm's auditor from Haughey, Boland & Co. were in attendance.

A detailed document on various options and issues surrounding the public offering had already been provided for the Board members to review, and served as the primary agenda for the meeting. Denis Brosnan began by formally presenting the newly revised corporate strategy for 1986–1990:

> To build a profitable and growing *international* Food Or-
> ganisation, thus providing farmer-suppliers and share-
> holders with continually improving returns.[15]

A lengthy discussion of the issues surrounding going public then ensued, and there was agreement that the growth envisioned in the corporate strategy could not be achieved without "a substantial injection of capital". It was further agreed that the plc route offered the best opportunity for raising the necessary amount of money.

The Board then reviewed in detail the "mechanics" of the proposed conversion:

- First, Kerry Group plc would be formed as a subsidiary of Kerry Co-operative Creameries Limited. It would subsequently acquire all of the assets and property of the former Kerry Co-op in return for a consideration of 72,000,000 "B" ordinary shares in Kerry Group plc. The Kerry Co-op thus became the equivalent of an investment holding company, with no direct operational connection to the Kerry Group. It also, at this point, owned 100 per cent of the share capital of Kerry Group plc.

- Next, a first placing of "A" ordinary shares in the plc was to be accomplished by allocating 9,100,000 (ultimately 10,350,000 shares) to existing shareholders, milk suppliers and employees of the Kerry Co-op, at a price of 35p per share. This would raise £3,185,000. It should be noted that there would be a bonus share issue of one share for every share held in Kerry Co-op, bringing the total issued share capital in Kerry Co-op to 7,200,000 shares. In effect, and before the placing of any "A" shares, each co-op share would equal 10 shares in the plc.

- Finally, the Kerry Group would arrange an additional offering of 8,500,000 "A" ordinary shares to institutions and the general public (at approximately 70p per share), to raise nearly £6,000,000. (This was later revised downward to an 8,000,000 share offering.)

- At the end of this initial phase of the re-capitalisation scheme, the ownership structure of the Kerry Group would be:

  ◆ 72,000,000 "B" shares held by Kerry Co-op (80 per cent)

  ◆ 10,350,000 "A" shares held by shareholders, suppliers and employees (11 per cent)

  ◆ 8,000,000 "A" shares held by institutions and the public (9 per cent).

- At no time would "A" ordinary shares equal or exceed the number of "B" ordinary shares. In other words, Kerry Co-operative would always retain control.

- The Board of Directors of the plc would include the Board of the Kerry Co-op, with the addition of Denis Brosnan, Denis Cregan, and Hugh Friel, and a provision for two "suitable" outside Directors. The plc Board would then total 20 members. It was also noted that financial institutions would probably insist that service contracts be entered into between the plc and the three executive Directors (Brosnan, Cregan and Friel) for a minimum time period. They would also insist that Brosnan be appointed Managing Director with a minimum five-year contract.[16]

Just prior to the Board's vote, it turned to the last page of the extensive briefing document that had been prepared for them. It was a final summing-up from Denis Brosnan:

I am presenting this final document without a recommen-
dation as was always my intention. That need not be taken
that I do not have a personal view and strong conviction
on what would be *financially* best for the Kerry shareholder and supplier. However, control, whether it be apparent or real and, in particular, control in co-operatives,
has and will always be an emotive issue. Even in Kerry, we
see this each year at election time. It is only the 15 Board
members of Kerry Co-op can weigh up and decide between the political and financial [interests]. I said at the
start we had reached a crossroads; in the financial interests of all at Kerry Co-op and, in particular, the milk supplier, we should go on. The co-operative dimension
probably says not. The decision is the balance between
politics and economics. If the Board and the Kerry shareholder wish to see continued growth and better returns
for all, that Kerry milk supplier, shareholder, present employees and even potential employment, they will have to
dilute some of their powers and control so as to bring in
outside investors. The work management has done as
shown in all the preceding pages has been in keeping the
maximum control yet making sufficient attractions for out-
siders to invest.[17]

The Board agreed to the proposals put forward by management,
and the timetable was set in motion. Meetings with farmers and
shareholders and their advisory and representative committees
were planned for later in December (1985) and January (1986).
Special shareholder meetings were to be scheduled for February.
Share offerings were expected to be made to shareholders in May
and to institutions and the public in October. The Kerry Group plc
was about to be born.

Public and Market Reaction

As is characteristic of the Kerry organisation, the plan for a public
offering had been intentionally and broadly signalled long before
January 1986. Speculation about a public offering had gone back at
least to the purchase of Denny's in 1982, and had already been
frequently discussed in the agricultural media. The announcement
of the planned offering was therefore no bombshell; it was simply

the final outcome of a very long internal gestation process. Despite the well-organised choreography of the plan, however, there was still a great deal to do. The complexities of the tax codes, the application of the Industrial and Provident Societies Act, and dealings with the Registrar of Friendly Societies all represented a labyrinth that would have to be navigated. More importantly, perhaps, shareholders would have to be properly briefed, and the financial community would have to be educated, wooed, and ultimately sold on the benefits of purchasing a shareholding in Kerry Group. It is important to understand that the financial community in Ireland was not, in general, well informed about the activities of the agricultural co-operative sector, even a financially successful one such as Kerry Co-op. Despite his success, Denis Brosnan was hardly a household name in financial circles.

But perhaps Brosnan possessed that self-same characteristic that Napoleon claimed to value above all else in his generals: luck. Brosnan was chosen in January 1986 to be the *Business and Finance* Man of the Year for 1985.[18] If nothing else, it provided an excellent introduction (for Brosnan and for the new Kerry Group) to the Irish financial community and a useful platform for the communication effort that was to follow.

Kerry management conducted a very extensive campaign, sponsoring nine regional meetings throughout the county to bring the co-operative shareholders a first-hand view of the proposal. It was, in fact, reminiscent of the series of meetings held throughout Kerry in 1973 when Kerry Co-op itself was being formed. At each meeting, there would be a request for a vote, or rather a non-binding poll, to determine the amount of support or opposition there was for the proposal. The proposal was unanimously supported at all but two of the centres, and at those two, the combined vote was in the order of 1,500 votes in support to 11 votes against the measure. Clearly, the proposal would be endorsed at the special meetings of the co-operative membership that were scheduled for February. An editorial in *The Kerryman* newspaper in January probably provides an accurate summary of the general mood in Kerry:

> No doubt some people will say it [the Kerry Co-op] is getting too big for its boots; that it is over-stretching itself. However, the people who have closely watched it grow

from an infant in 1974 to its present size will have full confidence in the group's proposal. . . . We need people who are
prepared to face up to the challenges of modern life and
who are confident that they can succeed. It's not going to
be roses all the way for Kerry Co-op as it faces into the
challenge of the future. But the performance to date suggests that the co-op people know what they are doing in
going to the public for funds. And that there is enough confidence in them for that public to give them all the funds the
Co-op needs to grow bigger and stronger and to add to the
economic strength of our county and country.[19]

The stellar loyalty that Kerry management had received over the
past decade from their shareholders was still firmly in place. This
was so despite the fact that there were no "free" shares being distributed; shareholders who wished to own a direct stake in the new
public company would have to dig down into their pockets yet
again to pay 35p per share. Realistically, one could have expected
Kerry farmers to demand free shares since, after all, it *was* their
company. But the 35p offering price (discounted though it was)
was intended to do more than just raise finance; it was also predicated on the assumption that anything that is free is never fully appreciated.[20] Anyone who wished to participate fully would have to
put up their money. In Kerry, they had done so in 1974 when the
co-operative was formed. In 1978, they had answered a further call
for capital in order to expand the Listowel factory. It appeared that
they would answer the call yet again in 1986. Farmers, as a class,
were hardly known for being risk-takers, or for being at all free
with their money. It should be remembered that, for the vast majority of these farmers, their investment in Kerry shares was their
first foray into the world of investments, equities, stock markets,
P/E ratios, and the often bewildering array of financial tools and
analyses that surround publicly traded companies. For most of
them, indeed, it was (and would remain) their only such investment. The willingness of Kerry farmers to back their enterprise so
completely thus represented a genuine anomaly, but one entirely
consistent with the solid support the enterprise had always enjoyed in its home county. Hugh Friel remembers that:

At this time the idea of creating enormous wealth was not
being promoted. We did not at any meeting promote the
concept of creating a lot of wealth, but we promoted the
idea that you can grow with the business. We did not promote the idea that you are going to get rich on this.[21]

Clearly, support on the home front was, and would remain, rock
solid. The plan was approved at a Special General Meeting in February, and the offering of 10,350,000 shares in July 1986 was over-
subscribed and strictly allocated. At the very attractive issue price
of 35p, the issue raised £3.6 million before expenses.

The reaction from other quarters, however, ran the gamut from
reasonably supportive to downright hostile. Certainly, the reaction
from certain other co-operatives could have been predicted. From
its beginning as a latecomer to the ranks of major co-ops, Kerry
had always been the rambunctious upstart of the co-operative
movement. It had never been accepted, nor had sought acceptance, as a member of the "club" and cared little for the subtle
understandings and "gentleman's agreements" that often characterised competition within the co-op sector. If anything, its very
success had made many of the other major co-operatives look bad
in comparison. Kerry had already fought the "milk wars", begun to
sell its products directly to customers rather than through Bord
Bainne, and had the audacity to take an office in the John Hancock
Tower in Chicago. It did not play cricket. It was brash and aggressive and, in the eyes of many stalwart co-operators, over-
confident. It is fair to say there was little love lost between Kerry
and at least some quarters of the co-operative scene. Samuel Johnson once said that "the Irish are a fair people, they never speak
well of one another". This was widely evident in co-op circles as
Kerry made plans for its public offering, for it was suffering a serious bashing from other co-operatives behind the scenes. Fund
managers in Dublin were well provided with negative stories
about the Kerry offer, and the generally articulated expectation by
many in the co-operative sector seemed to be that Kerry's plan
would not work. An article in *Business and Finance* even reported
that "senior figures in the co-op movement already hope that he
[Brosnan] will fail" and hoped that the Kerry farmers would vote
down the proposal.[22] Indeed, a successful Kerry flotation on the

stock exchange would mean generally gloomy news for some other major co-ops that were in a very weakened financial condition at the time. Given their relatively depressed financials, it could have been a tough sell for them to come to the stock market at all, had they chosen to attempt it.

The negative reaction from the co-operative sector was not, however, unanimous. Jim Moloney, the Director General of ICOS, had been consulted by Brosnan very early on in the process and had become a strong supporter of the proposed flotation. This support was more than merely a kind word. Just as he had done in 1973 (when the co-operative was first forming), Moloney (along with two of his ICOS colleagues, Malachy Prunty and Joe Gill) joined with Kerry's management in December and January, taking the case to the farmers at a series of meetings around the county. His active promotion of the plan, coupled with his long record of honourable service to the co-operative movement in Ireland, did much to allay the fears of many farmers who might otherwise have been concerned with the erosion of their control of the enterprise. Moloney was also highly respected for, among other things, his gift of common sense. His evaluation of this plan, too, was logical, straightforward and eminently practical:

> Not everybody at ICOS, and not everybody in the co-operative movement, would have supported this plan, but my basis was this: I looked at the market situation and it was very clear to me that to be solely dependent on a small Irish market of 3½ million was going to be a very serious limitation to any development. If co-operatives were going to expand, they would have to serve a wider market in the UK, the rest of the European Community, and the United States. Their competition was going to come from the multinationals that had access to sources of capital that co-operatives did not. Even amalgamations of co-operatives would not have allowed them to face this. I supported the plan that Kerry put forward and I went around to meetings of Kerry shareholders to support it and recommend it. But this was not a route for everybody, and not a route for the faint-hearted.[23]

For his part, Brosnan had no second thoughts. The dissenters' objections seemed more "sour grapes" than substance. He was convinced that, within a few years, those who were now badmouthing the proposal would be imitating it. Said Brosnan:

> We have led the way for the past five years with R&D, quality products, diversification. What we did five years ago they are all doing now. We are leading the way to the plc as well.[24]

Getting the Issue Away

Ultimately, however, it was the reaction of the financial markets that would determine the success or failure of the Kerry offering. Kerry's campaign began in earnest during the first week of October 1986 with the publication of a prospectus for the placing of 8,000,000 "A" shares at a price of 52p per share. The size of the offering and the placing price had both been pared down from Kerry's earlier expectations, and would yield approximately £4,000,000 net of expenses. This was quite a small issue, even by the standards of the Irish Stock Exchange, and the amount of money involved could not be considered in any way "serious". It was the novelty of the issue rather than its size that was of interest to the market. Kerry initially was not seeking a full listing for its shares, but rather went the route of the USM (Unlisted Securities Market) which required only 10 per cent of the firm's shares to be sold to obtain a listing. The more modest scale of the initial public offering of Kerry Group might also be partly attributed to a number of other factors. One factor was that, quite simply, the market timing was not the best. Although the Irish stock market had been fairly buoyant during the first part of the year, it was more "fragile and uncertain" by October.[25] In a relatively bad market, it was unlikely that any sort of premium for the shares would stick. Even the offering price of 52p (itself steeply discounted from where Kerry management had valued the shares) was considered by some institutions to be too high.

Kerry may also have suffered from a more prevalent market scepticism about food companies generally, and co-operative food organisations more particularly. The few Irish food companies that had been listed in the past, such as Jacob's Biscuits, Bacon Company of Ireland and others, either had not survived, or continued as "supremely indifferent performers" at best.[26] Although both Denis Brosnan's leadership and Kerry Co-operative's successes had been nearly legendary in co-operative circles, they were little known to the financial community at large. While Hugh Friel had counted on Kerry's stellar track record to add a few points to its projected P/E ratio, to market analysts Kerry had virtually no track record at all. In fact, many fund managers had only recently been introduced to Kerry by J. & E. Davy, the stockbrokers for the issue. John O'Reilly, a former journalist who had pioneered coverage of the "agri-business" industry in Ireland, had joined Davy's at about that time and was deeply involved in "getting off" Kerry's public issue. He remembers that:

> People were watching and waiting. I can remember that at the institutional presentation, Denis Brosnan made a very firm commitment to deliver 15 per cent compound growth in earnings for the next five years. The institutions were impressed with that, but they didn't know him. He had no track record as far as they were concerned.[27]

Aside from a bad market and general negativity about the historical performance of food companies, other concerns surfaced. One widely voiced fear was that Kerry farmers, who had recently bought over 10,000,000 shares at 35p, would take the opportunity to turn a very quick profit by unloading their shares. Given the placing price of 52p to the public, this would represent a very attractive gain of almost 50 per cent for them. It would, however, also represent a considerable drag on the 52p offering price itself, and thus an unpleasant prospect for fund managers already unhappy with the 52p price. Given the novelty of the offering, there was little evidence to substantiate the concern, or indeed to rebut it. Hugh Friel, at the institutional presentations, did his best:

> At the presentations we made to the institutions, they would ask, "Hey, what about these farmers? These guys are going to dump their shares!" I answered that "I'm not from County Kerry, but I've been here long enough to

know them very well. From what I know of these people,
they don't sell things, they buy things!"[28]

The fact that the company would still be 80 per cent owned by
Kerry Co-op was also a recurrent concern. Can you have a business where the owner and the supplier (and often customer) are
the same? Would there be a conflict of interest between the milk
suppliers (anxious to get the highest price possible for their milk)
and the shareholders (whose best interest might suggest that a
lower price be paid)? Was there a likelihood that the minority
shareholders in the plc (less than 20 per cent of the ownership in
total) could be squeezed? This was not an issue that could be de-
finitively resolved. It was up to Denis Brosnan and Hugh Friel to
offer what assurances they could and put their own personal
credibility on the line. For their part, J. & E. Davy had to extend
their own not inconsiderable goodwill as well to reassure fund
managers and institutions.

Well below the surface, as well, may have lurked some element
of the old divide between those who lived in the "Pale of Dublin"
and those from the "Wilds of Kerry". Dublin, in business and
commerce as well as in politics and the arts, has been accused in
the past of having at least a mildly patronising attitude towards
what, and who, come to them from the provinces. In evaluating
Kerry's public offering, could there have been some element of
Dublin snobbery? There is little overt evidence to suggest that
there was, but similarly little reason to dismiss the possibility out
of hand. Dublin, despite its recent growth and its status as a cosmopolitan, capital city, is a very small place — a big city with a
small town feel. It is a city with few secrets (I still remember the
title of a favourite book about Dublin titled *Mind You, I've Said
Nothing*) where a "wink" is still "as good as a nod". This would
have been the case in the Dublin financial community even more
so in 1986 than it is today, particularly among the "insiders". Did
any of this even tangentially affect Kerry's offer? We will have to
content ourselves with conjecture.

Moving to the more concrete from the highly speculative, it is
probably fair to suggest that the issue of the pricing of the shares
may have represented the major irritant in the offering. The prob-

lem was recounted in *Business and Finance* shortly after the offering:

> There is no doubt that there was a lot of unhappiness
> about the price that had to be paid to take part. Many
> people thought it was dear and Denis Brosnan was defi-
> nitely pushing his luck. The institutional view tended to
> centre about a price of around 45p a share, with the Kerry
> camp wanting 55p a share. In the end it was felt that 50p
> might be a reasonable compromise, but the Kerry side
> pushed it to 52p. This was felt to be too high by many. It
> gave a [P/E] ratio nearer to 10.4 times earnings, whereas
> some felt that eight or nine times earnings would be rea-
> sonable under the circumstances, given the current Kerry
> position and future uncertainty.[29]

At the time, Davy's denied having to "twist arms" to get the issue
off. Kyran McLaughlin, a J. & E. Davy Director, said at the time:

> There was no real arm-twisting to get people involved.
> You can only do that on rare occasions — otherwise you
> use up your goodwill rather rapidly.[30]

Still, they had to work very hard to ensure a successful flotation. It
was tough going. The issue, although small, was trickier than most,
and the pricing issue caused friction. A number of institutions declined to participate in the offering, and the shares allocated to
them were quickly reallocated. Still, on Monday, 1 October, the
phone calls were made and the entire share issue was placed. Disappointing as it was to Kerry that the shares could not be issued at
a premium to book value, they had learned a great deal in this first
time coming to the market. For Hugh Friel, he had learned a difficult lesson concerning the importance of price in an initial flotation:

> When you are getting a flotation off, price does not mat-
> ter! That is a very important concept, but was difficult to
> grasp at the time. We were as wrong as they [the institu-
> tions] were wrong. It was over a matter of 2 pence! Price
> should not have mattered. Yes, it was the first time we
> were going to sell our silverware, but it doesn't really

matter. It's a non-issue. The most important thing is just to get the issue away.[31]

The Importance of Going Public

It had been a long and circuitous road to complete the public of-fering. It had taken a lengthy period of time and consumed a seri-ous amount of effort. The novelty and the general uncertainty surrounding it were yet to dissipate. The disagreements over price, and the less than wholehearted embrace of the offering by many institutions, no doubt still rankled to some participants. Yet, at the end of the day, it could only be considered a highly suc-cessful effort, for all of Kerry's most important objectives had been met. Some £7.5 million in capital had been raised for Kerry to be-gin its march on the acquisition trail in earnest. More importantly, Kerry now had a convenient vehicle for the efficient raising of yet more finance, for this was always intended to be only its first sally into the equity market. The flotation of the Kerry Group provided the missing link in what it later called its "equation for growth". Frank Hayes, Kerry Group's Director of Corporate Affairs, later summarised the process, and the result, this way:

> The Board of Kerry Group and its management realised that the future lay with strong diversified businesses ca-pable of competing in a world market. In terms of the food sector Kerry viewed this as a momentum towards the de-velopment of large international companies, financially strong, with a significant share of any market in which they chose to compete. A five-year corporate plan was defined and agreed by the Board, research and development be-came a priority, overseas offices were opened and the quiet search for suitable acquisitions began. Kerry was determined to become a large-scale food business and an appropriate management structure was put in place to cater for this strategy. Kerry's strategy was based on an equation for growth which read: Strategy x Capability x Capital = Sustained Profitable Growth. The organisation was and indeed remains convinced that where one of the elements in this equation is missing, the result at best is zero profitable growth.[32]

By 1986, Kerry had already defined its strategy and developed many of the necessary capabilities to effect it. What had been missing was, quite simply, the money. With the successful public offering, the "missing link" of adequate capital was now in place. Going public had yet again solidified Kerry's reputation as an innovator and risk taker, and its stock market listing (it would shortly be listed on the Dublin and London Stock Exchanges) provided it with a platform for future growth. As a public company, of course, disclosure and reporting rules would be more onerous, but also would provide Kerry with a far more conspicuous profile; its future results, good or bad, would be widely reported and analysed. If Kerry were able to meet its firm commitment to a 15 per cent compound rate of growth in earnings, it could be assured that the financial world (at least in Ireland) would know about it! For Kerry's farmer-shareholders, at least some portion of their ownership stake in the enterprise was now liquid, fully tradable, and with an easily determinable market value. In a very real sense, some of the wealth that they had created and stored in the Kerry Co-operative structure had now been "unlocked" and made available for them to use as they personally saw fit. Similarly, employees in the Kerry Group now had their own tangible stake in the enterprise.

I spoke one day with a lorry driver for Kerry Co-op who for years had been collecting milk from farms throughout the county and delivering it to Listowel for processing. He mentioned in passing that in the early years of the Co-op, it had always been the milk price that was the prime item of discussion brought up by the farmers as they waited for the milk to load. And the weather. After Kerry went public, however, a third item of regular discussion seemed to have crept into the "top three" conversational items. The weather, the milk price, and Kerry's latest share price now constituted the ruling pantheon of the Kerry dairy farmer's conversation!

Kerry's public offering, radical as it may have been in 1986, reflected only the *first* step in the gradual evolution of the firm from a co-operative to a publicly owned multinational company. Due credit must be given to the manner in which this transition was accomplished. In future years, the co-operative's stake in the enterprise was diluted in a sensible way over an extended period of time. It was a careful, thoughtful, step-by-step process. Change was signalled, discussed, and understood well in advance, allowing plenty of time for people to find their feet. The structure did not change massively overnight. Electoral processes within the co-operative remained intact. Even in 2000, the co-operative still retains 37 per cent of the outstanding shares in the plc (and the co-operative Board of Directorss currently appoints nine of the twenty members of the plc Board).[33] It was a smooth transition from co-op to plc. In the final analysis, Kerry's very modest first offering on the stock market set the tone for the gradual, incremental changes in its structure over the following 14 years. Of course, Kerry, in a sense, had already been preparing for this transition for years. With its commercial and outward-looking market orientation, it was perhaps far better prepared than most to make the transition. Reflecting on going public, Denis Brosnan has offered that:

> It is easy to convert [to a plc]; that is simply going through a technical formula. What some have not realised is that being a plc, with a good status and a good rating, demands discipline. The first major discipline it calls for is to have stability of profits. This means you have to move out of the commodity businesses, and into those business segments that will give you significant growth in profits. By the time Kerry went plc in 1986, I think we had been practising how to be a plc, a good plc, since the early 1980s, after the collapse of our milk supplies.[34]

Despite their initial negativism, the other major dairy co-operatives in Ireland observed the successful Kerry flotation with considerable interest. Of course, some leaders of major co-ops had already had a field day denouncing Kerry from the pulpit for destroying the fabric of the co-operative movement and undermining co-operative philosophy. Others had gone so far as to declare that their own co-operative organisations would go public (in the words of one) "over my dead body". As such outbursts were remembered later, they surely lent credence to the old adage about being careful with one's words, for they may have to be eaten later! It was a supreme irony that, within 12–18 months of Kerry's flotation, a second major dairy co-op was queuing up to go the same route. By 1990, Avonmore Co-operative, Waterford Co-operative, and Golden Vale had all gone public. Before Kerry went public in 1986, all of the "Big Six" in the Irish dairy industry were co-operative organisations. By 1990, four enterprises had a plc structure, while the other two co-operatives, Ballyclough and Mitchelstown, had amalgamated to form Dairygold, the largest "pure" dairy co-operative of any substantial size remaining in Ireland. Additionally, the IAWS (Irish Agricultural Wholesale Society), which was founded in 1897 with Horace Plunkett himself as the first chairman, went public on 25 May 1988 following what was essentially the "Kerry model" for plc conversion. A smaller co-operative, the Donegal Co-op, later did a complete conversion (similar, technically, to Golden Vale) on 12 December 1997.

If going public supplied Kerry with the missing link it needed to ensure its own organisational success, it also permanently changed the role of co-operative structures in the Irish dairy industry. In the view of this writer and others, such change was entirely consistent with the very practical, and pragmatic, orientation of the founders of the co-operative movement in Ireland. The movement was never intended to reflect a woolly-eyed ideology, indeed a theology, which could not be questioned. It was intended as a principled response to specific social and economic conditions. A publication of the Centre for Co-operative Studies at University College, Cork has addressed it this way:

> Co-operative principles and practices are not fixed immutable sets of standards carved in stone but legacies derived from different historical circumstances which are not always appropriate to present conditions. Co-operative principles and practices must constantly be re-evaluated in view of the changing social and economic conditions under which they operate.[35]

Co-operative organisations were processes, and vehicles, for achieving very specific objectives. These objectives, and not the vehicles originally devised to achieve them, are what are truly enduring. They hark, quite simply, back to the original rallying cry of Plunkett and his disciples: "Better farming, better business, better living!" There is a very strong case to be made that the conversion to publicly owned enterprises, as pioneered by Kerry and in response to the specific circumstances it faced, was the right thing for its milk suppliers, its investors, and its community.

Jim Moloney, as thoughtful and insightful an observer of co-operative organisation as there is, reflected upon it this way:[36]

> I've often said to myself over the past fifteen years, what would Horace Plunkett think of what we are doing? Are we "selling out" the co-operative movement? I know I've been accused of that. But the world has changed quite rapidly, and so have farmers. Farming has become a business, and the best farmers are among the best businessmen. This requires the co-operatives to which they are selling their produce to keep abreast of the times, and to look at larger international markets. The size and population of Ireland make this inevitable. In order to exploit this opportunity, some form of financing related to public ownership is, in my view, necessary. Now, some might think otherwise, and that is all to the good. Let's have a debate on it. But in the absence of any other way at the moment, I see this as a necessary development. What it comes down to, I think, is this: Do you prefer to have 100 per cent ownership in your own co-operative which is limited in its growth possibilities, or do you reduce your ownership in a group which will have a greater share of markets and profits? Now, I can't predict the future, but I have seen that some traditional co-operatives, particularly in some European countries, have lost out to the multinationals, particularly in the added value area. In my view, it is better that a farmer-owned co-operative should evolve into a publicly owned multinational, with certain safeguards. That is my philosophy on this; it might be a bit tangled, but that is what it is.[37]

Notes

---

[1] "Milk Co-operatives Walk Financial Tightrope", *Aspect*, March 1986, p. 15.

[2] An unidentified "senior figure in the co-op movement", quoted in "Denis Brosnan: Man of the Year", *Business and Finance*, 9 January 1986, p. 16.

[3] This objective was debated and approved at a Special Meeting of the Board of Directors held in Head Office, Tralee, 19 April 1983. It is reflected in the minutes of the meeting.

[4] Danny Miller (1990), *The Icarus Paradox: How Exceptional Companies Bring about their own Downfall*, New York: HarperBusiness.

[5] Jim Moloney, personal interview, 9 July 1999.

[6] Internal Kerry Co-op documents prepared by Hugh Friel for a meeting of the Board of Directors on 9 December 1985.

[7] Minutes of Special Meeting of the Board of Directors, Kerry Co-operative Creameries, Ltd., 19 April 1983.

[8] Minutes of the 10th Annual General Meeting of Kerry Co-operative Creameries, Ltd., 15 May 1984.

[9] 1983 Annual Report of Kerry Co-operative Creameries, Ltd., Chairman's Statement, p. 3.

[10] Hugh Friel, personal interview, 31 May 1999.

[11] Minutes of Special Meeting of the Board of Directors, 19 April 1983.

[12] Hugh Friel, personal interview, 31 May 1999.

[13] Brendan McGrath, "Reduced Co-op Holding Dominates Kerry AGM", *The Irish Times (on the Web)*, 28 May 1996.

[14] Minutes of Special Meeting of the Board of Directors, 9 December 1985.

[15] Ibid.

[16] Ibid.

[17] Internal Kerry Co-op documents prepared for a meeting of the Board of Directors on 9 December 1985.

[18] "*Business and Finance* Denis Brosnan: Man of the Year", 9 January 1986, p. 16.

[19] *The Kerryman*, "The Kind of Spunk that We Need!", 10 January 1986, p. 10.

[20] Hugh Friel, personal interview, 31 May 1999.

[21] Hugh Friel, 31 May 1999.

[22] *Business and Finance* (1986), "op. cit.

[23] Jim Moloney, personal interview, 9 July 1999.

[24] *Business and Finance* "Denis Brosnan: Man of the Year", , 9 January 1986, p. 19.

[25] Bill Murdoch (1986), "Business Opinion: Low Key Debut for Kerry Co-op on Stock Market", *The Irish Times*, 29 September 1986.

[26] John O'Reilly, personal interview, 10 January 2000.

[27] Ibid.

[28] Hugh Friel, personal interview, 31 May 1999. Indeed, history has borne him out. In the 14 years since the public issue, and even as the number of Kerry shares outstanding has grown, the stock continues to be very thinly traded. In fact, its lack of trading volume and liquidity has been a source of complaint for many institutions!

[29] "Guess Who Didn't Come to the Kerry Party", *Business and Finance*, 9 October 1986, p. 3.

[30] Ibid.

[31] Hugh Friel, personal interview, 31 May 1999.

[32] Frank Hayes (1986), "Kerry Group: Building an Irish multinational", in *Food for Thought*, a limited edition publication of the 1986 Listowel Quality Food Fair, p. 10.

[33] Of the twenty members of the Kerry Group Board of Directors, nine are appointed by the Kerry Co-op Board, five are Executive Directors, and there are six others.

[34] Denis Brosnan, personal interview, 11 October 1999.

[35] Bob Briscoe, Susan Grey, Paul Hunt, et. al. (1982), *The Co-operative Idea*, Cork: Centre for Co-operative Studies, University College Cork, p. 14.

[36] It is important to note that Moloney joined the Board of Directors of the IAWS in 1981, and was a member of the Board when IAWS went public in 1988. He later became chairman of IAWS Group plc in 1991, a capacity in which he continues to serve.

[37] Jim Moloney, personal interview, 9 July 1999.

Chapter 8

The Evolution of a Multinational Corporation

We have got to lift our heads above the borders of this small country. It's a big world out there! — Denis Brosnan

Although plans for the public offering dominated the thinking of some of Kerry Group's senior executives through late 1985 and into 1986, others were well on their way towards implementing various elements of the company's plan to become a substantial international food organisation. As was the norm at Kerry, activities were proceeding simultaneously rather than sequentially, and no one was waiting for the public issue to be completed before moving decisively on other fronts. It may be useful to recount the position of the company at the end of 1985. It was clearly continuing to outperform its peer group in Ireland. The strategic planning process was, by now, well established, and a high level of clarity of purpose was beginning to emerge. Kerry's managers were focusing upon the task ahead but still, there were considerable challenges. First, the prospects for growth in the traditional dairy business were increasingly limited. The introduction of milk production quotas by the EC in 1984 had marked the final end of the boom in production of the 1970s and had ushered in a new era of limits, with farmers facing substantial penalties (the EC superlevy) for production above quota. Second, Kerry had made its first independent forays into foreign markets with the opening of small offices in Chicago and Luton (outside of London) but was finding the initial going very, very slow. In the US, having sundered its ties with Erie Casein, Kerry was in effect building a business almost from scratch. It had also become increasingly clear that if it did not want to be merely an exporter of commodity dairy products like casein, it would need to find a way to break into the newly emerging food ingredients industry. In the United Kingdom and Ireland, the focus was to be on consumer foods. Although progress in the Irish market had been good, the market of 3½ million consumers was limited. The UK market was far larger and more lucrative, but also more difficult to crack. UK market demographics were very stable, retailing and supply arrangements were deeply embedded, and Kerry was an unknown upstart in a field of very established players. Clearly, external acquisition would be required, something on the magnitude of a "Denny's" purchase in the UK. But, the efforts to turn around Denny's, while ultimately successful, had been bruising. Kerry no longer had any illusions about the difficulty, expense, commitment and patience required in turning around an ailing consumer business.

At least, as the Kerry Group executives looked forward, they could rely upon considerable continuity at the board level. Michael Hanrahan, in situ since 1980 as the Chairman of the Kerry Co-op, moved into the Chairmanship of the new plc. He was joined on the board by, among others, Eddie Hayes, Patrick (Patsy) O'Connell, and Alexander (Sonny) O'Donnell, all founding members of the Kerry Co-op. Accordingly, there was a high unity of purpose between the board and management which, to some extent, permeated the entire organisation.

In a nutshell, the challenge during the period of 1985–1987 was clear: to begin to execute in earnest the strategic objective of becoming an international food organisation through internal growth and external acquisitions.

Going it Alone in the USA

Kerry had attended its first food ingredients trade show in the United States in Anaheim in June 1984, not long after the opening of the Chicago office. The annual IFT (International Food Technologists) Show was an important showplace for firms in the food ingredients industry, particularly for Kerry as it attempted to build an identity for itself in this new territory. Everyone in the industry was there. The IFT was a place to display one's wares, meet potential customers, size up the competition and their products, listen to customers articulate their needs, and generally meet, greet, network, and learn. But Kerry, not even a blip on the radar screen of the industry, was taking the 1984 event even a step further. They were also on the lookout for acquisition candidates, and they were not necessarily thinking small. The annual IFT meeting was a good opportunity to size up potential candidates.

Not for the first time, however, Kerry's ambitions may have exceeded its immediate resources, and its representatives needed to be particularly resourceful to reap the maximum gain they could from the event. At that first "food show", Kerry had only a small booth, nothing more than a tabletop really, and its only representatives were Denis Brosnan and Finbarr O'Driscoll.[1] They had made only one small request of the organisers: that their booth be placed next to the Beatreme Specialty Products' booth, since they would be the biggest at the show. In fact, the Beatreme exhibit that year was the largest in the history of the show. Brosnan and O'Driscoll figured that with proximity, they could "feed off" Beatreme at the show, catching their customers as they came and went and perhaps culling a few. Beatreme, a unit of the giant Beatrice Foods Company, was the premier food ingredients company in the North American market at the time, the "big name" in the industry, with a wide range of product applications and an impressive array of blue-chip accounts. Their exhibit that year had particular lustre since Beatrice was in the midst of a corporate-wide "We're Beatrice" campaign that sought to pull together all of their far-flung brands into one recognisable brand portfolio. As the 1984 Olympics (of which Beatrice was a prime corporate sponsor) were being held in nearby Los Angeles that year, the trade show in Anaheim perhaps received special attention. Beatreme itself was truly a *specialty*, rather than a *commodity*, food ingredients business, with a focus on value-added, highly specific applications for the food industry. If there were a company upon which Kerry wanted to model itself in the ingredients business, Beatreme was the one.

There must have been a certain David and Goliath element at play at that first food show. Kerry was not, by any means, a serious player in the ingredients industry. While Brosnan and O'Driscoll manoeuvred to steal a few Beatreme customers, they were at the same time mindful that Beatreme was also a Kerry customer (they'd been selling casein to them, through Erie Casein, for a number of years). Actually, there was a lot of banter, and Brosnan remembers that:

> I know at that stage that the Beatrice guys thought we were very funny . . . these two Irish guys. They didn't mind us taking their customers, or at least enticing their customers![2]

Jack Warner, who was soon to become President of Beatreme, had already been a guest of Kerry in 1983, when he and about 20 North American customers were treated to a visit to Kerry and to Kerry Co-op's facilities in Ireland. Bob Kasik, Beatreme's worldwide Technical Director, was also in the booth that year. Both Warner and Kasik were to figure prominently in the Kerry–Beatreme relationship for years to come. Amid the kidding and banter at the show, the Kerry guys sent over a message to Beatreme to "send over the customers now, because we'll own you one day!"[3] It was more than a little like the mouse eyeing up the elephant, but the message sent over by Kerry was only partly in jest. Equally improbable perhaps was that Beatreme itself, long a small, stable but very profitable division of Beatrice, was about to embark on a wild ride of its own.

Meanwhile, there was the constant pressure to sell casein into an already oversupplied commodity market. Through aggressive pricing, Kerry was able to "move" the casein in the marketplace, but it was clear that this dependence would have to end. What was unclear was specifically what would replace it. O'Driscoll, the first Kerry employee to relocate to the States, took the lead in this regard. He spent most of his time on the road, cultivating customers, entertaining buyers, spending time in the marketplace. Throughout all this, however, it was *learning* that was paramount — about casein applications, ingredients, shortenings, powders, creamers, cheese powders, customers and their varied price tolerances, and other ingredients companies. Quality was also an issue, and Kerry made efforts to build a reputation for superior technical support, since it could help support a pricing premium.

And constantly there was the investigation of opportunities, the search for a faster way into the ingredients business. Stan McCarthy remembers that:

> We started out looking at areas that were relatively familiar to us, such as animal feed, the pet food industry, or veal feed. We looked at business that was somewhat casein-related, given that we did not understand all the applications for casein, and considered whether we could contract manufacture our casein by putting it with other ingredients and selling it to these various applications.[4]

By 1986, Kerry was using contract manufacturers in the States to produce some of these applications, but still had no manufacturing presence of its own in the USA.

By this time, Michael Leahy, who had been involved with production in Listowel since it opened in 1972, was flying back and forth between Ireland and the States, joining Finbarr O'Driscoll in the search for a suitable acquisition. They travelled around the country constantly, looking at potential businesses to acquire and inspecting spray-drying (the prime technology employed in manufacturing specialised food ingredients) plants, but nothing seemed to fit the bill. Oddly enough, one of the operations they inspected was a facility in Owen, Wisconsin that was, at the time, a part of Northfield Industries. The plant had some significant operational problems and Kerry chose not to buy it at the time; years later, ironically, it wound up as a part of Kerry's North American organisation.

Kerry was beginning to pick up business in the States, selling to customers like Kraft, Beatreme, and Pillsbury. However, it was still selling products at the low end of the food ingredients pyramid, products that were less technically sophisticated with limited margin opportunity. Leahy remembers that:

> We couldn't just go into General Mills and sell them emulsifier, which was a very important component of their cake mixes. They were buying from Beatreme. We couldn't just walk in and say "we'd like to supply your

factory". They'd say, "Who the hell are you? What technology do you have?" We were able to pick up some of
the low-tech business, but it became clear to us that it
would be very difficult for us to grow in this business.[5]

Upgrading the business in the States would be a major and time-
consuming undertaking. It would take years to develop the technology, gain the necessary in-house expertise, expand the product
offerings, build up the client base, and ultimately achieve sufficient scale to do this economically. Given Kerry's ambitious
growth objectives, and remembering management's personal
commitment to achieving them, there was little enthusiasm over
such a patient, "go slow" approach. A far better strategy appeared
to be the acquisition of a company in the USA. With the public issue successfully executed by the end of 1986, additional capital
raised, and the vehicle in place to raise more if necessary, the time
seemed right. Clearly, the obvious candidate was Beatreme. Brosnan had always been impressed with Beatreme. He was fascinated
by what they were doing. They were pioneers in spray-drying all
sorts of products: shortenings, cheese powders, and other processed food ingredients with which Kerry was unfamiliar. Looking
through Beatreme's catalogues and product literature, their technology, their client base, and their range of product applications,
it was clear to Brosnan that they were the ideal vehicle to spear-
head Kerry's entry into both the lucrative specialty food ingredients industry and the crucial North American marketplace.

Kerry had been drawing up lists of target acquisitions since
about 1984, and Beatreme was a perennial favourite. It was
brought up at board meetings as a potential acquisition in early
1985. Initially, Beatreme was simply not for sale. Inquiries, however, were made repeatedly, and Brosnan and O'Driscoll, in particular, stayed in close touch with Jack Warner, then the President
of Beatreme. When Brosnan came over to the States for the IFT
meetings in 1985 and 1986, he and O'Driscoll met with Warner, but
the meetings went nowhere. One lasted no more than three to four
minutes, for there was simply no interest in selling. By the end of
1985, however, any possible acquisition of Beatreme had grown
even more complicated. Beatreme, through its parent Beatrice
Foods, had become a pawn in the M&A (mergers and acquisitions)

mayhem of the mid-1980s. Although the story will be detailed more fully in Chapter 9, the basic outline is as follows. Beatrice was taken private by a leveraged buyout (an LBO) led by KKR (Kohlberg Kravis Roberts & Co.) in late 1985; at that time it was the largest LBO in history. Since the intent of the LBO was to buy the company using a huge amount of debt (typically "junk bonds"), and then sell off various parts of the company to pay down the debt, KKR began to dismantle Beatrice. Beatreme wound up "packaged" with a number of other Beatrice divisions and sold to a group of investors led by Don Kelly, called E-II Holdings, in June 1987. E-II itself (including Beatreme) was in turn gobbled up by American Brands in January 1988. Throughout this period, Kerry tried to get to Beatreme, but it was simply inaccessible. It was "in play", but submerged as part of a larger "bundling" of companies, buried in the deck of cards in a very high stakes card game. Not to push the analogy too far, but it should also be noted that professional gamblers and card sharks were playing the game, and not anyone with an even remote interest in running a food ingredients company. Even early on in the process, Kerry had tried to go in through the "back door" by putting Karl Obenauf, who had retired as the Chief Executive of Beatreme in 1983, on retainer as a consultant. But there had been no interest on Beatrice's part. Since Beatreme was not for sale, Obenauf's charge from Kerry was to find a Beatreme "lookalike", but he kept coming back and saying, "There is no Beatreme lookalike; the only one to buy is Beatreme."[6] Unfortunately, Kerry could not get to it.

By the end of 1986 there was considerable pressure to find a way to enter the ingredient business in North America, but the two primary options had been stymied. Kerry had not been able to buy a complete business (specifically Beatreme) and had not found a manufacturing facility that met its requirements. The only remaining option was to go to a "greenfield" investment; that is, Kerry would build its own facility and begin to build its presence from there. If Beatreme would not sell to them, then Kerry would compete with them. At the time, Kerry was storing casein in a warehouse and shipping it around the country; it was decided to look for another facility to serve as a warehouse and distribution centre, install some dry mixing equipment, and perhaps add a spray dryer a year later. This is what led them to Jackson, Wisconsin.[7]

The Jackson facility was owned by Sherwood Medical, a division of American Home Products, and had been built in the early 1980s. Sherwood had moved its operations to Mexico, and removed all its equipment from the plant. When Kerry looked at it, it was an empty shell of a manufacturing facility. Still, it was modern, well located on about 30 acres of land on a state highway only 40 minutes from downtown Milwaukee and, best of all, priced at a very attractive $1.65 million. This was a price that was considerably less than the cost of new construction. Kerry purchased the Jackson plant in April 1987, and immediately embarked on an all-out effort to get the plant up and running. The investment in Jackson (which totalled about $10 million) was, in a real sense, the tangible manifestation of a "shot across the bow". It was a signal to Beatreme and the rest of the specialty ingredients industry that Kerry was committed to becoming a serious player in the industry, and was prepared to invest equally serious amounts of money to do so.

Time, of course, was of the essence. The sales and administration staff was relocated from Chicago over the course of about a year, and Stan McCarthy took on the new title of Vice President of Commercial Affairs. Michael Leahy moved his family to Milwaukee from Ireland, and took over the post of Vice President of Operations. His primary responsibility was the engineering of the facility and the ordering and installation of the equipment. Pat O'Neill, the company's chief engineer, virtually lived in the States while the plant was being fitted-out. Dryer operators from Listowel provided assistance in the commissioning of the spray dryer. By September 1987, the dry-mixing plant was running; by June, 1988, the spray dryer had been installed and the manufacturing facility had been fully commissioned. Finbarr O'Driscoll, still the President of Kerry Foods, was actively involved on the sales side, and heavily focused on building an ingredients sales force. He succeeded in luring a few salespeople from Beatreme who were experienced in the industry, knew the customers, the competition, and importantly, knew a thing or two about Beatreme. So, by the middle of 1988, Kerry at last had a business "on the ground" in the US, had built the bare bones of a sales force, was developing its technology, and was building its image as a serious competitor. It was also competing directly with Beatreme.

Even then, progress was slow. Stan McCarthy remembers that:

> It is no exaggeration to say we hadn't enough business;
> we had aspirations of business. We did not have enough
> business to keep the dryer busy. We were beginning to
> build inventory and fill the warehouse. We were compet-
> ing with Beatreme, and we knew we were creating quite
> an impression in the marketplace as people spending
> money in the new specialty ingredients business. But suf-
> fice it to say that, at that point, our bark was better than
> our bite.[8]

In 1986, demand for rennet casein had dropped off considerably
due to a bad market environment for casein's principal user, the
imitation cheese industry. Now, competing with Beatreme in 1987
and into 1988 in more specialised food ingredients, Kerry was
having some success but it was painstakingly slow, and incremental. Building an ingredients business in the US was going to be
a very long-term proposition, unless the right acquisition came
along. Throughout the entire period of starting its own North
American operation, Kerry kept relentlessly tracking Beatreme as
it changed hands from one short-term owner to another, waiting
for the opportunity to take a crack at purchasing what they saw as
the crown jewel of the industry. Although Kerry did make a small
acquisition in the United States in early 1988 with the purchase of
Primas Food Ingredients, it was not at all clear that the opportunity
to acquire Beatreme would ever present itself.

Entry into the Beef Business

Before the mid-1950s, farmers in Ireland had typically sold their
livestock at fairs in the streets and squares of their provincial
towns. The haggling and negotiating proceeded in a time-
honoured fashion that had been unchanged for generations. A single buyer and a single seller negotiated the sale of a single animal. Although it was colourful, complex, richly patterned, and a
good draw for the tourists, it was not terribly efficient. It was an
anachronism that the rest of Europe had long ago relinquished.
During the 1950s, both the IAOS and the NFA (National Farmers
Association) had stepped in to encourage farmers to organise their
own "marts" as co-operative organisations. Marts were basically
systems whereby farmer-members could bring their livestock to

auction, with the marts serving as centralised clearinghouses for dealings with buyers. A few expanded into beef processing, building their own factories for the export of meat rather than selling live cattle. Farmers in the Cork Co-operative Marts were the first (later followed by Golden Vale Marts (unrelated to Golden Vale Creameries) and NCF Marts), building a new factory in Midleton, County Cork, and a new organisation, International Meat Packers (IMP).

By 1985, however, the Cork Marts (IMP) were in serious financial difficulty. In fact, it was the last Irish co-operative involved with the beef business, all of the remainder having already fallen into the hands of private owners. The Irish beef industry itself was being concentrated more and more into the hands of just a few investors (chief among them Larry Goodman), creating fears of a virtual monopoly. The ICOS, as well as the government, was anxious to keep IMP in co-operative hands. Kerry, as the most successful co-operative in Ireland at the time, clearly felt the pressure from them and from the farm lobby to step in. Clover Meats, another beef processing co-operative, had already gone under. Kerry had made a bid for several of Clover's brand names, but did not attempt to buy the assets, preferring to wait for IMP to become available.[9] The fact that Denny's was only just turning the corner to profitability in 1985 may also have made Kerry more circumspect with regard to moving too quickly to acquire another failing meat company.

Government or farm lobby pressure, however, was probably not the primary motivator for Kerry's entry into beef. There were commercial attractions as well. First, there was the general impression that Larry Goodman and the other barons of the beef business were making a lot of money. If they could, why not Kerry? (This, with the benefit of hindsight, should not have been a rhetorical question, for within several years Goodman's beef empire was to fail in spectacular fashion. By that time, as well, Kerry would have been well able to answer that question itself.) Second, it was an agribusiness venture that was consistent with Kerry's agricultural heritage, with apparent relevance for its farmer-shareholders. If it worked out, it might also nicely complement its pigmeat business at Denny's and Duffy's. Third, Kerry was back on the acquisition trail in earnest, but had been unable to come up with anything of substantial size in the US or the UK. IMP was on its doorstep for the taking, and the initial investment was not large; it would not preclude other acquisitions. Finally, Kerry had the confidence that they could build this beef business into a substantial, profitable food enterprise. Although they understood that beef was not the most lucrative of businesses, their hard won success at Denny's had proven to them that they could take an ailing business and turn it around.

Kerry finally moved, in March 1986, to purchase an 80 per cent stake in the assets of IMP (in Midleton), and a related facility, Convenience Foods (in Tallaght, County Dublin) for a reported £5.8 million, with Cork Marts retaining a minority interest. It was an amicable purchase, with the Cork farmers pleased that they had been able to sell to another co-operative (albeit one that would soon be a "hybrid" co-op/plc) rather than one of the private "beef barons". The Midleton factory had already closed its doors in 1985; it produced primarily for the commodity beef trade. Convenience Foods, however, was a modern plant that produced processed beef products like hamburgers, and had continued trading throughout Cork Marts' financial troubles.

Kerry from the beginning invested capital in modernising and upgrading the Midleton facility, and reopened it in June 1986. It also brought in Kerry management from its pork meat division and experts from Europe to help train workers in the latest, most efficient methods. In the commodity beef trade, being the low-cost producer meant everything. Convenience Foods, however, offered better possibilities to effect Kerry's plans to develop consumer branded prepared beef products that would find their way onto the supermarket shelves. Kerry began to focus R&D efforts upon transforming beef from a *commodity* to a consumer *branded* product.

Proving that, once again, timing is everything, it happened that 1986 was a very good year for the beef industry in Ireland. Even Kerry's new beef business turned a profit, for as Brosnan admitted not long afterward, "You couldn't lose money in beef in 1986.[10]" Some 40,000 cattle were processed through Midleton during the second half of 1986. This stroke of good fortune notwithstanding, Kerry's entry into beef was problematic almost from the very beginning. Perhaps three to four years earlier, as a co-operative, the beef business might have been a sensible fit for Kerry. Now, as a public company with commitments not only to sales revenue but also to consistent profitable growth, any such fit was far less obvious. Looking back, Hugh Friel saw that:

> It [the beef business] didn't cost us a lot of money, but it did cost us a lot of pain. It was a serious distraction, with a great big bundle of turnover and next to no profits. If you were lucky, you made a miraculous two per cent! It was not a business for an organisation like Kerry, but it took us a long time to get out of it.[11]

With the benefit of hindsight, the fundamentals of the beef industry were never going to be right for Kerry. Kerry was now a plc that had committed itself to achieving operating margins in the area of 10 per cent; the beef business, which was a big chunk of the total turnover, was getting about 2 per cent, with luck! It was, by its nature, a commodity business. Branding of beef was virtually unknown, and apparently ineffective. Price was king, and quality, delivery, and dependability of supply were all secondary factors. Those who made money in the industry made it by cut-throat trading, buying and selling on razor-thin margins, selling into EC intervention, or exporting to foreign governments (and taking advantage of export credits and other incentives). Customer relationships, such as they were, were strictly transaction by transaction. Opportunism was paramount, and thus it was an industry dominated by individuals. Neither co-operatives nor corporations had had much luck in it. Demand was notoriously fickle, and the market went through cyclical periods of boom and bust. Many of the common business practices employed in the industry were questionable at best. Much of the industry's dirty laundry, in fact, was subsequently well aired during the hearings of the "Beef Tribunal" during the 1990s. The Tribunal documented abuses ranging from quality, health and safety issues in the slaughtering and packing houses, to the use of questionable payments to gain large export orders, to the wholesale abuse of intervention and export credit programs. It was a very messy business, and one that didn't mesh well with either Kerry's new status as a plc or its organisational culture.

As it turned out, 1987 was a difficult year in the beef industry, down significantly from the second half of 1986. Kerry's beef business suffered from lower supplies and higher cattle prices that further pinched its already tight margins. Efforts to increase efficiencies and lower overheads at the two beef processing facilities were ongoing, but it had come to be accepted that the learning curve was going to be a long one. R&D and marketing efforts were focused upon creating a market for added value beef products on the supermarket shelves. With the warning signals becoming ever clearer, Kerry girded itself for another long and protracted effort. Granted, there was never any question of Kerry adapting its style to fit that predominant in the beef industry. Neither was there any question that Kerry would cut and run at the first sign of difficulty.

Indeed, Kerry would not be the first or the last organisation to engage in what some academics have termed "an escalating commitment to a failing course of action".[12] Unwilling to depart from the beef industry with undue haste, and certainly not until it had thrown everything it could at it, Kerry embarked upon a series of acquisitions that effectively "upped the ante". It was what Brosnan called a "growing up phase" for the company:

> We got in deeper and deeper. We doubled and trebled in size. We wound up doubling the bet. We kept upping the ante. We purchased South West Meats, Meadow Meats, and then Tunney Meats. We kept going deeper and deeper, until we finally said "that's enough", and looked for an opportunity to get out.[13]

This "escalating commitment" was first manifest in the purchase, in February 1988, of South West Meats from Unigate for approximately £4 million sterling. Located in Somerset in the UK, South West had relatively modern facilities for the processing and packaging of red meats and already distributed its "value-added" consumer packs to major supermarket chains in the UK and Europe. South West was seen as a vehicle for Kerry to begin to change its beef business from a commodity business to a higher value, consumer branded business. Importantly, it offered access to the supermarket shelves of the major UK multiples, access deemed critical to any fundamental reshaping of Kerry's beef business. In 1988 there were continued decreases in throughput at Midleton, but reasonably good growth in both the South West and Convenience Foods businesses. Despite acceptable gains in turnover, however, margins were razor thin. In October 1988, Kerry acquired McCallum Meats Ltd., located in Portsmouth in the UK. McCallum specialised in serving caterers, institutions, airlines, restaurants and hotels, providing one more value-added outlet for the firm's various meat products.

Even though trading in beef improved during the following year, particularly in expanding trade in the UK, and cultivation of a successful export market in Germany, margins remained low. The Midleton facility was particularly problematic. As a commodity beef producer, it still remained a factory that had no stable markets, compelled to sell its product under auction-like conditions. This deficiency led to subsequent investments in Meadow Meats in Rathdowney and Tunney Meats in Clones in 1991 that will be detailed in subsequent chapters.

Searching for a Breakthrough in the United Kingdom

Kerry's initial activities in the United Kingdom were modest, if not trivial. During the early years, Kerry exported small quantities of animal feed, calf milk replacer, specialised milk-based products, and dairy products through a small London export office. The business was marginal, more of a way to dispose of surplus stock than part of an overall strategy to develop a business in the UK. Kerry was doing bits and pieces of business in the UK, but it was without cohesion and devoid of any great seriousness of intent.

In February 1982, Kerry purchased a small cheese distribution company, Motto Food Company, Ltd. This operation, however, was closed down in 1983 due to the generally depressed conditions then prevalent in the cheese market and the poor prospects for improvement. Efforts, however, were afoot to identify other suitable acquisitions that would give Kerry a foothold in the UK, principally in branded consumer foods. These efforts were simultaneous with efforts taking place in North America to identify likely acquisition targets in the nascent food ingredients industry.

Although exports to the UK did grow through 1986, they remained very much a matter of opportunism rather than of focused strategy. With the addition of Duffy's in 1982, exports of prepared meat products to the UK, Germany, Holland and Belgium increased. With the acquisition of E.M. Denny Holdings in the UK, and Henry Denny and Sons (Ulster) in Portadown, Northern Ireland in 1987, scope was provided for the reestablishment of the Denny's bacon brand in the UK. Denny also had an office in the UK. Kerry's entry into the beef business with the acquisition of IMP in early 1986 brought with it an export business to the UK, along with an office facility located at Smithfield in the heart of London. Still, although exports were growing, Kerry's activities in the UK were widely scattered and fragmented. There was not yet a consistent strategy to develop a UK business.

It was only with the assignment of Michael Griffin to the United Kingdom as the Managing Director of Kerry Foods, Europe, that Kerry began to demonstrate a seriousness of intent to crack the UK market. They had now finally put down their marker in the UK. Looking back at those first years, and at the state of the consumer food market in the UK, Griffin remembers that:

> We had a lot of activity but personally, I was disappointed. It was harder to break into the UK than I had bargained for at the time. It was a very well-established market; the population of 56 million was static, they were eating what they had always eaten, and were not too disposed to trying new products. The suppliers to the supermarkets were well established too. It was very hard to break in. You knew that you might be getting "used" to make a price for the buyer, but the business would always stay with the existing supplier. It was very hard to rattle the cages. While we had lots of individual successes . . . in terms of a coherent, overall presence, it hadn't arrived.[14]

On arrival in the UK in February 1986, Griffin decided to base himself in the former IMP office in Smithfield, rather than the Kerry Foods office at Luton. The beef business had just been acquired, and Griffin assumed that, given the critical nature of the UK as a market for beef, he'd better try to understand it. After all, his experience to date had been on the dairy side of the business only (as MD of Dawn Dairies), and in the Irish market exclusively. He began to study the dynamics of the beef industry, particularly the ways that beef was marketed. Very basic, fundamental questions had to be addressed. What essentially "drives" the business? How important is quality? How important is consistency? The conclusion, to Griffin at least, was not promising. Nothing mattered but price! Beef was purely a commodity business. Kerry's strategy was to change this; their vision was that beef could be made a truly consumer food business. Their intent at the time was to focus their energies on supermarkets, and on building some sort of supplier relationship with the big multiples. But the IMP staff in Smithfield were "beef people", well acquainted with trading and selling carcasses and vacuum-packed joints, through a network of wholesalers, into processing and manufacturing. They hadn't a clue about supermarkets. Griffin decided that a whole new office environment was necessary, and created a new office in Uxbridge, North London. This consolidated the formerly separate offices for Kerry Foods, IMP and E.M. Denny Holdings and totalled no more than eight people.

The reality was that progress was agonisingly slow, and Kerry's staff was literally knocking on doors trying to get listings for their products into the major UK multiples such as Sainsbury's, Tesco, and Marks and Spencer. At this point in time, the Group literally had no retail business at all in the UK. Export sales had, for the most part, gone through wholesalers or, in the case of some milk-based products for the retail trade, through Bord Bainne. In 1987, however, subsequent to going public, Kerry discontinued the use of Bord Bainne for any of its UK exports. It was now fully committed to conducting its own marketing in the UK. But it was a tough go. Griffin, remembering those early years, recounts that:

> It was a very different environment. We were good observers, but maybe slow learners. It was a baptism of fire in a different, and dynamic, environment. What we tried to do in the first instance was to see what products we had within the organisation that we could sell more of in the UK. We traded in a bit of porkmeat, and we put a lot of time and effort into beef over a three to four year period. We also sold turkeys after we had bought Grove Turkeys in 1988, which also took a lot of our time, as we were again encroaching on a very well supplied market. But we also were looking back at our technical capabilities at Lis-

towel, searching for ways to leverage our capabilities at making low-fat butter.[15]

Then, in early 1987, a chance opportunity presented itself. Griffin and a few colleagues were manning a small Kerry Group exhibit stand at the IFE (International Food Exposition) in London. They had on display a few cuts of beef and a placard about their expertise at making low-fat butter. John Pearson, a food technologist at Marks and Spencer, was searching for a half-fat butter, and had heard about Kerry's low-fat butter spread on the Irish market, *Dawn Light*. He stopped by Kerry's stand, met up with Michael Griffin, and had sufficient interest to come out to visit the factory in Listowel. After some energetic efforts on the part of the development crew in Listowel, Marks and Spencer agreed to list an own-label version of *Dawn Light*, a new half-fat butter spread that they called *Sunglow*. The product began shipping before the middle of 1987 and, although the amount of business was quite small in itself, the importance of getting a product listing with Marks and Spencer was huge. It was the first dairy spread to come out of Listowel and into a major UK retailer; it would not be the last. When approaching other supermarket chains on sales calls, the fact that Kerry was producing something for Marks and Spencer was not insignificant; as Michael Griffin said, "At least they'd answer the phone, have a meeting, and at least listen to us!"[16] It was a major breakthrough. Kerry, though still a tiny player in the market, had at last achieved some measure of legitimacy, exposure and, importantly, access to the major UK multiples.

Griffin hired his first non-Irish recruit, Alan Onions, in September 1987 to build upon that slim Marks and Spencer business. His task was very broad: to expand the yellow fats and spreads business (produced and shipped from Listowel) in the UK. Onions had already dealt with Tesco, the giant UK supermarket chain, for a number of years through his previous employer. Through his existing relationships, he was able to at least get in the door with his wares. Specifically, he was trying to sell half-fat butter, basically *Dawn Light*. Onions got a polite rejection, but then the question, "But can you produce this?" It was a half-fat sunflower oil product. Said Onions, "I don't know but I'll find out. He [the fellow at Tesco] said, 'you've got three weeks to have samples in a kitchen trial'."

Onions ran back to Listowel, sat down with Eugene Corcoran, the
R&D Director at the time, and with the product development team
in Listowel was able to get the samples out on time. They were the
best samples in the trial. This got Kerry the Tesco "healthy eating"
business (Tesco's own-label, low-fat spreads). Interestingly, it was
also the first product made in Listowel using ingredients (sunflower oil) that came from outside the Listowel milk pool.[17]

It is important, at this point, to acknowledge the important contribution made by what was called the "spreads group" back at
Kerry's flagship plant in Listowel. Jerry Houlihan, the General Manager at Listowel at that time, noted how "the technology that the
Group had developed in the production of casein could also be
used to make low-fat, emulsifier spreads".[18] For years, people in
both development and production had sought ways to leverage
these increasingly well-honed technical capabilities in the development of other "added-value" products. From the beginning, this
included finding new things that could be done with traditional
butter. There was, throughout the 1980s, considerable ferment and
buzz, with all sorts of ideas and lots of pilot work on low-fat butter
spreads. At the time, "low-fat" butter was unknown in Ireland.
Along with the various pilot and product development work going
on, the group was developing a very serious technical capability.

For those most closely associated with this work, it was an "era
of great excitement".[19] Eugene Corcoran remembers how a small
group of people, including Mike Brown (Development), John
O'Brien (the production manager of the butter plant in Listowel)
and Jimmy O'Brien (Quality Assurance), would often meet on Saturday evenings at 6.00 just to go over the events of the past week
and compare notes (in relative tranquillity). A "can do" attitude
permeated the entire scene. They felt that, with spreads, they could
do anything.

Dawn Light, a 40 per cent butter spread launched in 1986 in
Ireland, was a pioneering product, but commercially perhaps a bit
ahead of its time. With less than half the calories of regular butter,
it certainly represented a notable technical achievement. More
importantly, however, it was this product that sparked the interest
of Marks and Spencer in early 1987, providing Kerry the opportunity it needed to further develop a spreads business in the UK.
With its low-fat butter spreads, and the patents that it held for their

production, Kerry was already well ahead of its competition. This was extended further with the development of a variety of vegetable-fat spreads for Tesco and other retailers in the UK and Ireland. Kerry's branded low-fat spread, Low-Low, became the leading brand in its segment of the Irish market

Stepping back for a moment, Alan Onions recounts that "we saw we had a technical, quality strength over all of our competitors who could supply own-label spreads to the UK".[20] Said Michael Drummey:

> We knew a lot about fat. We knew that we could do low-fat products. We became identified as people who could make yellow fats stand on their heads. If you are in trouble with a yellow fat, you go to Kerry. If you want the Alan Greenspan of the Fats business, Kerry is your man. End of story. [21]

By 1988, Tesco, Marks and Spencer, and Sainsbury's were all buying low-fat spreads from Kerry. It was the beginning of solid organic growth in low-fat, own-label spreads that has continued to the present day. This was own-label business exclusively; Kerry could not even dream of having a brand, in a market that was dominated by brands. To go up against the giants of the industry, the Unigates and Unilevers, would have been unthinkable at this early point in Kerry's presence in the UK, and the cost would have been entirely prohibitive. But the own-label business provided a back door entrée to the market, valuable exposure to retailers if not to consumers, and respectable profit margins. Of course, developing this business organically would take time. To make more significant and timely progress, clearly acquisitions would be necessary, but in the UK at that time they were very costly:

> We *knew* that we would have to acquire in this marketplace to become a force. But during the late 1980s, Hillsdown Holdings, Perkins, Hazelwoods, and others were buying anything that was saleable, and for very high valuations that simply didn't make sense. We never missed anything that was going, and we got a sniff at them, but we were just blown out of the water in terms of the price being paid.[22]

In fact, the entire food processing industry in the UK was beginning to embark on its own period of "take-over mania". What had been a very well-established and stable environment quickly became turbulent. While the high valuations made it difficult for Kerry to engineer successful acquisitions, many of the "successful" acquiring firms were themselves to become high-profile casualties as a result. Within a period of ten years, for example, the market saw the break-up and sale of United Biscuit, the take-over of RHM, the demise of Albert Fisher plc, the eventual break-up of the acquisition-hungry Hillsdown plc, the demerging of the Northern Foods dairy business from the value-added food business, the slimming down of Hazelwoods plc, the sale of the Unigate milk business, and the disbanding of the UK Milk Marketing Board, among others.

The fact that Kerry Foods in the UK was able to navigate its way through this mayhem, without getting caught up in it, and continued slowly building a respectable food business, was no small achievement in itself. This prudent and disciplined approach to growth in the UK, while perhaps difficult to adhere to in an "impatient" organisation such as Kerry, was ultimately proven successful. That Griffin and his Kerry Foods team in the UK saw it through, not without some difficulty, is to their credit.

They remained on the trail of another Denny's-type acquisition, but it failed to materialise. So Kerry's business in the UK focused on organic growth in own-label products in its prime area of competence, that of yellow fat spreads. In 1986–1988, it succeeded in loosening a brick here and a brick there, slowly building a yellow fat spreads business, and selling some beef, some pigmeat, some poultry, and a few other consumer products. The beef business continued to drain corporate resources. Michael Griffin says:

> With the benefit of hindsight, we put a lot of our energy and focus into trying to build a respectable red-meat business during this period of three to four years, when more experienced food companies like Unigate and Northern Foods had already exited this business.[23]

It was also at this point in late 1988 when food activities in the UK perhaps took a temporary back seat to major developments that were unfolding in North America. In the US, it seemed that the long awaited breakthrough might be at hand.

Notes

[1] Kerry at some point purchased Beatreme's old booth for about $10,000 and used it for several years.

[2] Denis Brosnan, personal interview, 1 June 1999.

[3] Ibid.

[4] Stan McCarthy, personal interview, 6 December 1999.

[5] Michael Leahy, personal interview, 7 December 1999.

[6] Recalled by Hugh Friel, personal interview, 31 May 1999.

[7] Michael Leahy, op. cit.

[8] Stan McCarthy, op. cit.

[9] Aileen O'Toole (1987), *The Pace Setters*, Dublin: Gill and Macmillan, p. 105.

[10] Aileen O'Toole (1987), op. cit., p. 106.

[11] Hugh Friel, personal interview, 31 May 1999.

[12] The phrase was coined, and the concept pioneered, by Professor Barry Staw. See, for example, Barry M. Staw and Jerry Ross (1987), "Understanding Escalation Situations: Antecedents, Prototypes and Solutions", in L.L. Cummings and Barry M. Staw (eds.) *Research in Organizational Behavior*, Greenwich, CT: JAI Press; Barry Staw and Jerry Ross (1989), "Understanding Behavior in Escalation Situations", *Science*, 246(4927), p. 216; or Barry M. Staw (1981), "The Escalation of Commitment to a Course of Action", *Academy of Management Review*, 16(4), p. 577–587.

[13] Denis Brosnan, personal interview, 11 October 1999.

[14] Michael Griffin, personal interview, 5 January 2000.

[15] Ibid.

[16] Ibid.

[17] Alan Onions, personal interview, 6 January 2000.

[18] Jerry Houlihan, personal communication, 26 October 2000.

[19] Eugene Corcoran, personal communication, 26 October 2000.

[20] Alan Onions, op. cit.

[21] Michael Drummey, personal interview, 6 January 2000.

[22] Michael Griffin, op. cit.

[23] Michael Griffin, op. cit.

Chapter 9

The "Big Deal" —
The Acquisition of Beatreme

May you live in interesting times.
(An ancient Chinese curse)

Beatrice's "Secret Division"

In his company history of Beatrice Foods, Neil Gazel wrote:

> Although its name never appears on a label, package,
> bottle, jar, or cap, at least one product from the "secret di-
> vision" of Beatrice is consumed each day by every person
> in the United States.[1]

The "secret division" so described was none other than the enterprise later known as Beatreme Food Ingredients. Based in Beloit,
Wisconsin, Beatreme was founded in 1906 as the city's first bottled
milk plant, under the name of the Surtevant, Wright and Wagner
Dairy Company. It merged with Beatrice Foods, eventually to become one of the leading food companies in the United States, in
1930. During the mid-1940s, Beatreme (known then as the Beatrice
Special Products Division) recognised a market need for powdered shortenings for the newly emerging cake mix business. It
was able to provide these products through utilising spray-drying
equipment that it had used to produce milk powder for the army
during the Second World War. After being spray-dried, these

shortenings had the characteristics of being "high-fat, free-flowing powders, which could easily be blended with flour, sugar, leavening agents, colours and flavours to obtain homogenous mixes with reduced mixing time".[2] By encapsulating the fat (shortening) and drying it into a powdered form, the fat would not leak into the cake mix boxes. The success of these new cake mixes that only need be combined with water was perhaps a leading indicator of the explosive growth of the convenience foods industry that was to sweep the United States in the 1950s and 1960s. Thanks to its technological capabilities, Beatreme found itself well positioned to ride the crest of this emerging market segment.

In pioneering the application of spray dehydration technology to these particularly hard-to-handle food ingredients, Beatreme effectively invented a new industry, that of specialty food ingredients. Over time, Beatreme expanded the range of products that could be spray-dried and rendered free-flowing and generally easier to process. Such dehydrated, processed ingredients also tended to have much longer shelf lives. Gazel notes that:

> The food industry found these powdered products attractive for a number of reasons. The advantages are that they are powdered, siftable, nongreasy, and free-flowing; mixing is faster; high-speed packaging is implemented; the fat content of the mix can be increased and the mix is still flowable; the powders need no tempering; and waste and clear-up times are reduced.[3]

Given such a range of attractive characteristics, it is easy to see how the speciality food ingredients industry was born.

Beatreme also began to spray-dry dairy and cheese products, expanding into dehydrated sour cream and butter. One particularly successful application of this technology was in the provision of powdered cheese for macaroni and cheese mixes. Other dehydrated specialty food ingredients, all of them focused upon satisfying very specific food needs, were to follow. Powdered shortenings, emulsifiers, dairy ingredients, cheese, sour cream, yoghurt, butter, margarine, flavouring ingredients, and fruit and cheese nuggets were just a few of the almost 600 food ingredients Beatreme was supplying to the food industry by the mid-1980s.

During this time, Beatreme remained a very small, but highly profitable, part of the huge and ever-expanding empire of Beatrice Foods. By 1985, sales revenues had reached approximately $93 million and net profits were typically in the range of 10–15 per cent. Beatrice itself had grown to become a huge conglomerate and one of the leading food companies in the United States, with sales of $12.6 billion and net profit of $479 million by 1984. Beatrice's philosophy had been one of decentralisation, and the management of Beatreme had generally been left alone to run the business relatively unhindered by corporate level interference. During the mid-1970s, Dell Food Specialties, a seasonings business also located in Beloit, was added to the Beatreme operation. Mixing, blending, and packaging equipment was added, and a new research and development centre was commissioned in 1983. Spray-drying plants in Covington, Ohio and Vesper, Wisconsin were also added to Beatreme, as Beatrice itself reorganised its operations into various business groupings in 1982–83. Thus, while other Beatrice businesses were being divested or incorporated into new business groupings, the operation in Beloit benefited from consolidation of some of the firm's specialty food activities.

Beatreme's inventive utilisation of spray-drying technology provided a new tool for the food industry to combine flavours, seasonings, colours, and textures for new easy-to-mix convenience foods that could be produced and stored efficiently and economically. Ingredients that had heretofore been very difficult to handle and process, had become, by virtue of being spray-dried, far easier to process, and could be combined in unique and creative ways to provide characteristics to fill very specific needs. Reaping the advantages of being the "first mover" in this new and growing industry, Beatreme was by the 1980s perhaps the largest spray-dryer in the world, and certainly the premier specialty food ingredients company in the United States. Importantly, it was also acknowledged to have some of the finest food technologists in the business and was often the first in the field with new innovations in food technology. In many ways, the distinct advantage that Beatreme possessed over its competitors resided in the competence and knowledge of its people, rather than in the quality of its equipment and facilities.

One other particular advantage that Beatreme had was the stellar, "blue-chip" quality of its customer base. Its customers included General Foods, General Mills, Kraft, Procter & Gamble, Borden's, Pillsbury, Hunt-Wesson and virtually every food company of any size in the US marketplace. This is incredibly important when one considers the lengthy period of time it takes to grow customer relationships, to develop products to meet specific customer needs, to foster trust in one's reliability and dependability as a supplier, and ultimately to begin supplying a product. Since most specialty food ingredients were, by definition, *specific* to the application needs of a *specific* customer for a *specific* product, once a food ingredient was specified in the formulation of a product it was very difficult to change. There were very high "switching costs" in moving from one supplier to another. In this industry, supplier–customer relationships were close, stable, and enduring. Absolute trust and utter reliability were highly critical elements of such relationships. On the other side of the equation, one of Beatreme's suppliers was Kerry Group, who had been supplying them with casein for use in shortening powders for spray-drying since the early 1980s. In comparing Beatreme and Kerry at the time, a distinct contrast is apparent. One may consider the specialty food ingredients industry as a pyramid. Beatreme's business was at the top, or apex, with more sophisticated, engineered, value-added ingredients (flavours, coatings, colours) that commanded healthy margins. At the base were the more commodity-like products (starches, oils, sweeteners, butter, and proteins). Clearly, Kerry was operating in the low-margin zone of this added-value pyramid, trying to climb the value-chain ladder. Given the embeddedness and durability of supplier/customer relationships, however, it was a very slow process.

Jack Warner had joined Beatrice in 1969 with a degree in food science and technology, and had been sent to Beloit expecting to spend a year or two there. His tenure, unexpectedly, lasted far longer than that, and in 1983 Warner was named President of Beatreme, succeeding Carl Obenauf. One of his closest associates at Beatreme was Bob Kasik, the Vice-President of Research and Technical Services. Kasik had joined Beatrice in 1967 in Research and Development, and had had a wide experience working in various functions throughout the Beatrice organisation. In particular, he had done pioneering work on formulated cheese and cheese flavours. Both were aware of Kerry Group as a supplier of casein, and had been over to the Listowel factory in connection with that relationship. They also knew, by 1983 or so, that Kerry had a keen interest in entering the North American market, and in the ensuing three to four years, that Kerry had its eye on buying Beatreme. It was also clear that Kerry was pulling out all the stops to learn what it could about the technology, the applications, and the customers in the food ingredients industry. But there was, understandably, scant interest at Beatreme's end in helping Kerry. Kasik remembers visiting Kerry's plant in Listowel in 1985, and being repeatedly asked in a variety of ways about certain of Beatreme's manufacturing processes. Kasik's basic reply at that time was, "I know, and you don't."[4] After all, the Beatreme business was growing reasonably well, and continuing to move "up market" to ever more specific, high-tech applications that provided far better margins than the more generic commodity ingredients. In general, things looked good. The same, however, could not be said of the situation at the parent company, for Beatrice itself was about to come apart at the seams.

The Break-up of Beatrice

Over the course of a history spanning more than nine decades, Beatrice Foods had grown to the status of a giant in the food industry by 1985. Ranked number 26 in the *Fortune 500*, Beatrice fielded dominant brands in a wide variety of industries, including yoghurt (Dannon), orange juice (Tropicana), canned and frozen Chinese food (LaChoy), water softening equipment and supplies (Culligan), rental cars (Avis), luggage (Samsonite), and many others. Through the years, it had grown through a combination of internal growth and development and selective acquisition of profitable companies in rapid growth segments. Its management philosophy for much of that time was characterised as "management by a feather";[5] operations were typically decentralised and operating units had considerable scope for decision-making as long as profit targets were met. "Hands-off at the top, and hands-on at the plant level" was the slogan, and one that had appeared to stand the enterprise in good stead for many years.[6] With the accession of James Dutt to Chief Executive in 1979, however, the philosophy of decentralisation was about to be consigned to the ash heap of history. By 1985, time was running out for Beatrice. George Baker and George Smith, in their excellent analysis of the KKR acquisitions of the 1980s and 1990s, are quite direct in their appraisal of Beatrice in 1985:

> The century-old diversified food, consumer, and industrial goods conglomerate had grown far beyond its original dairy business, largely through a series of well-executed small-company acquisitions beginning in the early 1950s. In 1975, *Dun's Review* named Beatrice one of the five best-managed corporations in America. A decade later it was a mess. Following the retirement of the architect of its diversification strategy in 1976, a series of boardroom brawls, along with a disastrous change in strategy, significantly weakened the performance and reputation of Beatrice. In 1979, a new CEO, James Dutt, went on an acquisition binge, buying large public companies for which the "fit" was dubious. The ill effects of his misconceived strategy were exacerbated by inappropriate organization. Attempts to centralize administration set the scene for a disastrous attempt to centralize marketing programs, as well.[7]

This attempt to reposition Beatrice into a more marketing-driven, centralised and focused operation resulted in the divestiture of many businesses, the consolidation of others, and the acquisition of still others. Beatrice embarked upon a huge advertising campaign, showcased in the coverage of the 1984 Summer Olympics in Los Angeles, aimed at creating a new corporate identity and displaying prominently the various companies that shared the "Beatrice umbrella". Such an investment was expensive, with more than $30 million spent on advertising at the Olympics alone.[8] Dutt himself grew increasingly autocratic and remote. The management style brought in by Dutt resulted in the departure of more than a few senior managers, and morale at the headquarters was low. An *Industry Week* article about Dutt in 1984 presents this new management style well:

> A framed cartoon behind his desk in Chicago illustrates his new management style. It shows the head of a com-

pany at a table flanked by his management team. The caption reads "All of those opposed signify by saying, I quit."[9]

Beatrice, well run for so long, now seemed a company without a vision.

Yet Beatrice, as an operating organisation, was by no means in dire straits. Although it had its share of operating issues, it remained a strong and profitable company. Rather, it was in the high stakes world of the boardroom, of mergers and acquisitions, of corporate raiders and "white knights", of LBOs (leveraged buyouts) and junk bonds, and ultimately in a very personal game of power and ego that Beatrice was ultimately lost.

The decade of the 1980s had spawned a boom in mergers and acquisitions, fuelled in large measure by a relatively new financial innovation, that of the leveraged buyout, or LBO. In an LBO, a well-established, stable, cash-generating company would be bought out and taken private by investors who might, or might not, include company management. Such buyouts would be financed largely by debt (hence the "leveraged" buyout), usually through the issuance of high yielding "junk bonds". Naturally, the quality of the assets and the reputation of the investors would determine the risk of a default on the bonds, and the yield that would have to be paid to compensate bond holders for the perceived risk. The beauty of this technique, to investors at least, was the fact that it was done using, literally, other people's money. The bondholders would supply the cash for the purchase, while the company's new owners would use the cash flow from operations to service the heavy debt load. It was to be expected that investors would take steps to increase efficiency and cash flow very quickly through programmes of rationalisation and restructuring. In the meantime, the company would often be dismantled, with various units sold off to the highest bidders and the proceeds used to retire the debt. If successful, the investors would be left with the debt liquidated and sufficient remaining assets to either sell off when the opportunity arose or to operate for a continuing return. Of course, this was only possible in cases where the "break-up" value of the firm's individual pieces was higher than the market price for the firm's stock.

LBOs, however, did not enjoy a particularly positive reputation with employees, the media, and the public at large. In the drive for increased efficiency and improved cash flow, many workers were made redundant, facilities closed, capital investments reduced, and over-funded employee pension plans raided. Nor were management of target companies particularly pleased (unless they themselves were investors), as the prospect of a restructured organisation often meant a wholesale clearing of the executive suite. It could not have been a pleasant prospect for Beatrice, long a firm noted for its own successful acquisitions, to find itself on a "short list" of target companies that might be bought and "broken up" at some considerable profit.

In July 1983, Esmark Inc., a conglomerate with significant interests in the food industry, bought out Norton Simon Inc. for $1.02 billion, prevailing over an offer made by the investment firm of Kohlberg, Kravis, Roberts & Co. (KKR). Led by its chairman Donald P. Kelly, and like Beatrice based in Chicago, Esmark was enjoying a dizzying rate of growth. It had also taken a position in Beatrice stock, a move that apparently disturbed Beatrice's CEO, James Dutt. Beatrice bought back the shares at a slight premium. Later, in May 1984, Kelly crafted a deal whereby he and KKR would jointly take Esmark private, but Dutt had other ideas. Within a few weeks of the Kelly/KKR offer, Dutt brought Beatrice to the table and outbid them for Esmark, paying a considerable premium over its market price. The previous Beatrice CEO, William Karnes, had advised Dutt to stay away from Esmark, because "it is too big, the debt will be too big, the company has too many commodity items . . .".[10] Nevertheless, Beatrice now had to digest Esmark, as well as manage a huge burden of long-term debt totalling some $4.5 billion carrying interest rates of from 12–14 per cent.[11] In the meantime, Dutt had immediately fired Kelly and his management team at Esmark in a manner that clearly left bad blood. (Employees told stories, real or apocryphal, of how Kelly was "frog marched" out of the building.) Dutt began a program of divestiture and consolidation, but the Esmark purchase began to literally sink the Beatrice operation. Earnings were down, the share price flat, senior executives were leaving in droves, morale was abysmal, and the financial community and media were increasingly critical. An editorial in Crain's *Chicago Business* summarised "Jim Dutt's Sorry Record" and suggested that:

> Mounting evidence over the past months leads us to conclude that Mr Dutt, driven by a private vision and an unexplainable impatience, is on his way to ruining an important Chicago company. Indeed, the evidence of adversity has become so compelling that one already can question whether outside directors have effectively exercised their oversight responsibilities.[12]

By August of 1985, Dutt was gone, but Beatrice was out of time.

In October 1985, Don Kelly partnered with KKR again, this time with an offer to purchase Beatrice. By April 1986 it was all over, and Kelly and KKR had taken Beatrice (now called BCI Holdings) private in a leveraged buyout for $6.2 billion, the largest such deal in American financial history at the time. Kelly took over as Chairman at Beatrice, bringing back with him many of the other top Esmark executives who had been deposed by Dutt. In succeeding months, BCI staged one of the largest corporate sell-offs in history, divesting itself of companies, shedding overhead and decentralising operations again. In May 1987, BCI spun out the remains of Beatrice into two parts, and Kelly took 14 Beatrice companies in the "Specialty Foods" Division and the "Consumer Durable Goods" Division (including such well-known products as Stiffel lamps, Culligan water treating systems and Samsonite luggage) to form a new holding company, E-II Holdings, Inc. (It is said that Kelly tried almost everything to get the Esmark name back, but he couldn't, so E-II had to suffice.) Strangely enough, buried in the E-II operations along with all the "non-food" businesses was Beatreme Food Ingredients.

Kelly fully intended to push forward with E-II as an investment vehicle, making plans and lining up funding for an acquisition spree. Events, however, took a surprising turn. E-II made a try at acquiring the giant American Brands in late 1987, accumulating 6.4 per cent of its outstanding shares at one point. American Brands, a diversified tobacco and food concern, then responded with the first successful use of the so-called "Pac Man" defense (taken from a video game where you must gobble up your opponent before he gobbles you up) by acquiring E-II for $1.2 billion in February 1988. Kelly had kept E-II for less than a year. American Brands immediately made plans to sell off the former Beatrice specialty food businesses, one of which was Beatreme Food Ingredients. Once again, Beatreme was "on the market", but as part of a package of specialty food businesses.

By this time, Beatreme had experienced four distinct sets of owners in less than three years (Beatrice, KKR, E-II and American Brands), although surprisingly the rapid changes in ownership structure had not appreciably trickled down to day-to-day operations. At least the business was holding its own, with annual sales growth of approximately 6 per cent over the 1985–88 period. Given the dynamic nature of the industry, however, real growth should and could have been far higher. But with the exception of some capital provided by E-II for the installation of a new dryer, there was little capital available for growth. Except for Jack Warner and his staff, however, the impact of this probably did not percolate down to the entire workforce, except to create a general sense of uncertainty. After all, a steady succession of owners with scant interest in operating the business and a planning horizon of months rather than years was not likely to inspire confidence.

At about this time, in Spring 1988, Warner, Kasik and some others in the Beatreme management group investigated doing a management buyout themselves, going so far as to get support from local banks who were anxious to try it. The management group itself, however, had far more of an operating than a financial orientation, and felt it lacked the necessary financial sophistication to pull off such a venture. It seemed to them a high-risk proposition and nothing ever came of it.[13] Nor was Kerry Group entirely out of the picture. Despite having set themselves up in competition with Beatreme with the new facility in Jackson, Brosnan and O'Driscoll were regular callers to Beloit, making clear their continuing interest in buying Beatreme. The trouble was, with all the changes of ownership, Kerry could not seem to "get at" Beatreme.

The Pursuit of Beatreme

Since initially targeting it in 1983, Kerry's pursuit of Beatreme was characterised by rejection, frustration, perseverance, and ultimately some measure of luck. But Kerry's stalking of Beatreme had also been relentless. A number of approaches had been made, going back as far as 1985, but had been rebuffed. Even Carl Obenauf, the recently retired president of Beatreme who had been engaged to approach Beatrice and Don Kelly on behalf of Kerry, was unable to generate any positive response. At this point, Obenauf was liasing closely with Michael Ryan, the Financial Controller back in Tralee, and Finbarr O'Driscoll. Nevertheless, Beatreme remained at the top of Kerry's list. Given Kerry's critical need to break into the ingredients market in the States, Beatreme offered the best vehicle to achieve it. Yet, like a lover condemned "to woo, but never win", Kerry's pursuit of Beatreme seemed that it would go unfulfilled. But similarly, the more inaccessible Beatreme seemed, the more desirable it became!

Already, by the beginning of 1988, the Beatreme purchase had been studied ad nauseam at Kerry headquarters in Tralee, using all the information that could be gleaned from various formal and informal sources. For its part, Kerry's Board of Directors had been fully convinced. Even during the public flotation of Kerry Group in 1986, discussions of the acquisition of a company much like Beatreme had surfaced. There was little uncertainty that Beatreme was "the one", for the merits of an acquisition seemed clear:

- It was the leading firm (approximate 12 per cent market share) in the relatively fast-growing food ingredients industry (a sector characterised by high barriers to entry) in the largest market in the world.

- Its product line was the most extensive, and its R&D function the largest in the industry. New products represented a growing percentage of their sales and profits.

- Its customer base was extensive, including *all* leading US food companies, and remarkably loyal.

- Compared to Kerry Group, its margins (approximately 10 per cent net profit on sales) were appreciably higher.

- Kerry saw opportunities to improve Beatreme's performance through better marketing, operational efficiencies, and integration with other Kerry operations. Kerry had no doubt whatsoever that they could further grow and develop the business.

The only real question marks were 1) Would Beatreme ever become available, and 2) If so, at what price?

During Beatreme's days as part of Beatrice, it was simply not for
sale. When Kelly and E-II took over Beatreme in May 1987, they
were less interested in selling, and more interested in going on the
acquisition trail themselves. Jack Warner remembers the plans
being made to become "another Beatrice" through such acquisitions.[14] Again, Beatreme was simply inaccessible. But with American Brands' purchase of E-II in January 1988, there finally seemed
to be an opening. American Brands had no interest in retaining
most of the 14 former Beatrice businesses it had bought with E-II,
particularly the specialty food businesses, since they had only recently exited the food business themselves to concentrate on tobacco, liquor, financial services and home and office supplies. Michael Ryan quickly contacted Dick Lauder, Development Manager
for American Brands, and outlined Kerry's serious interest in Beatreme. In response, American Brands had "good news" and "bad
news". The good news was that, yes, they would be happy to sell
Beatreme to Kerry. The bad news was that they would only sell it to
Kerry as part of a 14-company "bundle" of all the E-II companies,
for a price tag of $950 million. Needless to say, this was not on. The
market capitalisation (total market value of all outstanding shares)
of Kerry Group at that time was only approximately $100 million.

Regardless of how outlandish such a purchase may have
seemed, Kerry stayed doggedly on the trail. It discussed with a
number of banks their possible participation in such a transaction,
and continued to negotiate with American Brands to amend their
position. At one point, American Brands relented somewhat by
proposing that they would sell ten of the companies, all food companies, as a package for a price of around $700 million (and
American Brands would then dispose of the other four). This was
only slightly more attractive than the initial proposal, but nevertheless Hugh Friel brought it back to the board of directors for discussion. There is a funny story that is told in connection with this
particular discussion. There was a member of the board of directors who had a habit of saying "that's right", very rapidly and constantly in the course of a typical conversation as a sort of polite response to the speaker. On this occasion, Brosnan was presenting
to the board the American Brands' proposal to sell Kerry the bun-

dle of ten companies, as well as Kerry's desire to buy only Beatreme. In the course of Brosnan's description of the offer to sell all
ten companies, this board member repeated "that's right". Brosnan jokingly said, "What do you mean? Do you mean we should go
for the big one? All ten companies?" The board member, without
missing a beat, responded, "That's right, Denis. Go for the big
one! We might as well bury the handle with the hatchet!" This is
indicative of the sort of support for the purchase of Beatreme that
existed on the board. Kerry, in any event, was in no position to
make such a purchase. Convincing a merchant bank to underwrite
it, at a certain level, was an option that Kerry was willing to explore, but it would have been messy, difficult, and time-
consuming. As another alternative, an "off balance sheet" purchase was discussed with Ned O'Callaghan, Kerry's banker from
the AIB, whereby a new company would be set up for the purchase, owned 45 per cent by AIB, 45 per cent by an investment
house, and the remaining 10 per cent by another investor. Although this may have been one mechanism for Kerry to get at
Beatreme without taking on an inordinate amount of debt (it was
already highly leveraged), it quickly collapsed. Such an investment would have run afoul of US securities laws. In any event,
events were moving far too quickly for any of this.

American Brands brought in Morgan Stanley to sell the bundle
of businesses, and by May 1988 they were actively shopping the
business around. Jack Warner remembered that the process of
putting the company on the auction block was surprisingly "black
and white". Morgan Stanley came to him with an inventory of
questions about sales, market share, customers and profits that
were duly answered, tallied, and put into the equation. The business was going to be sold "by the numbers". Already Burns Philp,
an Australian food ingredient company, and the New Zealand Co-
operative had both expressed interest in making a bid. Kerry was
not the only company that saw the possibilities in Beatreme.

In late May, Brosnan, Friel, and Ned O'Callaghan from AIB travelled to the States to meet informally with Jack Warner and take a
look at the plant in Beloit, albeit from a distance. O'Callaghan recounted this experience:

> The 23rd of May was a ferociously hot day. Denis, Hugh
> and myself sat in a car on a rail siding looking at the fac-
> tory in Beloit. We couldn't go in; we did not have access at
> that point. But it wasn't the most prepossessing factory
> you ever saw.[15]

There is something almost metaphoric about this description of
gazing at an old factory from afar, but certainly by this time Brosnan, Friel and Kerry's top managers in America already knew a
fair amount about Beatreme. But would they ever get to use it? In
the middle of June, opportunity at long last knocked.

On 13 June, Michael Ryan received a call from Morgan Stanley
informing him that American Brands had sold the bundle of companies that was E-II to the privately held Riklis Family Corporation
(controlled by private investor Meshulam Riklis). Ryan immediately
began efforts to contact Paul Weiner, the CFO for Riklis, but to no
avail. He followed up with a letter outlining Kerry's very serious
interest in acquiring Beatreme, but there was no response. Finally,
on 1 July, Ryan succeeded in catching up with Weiner, who told him
the acquisition was not yet complete, but that he (Ryan) should
follow-up with him in thirty days. Meanwhile, Denis Brosnan wrote
to Ed Gustafson, who had been Kelly's right hand man at E-II and
was well known to Jack Warner, outlining Kerry's interest. Finally,
on Friday, 22 July, an appointment was arranged to meet with Riklis
on Monday morning, 25 July. The combined efforts of Michael Ryan
and so many other Kerry managers had at last yielded the opportunity Kerry had sought for so long.

Brosnan and Friel wasted no time. By Sunday, they were on an
aeroplane to New York. After breakfast on Monday with Steve
Green, who functioned as a right-hand man/partner in the Riklis
enterprise, they were picked up by Meshulam Riklis and brought
to his office at the Trump Tower. Riklis was very clear. He had no
interest in running the business; he was after cash. Riklis himself
said that he had no information about Beatreme, repeating that
"you guys probably have more information on it than I have".[16] He
didn't put a price on it, but gave Brosnan and Friel the rest of the
week to go out to Wisconsin, look over the facilities, talk to the
management, inspect the books, and come back with an offer on
Friday. To add a sense of urgency, Riklis also threatened to bring in

Shearson-Lehman to put together an option to sell the various parts. So time was of the essence but, for the moment, Kerry held the inside track. Other potential suitors had yet to react.

Brosnan and Friel were greeted by Jack Warner on their arrival in Beloit, and began a very quick study. It is probably fair to suggest that Kerry may have been considered a "white knight" by this point. Having gone through a succession of owners, and on the selling block again, Beatreme management was generally eager for some sense of stability. It seemed far preferable to be a large and important division of a relatively small company that had ambitious plans for growth in food ingredients than to be lost as a relatively small, "secret" division of another big, diversified conglomerate. As Brosnan and Friel went about their task, they did so with the help of allies and friends, rather than having to contend with the reluctance of a competitor. They had complete access to all the numbers and documents. Since they also had to see the facilities in Covington, Ohio and Vesper, Wisconsin they piled into Bob Kasik's GMC Suburban (what might be called a "van" in Ireland) and drove there, discussing the business and running their numbers as they trundled along the highways of the midwest. It was an unorthodox way of getting around, but it served the purpose. They had only a few days to work things out. Actually, the production facilities were not at all impressive, but that merely confirmed what they had already been told. Kerry unquestionably still wanted Beatreme, warts and all. At least, they could tell the bankers that they had been out to inspect the assets.

Back in Ireland, Ned O'Callaghan at AIB knew that Brosnan and Friel were in America to negotiate with Riklis. This was all highly confidential at the time, but O'Callaghan, as the principal banker, was asked to be ready to travel back to the States, depending on how things went with Riklis. O'Callaghan recalled that:

> I got a phone call from Michael Ryan (the Group Financial Controller), and I remember it quite well. Denis and Hugh had been allowed in to see the plants, and Michael said, "the smoke signals are strong". I remember that phrase. It meant I'd soon be going to America again.[17]

Beatreme had sales of $110 million in the fiscal year 1988, with operating income of around $10.9 million. Income for 1989 was projected to be lower due to some non-recurring expenses, but generally Beatreme could be counted on for $11–12 million in operating income. (Table 7 includes sales and profit information for 1984–1988.)

Table 6: Beatreme Financial Data, 1984–1988

	1984 ($ Mil)	1985 ($ Mil)	1986 ($ Mil)	1987 ($ Mil)	1988 ($ Mil)
Sales	$85.3	$92.0	$96.0	$103.6	$110.0
Trading Profit	7.3	7.7	10.1	11.5	10.9

Before returning to New York, Brosnan and Friel met with Ed Gustafson, Jack Warner's direct boss who was still heading the E-II companies. In evaluating the price for the company, Brosnan and Jack Warner had agreed that it was worth $100 million, comfortably, and probably more. Riklis would want significantly more. With operating income of around $11–12 million, and interest rates that averaged 11–12 per cent at the time, it seemed the newly acquired business could support something less than $120 million in debt. A lot hinged on how much, and how quickly, Kerry would be able to grow Beatreme's profits. The other major question at this point was, how much money did Riklis want to part with Beatreme? Jack Warner remembers the meeting in a conference room at the divisional headquarters in Beloit:

> Denis said he could do $120 million, and I think Ed [Gustafson] said, "That might get it or it might not, but if you can do $130 million, I can pretty much guarantee that you've got a deal". So Denis said, "okay". Basically, we reached agreement on the number here in Beloit. It was a gentleman's agreement. Later on, you'd go back and evaluate the numbers and perform your due diligence.[18]

The $130 million was tight, but it was "doable", particularly if Kerry could grow and develop the business, as it believed it could. Brosnan and Friel returned to New York on Friday, and met with Riklis. Riklis had a very high profile in the financial community as a sharp character with a penchant for bold actions; he was unquestionably shrewd. In this instance, he called Kerry's bluff: Kerry could agree to a price of $130 million now and they would have a deal, or they could hold out for a lower price and see what happened. Of course, Brosnan and Friel knew that Beatreme had other suitors who, given time, were likely to respond with some sort of an offer. Brosnan and Friel could think about it overnight, but Riklis wanted an answer the next morning. Brosnan remembers that:

> There were Hugh Friel and myself walking the streets of Manhattan, trying to decide on our own whether to go with it. It couldn't be justified purely on the historical numbers! If it were up to the financial guys, they'd have said "no way".[19]

One consideration was that the net asset value of Beatreme was in the area of $37–38 million, meaning that Kerry would be paying nearly $92 million in goodwill. This would likely be considered by the financial community in Ireland to be a huge premium, and Brosnan and Friel would still have to return to Ireland and arrange the finance. Of course, such a reaction would be based on a response to the historical numbers; the sense at Kerry was that they could improve those same numbers rapidly, and substantially. They were willing to bet on it. The next morning they met with Riklis and agreed to buy Beatreme for $130 million. Riklis asked, "Do you have the money?" and Brosnan replied, "We'll get it." Brosnan wanted to put something in writing concerning the terms of the agreement, but Riklis said "Nah, it's all right", and they shook hands. "My word is my bond," said Riklis.[20] Although Brosnan and Friel didn't know it at the time, Riklis apparently had a well-known aversion to signing things.

There is a story, probably apocryphal but now part of the Kerry mythology, about Brosnan and Friel coming down in the elevator of the Trump Tower having just shaken hands on the deal. Friel turned to Brosnan and said, "You know, we don't have the money", and Brosnan replied, "We'll get it; the farmers of Kerry won't let us down!" Farmer support, however, was not the issue. It was the support of the bankers, in the very tangible form of loans, that was critical. Although the support of the farmer-shareholders was always important, the more pragmatic and immediate question was whether the banks would support the purchase. The $130 million price tag for Beatreme exceeded the entire market capitalisation of Kerry Group, and the premium of over $90 million paid for it could be considered by generally conservative lenders to be excessive.

The purchase of Beatreme was a huge risk in the sense that it was literally a make-or-break bet, a huge raising of the ante. The future of the Kerry organisation would be quite literally on the line. For better or worse, it would be yet another turning point in the history of the Kerry Group. But the risk was a "responsible risk"; the bid for Beatreme was the end result of years of planning, study, and analysis. Kerry knew what they were getting, and what they wanted to do with the acquisition. They had a high level of confidence in their ability to execute their plans for Beatreme. To an outside analyst, it might appear a gamble, but to insiders at Kerry it was anything but a gamble. It would be misleading to use such terms as "sure thing" or "can't miss", but in the greater scheme of things, Kerry felt they were getting a clear winner. Part of the challenge for Kerry, however, was that not only would they have to make this acquisition work in the long term, but they'd have to show significantly improved short-term returns as well. The debt burden created by the purchase would be heavy, and would have to be serviced by Beatreme's profits, or the entire Kerry Group financial performance would be in jeopardy. Quite simply, the Beatreme acquisition would have to work fast; it could not take anything like the toll, or the time, that the Denny's acquisition had taken some years before.

Brosnan and Friel returned to Ireland with a handshake agreement but nothing on paper. They had to set in motion the due diligence process and line up the finance for the transaction.[21] Riklis had made it clear that he didn't want this transaction to drag on forever. At this point, the pending deal would remain strictly confidential, but due to the size of the transaction, shareholder approval would be required before closing the deal. Time was of the essence, since other suitors were clearly interested in buying Beatreme; Kerry's big advantage was that they had got there first. The major fear in Tralee was that someone else would nip in to buy the business, stealing it away from Kerry. After all, the only agreement was a handshake.

Clearly, the Board of Directors supported the acquisition and accepted management's assurances that the numbers were "there". After all, this was the key element of the group's strategy to become a substantial international food organisation and represented the bold step that had been discussed for many years. There may have been a few raised eyebrows at the size and cost of the deal, but there was utter confidence in management's judgement of its merits. Similarly, the shareholders would clearly support it, particularly since Kerry Co-op (represented by the same men who sat on the Board of Directors of the plc) still held 67 per cent of the share capital in the Kerry Group and would vote in favour. Aside from the possibility of another suitor stepping in to complicate matters, the most critical factor in closing the deal would be getting the finance. Despite Kerry's strong track record, the support of its banks for an acquisition of this size could not be taken for granted.

Closing the Beatreme Deal

AIB (Allied Irish Banks) had inherited a reputation as a "co-op bank" from one of its three constituent banks (The Munster and Leinster Bank) and had made it a point to aggressively pursue business in the co-operative and agricultural sectors. Its relationship with Kerry began with the provision of a loan facility of £2.85 million to the new Kerry Co-op in 1974, when P.J. McGrath, the regional manager for Munster, took a personal interest in the efforts of the Kerry management to build this new co-operative organisation. In the context of the times, £1.7 million had been a substantial sum, and it had been vital to getting the co-operative up and running. The relationship had matured over time, and had proven to be a good one for both Kerry and AIB. In fact, for years afterward when P.J. McGrath would visit Ted Sheehan, AIB's branch manager in Listowel, he'd always ask, "How are 'my boys' doing?"[22] But such confidence had not been built on goodwill alone. Ned O'Callaghan remembered his first encounter with the Kerry Co-op, sometime in 1974:

I was sent off down the country one day to a co-operative
(not the Kerry Co-op) that was about to build a new facility. I met with them, and reported back to the Regional
General Manager, P. J. McGrath, who was the bank's most
respected and informed authority on agribusiness. He
said to me, "Show me the figures." He then went over to
the filing cabinet, took out a couple of files, and said,
"These are files from a couple of young fellows below in
Kerry who are starting a facility in Listowel. If your figures
are better than theirs are, they're worthless. If your figures
are as good as theirs are, you're exaggerating. If your figures are a little bit behind them, they are very good![23]

O'Callaghan, who himself had been assigned to the agribusiness
side of the bank in 1976, had stayed with the Kerry account since
that time. Typically, he'd meet with Kerry management twice a
year — in the spring to review the loan facilities in place for the
year and the prior year's results, and again in the autumn to touch
base. Such meetings would be reported to the bank's board, as a
matter of course. Year after year, O'Callaghan remembered adding a comment to the effect that "these clients have never made a
commitment that they did not honour in full".[24] Over the years, the
facilities provided had grown significantly to about £40 million and
the bank had participated as a banker in most of Kerry's major initiatives. This included serving as guarantor to the state of Wisconsin for an industrial revenue bond used to fund the purchase of the
Jackson, Wisconsin manufacturing facility. Now AIB was to serve as
the lead bank in the financing of the acquisition, and Ned
O'Callaghan, always a strong supporter of Kerry, was to play a
prime role in putting together the loan package. In that capacity,
he travelled to the States again in August to look at the assets, get
comfortable with the proposed acquisition, and gather information
to make a presentation to the AIB board on the merits of the deal.
Given the relative size of the purchase in an Irish context, the fact
that it was an ocean apart from Ireland, and in a very unfamiliar,
even unknown, industry, it would have to be a very thorough and
persuasive presentation indeed. O'Callaghan remembers:

On the first of August, I was off to America again. I went in
with Stan McCarthy to see the plant in Beloit. It was an-

other blistering hot day. It was a small plant, compared to the massive processing operation in Listowel. I remember Stan said to me standing outside in the yard, "There's nothing in there, only people." We agreed on that, and only wondered, "Are they good people?"[25]

His next stop was Jackson, to meet with Finbarr O'Driscoll:

I remember going in to Finbarr, who was sitting in this massive leather chair, the monarch of all he surveyed. He leaned back and said something like, "So, you are going to give us the money to buy this place!" I said something evasive like, "Well, I don't know, we'll see." "You'll have to do it," he said. "We'll never get anywhere in this bloody place if you don't." He told me his experience was that it took five years between identifying a customer and maybe eventually getting some business. If they had Beatreme, it would be a great leap forward, because Beatreme had a lot of captive customers. They had no doubt they could develop and expand the business.[26]

O'Callaghan carried on to visit several of the other facilities, none of which were particularly impressive in themselves. It was becoming clear to him that it was not the physical plant that was important; the fixed assets provided little clue as to the value of the business. Rather, it was in the capability of the people — particularly the accumulated know-how of their technical and product development people, and the quality of their existing customer base — that the true value of Beatreme resided. Kerry felt that they had the keys to unlock these capabilities and move this business forward very quickly. With his knowledge of the Kerry track record back home, and his own confidence in the ability of Kerry's management to deliver on its promises, O'Callaghan was growing more and more comfortable with the acquisition. He set about gathering all the data he could muster, and not just the usual financial data concerning the business. He brought back to Dublin photographs of the plants, various product samples and promotional materials to help him explain this new and alien business to the AIB board, and bits and pieces about the history of Beloit and of the factory itself. He did not omit the fact that, like Kerry, Beatreme had begun in the milk business as well. Professional valuations of the property were solicited, and even second opinions were sought (even though Kerry couldn't understand the logic of what seemed to them duplication). In addition, Kerry's legal advisors for the deal were one of the best law firms in Chicago, Mayer, Brown & Platt, while AIB were represented by a New York law firm. Although Kerry's managers were often exasperated by their meticulous approach and apparently glacial pace, they were a well-regarded firm with whom the banks were comfortable. Once these attorneys gave their blessing to the loan agreement, the board of AIB were satisfied that all the critically important legal safeguards relating to the transaction had been properly addressed. Armed with all this, O'Callaghan brought the proposal to the executive board of AIB, who approved a loan of $35 million over and above the existing loan facilities of approximately £40 million provided to Kerry. This brought the bank's total exposure to the Kerry Group to about £65 million which, at the time, was certainly one of the largest such loan facilities ever provided by the bank to any commercial company in Ireland.

The financing package assembled for the acquisition totalled approximately $125 million. AIB provided $35 million, Ulster Bank Ltd. provided $30 million, the Bank of Ireland and ABN (Algemene Bank Nederland) Ltd. provided $20 million each, and the £20 million of equity raised in September 1988 rounded out the package. The deal was closed in October in New York, in offices at the World Trade Center. There were a few hiccups in the process of closing, as is quite normal. There were problems with First Bank. Since the loans were put on the balance sheet of Beatreme, there were issues of whether the banks could go after Kerry Group in the event of default, and when. There was a timing issue with the money reaching Ricklis by the promised date and time (a point on which he insisted). Ned O'Callaghan wrote years later that:

> It was a wet and windy evening and the work went on well into the early morning. It was a new experience for us working in a skyscraper building that seemed to groan and grind as it swayed imperceptibly in the wind. Nor was the groaning and grinding confined to the building, as negotiation on the details continued. It was something of a

stormy night in more ways than one. However, more importantly, when the work eventually ended there was no storm damage but a lot of progress. Something had been built rather than blown away.[27]

The details were finally worked out in some satisfactory manner, and the deal closed. Afterwards, everyone went for lunch at Windows on the World, the famous restaurant on the top floor of the World Trade Center. There was no euphoria, but a shared sense of accomplishment. For the bankers, it had been a well-crafted deal, professionally structured and executed. For Brosnan, Friel and the other Kerry managers, it was the beginning of an entirely new phase in the history of the organisation. Friel remembers that:

> It was a very good deal for Kerry. It brought us to a new level. It really was the start of our ingredients business. Prior to that, we were only dreaming about ingredients, but we were actually a million miles away from where we eventually found ourselves.[28]

Interestingly, after the deal was closed, the CFO for Riklis gave Hugh Friel a telephone number and said, "If you want to make $15 million, contact that guy".[29] Apparently, Kerry's fears about someone else outbidding them for Beatreme had not been ungrounded. Subsequent to the agreement with Kerry, Riklis had been offered $15 million more than Kerry for Beatreme. Riklis, however, had remained true to his word, and the handshake agreement held. Whatever risk Brosnan and Friel had taken in so quickly "locking in" the deal with a handshake had already been amply rewarded.

Notes

[1] Neil Gazel (1990), *Beatrice: From Buildup through Breakup*, Urbana and Chicago, Illinois: University of Illinois Press, p. 119.

[2] Carl Obenauf, quoted in Gazel, op. cit., p. 120.

[3] Gazel, op. cit., p. 121.

[4] Bob Kasik, telephone interview, 18 February 2000.

[5] Gazel, op. cit., p. xvi.

[6] Ivan Bull, in his Foreword to Gazel, op. cit.

[7] George P. Baker and George David Smith (1998), *The New Financial Capitalists: Kohlberg Kravis Roberts and the Creation of Corporate Value*, Cambridge: Cambridge University Press, p. 83-84.

[8] Gazel, op. cit., p. 182.

[9] Gazel, op. cit., p. 174, quotation from *Industry Week*, 11 June 1984.

[10] Gazel, op. cit., p. 185.

[11] Gazel, op. cit., p. 187.

[12] Gazel, op. cit., p. 194.

[13] Jack Warner, personal interview, 6 December 1999.

[14] Ibid.

[15] Ned O'Callaghan, personal interview, 8 July 1999.

[16] Hugh Friel, personal interview, 31 May 1999.

[17] Ned O'Callaghan, personal interview, 8 July 1999.

[18] Jack Warner, personal interview, 6 December 1999.

[19] Denis Brosnan, personal interview, 1 June 1999.

[20] Hugh Friel, personal interview, 31 May 1999.

[21] "Due diligence" is the formal process whereby the financial statements and other operating information of the target firm are reviewed, certified and warranted to insure that there has been full and complete disclosure of relevant information. It is not unlike an audit, although it is performed in the service of the buyer and not the target firm. It can often be a relatively time-consuming operation and conceivably can reveal information that would cause the purchaser to return to the bargaining table to renegotiate the purchase price, or even abrogate the transaction.

[22] Ted Sheehan, personal interview, 8 October 1999.

[23] Ned O'Callaghan, personal interview, 8 July 1999.

[24] Ibid

[25] Ibid.

[26] Ibid

[27] Ned O'Callaghan, private communication, 21 June 2000.

[28] Hugh Friel, personal interview, 31 May 1999.

[29] Ibid.

Chapter 10

Building an Ingredients Business

The Melting Pot: Integrating the Beatreme and Kerry Businesses

On 22 October 1988, the day before the deal was finally closed in New York, the Board of Directors of the Kerry Group arrived in Beloit to tour their new acquisition. Actually, the visit had been timed to occur on the *same day* as the closing, but the closing had been delayed by a day. This sort of visit was typical of the Kerry organisation; it had always been important that its farmer-shareholders had a very good idea of precisely *what* they owned. So in a way, the Board members, all Kerry farmers, were the first of the Kerry team to physically show up on Beatreme's doorstep. At a dinner at the Wagon Wheel restaurant near Beloit that night, the Board were toasted as the new owners of Beatreme with Guinness stout and some Irish entertainment, both brought in from Chicago. Jack Warner had had to scramble, as a good host, to bring in something appropriately Irish for them! He needn't have bothered. The Kerrymen disparaged the "stage Irish songs" and preferred to sing their own ballads, which they did into the wee hours of the night. As for the Guinness, most preferred Budweiser. They said that Guinness did not travel well. Nevertheless, it was a very successful evening. Warner's wife Janice sat next to Eddie Hayes and a few other Kerry farmers for most of the evening. She later told her husband that she hadn't understood 10 per cent of what they were saying, but had a marvellous time anyway because of the general enthusiasm.

Certainly, there was good reason for enthusiasm. Kerry had acquired a gem of no little value. In the words of Stan McCarthy:

> The acquisition of Beatreme brought us to a whole new
> level. Beatreme had mastered the technology that we
> were only beginning to touch. They had a serious capa-
> bility in terms of their people. They were the "name" in
> the industry. We at Kerry had been making noises, but
> they had the bite! With this purchase, we immediately
> gained stature in the industry.[1]

The fusion of the two organisations promised additional benefits. Clearly, it brought new life to the Beatreme organisation, and renewed energy to the Kerry organisation in America. The combination of Beatreme's stature and Kerry's desire promised any number of synergies. To get the most out of Beatreme's superior technology and impressive list of customers, Kerry brought with it certain disciplines — for example in accounting and logistics — that could have an immediate impact on the bottom line.

The Kerry team formally came on board in January 1989. Throughout the preceding five years, even as Beatreme had passed through the hands of a succession of owners, the impact of such changes, except at the very highest executive levels, had been scarcely discernible. Commercial life and business went on as before. With the arrival of Kerry, however, the change would be substantive, immediate, and widespread. For Kerry, this was no passive investment. They had literally bet their entire future as an organisation on this purchase, and there was no slack for failure. Unlike Denny's, which had taken years to straighten out, the Beatreme acquisition had to provide a profit in excess of its cost of debt very, very quickly. Of course, unlike Denny's, Beatreme was a profitable business, but Kerry had paid a substantial premium for it and the debt now had to be serviced. At a purchase price of $130 million, at interest rates averaging 12 per cent, Kerry would need a profit of approximately $15–16 million just to break even on its investment. Beatreme's profits in 1988 had been just under $11 million. Clearly, there was a double-tiered challenge: First, the debt would have to be serviced out of the Beatreme business; there was little willingness to let the Beatreme operation be a drag on the overall corporate income statement. Second, Kerry had already promised that it would develop and grow this business well beyond its current boundaries; this would also have to happen before the purchase could be declared a success.

The immediate challenge for 1989 was the integration of the two businesses: Kerry, with its North American sales of approximately $60 million, and Beatreme with its $110 million in sales. The Jackson plant had only come on line in August 1988, and had plenty of idle capacity. Additionally, Beatreme's Vesper (Wisconsin) plant had also just added another dryer, creating even more idle manufacturing capacity. The newly merged operation now had a total of five manufacturing locations: Beloit, Covington, Jackson, Vesper and Dell Seasonings, also in Beloit, and achieving higher capacity utilisation would be an important component in Kerry's drive to be the industry's low-cost producer.

Of course, before the integration could proceed, the organisational structure and staffing issues had to be addressed. Even before the acquisition had been finalised, it had been decided that the headquarters of the newly merged organisation would be in Beloit. Naturally, there was uncertainty and anxiety among the staff of both organisations. After all, both the Kerry Group and Beatreme had functions and managers operating in parallel, and such duplication of responsibility would obviously need to be winnowed away. Still, there was no plan for any wholesale elimination of jobs, or for any systematic purge of the management ranks. The idea was that staffing issues would sort themselves out as the integration plan was put together and the groups began the process of coalescing into one organisation. As a first step, the Kerry expatriates in the US, located in Jackson, relocated to Beloit. With their arrival, staffing issues began to resolve themselves, one way or the other. One of the first to move in was Finbarr O'Driscoll who took over the sales and marketing function after the departure of Beatreme's incumbent vice president of sales. However, most of Beatreme's sales force stayed, while many of Kerry's sales force began to depart. Perhaps in many ways the writing was on the wall: Beatreme's sales team had far more experience, knowledge, and customer relationships than Kerry's relatively inexperienced team had. Since Beatreme's vice president of operations had already departed before Kerry even formally took over, Michael Leahy relocated to Beloit to take over that responsibility. Stan

McCarthy moved to Beloit to take responsibility for the logistics and planning functions. Later in the difficult first year of 1989, the financial controller for Beatreme also left, and Mark Earley, Philip O'Connor, and Margaret Davin, all from Tralee, came on board for varying lengths of time to help sort out the financial picture, with Earley remaining on as the new VP of Finance.

It was indeed fortunate, however, that the acquisition of Beatreme by Kerry had been strongly supported by both Jack Warner and Bob Kasik. The fact that both of these key executives stayed on, not only to help manage the transition but also to play leadership roles in the newly merged organisation as it moved forward, was of no little importance. Amidst the inevitable turmoil and culture clashes that accompany any large acquisition, particularly where there are differences in national as well as organisational culture, their presence inspired some amount of confidence on the part of the Beatreme workforce that the acquisition would indeed work out for the better. Warner, staying on as the president of the newly merged Beatreme Foods Inc., and Kasik continuing as the vice president of research and development, provided the balance and continuity that the organisation needed as it moved into the turbulent waters of integration. Warner's support was clear in a statement released to Beatreme employees on 30 September 1988, a few weeks before the closing of the deal:

> When the Riklis family bought us from American Brands, I had an opportunity to suggest who would be the best candidate to purchase us if they decided to sell. For the good of our business and our personnel, Kerry was the leading choice by far. I have known Denis Brosnan . . . for six years. He is one of Ireland's most dynamic business leaders. . . . Denis has named me President of the newly formed group, and at present, I do not see any major changes in the way we are doing business. The exception is that we need additional sales as fast as possible to fill our new dryers. Beatreme has finally found a home and Irish eyes are smiling![2]

Warner's vote of confidence in the newly merged group was genuine and accurate, but the notion that little would change was perhaps somewhat off the mark! Kerry was a "hands-on" organisation, with a penchant for acquiring businesses somewhat outside their field of expertise, jumping into the deep end and learning about those businesses from the ground up and inside-out, and quickly! They had done it with liquid milk, with Denny's and the pig meat business, with the beef business, and with the consumer foods business in the UK. Now it was time for them to get seriously involved with the evolving specialty food ingredients business. The Damocles' Sword of the debt service obligations for Beatreme's purchase lent a certain sense of urgency to the effort.

Brosnan spent perhaps one week a month, on average, in Beloit during that first year. Aside from his involvement with setting up the management team in Beloit, he was involved with many meetings dealing with virtually every phase of the business. Some meetings focused upon the implementation of the Kerry corporate planning process, while others focused upon shorter-term planning concerned with how the first year's forecast was going to be delivered. He also spent time visiting the plants and the sales force. The monthly planning meetings were not without a certain amount of tension, for in some ways it was a peculiar situation. Beatreme's managers had built the business, knew the industry intimately, had long relationships with a blue-chip list of customers, had developed new products, had systems, and could fall back on a wealth of experience. Yet the Beatreme organisation had its own problems with margin management, pricing, inventory control and overheads. Kerry, as the acquirer, had gambled a huge stake that these problems could be quickly fixed; with their typical terrier-like tenacity, they were prepared to get started, but they hadn't nearly the industry knowledge that Beatreme had. Neither could they take a back seat and adopt a "hands-off" approach. A middle way had to develop. It is said that the stress and strain of opposite poles create a tension that leads to growth. That is perhaps a fair metaphor for the dynamic that developed at Beatreme under the new Kerry regime.

One primary, short-term task was to improve margins quickly. Savings were found first on the input side. Tom Murphy, the Director of Purchasing in Tralee, came to the States to work with the Beloit purchasing group to attempt to reduce raw material costs appreciably. Some local staff were reportedly somewhat put-off by what they saw as a strong-arm style in negotiating with vendors.

Indeed, it may have been a more confrontational approach than that to which they were accustomed. Nevertheless, it did make it patently clear that there was now a new regime that was committed to driving down its costs, and vendors should expect to be pressed hard to defend and support their pricing if they wished to continue the relationship. Other reductions were made to trim overhead expenses where possible. By the end of 1989, there was also a fairly serious redundancy that removed about $1 million in costs, an event that probably raised more concern on the part of the workforce than any of the other changes. Redundancies (or layoffs in American terminology) had never been the norm at Beatreme, but in this case they did serve to lay further emphasis on the absolute commitment to reduce costs and achieve the necessary improvements in profitability.

On the manufacturing operations side, there were also issues. Michael Leahy's task was to re-organise the factories and improve efficiencies. The going, at least in 1989, was very rough, and there was little if anything in the way of cost reduction. Production was rationalised among the five plants; quite a few products were pulled out of the Beloit plant and reallocated to other plants that could produce them more cheaply. Beloit was left with the low volume, high value products that relied more upon the accumulated skill in the factory than upon volume efficiencies. A termination package was also offered that reduced the Beloit workforce by 10–15 workers. For that matter, the Jackson plant was for all intents and purposes still in a start-up mode, having just begun production in June 1988. As Stan McCarthy remembers, "It had its rough times. To say it worked smoothly would definitely be an exaggeration."[3] Says Jack Warner:

> It was pretty edgy, pretty edgy. There was some concern that first year about how successful this would be. We were right on the edge the first year.[4]

Michael Leahy remembers that :

> Obviously there was a lot of nervousness from the Beatreme people. We just came in, you know, and were taking the thing apart. And they said, "Jeez, what are they going to do next?" We were not the best communicators either.

> We didn't have the patience to sit around a table and ex-
> plain, step by step, what we were going to do, so that was
> a bit of a problem. The first year was very difficult; we
> didn't save any money in the factories.[5]

There was a culture clash to be addressed as well. It can safely be suggested, however, that it was *not* an issue of national culture. Indeed, being Irish in America in the late twentieth century was generally an advantage, an easy way to open a door and build a relationship. As a rule, Americans today are very receptive to the Irish, light years away from the "no Irish need apply" days of the late nineteenth century. There may have been the odd instance of communication problems on telephone calls to Tralee (as in "two peoples separated by a common language"). It was really a clash of *organisational* cultures that had to be managed. Beatreme was a highly structured company, with organisational charts and clear reporting lines. There were systems in place, and lines of authority, and communication lanes "up" and "down" the organisation. The Kerry approach, on the other hand, was far more informal; there were no organisational charts in Kerry! Finbarr O'Driscoll would say, "I don't want to see any boxes!" The obvious inference was that having "boxes" and organisational charts would limit and constrain people, and make them think and behave narrowly. In the Kerry culture, people would float to wherever attention was needed. There was plenty of personal responsibility and account-ability, but it was more *personal* and less *functional* in nature. One could almost take this back to the very earliest days of the Listowel factory, when everyone regardless of rank or function was ex-pected to pitch in wherever help was necessary. Such informality and lack of structure was very uncomfortable for the Americans at Beatreme. During the first year or two of the merger, compromises had to be reached to try to meld the best of both cultures.

On one side was Beatreme, who had the structures, the systems (not all of which were working well), the technology, the knowledge base, the people, the products and the customers. On the other side was Kerry, led by a tight-knit group of highly com-mitted and passionate managers, focused upon a strategy of con-tinuous growth, relentless improvements in quality and sustained increases in profitability. Even as they surveyed the various inte-

gration issues that had to be addressed, it was clear early on that
the opportunities to develop synergies in a merging of the two organisational cultures were significant. Jack Warner looked at the
possibilities this way:

> What did Kerry bring to the party? Well, stability for one
> thing. At the time, we just wanted to have a home. It was
> also obvious that we were going to play a hell of a bigger
> part [within Kerry] than in a $12 billion company like
> Beatrice. All of a sudden, we became of huge importance
> to this new company of which we were now a part. That's
> the way I looked at it. It was a great opportunity. I didn't
> know their corporate culture at the time, but I knew they
> took chances, that they did the best they could with what
> they had, and that they did things the right way. I think
> there was a great mix with our people. Kerry came in with
> their great discipline on the accounting side, and put ac-
> countants in all the plants to get the MAPICS system [a
> materials requirements planning and inventory control
> system] running by putting the right numbers into it. Al-
> most overnight, we had a 15–20 per cent gain in margin,
> just by getting that right. We had the systems, and Kerry
> had the wherewithal to make the systems work. Just by
> doing things right, we started making a lot more money.
> There was great synergy between us.[6]

Such magical synergy, however, did not happen overnight. In fact,
1989 was a disappointment and did not meet Kerry's financial expectations. This was serious. Towards the end of 1989, some of the
more aggressive actions were taken. Reducing overheads,
streamlining processes, biting the bullet on forced redundancies,
and taking an aggressive line on the purchasing side were all
pushed with renewed vigour. Pricing was also increased. One
manager recalled that Brosnan came in and said, "Come on, let's
push our prices." After all, demand for these products was not
price elastic; they were not commodities. They were highly engineered, key components which customers could not easily source
elsewhere. Of course, price increases would have to be justified,
but perhaps the $100 million or so in debt that Kerry needed to
service and pay down was sufficient justification in itself. Knowing
there were tremendous growth opportunities in the business,

Kerry Advisory Committee members visit Kerry's new plant in Jackson, Wisconsin in 1987.

Beatrice Foods personnel photographed at Snaxpo 1980, United States. Dave Nucifero, Dell Seasonings President and inventor of the BBQ snack seasoning; Jack Warner, Beatrice Foods Technical Services Director and current Chairman of Kerry Ingredients, US; Rich Degregori, Beatrice Foods Special Products Sales Manager and now President of Pioneer Mills, Jim Stroup, Dell Seasonings Broker; Wayne Skarda, Beatrice Foods; and Larry Nichols, Dell Seasonings Sales Manager.

Dell Food Specialties (a Beatrice Foods business) at Snaxpo 1975, the annual snack industry convention in the US.

Processing and Packing at Beatreme Food Ingredients plant, Vesper, WI.

Former Presidents of Beatrice Foods; Carl Obenauf (1978 – 1982), Al Alton (1965 – 1978) and Jack Warner – 1982 onwards.

Beatrice Foods
Spray drying of cheese powders circa 1950s.

Trade advertisement at Snaxpo '89 announcing the Kerry acquisition of Beatreme Foods.

Kerry US Headquarters located in Beloit, Wisconsin.

One of two Kerry Ingredients plants in Beloit, Wisconsin.

Specialist processing technology at Kerry's manufacturing facility in Owen, Wisconsin.

Spray drying technology at the Group's flagship dairy and ingredients plant in Listowel.

The story of Wall's began in 1786. By the early 20th century, demand for Thomas Wall & Sons products was such that Wall's opened its first factory in Battersea, London. Photograph illustrates sales van No. 6 of the original 10 purchased at the start of Wall's wholesale operation in 1903.

Premium sliced meat products in the Mattessons range.

Kerry Foods branded savoury product range.

Kerry Foods exhibits at IFE '96 in the Earls Court Exhibition Centre, London.

Kerry Foods Headquarters in Egham, Surrey, UK.

Kerry Foods', Shillelagh Co. Wicklow, state of the art manufacturing facility, commissioned in 1994.

Kerry Ingredients food ingredients technology.

DCA acquisition established leadership for Kerry in food coating systems and extended the Group's customer and geographic base.

Kerry Ingredients Europe at FIE '94 in London. Photographed with Ireland's Minister of State for Agriculture and Food Mr. Brian O'Shea TD are: Mr. Bob Kasik, Mr. John Buckley and Mr. Michael Wren.

Photographed in Paris at the presentation of the Sial D'Or 1996 Ireland Award to Kerry Spring.
Left to right: Mr. Liam Chute, Managing Director Kerry Spring; Minister Ivan Yates TD;
Mr. Paul-Louis Halley, President of CIES (Paris) and President of the Promodes Retail Group;
Mr. Daniel Juillard President du Directoire du Sial.

Kerry Ravifruit's Jean Francois Devineau demonstrates the Ravifruit range of natural fruit
products for the specialist artisinal, retail bakery, patisserie and ice cream sectors.

Inauguration of Kerry de Mexico facility in Irapuato in October 1995 by Mr. Vincente Fox, Governor of State of Guanajuato (Vincente Fox was elected President of Mexico in 2000).

Kerry Foods wins the Grocer IFE Business Excellence Award in February 1997. Pictured at the Awards were (l to r): John Beaumont (IGD Chief Executive), Iain Ferguson (Chairman Birds Eye Wall's), Michael Griffin (CEO Kerry Foods), Martin Totty (Vice-President (sales) Walkers), Tom Vyner (Deputy Chairman J.Sainsbury plc and President of the IGD).

Mick O'Kane working in Kerry's culinary centre at the Bristol (UK) technical research centre.

The Dalgety ingredients product range.

Kerry's purpose built crumb plant in Wittstock (near Berlin) Germany, acquired as part of the Dalgety acquisition.

Kerry's Malaysian food ingredients processing plant located at Johor Bahru.

Tanaiste Mary Harney TD opens Kerry Asia R&D facility in Johor Bahru. Photographed left to right: G. Heath, B. Lyons (Irish Ambassador to Malaysia), Tanaiste M. Harney TD, M. McCormack, T. Courtney (Enterprise Ireland).

Kerry Ingredients Australian Headquarters at Regents Park NSW.

Research and Development at Kerry's North Ryde laboratories in Australia.

Presentation of the Ireland-United States Council for Commerce & Industry Annual Award for Outstanding Achievement to Denis Brosnan on 20th November 1996 in New York. Left to right: D. Hamill (Consul General of Ireland), MJ Roarty (President, Ireland-United States Council), D. Brosnan and Senator G. Mitchell (Special Advisor to the US President).

Kerry Group — selected one of *Industry Week's* 100 Best Managed Companies in 1999 and 2000. Pictured here at the 1999 award presentation Mr Denis Brosnan and Mr John Brandt, Publisher and Editor-in-Chief of IW.

Inauguration of Kerry do Brazil in Tres Coraçoes on 15th August 1999. Left to right: Mr. Denis Brosnan, Mr. Pratini deMoraes, Minister for Agriculture and Food in Brazil, Mr. Joe Walsh TD Ireland's Minister for Agriculture and Food, and Mr. Jerry Henchy, President Kerry do Brazil.

Official opening of Kerry's €10 million research and development centre in Bristol (UK) on 12th May 2000. Left to right: Verle Grove (MD Commercial Kerry Ingredients Europe), Kevin Matchett (R&D Director), Minister Joe Walsh TD and Denis Brosnan.

On the occasion of US President Bill Clinton's visit to Ballybunion in September 1998. Left to right: Mai Maher (Lady Captain), Denis Brosnan (1998 Club President), President Clinton, Minister Charlie McCreevy TD.

Victorious Kerry Senior Football team – Millennium All-Ireland Football Champions.

Kerry Group plc Board of Directors 1999. Front left to right: M. Dowling, I. Kenny, D. Brosnan, M. Hanrahan (Chairman), D. Cregan, M. Harty and DT O'Sullivan. Middle row: P. O'Connell, T. McEnery, M. Gabbett, J. O'Connor, M. Griffin and B. Durran. Back row: D. Buckley, R. Fitzgerald, D. O'Connell, J. Brosnan, P. Healy and E. McSweeney. (not present, H. Friel and S. McCarthy).

Kerry's Worldwide operations 2000.

Kerry Group Executive Directors:
Denis Brosnan (Managing Director),
Denis Cregan (Deputy Managing Director),
Hugh Friel (Deputy Managing Director),
Michael Griffin (CEO Kerry Foods) and
Stan McCarthy (President Kerry Americas).

Brosnan also targeted certain products, like cheese powder, for renewed marketing efforts.

Throughout the integration, Brosnan stayed directly involved, particularly in the famous "planning meetings" that occurred in Beloit (as they did throughout the Kerry organisation) every two to three months. From the start, these meetings and their outcomes clearly set the tone for the new organisation. Randy McIntyre, (now the Senior VP of Sales at Kerry Ingredients), remembers his first impressions:

> What I remember most from those years are the planning meetings. I was promoted in late 1990 to regional manager, and started coming to the planning meetings in Beloit. This is where all of the major issues were dealt with and put right up front. Each department brought up its issues, what had happened, what was happening, what would happen, and what needs to happen in the future. . . . And there was always a simple list of specific actions to be taken. There were never more than ten actions and each action had a name after it, and a date.[7]

In 1990, these efforts began to bear fruit. Costs came down dramatically, price increases stuck, margins were improving and sales were growing. By 1991, the improvements and growth were dramatic, and the returns were beginning to exceed Kerry's original targets. The Beatreme purchase was beginning to pay off in a very big way. Said Denis Brosnan:

> Beatreme added a whole new dimension to our business. Our list of customers was a "Who's Who" of the food industry. Kerry was now the number one supplier of specialty food ingredients in the United States.[8]

Hugh Friel added that:

> Kerry had a capacity to embrace the details. Beatreme's technology and applications technologies were unrivalled. This, together with Kerry's strategic planning capability, meant that we were now poised to achieve new growth records in the world's premier consumer market. Subsequent results would bear this out.[9]

The Dairyland and Northlands (Owen) Acquisitions

Even as the Beatreme-Kerry integration was being sorted out, the ingredients group in Listowel was involved in negotiating several acquisitions (discussed in Chapter 13) including the purchase of Milac GmbH in Germany in 1990, and Eastleigh Flavours (1991) and Tingles Ltd. (1993) in the UK. The expansion of the ingredients business into the EC was now modestly underway. In the States, Kerry was getting ready to consolidate its purchase of Beatreme with the acquisition of several complementary businesses. Of course, initial work on this expansion plan had been done even before Kerry had entered upon the scene. Even back when Beatreme had been bought by E-II, Don Kelly and Ed Gustafson had planned to grow Beatreme's business via acquisitions. At the top of Beatreme's list of acquisition candidates from that time was a family business called Dairyland, based in Minnesota, that was a direct competitor of Beatreme.

Dairyland operated a business very similar to Beatreme's, although it had most of its manufacturing (spray drying) done for it by contract manufacturers and did only blending in-house. It specialised in dry cheeses and cream powders, dairy blends and ingredients for the health food market. They had an excellent reputation for technical innovation. Dairyland was privately held by the Sandoz family, with Tom Sandoz, son of the founder, as the principal owner. Jack Warner had been in contact with the family over the years, but there had never been much interest on their part in selling. They had, after all, been making some inroads among Beatreme's own customers. Then, at the IFT meetings in 1991, one of the senior executives in the company came to Warner and said, "Tom is ready to sell. Why don't you contact him?"[10] Dairyland at the time was doing about $67 million in sales. After discussing the deal with Denis Brosnan and Hugh Friel, Warner made an initial offer and, after he, Brosnan and Friel met face-to-face with Tom Sandoz, a deal was eventually agreed for $36 million. The deal was closed in the summer of 1991. Michael Leahy, commenting on the purchase, remarked that:

> Dairyland was a great purchase. It was run by a very good guy who had some very good managers who worked with him. (One of them is Verle Grove who is now Commercial

and Sales Director for our Ingredients operations in Europe, and another is Jeff Miyake in Sales.) So, we bought a company with lots of sales, making a pretty good profit, tightly run by some good people, and with hardly any assets! But we had lots of spare capacity in our factories, so we brought a lot of those products (that they had contract manufactured) in-house. We closed the one blending facility that they had. Of course, it took a few years to do all that, but it made money the first month we bought it.[11]

Ironically, if Kerry had been unable to buy Beatreme it would definitely have had to make a move to buy Dairyland. As a consequence, the entire specialty ingredients industry may have developed very differently. It would have been far more fragmented, with many smaller firms competing in various product and market niches. Happily for Kerry, things turned out differently, and according to Stan McCarthy, "Dairyland was the piece that totally consummated the value of Beatreme, and our leadership position in ingredients."[12]

In 1992, shortly after the purchase of Dairyland, Kerry bought the Owen, Wisconsin manufacturing facility of Northland Foods, jointly owned by a pair of co-operatives. The facility had two spray dryers and was doing contract manufacturing work at the time. The purchase price was in the region of $5 million. Although Jack Warner had negotiated the purchase, Brosnan continued his hands-on involvement with the operation, visiting the facility and suggesting that a freezer and cheese cooler including 20,000 feet of additional storage space be added.[13] Stan McCarthy remembers that Kerry had originally passed up an opportunity to buy it years earlier:

> Back in 1986, we were searching for a way to get into this ingredients business and were unable to find anything that fit the bill. The irony is that we looked at a facility in Owen, Wisconsin that was, at the time, a part of Northland Foods. It seemed to us to be a mess, and we decided we wouldn't go near it. Didn't we wind up buying it a few years later? We gutted it and reengineered it, and it's been a great facility ever since.[14]

By the end of 1992, then, Kerry had successfully removed a pair of competitors from the marketplace and merged their businesses under the Kerry/Beatreme umbrella. This reinforced the leadership position that Kerry had built in the specialty food ingredients industry in the US, making it more difficult for competitors and encouraging customers to come to Kerry for their products. The Dairyland purchase, in particular, was a near perfect fit with the Beatreme operation, and helped to "put the icing on the cake" of the Beatreme acquisition for Kerry.

The purchase of Beatreme represents a critical turning point in the story of the Kerry Group. In one fell swoop, Kerry was transformed from a minor player at the periphery of the food ingredients business, to the leading firm in specialty food ingredients. It changed from a largely regional player to a truly international, if not yet global, firm. It would never again be captive to either a commodity business or the narrow geographical confines of a small island economy. Beatreme became the platform from which Kerry would continue to grow, expand and develop. It also validated, in the eyes of many, Kerry's global aspirations and undeniable ability to achieve them. Building on the confidence it developed as a result of the successful integration, Kerry Ingredients would extend its already ambitious efforts even further in the future.

Notes

[1] Stan McCarthy, personal communication, 24 October 2000.

[2] Jack Warner, letter written for the *Beatreme Scene*, 30 September 1988.

[3] Stan McCarthy, personal interview, 6 December 1999.

[4] Jack Warner, personal interview, 6 December 1999.

[5] Interview with Michael Leahy, 7 December 1999.

[6] Jack Warner, personal interview, 6 December 1999.

[7] Randy McIntyre, personal interview, 7 December 1999.

[8] Denis Brosnan, personal communication, 23 October 2000.

[9] Hugh Friel, personal communication, 23 October 2000.

[10] Jack Warner, personal interview, 6 December 1999.

[11] Michael Leahy, personal interview, 7 December 1999.

[12] Stan McCarthy, personal interview, 6 December 1999.

[13] Jack Warner, personal interview, 6 December 1999.

[14] Stan McCarthy, personal interview, 6 December 1999.

Chapter 11

Building a Foods Business

It is generally granted that the purchase of Beatreme was a defini-
tive turning point in the history of the Kerry organisation, leading it
into an emerging, highly technical industry with significant growth
prospects. It was also the leading edge of Kerry's serious international expansion and development into a globally integrated firm.
With most attention focused upon Beatreme in 1988–89, however,
it would be easy to overlook the less dramatic but all-important
contribution that had been made far closer to home. The foods
business represented the fruit of Kerry's initial attempts to break
away from commodity trading and into branded consumer products where, by 1988, Kerry had already engineered some notable
successes. In Ireland, it had grown to a major player in a number
of dairy and meat categories, and a big fish, albeit in a very small
pond. Its Denny sausage brand and Duffy meat products were
leaders in the pork meat category in Ireland and, by 1985–86,
were operating quite profitably. Its milk and dairy products, produced in the five dairies that Kerry had acquired, and marketed
under the unified *Dawn* label, had made both volume and market
share gains in the face of stiff competition and a generally declining market. Finally, the entry into the beef business in 1986 had, if
nothing else, made Kerry a major player in the industry in terms of
volume, even though it had contributed little to overall profitability. Clearly, major efforts would have to be expended to bring the
beef business to the level of return that Kerry required of its food
businesses.

In the UK, Kerry was just beginning to build the foundations of a business, although it remained far too small to be considered a serious player in the UK foods industry. Its greatest success to date had been in providing own-label low fat spreads to the major multiples like Tesco, Marks & Spencer and Sainsbury's. These products, all variations on Kerry's own *Dawn Light* brand that was half butter, half fat, were produced in the Listowel plant. But organic growth, particularly in a brand-dominated market like the UK, was dreadfully and painfully slow. Perhaps the only option for getting into the market was through acquisition, as Kerry had already done in the smaller Irish market and was now doing in North America. Despite Kerry's best efforts, however, they had not yet been able to land a major acquisition. They were looking for a rough equivalent of Denny's, a firm with a "sleeping brand" on which Kerry could train its formidable strengths at garnering operational efficiencies and reinvigorating the product in the marketplace. Still, in late 1988, as this search was continuing with renewed urgency, there was little to cheer about.

Dawn Dairies

By 1988, Kerry's five regional dairies in Killarney, Limerick, Ballinahina, Galway and Moate had already been operating for three years as one integrated unit selling the Dawn brand of consumer dairy products throughout much of Ireland. Tuam Dairies in County Galway, acquired in late 1992, was later integrated into this structure. The range of milk products included non-fat, low-fat and whole milk and cream, assembled and processed in the regional dairies, and a range of butter products and low-fat spreads produced at the Listowel manufacturing facility. Liquid milk products were sold within Ireland, almost exclusively. Butter was sold both within Ireland under the *Dawn* label, and exported through Bord Bainne under the *Kerrygold* label (but only through 1987–88 when Kerry had its final "break" with Bord Bainne). Various low-fat spreads such as *Dawn Light* and *Low-Low* (sunflower spread) were exported as own-label products to Kerry's food business in the UK, where they came to supply most of the major UK multiples. Kerry's *Low-Low* spread, as well as *Kerrymaid* and *Move Over Butter* high-fat butter products, were also heavily promoted and marketed within Ireland. In general, Kerry could claim considerable success with its branded yellow fat products in Ireland. Along with its policy of intense marketing support, Kerry's technical capabilities in this area probably had no equal. It was also able to reap some advantages from the experience it was gaining in the UK market, adapting those lessons to the evolving marketplace at home in Ireland.

These successes notwithstanding, the consumer dairy market in Ireland was static at best and Kerry was hard-pressed to grow its business under such conditions. Similar to the rest of Europe, per capita consumption of liquid milk, eggs, butter and other dairy products was generally declining amidst concerns with cholesterol levels and increased emphasis on healthy eating. In the face of such difficult market conditions, the Dairies division focused upon the development of new packaging innovations (such as more modern, hygienic, single-serve packs) to increase convenience, low-fat products, and a wider range of flavoured milks, ice cream, and milk shake products. Additionally, in confronting lack of opportunities to grow volume appreciably in such a difficult market, Kerry's focus on efficiency and low-cost production succeeded in providing a competitive advantage and a tool for holding, and in some cases growing, the margin contribution of these businesses. The operations side of the dairy business in Ireland, including liquid milk assembly and packaging, in-house production of many primary packages (for example, in-house blow-moulding of plastic containers) and distribution systems, was continually emphasised to realise all possible economies. Similarly, a concerted focus on quality within the dairies sector led to Kerry's achievement of ISO 9000 Quality Certification for its five dairies in 1992.

Given the severe market constraints imposed by the static to declining Irish national market for traditional dairy products, it was imperative that Kerry expand into other categories that could provide volume growth. Such products, however, would ideally take advantage of the Dairies division's significant, and in some cases under-utilised, manufacturing and distribution capabilities. To this end, in 1993 Kerry acquired the assets of Kerry Spring Mineral Water based in Ballyferriter, County Kerry (on the Dingle peninsula). By the following June, Kerry had restarted production and was already beginning to breathe new life into the brand. The relaunch was highly successful, and *Kerry Spring* was able to take advantage of the overall growth being experienced in the Irish mineral water market. This growth in the bottled natural water category in Ireland highlights the extent to which the Irish consumer, within a relatively short period of time, responded to consumer behaviour patterns already at play in the US, UK, and continental Europe. Bottled water in Ireland had been successfully pioneered by Geoff Reid with the *Ballygowan* brand, against a background of sceptical cynicism. Very quickly, however, a multiplicity of brands were jostling for position on Irish supermarket shelves. *Kerry Spring*, benefiting from Kerry Group's strong marketing support and distribution channels, quickly achieved the number two position in this market segment. More importantly, Kerry's product development teams and marketers introduced an entirely new line of flavoured mineral water drinks to the marketplace. This move also proved highly successful, making *Kerry Spring* the premier brand in Ireland in the flavoured water category. *Kerry Spring* also began to achieve some success in the export markets in the UK and several other European countries. These exports reflected a nice bonus to the success already achieved in the Irish market.

In the same vein, the *Dawn* line of juices was introduced in 1994, further extending the Dawn Dairies line of products. Juice products have proven a very successful addition to Kerry's range of products distributed in Ireland. In addition to their range of low- and high-fat dairy spreads (from *Low-Low* to *Kerrymaid* to *Move Over Butter*), Kerry Foods has also introduced other dip products, grated cheese products, and other dairy-related products to enable them to compete broadly in the small, highly competitive Irish market.

The Pork Meat Business: Denny and Duffy's

Once the corner had been turned at Denny's in late 1984, and the operation finally began to run consistently in the black, there was literally no looking back. With production centred in the Denny's plant in Tralee and the Duffy's plant in Hacketstown, Kerry had become, by 1987, the premier supplier of consumer pork products in Ireland. There was still, however, unfinished business with regard to the Denny's business in Ireland.

When Henry Denny & Sons (Ireland) Ltd. was purchased in 1982, it secured for Kerry only the Denny's plant in Tralee and the rights to market the Denny brand in the 26 counties of the Republic of Ireland. The Denny family retained a manufacturing plant in Portadown in County Armagh, in Northern Ireland, as well as the rights to market the Denny brand throughout Northern Ireland and the United Kingdom (through a holding company based in the UK). Clearly, the acquisition of the remainder of the Denny's operation was of significant strategic importance. One reason, of course, was to take advantage of market opportunities in Northern Ireland and the United Kingdom, where Denny's had strong brand recognition. More importantly, however, was a very sound defensive imperative for acquiring the rights to the brand. It would simply be untenable for Kerry to promote the Denny brand to the three and a half-million consumers in the Irish market, without being able to reap the benefits of such promotion for the one and a half million consumers in the north. Nor could they accept that the brand itself could potentially be sold to a buyer who could then market under that brand name everywhere else in the world, with Kerry confined to the small Irish market. Additionally, it was a sobering prospect to consider what could happen if there were any quality problems with the Denny product being manufactured in the North (under the old regime, or under unknown new buyers). Any spillovers would certainly have serious consequences for Kerry's robust Denny business in the South. The Denny trademark had to be protected. Finally, it should be noted that the Portadown plant produced a wide range of pork meat and other pie products that were in fact nicely complementary to the existing Denny business in the Republic of Ireland.

Kerry purchased the fixed assets of Henry Denny and Sons (Ulster) Limited in Portadown in late 1987. The concern had actually gone into receivership in June 1986, but continued operating as a going concern until May 1987 (some five months before Kerry took it over), when it ceased business with virtually no notice to its customers.

It should be remembered that Northern Ireland, at the time, was going through a particularly difficult political period, and relationships between the different traditions in the province were volatile. Portadown itself was centre stage as these "troubles" swirled about, and the Denny facility itself was located roughly between the Catholic and Protestant communities. It was under these circumstances that Kerry moved in two young managers from the

Denny operation in Dublin: John O'Callaghan as plant manager and Mark Earley as financial controller. They arrived in Portadown on 8 December 1987.

Their first task was to get the factory going. There was no work force. The brand had by then been absent from the retail shelves for some five to six months. There were myriad issues to sort out. A work force had to be hired, at a wage rate that was suitable for the work that was being done, and "balanced" properly between workers from both the Catholic and Protestant traditions. Industrial relations were decidedly tricky, and making personnel decisions was not unlike negotiating a minefield. The former managing director returned for a time to help restart the operation, and several other capable managers returned to the business. Changes were made to the packaging, to bring it more in line with what was being marketed in the Republic of Ireland to the south, while remaining sensitive to the local conditions in the north. O'Callaghan recalls that:

> . . . those were very exciting times. There were always a hundred and one decisions to be made, and I was constantly drawing on the people in Tralee for help. Tom Murphy came up to help with purchasing. Michael Drummey assisted with the marketing effort. Denis Cregan was on the phone with me all the time, coaching me through a lot of decisions.[1]

The marketing side of the equation was somewhat problematic. The fact that Denny's had ceased business with little notice, and that the product had been off the shelves for five to six months, had left retailers in a generally inhospitable mood. In addition, it was difficult to predict the reaction to the "Irishness" of the "new" Denny's. As the vans loaded with product pulled out of the yard for the first time, it was anyone's guess what kind of reaction they would get. As the Kerry managers watched the vans pull out on that first morning in Spring 1988 in convoy-like fashion, many of them piloted by rookies who scarcely knew the routes or the outlets they would be calling upon, they hoped that at least they would all find their way back home before nightfall! One manager who was there that day remembered:

> The first van arrived back early, in fact too early, in the afternoon. We made a beeline for the back doors, which were opened to reveal that almost as much product that had left the factory at 7:00 a.m. was now back in the yard. The story was not much better from the others as they limped back. But, the vans went out the next day, and the next, and the next.[2]

Through sheer persistence, however, the team in Portadown overcame the initial problems and succeeded in building a substantial business. With the re-opening of the Portadown plant, their range of pie products was added to the full Denny line and marketed for national distribution. Later, quiches and other meat pastry products produced at Portadown were added to the line as well.

Similar to conditions in the dairy segment, the pork meat segment in Ireland was static at best during the decade of the 1990s. In order to gain market share in this competitive market, constant innovation in both product and packaging was the order of the day, and product extensions (meat pastries, sausages, bacon, shaved and thin sliced chilled meats, etc.) were relentlessly pushed to try to gain the maximum chunk of the Irish grocery spending. These efforts met with considerable success. Michael Drummey, who was the Marketing Manager of Kerry Group at the time and responsible for the expansion of the Denny business in Ireland, remembers that:

> After Denny's and the purchase of the other brands, we had become a major force in consumer retailing in Ireland. There wasn't a housewife's shopping basket going home on a Friday evening that did not have a Kerry product in it. Fresh milk, butter, spreads, sausage, bacon, poultry. . . . One of the objectives that I may have set myself, was that if the shopping basket at the time averaged, say, £32, then I wanted at least £3 of it to be in Kerry products. We wanted 10 per cent of the shopping basket.[3]

Nevertheless, the brand came under increasing pressure during the mid-to-late 1990s, as private label products began to make their first appearance on the Irish consumer scene. (Interestingly, however, private label products were never seriously developed in Ireland by the major multiples; Ireland thus remained a largely brand-dominated marketplace, and Kerry continued to focus exclusively upon the marketing of branded products in its home market. The UK, as we shall see, was a different story.) Consumer research and evaluation of consumer preferences and trends, combined with product development and a focus on customer service and quality, helped to maintain Denny's as the dominant brand in Ireland. More and more, convenience packs began to assume importance in the marketplace, and major television advertising became a key ingredient in the battle to maintain Denny's dominance. Also, as the category leader in pork products, Kerry took the lead in introducing category management as an important component in their marketing efforts both at home and in the United Kingdom.

By 1991, plans were also afoot to build a new processing plant. This new state-of-the-art facility was built in 1993 and commissioned in early 1994, in Shillelagh, County Wicklow at a total cost of some £19 million. A further £10 million has since been invested at this site, making it one of the most advanced factories of its kind, now employing over 600 people. The plant's capabilities encompassed both processing and cooked meats production. Major capital investments were also made in the Portadown plant.

Kerry's investment in the pork products category was their first move outside of the traditional milk and dairy business. It had been, at the beginning, a huge gamble, driven by necessity. The campaign to resuscitate Denny's had been long and hard. The experience had provided a crucible in which Kerry's resolve to succeed had been tested, and ultimately hardened, and where an entire cohort of Kerry managers was similarly tested and trained. The lessons learned were carried by them to many subsequent acquisitions. The Denny brand itself represented an important, and ongoing, success for Kerry, reinforcing the confidence that a "sleeping brand", if acquired, could, through hard work, vision, and perhaps a certain amount of luck, be re-invented, re-tooled, and re-launched successfully. Such confidence would have a great impact upon the future path of the Kerry Foods business.

Poultry

In June 1988, Kerry moved to enter what was for them a new consumer foods market with the purchase of Grove Farm and Ballyfree, the largest producer and processor of turkey products in Ireland. Kerry paid £20 million for the concern, a relatively high amount considering Grove Farm/Ballyfree's net asset value of approximately £8 million at the time. Turkey, after all, was still considered a seasonal dish in Ireland and the UK, and only beginning to emerge as a year-round food. Still, by the late 1980s, it was the fastest growing meat product internationally. Given the rising tide of consumer awareness and concern for healthy eating, turkey offered an alternative to the beef and pork segments in which Kerry already operated, and one with considerably better long-term growth prospects.

In the deal, Kerry acquired two processing plants at Smithboro, County Monaghan and Glenealy, County Wicklow. These facilities were modern and encompassed the full range of production activities including the breeding, growth, and processing of turkey. Kerry brought its own strong marketing and distribution strengths to a business where such attributes were in short supply. Given Grove/Ballyfree's production of fresh, frozen and various value-added turkey products (such as breaded turkey and small portion packs), Kerry had now, along with its existing pork and beef businesses, an impressive range of consumer meat products on offer.

The Beef Saga

The confidence that Kerry had built up as a result of their successful turnaround of Denny's, as already indicated, had numerous positive spillover effects elsewhere in the business. It may, however, have backfired in the beef business. It is one thing when the fundamental building blocks of a successful business exist and what is needed is the development of the systems, the people, the programs, and the strategies required to build upon those fundamentals to the best effect. This had been the case in pork. It was not the case in beef. The experience of Denny's had taught Kerry's managers that if they analysed the business thoroughly, planned carefully, executed well, threw everything they had at problems, and stayed with it doggedly and relentlessly, they would achieve their goals. Kerry's experience in the beef sector, however, served to demonstrate that there is an exception to every rule.

Through 1990, Kerry's focus in beef had been on the value-added side, concentrating mightily on changing beef from a commodity product to a product that could be branded and promoted to the retail trade in a manner similar to pork meat. Its purchase of South West Meats from Unigate, and of McCallum Meats Ltd., both in the UK, had been done with the aim of pushing the business further along the value-added continuum. South West Meats, after all, had a franchise with Marks & Spencer, providing critical access to a high-end retail outlet. McCallum, with its focus on the catering business, seemed to offer yet another avenue to develop the value-added in beef, this time through providing beef to the catering trade. By 1990, Kerry was claiming some success in reducing its reliance on commodity trading of beef, but it was modest at best. In general, beef remained a commodity business with razor-thin margins. The big Midleton plant bought by Kerry from IMP still needed other outlets for its beef: South West and McCallum themselves could not provide markets of sufficient size to take all Midleton's production. The result was more sales into intervention (through the existing EEC mechanisms) or more beef sold in spot, commodity transactions with little profit. Kerry, particularly now as a plc, had made serious commitments to its shareholders with regard not only to growth in *turnover* (to which the beef business made a solid contribution) but far more importantly to growth in *profitability* (on which the beef business was a considerable drag).

The Kerry organisation, however, was not prone to run from a fight or slink away after a few hard rounds, and its approach to its "beef problem" was predictable. Simply, it would invest whatever was necessary, in capital, in people, in management attention, to make beef a profitable business. In June 1991, Kerry upped its ante on beef again with the purchase of Meadow Meats (in Rathdowney, County Laois) from Guinness. Guinness had bought the business a few years earlier from another financially troubled co-operative, Golden Vale Marts (unrelated to Golden Vale Creameries). Guinness, under the *Meadow* brand, had been able to move the brand away from the commodity meat business and onto the supermarket shelves, selling branded products to Tesco and other supermarkets. Yet, in the context of Guinness's overall business, it was not significant, and was certainly not in their future plans. After running the operation for a few years, Guinness offered it for sale and Brosnan, eager to acquire the *Meadow* brand, picked it up. On the surface, the Meadow Meats purchase seemed the missing piece of the puzzle. IMP's Midleton Plant had brought a lot of production, but no markets. Meadow Meats now promised to afford an opportunity to supply those markets. Ned O'Callaghan, observing the beef business closely from his position at AIB, commented that Brosnan felt he had at last "squared the circle" in beef.[4]

Increasing the stakes on beef yet again, later in 1991 Kerry bought Tunney Meats, a small meat business in Clones, County Monaghan that had the same sort of beef required by Meadow. Kerry now had a total of four locations in the Republic of Ireland engaged in the processing of beef (Midleton, Clones, Rathdowney and Waterford), and had unified all of its red meat operations (which would soon also include the processing of lamb) under the *Meadow* brand.

The year 1992, in particular, was a bad one for the beef sector. Despite an increase in turnover from £177 million to £204 million (due to a full-year contribution from Meadow Meats and Tunney Meats), net margins remained unsatisfactory. *Management*, an Irish business publication, interviewed Brosnan on the subject of beef in mid-1992:

> [Brosnan] says the beef industry is at a crossroads. Despite Kerry's best efforts to make added value products for supermarkets across Europe, he says margins this year will be one per cent or less. In not so polite terms, he talked about the ridiculous situation where the group's former Tunney Meats plant in Monaghan, which is a low-cost centre of intervention beef production, is the most profitable in the group . . . BSE, or the notorious mad cow disease, has shut Ireland out from certain markets and the level of international competition will result in margins of less than one per cent in the current year. . . . [Brosnan] indicates clearly that Kerry could be forced to review its overall commitment to the beef sector if the situation does not improve. However, Kerry will not make any "fast decisions" on that difficult question, he adds. "At the moment we are hanging in to see what will happen."[5]

Meadow succeeded in gaining additional business on the continent, developing new markets in Italy, Germany, France, the
Netherlands and the United Kingdom, but 1993, in fact, brought a
decrease in beef turnover to £194 million. Margins improved
somewhat, but remained in the range of 1–2 per cent, well shy of
Kerry's criteria for retention of any business. There were plenty of
reasons for the volume decline, including currency issues and EU
export subsidies that distorted normal trading patterns and drove
up the cost of beef in Ireland, impacting Meadow Meats' raw material costs for their specialty beef products. But awareness of the
reasons for the dismal performance of the beef business was little
consolation. The hard reality of the impact of that performance on
the overall Kerry Group's financial performance was clear.

Time was finally running out for the beef business. Kerry had
been involved with beef since early 1986, and in almost nine years
of throwing everything it could at developing the business, it had
still come up short. Nor were either the short-term or the longer-
term prospects for future results significantly better. Says Brosnan:

> It was a mistake to go into beef, but beef was probably
> part of our "growing up" phase. Like everything else, we
> thought we could improve our lot and turn it into a busi-
> ness. We gave it everything, but the margins in beef just
> didn't mesh with being a plc. You can't have a mission
> statement saying you'll achieve 10 per cent operating
> margins when a big chunk of your business is getting 2
> per cent. It just doesn't work. But look at the other side of
> it, one of the great decisions we made was to cut and run![6]

The decision was made to exit the beef business. Says Ned
O'Callaghan:

> Denis knew that if he couldn't crack it, nobody could
> crack it. So, he got the hell out. He didn't hang around
> waiting for the best price. He got out. He would say he was
> lucky to get out at the time he did, but I think you make
> your own luck![7]

Kerry began to execute a phased withdrawal from the beef industry,
and in July 1994, sold what had been its first investment in the beef

business, the Midleton processing plant, to Dawn Meats (no relationship to Kerry's Dawn Dairies brand). Kerry's beef sales in 1994 declined to £148 million, as it reorganised and consolidated its beef activities in its three other plants, focusing upon value-added business directed at the major multiple retail accounts in Ireland, the UK and the rest of Europe. Still, it was only a matter of time until it was clear of the industry entirely. In November 1995, Kerry sold its processing plant in Monaghan to Anglo-Irish Beef Processors (part of beef baron Larry Goodman's Irish Food Processors Group).[8] The following month, it sold its remaining Meadow Meats facilities in Rathdowney and Waterford to Dawn Meats. By the end of 1995, Kerry had exited the beef business.

Before leaving the discussion of Kerry's adventures in the beef trade, however, let us look at the bizarre story of South West Meats.

Kerry in the UK — South West Meats

Kerry's only beef plant in the UK, South West Meats Limited, was located in Chard in Somerset. In the early 1990s it had basically two streams of commercial activity: it bought in beef and lamb which it processed for some of the larger supermarket chains; and it tendered for and was awarded contracts to process and sell beef into intervention.

Intervention is a market support programme which is operated under the EU's Common Agricultural Policy, whereby Executive Agencies in each Member State, under set market conditions, purchase and store specified agricultural products. It was this intervention that resulted in the various beef, butter and skim milk mountains that were much written and spoken about in the late 1980s and the early 1990s.

In the United Kingdom, a Statutory Board, known as the Intervention Board for Agricultural Produce (IBAP) was charged with the overall responsibility for supervising and implementing intervention schemes there. How these schemes operated was that if the EU wanted to intervene in say, the beef market, it publicly sought tenders for the supply of beef to intervention. Interested companies tendered and if successful they purchased beef of certain stipulated quality on behalf of the EU.

Some tenders required the beef to be put into intervention with bone-in, others required it to be boneless. The successful tenderers were paid a set rate for deboning, cutting it into specified cuts, packing it, having it blast-frozen and delivered to storage, which IBAP would arrange on behalf of the EU. All aspects of this process were carried out under very strict rules and specifications and under veterinary supervision.

In the early 1990s, IBAP became suspicious that South West Meats was not performing its tenders in accordance with the specifications and intervention regulations. Its suspicions were heightened by the allegations being made in Ireland at the time against some Irish beef processors. IBAP decided that an in-depth investigation of South West Meats's activities was required. It sought the assistance of senior officers of Her Majesty's Customs and Excise. The Customs officers and IBAP officers planned and carried out a dawn raid on the South West Meat plant in Chard on the morning of 23 July 1991 assisted by a team of police officers. Simultaneously as the raid was taking place, several employees of the company were arrested. One employee of North Yorkshire Lamb, who was based in Thirsk in North Yorkshire, was also arrested and brought to Chard. The Customs and Excise officers and IBAP officials conducted an exhaustive and unrestrained search of the Company's premises at Chard and Thirsk. In the process, the Company's employees were subjected to verbal abuse and intimidation and confidential and privileged documents were seized and taken away in vans.

South West Meats Ltd. sought the intercession of the Courts in England including the Court of Appeal, which decided that the actions of the Customs Officers and IBAP amounted to "a deplorable abuse of power by public officials" and it awarded South West Meats Ltd. what are known in legal terms as exemplary damages. It is extremely rare for such damages to be awarded but the Court concluded that the extent of the abuse of power in this case was such that they were fully warranted. The case was widely reported in English legal journals.

It became clear at an early stage of the investigation that one of the key issues in the case was the fact that there was not the type of business relationship between South West Meats Limited and IBAP that one would expect between two organisations engaged in the level of trade that was involved here. This factor gave rise to a high level of misinformation being generated. Management, in order to redress this weakness, decided to appoint the late Dan O'Halloran as its Liaison Manager with IBAP and relationships between the two organisations improved greatly. He conducted a thorough investigation on the Company's behalf in co-operation with IBAP into all the allegations that were being made. After a protracted period of investigation, the Crown Prosecution Service entered a *nolle prosecui* in respect of each of the employees who had been charged and they were awarded their costs.

Kerry in the UK — The Purchase of Millers and Robirch

As the excitement surrounding the acquisition of Beatreme built through the end of 1988, Kerry Foods in the United Kingdom became, for the moment, something of a "second front" in Kerry's international expansion efforts. This, however, was more by circumstance than by design, for the Foods Division was also fully committed to growth via acquisition. Unfortunately, it had thus far come up short. Nevertheless, the Division continued to push forward, focusing upon organic growth of its products, sourced in Ireland. On the beef side, the purchase in the UK of South West Meats (a beef cutting plant) provided some opportunities to further build a relationship with Marks & Spencer, who were a customer. Also, the purchase of Ballyfree and Grove Farms in Ireland led to attempts to market cooked turkey products in the UK. On the yellow fats side, products sourced from Listowel were sold as own-label products to many of the major multiples in the UK.

Kerry correctly identified at the time that the retail trade in the UK was in fact progressing down the route of more own-label (private label) products, and Kerry's yellow fats business in the UK was nearly totally own-label. Kerry's resolute policy in the UK had been to develop a strong reputation with the major multiples for providing the highest quality yellow fat (own-label) products to compete with the major brands. Kerry eschewed the branded route with yellow fats, not only because of the tremendously high costs involved with marketing a branded product, but also in the belief, subsequently proven right, that the major multiples themselves would emerge as the biggest "brands" in the UK retail food industry. The strategy employed by the major retailers was simple. (Some will argue convincingly that most effective strategies are!) They would help support the launch of new branded products, would wait to see if they were successful, and if they were, would look for a producer/supplier who could very quickly provide an "own-label" alternative. Kerry, with its technical expertise in yellow fats, became the supplier of choice for the production of own-label products in this category. Not only was the own-label business moderately (but not wildly) profitable for Kerry, but the organisation gained a great deal of knowledge and experience in both technical product development activities and, most importantly perhaps, in grocery marketing. This knowledge, gleaned from their relationship with several of the most progressive retailers in the world, would prove useful to Kerry even beyond the UK.

Naturally, the margins on branded products were higher, so, with the exception of yellow fat products, Kerry continued to search for a way to establish a presence in branded retail categories. Although Kerry did manage to introduce some minor branded products to the UK supermarket shelves (for example, *Tea-Break*, a tea whitener sold under the Kerry name), in general, it was simply too expensive to attempt to launch a brand in the UK. The only way to go the branded route was to *buy* a brand.

Kerry did press forward, in 1990, with the acquisition of A.E. Button and Sykes, two UK producers and marketers of duck and goose products. These "specialty meat" products were marketed under both own-label and Kerry's own *Watermeadow* and *Chinatown* brands. Also in 1990, Kerry acquired North Yorkshire Lamb Company, adding lamb to its range of meat products. These three relatively small purchases represented a continuing "chipping away" at the UK retail food market, as Kerry searched for those "loose bricks" that would provide the market access they sought. In late 1990, however, it seemed that they had found it. Booker, a large UK food distributor, was engaged in an effort to dispose of a number of poorly performing companies it had acquired just the previous September with its acquisition of Fitch Lovell, a small food group. Booker had made the purchase to acquire particular product lines, and was anxious to divest itself of the remaining companies. Among them were W.L. Miller and Robirch, manufacturers and distributors of a variety of meat pies, pastries, sausages and savoury products. Both companies operated fleets of vans that called on retailers throughout the United Kingdom, and Millers in particular had a good-sized business with Sainsburys, one of the major

UK multiples. The remainder of its business was with smaller, independent groceries located primarily in the South of England. Robirch operated a similar business, calling on small retailers primarily in the Midlands. Millers and Robirch offered a couple of regional brands, two manufacturing facilities at Poole and Burton-on-Trent, and a more or less national distribution system, although one focused upon the smaller, independent retailers (in a market that was now consolidating around the large multiples).

They were acquired on 31 December 1991 for Stg£26.5 million. With this acquisition, Kerry now had its first full-scale manufacturing facilities in the United Kingdom, producing meat-filled pastry products. It had finally bought its way into the consumer food business in the UK, although granted at a very modest level and for a very full price. At the very least, the purchase of Millers and Robirch served notice that Kerry was determined to crack the UK market, committed to becoming a player, and clearly engaged for the long haul. It was a strong signal that amply communicated Kerry's seriousness of intent in the UK market.

Implicit in the Millers and Robirch purchase was the idea, or at least the hope, that it could become "another Denny's". That is, the business could be revitalised, operations rationalised, and the brands re-launched to become Kerry's first real entry into the branded UK consumer market. Michael Drummey was invited to come over and evaluate this possibility, but his appraisal was a sobering one. He didn't mince words:

> Michael [Griffin] asked me would I be interested in coming over and having a look at them. One look was enough . . . there was no way we were going to make national brands out of them. It was a different geography, a different business structure, a different everything. It was never going to be a possibility. What we had to do was to try to make money out of the business, as distinct from trying to make assets out of the brands. For a start, we got rid of Robirch. There was a lot of opposition to it, and we had to sell people on the idea that there was no way two brands could survive in the evolving retail industry in the UK.

Drummey's assessment was made in full recognition of the rapidly changing structure of the UK retail food industry. The independent retail business in the UK was contracting rapidly, as more and more retail activity was consolidated in the major UK multiples like Tesco, Sainsbury's and Marks & Spencer. These multiples, for their part, were not particularly interested in dealing with multiple sources for their products, a fact that worked to the detriment of businesses like Millers and Robirch, who had a fleet of vans that (by this time) scarcely called on supermarkets at all. The retailers preferred to sell their own-label substitutes, delivered to the store by their own transport, having been delivered first by an own-label supplier to the retailer's central depot. By the time of Kerry's purchase, Sainsbury's, who had been Millers' major customer, had already moved most of their business out, which was a major setback as well as a considerable surprise. Kerry's challenge was, thus, a substantial one. It had two businesses that were now almost entirely focused on a rapidly declining market segment, that of independent retailers (grocery stores, butcher shops, etc.). The acquired facilities had suffered from underinvestment for years. The van sales operation was badly in need of rationalisation and refocusing. The wide and overlapping product range had to be streamlined. Quite simply, there was a lot of work to do.

With a deepening recession and reduced retail expenditure in the UK, 1991–92 was a rough period for the Millers and Robirch businesses. The Robirch brand was dropped, and products consolidated nation-wide under the Miller brand. The number of products was greatly reduced. Significant investments were made in upgrading the manufacturing facilities at Poole and Burton-on-Trent, and production at both facilities was rationalised. With the continuing decline in numbers of small, independent retail outlets, energetic efforts were made to cultivate catering, cash and carry, and other wholesale accounts to be served by the 175 refrigerated vans operating out of depots throughout the country. Nevertheless, it was increasingly clear that to be successful in its chosen markets, Kerry would need to begin supplying the major multiples like Sainsbury's, Tesco, Safeway, and others who wished to be serviced only at their large, centralised distribution centres, and whose criteria for quality and service were increasingly rigorous.

Kerry had, however, already built a relationship with the multiples through its yellow fats business (dairy spreads), and through its beef business, although both were quite different from the savoury meat category into which Kerry was trying to break. Nevertheless, there was a dialogue, and one that Kerry continually nurtured. Interestingly, this category had always been dominated by strong brands, but that was now beginning to change as the major multiples increasingly needed to compete in each category across an entire spectrum of prices and quality. Considerable pressure was already being felt from other large cut-rate discounters that were beginning to move into the UK retail market. At this point, Kerry's good relationships paid off. Terry Leahy, the CEO of Tesco, the number two retailer in the UK at that time (they are now number one), called Michael Griffin in August 1993 with an offer and a distinct challenge. Griffin had been continually after Leahy, complaining that Kerry had had no opportunity to supply them with sausages or meat pie and pastry products. Leahy finally decided to give Griffin the opportunity he was looking for, perhaps because no other manufacturer had been willing to accept it. Leahy was very specific about what he expected. Griffin remembers that:

> . . . he wanted five to six products, a pork pie, a pack of sausages, one or two meat pies, and a savoury pie. He wanted to sell them at a specific price, he wanted them with some kind of a brand, and he wanted them on his shelves within one month.[9]

Griffin grabbed at the opportunity. Within a week, mock-ups of the packaging had been done, and a brand for the products had in fact been found. The old Clover brand had been bought from the bankrupt Clover Meats in Ireland years before, and put away for a rainy day. Within a month, Tesco had their exclusive, own-label Clover products supplied to them by Kerry Foods. These products became part of a range of hundreds of products known as "Tesco Value" products, launched specifically to battle with the discounters head on, and a key aspect of Tesco's strategy to achieve leadership among UK retailers. It was an important breakthrough, and helped enormously to cement an ongoing relationship with Tesco. It represented Kerry's first important break into value-added consumer foods at Tesco and, on the back of that, Kerry was able to get other products listed and build a serious franchise with them. Of course, one thing also leads to another. This was the real beginning of Kerry's own-label foods business in the UK. It had been a long time coming.

In a business in which brands had been dominant for years, own-label products were now growing rapidly. At the same time, big retailers, some of whom owned and managed manufacturing units of their own, decided to concentrate fully on what they did best, that is, sell food. Their exit from food processing left something of a vacuum, and Kerry was there to help fill it. Some food manufacturers resisted the growing trend towards private label products, feeling that such sales would only cannibalise sales of their existing brands. Kerry, with no major brands at risk, faced no such problem and found itself well positioned to cater to this increased demand for private labels. Increasingly, it assumed a leadership position in the manufacture of own-label savoury products for the major multiples. Additionally, its original Miller and Robirch (consolidated under the Miller brand) van fleets were eventually consolidated as a separate direct sales business unit, focusing upon the distribution of convenience foods and snacks to the independent retail sector. Here, the emphasis was placed squarely on quality and service, with Kerry handling stocking, returns, replenishments, and general management of the category for the independent retailer, assuming the role of leading UK distributor in this sector.

In early 1992, Kerry Foods had moved into a new UK headquarters at Egham, outside of London, into a stately building named Thorpe Lea Manor that had recently been vacated by Baxter Healthcare. Michael Griffin remembers looking through the iron gates that encircle the building and grounds and thinking, "we wouldn't dare go there". However, when they brought Denis Brosnan to see it he went for it right away.

> It's the right kind of building. We need to make that kind
> of a statement. We've got to have THAT place![10]

The symbolism was unmistakable, just as it had been when Kerry rented offices in the Hancock Building in Chicago in 1984. The choice of sites was meant to emphasise again that Kerry was a serious player in this market, a quality organisation, first class in every way, and in the UK market for the long haul. The Egham office was quite a bit larger than Kerry needed at the time, since many of its UK operations were still spread throughout various locations in the country. Headquarters staff had the luxury of stretching out comfortably in a half-empty building. Today, in 2000, the building is bursting at the seams. One reason for that was the reorganisation of the various consumer foods businesses in Ireland and the UK into one business, Kerry Foods, in early 1994. Denis Cregan assumed responsibility for all of Kerry Foods as Chairman, with Michael Griffin as Managing Director, presiding over a new strategic business unit (SBU) structure. Most non-manufacturing activities in the UK, such as sales, administration, finance and marketing, were moved to the Egham headquarters. Other operational activities remained based at the various manufacturing facilities in the UK and Ireland. The consolidation of food operations in Egham was prescient, for Kerry was gearing itself for what they predicted would happen as the structure of retailing evolved. Indeed, within a few years Tesco, Marks & Spencer, and other large UK grocery retailers had expanded into Scotland, Northern Ireland, and finally the Republic of Ireland itself. Kerry Foods, with its many scars from years of battle among the manufacturing and retailing giants in the UK, and with its exemplary reputation for service and commitment to the market and the consumer, was well positioned to take advantage of this evolving retailing structure.

By the beginning of 1994, then, all of Kerry's consumer foods operations in Ireland and the UK had been combined under the one Kerry Foods umbrella. The new SBU structure, at the time, had five business units and was headquartered in Egham. The Pork Products business in Ireland was based in Dublin, with four plants in Ireland including the newly commissioned plant at Shillelagh in County Wicklow. The Dairies unit was also based in Ireland, where it had been moved back to the Tralee headquarters, with its five Dawn dairies, its Kerry Spring mineral water facility in Ballyferriter, and its consumer dairy products (full fat and low fat spreads) still sourced out of Listowel. Specialty Poultry Products were based in Norfolk in the UK, with manufacturing sites throughout the UK. Savoury Foods (Millers and Robirch business) was based in Egham, with manufacturing sites throughout the UK and Ireland. At this point, the beef business at Meadow Meats had been broken off separately and was based in Dublin.

In the UK, considerable work had been done to put the Kerry "stamp" upon Kerry Foods' activities there. Extra help had been drafted from throughout the Kerry organisation, new systems had been developed, the SBU structure had been put into place, and the rationalisation of Millers and Robirch activities had been largely completed. The yellow fats business was continuing to grow organically. The capability — that is, the people, the management structures, and the resources — seemed to be in place. Yet still, the big "breakthrough" had yet to arrive. Recalls Michael Griffin:

> We had lots of success to show on yellow fats, a fair amount of success on the cooked poultry business out of Ireland, and lots of individual pieces, but we were only scratching away at the surface. You could probably have closed Egham at that time, and given the responsibilities back to the individual businesses, and they'd probably just have kept running along. As it turned out, the major breakthrough was around the corner.[11]

For nearly a decade in the UK, Kerry's progress had been slow, difficult and undramatic. By the end of 1994, this would all change.

Acquisition of Mattessons and Wall's, 1994

It is a risky business, in the new age of variety and diversity engendered by our globalising world economy, to cite any one food as being the "national dish" of a particular country. But if England were to claim a national dish, a strong argument could be made in favour of "bangers and mash", the colloquial term for sausage and mashed potatoes. The term "banger" itself refers to a peculiar propensity of sausages during the Second World War in Britain. Under the constraints of wartime rationing, sausages included a large amount of water that, when heated, turned to steam that escaped the sausage with a loud "bang". Even today, the total sausage consumption in the UK is something on the order of 300,000 tons per annum, or approximately 12 pounds per man, woman, and child.[12] In the UK, the best known, typically fresh and only lightly seasoned, traditional English sausage, or "banger", was the

Wall's sausage. In fact, the term "banger" and the name "Wall's" were nearly synonymous.

Wall's was a venerable firm, founded by a Richard Wall who had apprenticed himself to a pork butcher in London in 1786. By 1834, the shop was called "Wall's" and the business was well on its way to achieving the status of an institution. Wall's had already received warrants as suppliers of pork to the royal family, and the sausages that they made were famous throughout London, so much so that he had to move the business to new premises at 113 Jermyn Street in order to cater to the thriving trade. Over time, the business, now called T. Wall & Sons, Ltd., continued to expand its array of sausages, pies and cooked meats (not to mention ice cream), acquiring other manufacturers, extending its distribution throughout the United Kingdom and opening six manufacturing plants throughout the country. T. Wall & Sons itself was subsequently acquired in 1920 by the enterprise that was to become the giant Unilever company.

The story of Mattessons Meats, on the other hand, was of more recent vintage. It was started in 1947 by Richard Mattes, who bought control of an existing meat processing facility in North London. Mattes, a German who had learned the sausage-making trade in Europe, was convinced there was a market in England for the "continental" sausage. This sausage was more highly spiced and seasoned than the plainer, traditional English variety, and included various varieties of salami, German wursts, pork rings and highly spiced sausages. Mattes' intuition was correct, and the demand for continental meats grew, along with Mattessons Meats. In 1965, however, Mattessons Meats, headed at the time by Werner Mattesson, the son of the founder, was itself acquired by Unilever.

For the next 21 years, Unilever ran Wall's and Mattessons as independent business units. Mattessons continued to press its leadership in the market for continental sausages and consumer meats, and took credit for many product innovations such as the introduction of the first meat "spreads" in tubes (1966), the first pre-packed sliced meats (1970) and the first paté into the UK market. It was also a pioneer in the introduction of refrigerated vans in the early 1970s.[13] By the mid-1970s, Mattessons had built a market share of roughly 35 per cent, largely due to its extensive distribution system of vans that delivered directly to shops. With the decline of the independent retailers and the advent of the central distribution

systems favoured by the "multiples", however, market share began
to erode.[14] Nevertheless, left to its own devices and run independently within the Unilever organisation, Mattessons remained a
highly profitable business.

Wall's, however, despite its proud heritage and its status as
something of an English institution, was not only losing money, but
doing so at an ever-increasing rate. In January 1986, in an effort to
turn around the Wall's business by realising what economies of
scale and scope they could, Unilever combined the two entities
into Mattessons and Wall's, Ltd., and integrated their headquarters
and sales functions. They followed this with a Stg£25 million rationalisation plan, which included the closing of factories at Southall in
London, Chippenham in Wiltshire and Dyce in Scotland, the construction of a new, modern production facility in the Midlands, and
the addition of several new distribution centres. Approximately
2,000 jobs were lost as part of this restructuring. Ultimately, however, it was a failed endeavour. The integration of the Mattessons
and Wall's management groups never fully succeeded, and the expected economies from the restructuring never came to fruition. In
1991, Unilever reorganised the operation yet again, and incorpo-
rated Mattessons and Wall's into its Van den Bergh Foods subsidiary, which ran a highly successful core business in branded margarine and low-fat spreads, liquid oils, meat snacks, detergents, ice
cream, and other consumer products.

Van den Bergh was widely acknowledged as the foremost retail
marketing company in the UK, and perhaps the leading exponent
of consumer marketing as a discipline and an art. They had a well-
earned reputation for training and developing the "best of the
best" in marketers, shaping them into a mould that was uniquely
Van den Bergh. In the quality of their research, the care of their
planning and the power of their product launches, they had no
equal.

Again, the match simply did not work, and the Mattessons and
Wall's business was never fully integrated into Van den Bergh.
However, Mattessons and Wall's did not appear to figure importantly in Van den Bergh's future plans, and there was little likelihood that even with their sterling credentials, they would be able
to turn around the troubled enterprise. Mattessons and Wall's
again lost money through 1992, and Unilever finally decided to get

out. Unilever already knew that, in the Kerry Group, they had at least one interested buyer.

Kerry's designs on Mattessons and Wall's were nothing new. Almost five years earlier, Michael Griffin and Hugh Friel had made overtures to Guy Walker, the chairman of Van den Bergh, regarding their plans for Mattessons and Wall's. The message at the time had come back loud and clear from their merchant bankers, Morgan Grenfell, that "you couldn't afford it"![15] Kerry continued to express its interest, and in September 1993, Guy Walker wrote to Friel that he did not wish to take the matter any further. But, on 7 April 1994, Walker wrote to confirm that they were now prepared to open discussions regarding the sale. Kerry subsequently sent a questionnaire to which Van den Bergh responded. This set the ball rolling. By that time, Kerry had had ample opportunity to study Mattessons and Wall's and were convinced that it would be a perfect fit. There was no question but that they would bid on the business.

Initially, Kerry's offer was rejected, and Van den Bergh provided additional information in order to justify a higher price. It was not until 24 July that the acquisition was agreed in principle, subject to satisfactory completion of the due diligence process.

The acquisition, however, would hardly be without risk. As additional information had been digested it became clear that Mattessons and Wall's financial performance had been less satisfactory than expected. Unilever had made many efforts to turn the Mattessons and Wall's operation around, all to no avail, and some analysts had speculated that losses at the subsidiary ran into the millions. Kerry was not remotely of the same size as Unilever, and could not absorb losses such as this for any period of time; they would have to turn the operation around very, very quickly. There would be restructuring costs involved, as well as additional investments in facility. Kerry would also be absorbing a work force of about 1,100 people, with potential redundancy costs in the millions of pounds.

Yet the attraction for Kerry was overwhelming, and Kerry's appetite for Mattessons and Wall's had, if anything, intensified since they first set their sights upon it. Considerable thought had already been applied to both the physical and financial aspects of a reconstruction of the business. This was the "Denny's" equivalent that they had been awaiting for so long. The Mattessons, Richmond and Wall's brands were well known on the UK supermarket shelves, and represented an entrée into the value-added, branded consumer business in the UK that they had coveted for so long. Indeed, even though the level of advertising for Mattessons had declined precipitously, consumers' "level of recall" for Mattessons remained very strong. It may be difficult to overestimate Kerry's enthusiasm. Michael Drummey described the general reaction at Kerry like this:

> When the opportunity came to buy Mattesson and Wall's, we went for it baldheaded. We knew that we had a couple of gold nuggets there. It was a marketing person's dream! The emotional value that Wall's, Richmond and Mattessons had was positively captivating, at least as far as I was concerned. We knew we could take these brands and resurrect them and do some very good things with them. Here we had an opportunity to capture a British icon, for after all, the banger is to England what spaghetti is to Italy![16]

Michael Griffin was equally enthusiastic, but conscious of the downside as well:

> For us, we had a team ready to play in a bigger arena. We would be coming into a major UK branded business for the first time. We didn't have that exposure yet, but we were dying to have a cut at it. Still, we were a little apprehensive over whether we'd be able to turn it around or not.[17]

It was clear that the Kerry belief in the values locked in the brands, and its own proven ability to achieve a seamless integration of the business, were the key elements upon which success would depend.

The negotiations became protracted and complex. A meeting in Burgess Hill on 19 August, led by Denis Cregan on the Kerry side, ended abruptly and there was a consequent lull in the dialogue. However, both sides had an equally strong desire to complete the deal, and it was agreed that all outstanding issues were to be somehow resolved by the end of September. Philip O'Connor from Kerry and Bill Allen from Mattessons and Wall's were detailed to come to mutually acceptable agreement on the matters which were unresolved. It was October, however, before agreement was reached with Van den Bergh on the myriad of details associated with the acquisition. For example, within Unilever there were many arrangements whereby business units such as Mattessons and Wall's benefited from use of a central pool of corporate resources. These, of course, would not be transferring with the business, which meant that some measurement of the value and cost of such services would have to be factored into the acquisition price. This was a complicated and difficult task. Nevertheless, the will on the part of both parties was sufficiently strong to ensure that, even though two target completion dates were missed, the contract was finally signed at the Unilever headquarters in Blackfriars on 11 November 1994.

Mattessons and Wall's, with sales of approximately Stg£80 million in 1993, would double Kerry Foods' sales in the UK. The acquisition would add six well known UK brands (Mattessons, Wall's, Richmonds, Lawson, New York Deli and Valley Farm), two manufacturing facilities at Manchester and Durham, and (another) nation-wide distribution system (with van sales).[18] Operationally, the many overlaps between Mattessons and Wall's and Kerry's already rationalised Millers and Robirch manufacturing and distribution systems would provide considerable opportunity for savings and establish the only nationwide chilled meat sales operation in the UK.

The purchase price has never been disclosed by Kerry or Unilever, but media reports at the time suggested that Kerry may have paid something less than Mattessons and Wall's roughly Stg£25 million net book value. A discounted price, in fact, was assumed, given the obvious restructuring costs as well as the fact that, as one writer dryly noted, "Mattessons and Wall's 'clearly wasn't a favourite son' from Unilever's perspective."[19] Within a day or two of the acquisition in November, Kerry managers were already deeply engaged in moving the business forward, already spending money on developing the brands. Product quality was quickly upgraded, distribution was rationalised, sales forces were combined, administrative responsibilities were consolidated in Egham, and the entire operation was quickly tightened up.

By the end of 1995, the task of integrating and rationalising the new business in the UK was substantially complete. The upfront work that Kerry had done in developing systems and structures after the purchase of Millers and Robirch had been put to good use in the integration of Mattessons and Wall's. The business provided a profit in its first full year of operation. Says Michael Griffin:

> We got a lot of things right with the Mattessons and Wall's business, and the integration with the Millers and Robirch business. We surprised the retail trade and the food industry with the success we had. Before that, with only Millers and Robirch, we were seen as being on the periphery, one of the pack, and no great threat to anyone. But the job we did with Mattessons and Wall's won us a lot of respect. Personally, I think it is the best acquisition the organisation ever made![20]

Kerry in the UK already had an existing operation with its Millers and Robirch business, and had worked hard to develop good relationships with retailers. Mattessons and Wall's customers had proven to be very loyal to their brands, when they could find the products! Kerry's first significant accomplishment was thus in ensuring that the Mattessons and Wall's brands achieved nationwide distribution. Kerry also worked with great energy to improve Mattessons and Wall's listings, and made major investments in quality. Once product distribution had improved, Kerry began to focus advertising campaigns in support of the brands. Wall's, for instance, was put on national television again after an absence of some years. Additionally, Kerry began to invest in "category management" programmes, designed to assist retailers to realise the best performance possible from their sales of Mattessons and Wall's products. Finally, Kerry focused clearly upon consumer needs, and significant resources were expended on product innovations designed to meet contemporary consumer needs for convenience. All of these initiatives helped to further develop excellent relationships with retailers. Says Fliss Cox of Kerry Foods, "We built upon these relationships, and this helped us to make Mattessons Wall's a success, very quickly."[21]

The acquisition of Mattessons and Wall's represented the end, and the beginning, of another chapter in the evolving history of Kerry Foods. Kerry had set their sights upon what, to them, was a glittering prize, and despite delays and impediments had finally achieved it. With Mattessons and Wall's, Kerry brought off a deal which, in terms of its strategic significance, its value, and its subsequent profitability, could without too much hyperbole be considered another sparkling jewel in the Kerry crown.

In 1994, before the first full year of Mattessons and Wall's results, Kerry Foods had a turnover of £322 million, with about 60 per cent representing sales in Ireland. By 1999, total Kerry Foods turnover was in the neighbourhood of £700 million. This growth, which was almost exclusively in the UK, has exceeded Kerry's primary, and very public, commitment to a doubling of its sales revenue every five years. As Kerry looks to the future, clearly the growth imperative will be even more critical, and Kerry Foods will be driven to increase in size and scale even further.

Notes

[1] John O'Callaghan, personal interview, 27 March 2000.

[2] Michael Drummey, personal correspondance, 26 July 2000.

[3] Michael Drummey, personal interview, 6 January 2000.

[4] Ned O'Callaghan, personal interview, 8 July 1999.

[5] *Management*, "Kerry's Ingredients for Success", September 1992, p. 15.

[6] Denis Brosnan, personal interview, 7 October 1999.

[7] Ned O'Callaghan, personal interview, 8 July 1999.

[8] Brendan McGrath, "Kerry Group Pulls Out of Meadow Meats", *The Irish Times*, 21 December 1995, p. 16.

[9] Michael Griffin, personal interview, 5 January 2000.

[10] Michael Griffin, personal interview, 5 January 2000.

[11] Michael Griffin, personal interview, 5 January 2000.

[12] Information provided by Kerry Foods.

[13] "The Mattessons Story" from an internal Kerry Foods informational handout.

[14] "The Mattessons Story", op. cit.

[15] Michael Griffin, personal interview, 5 January 2000.

[16] Michael Drummey, personal interview, 6 January 2000.

[17] Michael Griffin, personal interview, 5 January 2000.

[18] Richmond's Irish sausage was an interesting brand as well. While Wall's was the major sausage brand in terms of awareness, Richmond outsold it to the extent that as a single brand, Richmond was the market leader. Richmond was an anachronism in that, although it had its own particular flavour and texture characteristics, it was by no means similar to what a consumer would associate with "Irishness". In fact, Richmond, a small town in Yorkshire, was far removed from any location that would suggest an Irish history or tradition.

[19] Paul O'Kane (1994), "Kerry Group Acquisition to Double UK Turnover", *The Irish Times*, 6 July 1994, p. 12.

[20] Michael Griffin, personal interview, 5 January 2000.

[21] Fliss Cox, personal communication, 25 October 2000.

Chapter 12

On the Home Front in Kerry, 1980–1999

*The Kerry farmers have been with us all the way through.
They invested in the Group at the very start, and have seen
the success of the Group since then. They are our people,
and we care about them. There is a great pride in that.*
— Michael Hanrahan, Chairman, Kerry Group[1]

This chapter examines a number of issues back on the "home
front" in County Kerry. Although no longer a significant contributor to the financial results of the enterprise, dairy farming in Kerry
remained inextricably linked with the character, the ethos and the
culture of the Kerry Group. The face of farming in Kerry, too, had
changed considerably. Additionally, a pair of court cases, with
their roots in the very early days of Kerry's history, also played
themselves out at home. Both the Fry-Cadbury case and the Bord
Bainne case offer insights into the nature of the Kerry organisation.
Finally, the issue of farmer control of the Kerry Group has been as
important as it has been highly emotional. The important 1996 decision to reduce the co-operative shareholding below the 51 per
cent majority threshold is also examined in this chapter.

Kerry Agribusiness

Since the collapse of the milk supply in 1979 first impelled the then Kerry Co-op along a path of diversification, acquisition and expansion, the Kerry organisation had travelled far afield from its roots on the dairy farms of County Kerry. To an outside observer, bedazzled by the rags to riches quality of Kerry's growth and diversification, it would be easy to overlook the continuing role of the "agri" business over the past 20 years of the organisation's life. Still, just as the roots of a tree may grow stronger and deeper even as trunk, branches and leaves grow, arch and stretch, the roots of the Kerry Group remained well embedded in its native Kerry soil. Even as the group had grown less and less reliant upon the production and processing of milk, to the extent that it was scarcely a side-show within the overall commercial activities of the enterprise, Kerry's commitment to its agribusiness activities, and to its farmer-suppliers, did not slacken.

The tangible vehicle for the organisation's ongoing relationship with its farmer-suppliers has been the Kerry Agribusiness Division, as it is called today.[2] Through the early 1980s, certainly, the emphasis had been placed squarely on increasing milk production, improving quality and upgrading farm facilities. Under the leadership of Tim Lyons and his colleagues in the Farm Services Division, and with the continued help of the Kerry County Agricultural Advisors, the dairy industry in Kerry had come a long way in the short space of ten years. The milk yield per cow had grown from 497 gallons in 1974 to some 720 gallons in 1984, an increase of 45 per cent. Quality and hygiene standards were dramatically improved, in reaction to both Kerry's needs for quality milk inputs and to pending EC standards.

The brucellosis eradication campaign, however, had many impacts, both immediate and lasting, upon Kerry farmers. Clearly, the nearly 16 per cent decline in production from 1978 to 1981 had important repercussions for the Kerry organisation itself, as it embarked on a crusade to literally remake and "re-imagine" itself. Closer to the ground, however, the volume crisis changed the dairy industry in Kerry as well. First, it dramatically reduced the number of active dairy farmers in the county. The roughly 7,300 dairy suppliers to the Co-op in 1978 were reduced to 5,800 in

1982, a decline of over 20 per cent. Secondly, and perhaps more importantly in the long term, was the fact that Kerry farmers would literally never have the time to rebuild those volumes, as EC quotas on the production of milk were introduced in 1984. These quotas were based on 1983 production volumes, and even though Kerry farmers had been able to recover a good portion of their volume loss due to the eradication scheme, they were well behind where they would have been otherwise. Yet those relatively low Kerry volumes became the basis for all future production. Kerry farmers had now entered the new "age of limits" brought in by the EC. Having reaped the rewards of nearly ten years of EC membership by virtue of the higher EC milk prices, Kerry farmers and their co-operative now had to deal with the downside of membership. To many farmers, it did not seem fair. Although they had improved their milk yields and quality considerably over the past ten years, they were still below the EC averages. Ireland, after all, had been a latecomer to the EC. The farmers in other member states had had far more time to enjoy the benefits of membership and to improve their efficiency. To Irish farmers, Ireland (and Kerry) had natural advantages for the development of a highly efficient dairy industry, and the EC should let it specialise in and develop this sector. This, of course, would mean the ability to achieve sufficient size to reap full economies of scale. But this was not to be. The EC introduced the superlevy system in 1984, which authorised sharp penalties for countries (and ultimately the individual producers) that exceeded the mandated EC quota limits.

It was, indeed, the end of an era in Kerry agriculture. This was driven home vividly, and sadly, by the death of Tim Lyons in June 1984. If Kerry farmers had ever had a guru of improved production techniques, quality and yields, it was Tim Lyons. The Kerry organisation had lost one of its leading lights at the young age of 49, the farmers had lost a powerful advocate, and the county had lost a genuine hero.

Kerry, whose suppliers had delivered 87 million gallons of milk in 1978 (98 million gallons, if deliveries from federated co-operatives are included), would not achieve such quantities again. With increased quantities no longer the answer to farmers' efforts to improve their incomes, the focus on profit now turned to cost control. The Agriculture Division at Kerry had itself been hurt by the reduced requirements for feed, fertiliser and other farm inputs, lower levels of agricultural trading and reductions in cattle breeding. It also had an infrastructure for milk collection, assembly and farm trading that was now larger than it need be. A rationalisation program was introduced at the end of 1981 and completed during 1982. Some of the smaller farm stores were closed, and others reduced to two- or three-day-a-week schedules. Similar steps were taken with branch creameries. Excess transport was taken off the road. Alternate day collection of milk was introduced to more and more locations. For many farmers, the entire notion of not having daily collection of milk was a difficult one to swallow. Finally, further efforts needed to be made to expand the use of bulk collection of milk at the farm. Even through 1980, probably no more than 10 per cent of the Kerry Co-op milk was actually picked up at the farm by bulk tankers.

None of these rationalisation steps was accomplished without some level of resistance. The closure or reduction in hours of some of the farm stores and branch creameries was a particularly emotive issue. Local farmers had deep and emotional attachments to these establishments that had little to do with economic logic. Liam Chute, who had succeeded Tim Lyons at the Ag Division, remembers one occasion:

> We had to do some unpalatable work but at times it had its lighter moments. I remember going out to Kilgarvan one night. We were rationalising the Kenmare creamery at the time, which was small, only about a million gallons. When I arrived at the meeting place, the place was packed, so I had to park all the way up the road. I said to a guy, "What's going on here tonight?" and he said "Oh, there's a fella coming down here from Kerry Group, and we're going to sort him out!" But this was not that unusual. We would go out, and we'd get attacked. That's the way it went. We accepted that. It was par for the course.[3]

Rationalisation was difficult, but necessary. Inefficient practices could not be sustained in the new and competitive environment. After all, the days of the Dairy Disposal Company and the crossroads creamery were long over. But, if there was some stick given with regard to this aspect of the rationalisation plan, there was an even larger flap a few years later with the advent of bulk storage and collection.

By 1990, particularly in view of the increasingly stringent quality criteria of the EU's Dairy Hygiene regulations, the time had come to expand the use of bulk refrigeration, storage and collection to the many small farmers who made up the major constituency of the Kerry Co-op. Up to two-thirds of the co-op's farmers, in fact, could be considered in this category, with quotas of less than 20,000 gallons a year.[4] The Agriculture Division's plan was for all farmers to purchase special refrigerated tanks for the storage of their milk (financed by low interest loans from Kerry), and to convert to a three-day-a-week schedule of collection. This raised some considerable concern on the part of many of these small farmers, for a variety of disparate reasons. First was the expense of the tanks. For many farmers, they simply could not or would not see the benefit of refrigeration. Given their small quotas, they felt it would take far too long to pay back the investment. To others, it was another measure designed to drive out the "small man" in favour of the larger farmers who were able to achieve the benefits of scale. For still others, it became enmeshed in Kerry farm politics, with Kerry Group's plans becoming a lightning rod for a political row between representatives of the IFA and the ICMSA.[5] Finally, and perhaps most important of all, the drive turned out, quite simply, to be ill-timed. Just as bulk refrigeration was being introduced in earnest, the milk price had declined precipitously, even with the Kerry Group subsidising their prices to farmers to a substantial extent. By this time, Dick O'Sullivan had succeeded Liam Chute as the head of the Ag Division. In May 1990, he attended a highly emotional meeting of about 700 dairy farmers organised under the aegis of the Kerry IFA at Ballygarry House Hotel, near Tralee. At this meeting, a succession of speakers demonised Kerry Group, all but accusing it of trying to force small farmers off their farms. One newspaper account said that:

> Two curly-haired Kerry "garsoons" in the front rows at the meeting of seriously worried farmers in Tralee recently were singled out for special attention. "What future have they on the land?" asked a leading IFA officer. "Will they be able to follow their fathers and grandfathers into

farming?" Nobody in the audience of well over 800 in the ballroom of the Ballygarry House Hotel said "yea" or "nay" but, by their stony silence, they answered the question in their own way.[6]

In addition to O'Sullivan, several Kerry Co-op Directors (Dan Barry and Tom Carroll) attended the meeting, at the invitation of the IFA, and mounted a spirited defence of the Kerry Group in difficult and highly politicised circumstances. They noted that Kerry Group was cross-subsidising the milk price to farmers, to the tune of £3–4 million, with profits from other parts of the organisation's activities. Even though it did not cover the entire price drop to farmers, it tempered it considerably. Amidst all the criticism of Kerry Group, and particularly of Denis Brosnan, Director Dan Barry stood up and said, "I can tell you, Denis Brosnan is the greatest man that ever struck the dairy fields in Ireland and that is well known throughout the county".[7] Dick O'Sullivan summed things up:

> Why shouldn't our people have the benefit of the best quality milk just because they are small? I don't care if they are 10,000, 20,000, 30,000 or 50,000 [gallons], the spirit in Kerry that started it will make sure that those people will get an equal opportunity and we'll see that they do. I said that nobody will be put out of business because of refrigeration if they genuinely want to stay in it, and I meant it, and it will happen.

> We have given a loan scheme. . . . We have a branch structure that others have taken out in the name of efficiency — but we haven't. Why have we left it there? Because our branch manager is the link with our farmer. In actual fact in many cases he is also a banker and this year I have no doubt that he will be used to the full in that capacity. . . . Nobody has mentioned the fact that we collect milk from West Cork to Lisdoonvarna, through areas where others would shrink before they would even visit, never mind bring 6,000 gallon trucks through it and we never charge a penny for that collection. My last message to you is this: you can rest assured, all of you, that all farmers will have the benefit of refrigerated and top quality milk in the years ahead.[8]

This tempest in a teapot blew over, and refrigerated bulk storage and alternate day collection became the norm. The incident is indicative, however, of the bumps on the road as Kerry farmers faced up to the economic realities of a new time. Progress was continuous, but it did not come easily. Nevertheless, it should be emphasised that the Kerry Group enjoyed, generally, very strong support from its farmer-supplier constituency. Of course, there were grumbles from time to time about elements of the various rationalisation schemes, the ups and downs of the milk price, whose son or daughter did or didn't get a job at the Co-op, and the myriad issues, great and small, that afflict any organisation (particularly those with a co-operative dimension). But Kerry farmers as a group were staunch supporters of the Kerry Group even as it directed its activities further afield from the dairy industry. Indeed, who would know better than the farmers themselves the limited prospects for the dairy industry?

Most observers of the dairy industry in Ireland, however, will tell you that there is one element, and one element alone, that ultimately dictates the quality of farmers' relationships with their company (or their co-operative). First, last and always, it is the price that they receive for their milk. Any successful relationship with farmer-suppliers must begin and end with this. From the very beginning, in 1974, the Kerry Co-op had made it a point to pay a better price for milk than what the Dairy Disposal Company had been paying. In those early years, when farmer support was critical to get the enterprise off the ground and united behind a common purpose, maintaining a high milk price was a key element in maintaining farmer loyalty. Still, there was a thin line to be walked as well. Money had to be retained in the business for growth and development; not everything could be returned in the milk price. Similarly, some money would need to be held back in good times to be held in reserve for the bad times. This was only logical. Luckily, the early years of the Kerry Co-op were set within the context of the EEC, and the gradual adjustment of milk prices upward to EEC levels. This stroke of good fortune gave the Kerry organisation the necessary space to increase farmers' returns regularly, while holding back some portion for capital investment and general reserves. For example, in 1974, the average price paid per gallon of milk was 24.3 pence per gallon; seven years later, in

1981, the average price was 61.2 pence per gallon, an increase of over 250 per cent. When combined with the increases in both productivity and herd size (at least through 1979), one can appreciate the relative bonanza that Kerry farmers realised during those early years.

After brucellosis eradication, the end of the adjustment period to EEC prices and the application of the quota system, this degree of "running room" was much reduced. The development of the milk price was a delicate balancing act between trying to provide a reasonable and fair return to the suppliers, and attending to the legitimate needs of other, more lucrative businesses within the overall Kerry enterprise. Not surprisingly, although not always the highest, Kerry's prices have most often been in the first tier of milk prices.

As the Kerry organisation has met its targets for growth and profitability, it is evident that at times some of these profits have gone towards "subsidising", at least to some extent, the milk price paid to its farmers. At Kerry, it is taken as a matter of loyalty that the organisation will "take care" of those farmers who took a chance on an infant co-operative back in 1974, and that one way of accomplishing this is through the milk price. More pragmatically, it also helps ensure the continued strong support from the membership of the Kerry Co-operative itself, who still maintain a significant stake (37 per cent) in the Kerry Group enterprise. Of course, this also has the effect of putting additional pressure on other Irish milk processors to maintain a high milk price. From time to time, there have been complaints that Kerry, through its high milk price, is trying to take over the milk business, but this can hardly be true. With Kerry's dependence on its milk processing for achieving growth and profits lessening with every passing year, the impact of movements in the milk price has reduced correspondingly.

By 1999, the number of milk suppliers to Kerry had declined to approximately 3,500 and Denis Brosnan had already predicted that number would further decline to 2,400 by 2004. Bulk tankers (either at the farm or at assigned collection points) now collect almost all supplies of milk. New schemes such as the Protein 2000 Programme and the subsequent Focus on Profit Programme have been advanced to pay for milk on the basis of its protein, as well as its butterfat content. The strict imposition of the EU Superlevy system has changed the way farmers run their farms, as they constantly monitor and attempt to forecast their production to match it with their available quota. Farmsteads are consolidating, increasing in size by either purchase or lease of available land and quota. Yields have steadily increased, quality standards continually upgraded, and farmers themselves have become increasingly better educated. Farming has become a highly technical endeavour. There are no more donkey and carts to be seen on the roads of Kerry, with a pair of milk churns clanking in the back, headed for the creamery. The face of dairy farming in Kerry is utterly changed.

The Dispute with Fry-Cadbury

In the midst of that pivotal period of 1979–1980, while the Kerry milk supply was contracting and the organisation was moving towards dramatic and fundamental changes in its strategic direction, a dispute unexpectedly arose with Fry-Cadbury. It is ironic that, at a time when the organisation was beginning to move well beyond the confines of its core business and its home location, it was simultaneously pulled back into a messy dispute that had its roots in the very birth of the Kerry Co-op. On one level, this legal altercation with Fry-Cadbury could be viewed as a mere distraction, a sidebar to more important themes of organisational life and history. On another level, however, Kerry's handling of the Fry-Cadbury affair may be instructive in revealing something of its organisational ethos generally, and its combative approach to litigation specifically.

It will be remembered that Fry-Cadbury (Ireland) Ltd. had built the first milk processing plant in Rathmore, County Kerry in 1948. This plant, which produced a chocolate crumb confection for further use by the firm's confectionery operation in a Dublin factory, had been dependent since its opening upon a reliable supply of milk from the creameries of Kerry, most of which were owned and operated by the Dairy Disposal Company. As the campaign for the formation of a countywide Kerry Co-operative gathered steam in 1973, there were concerns about the continuation of that supply of milk to Rathmore. This, of course, was also a matter of concern for the government. Fry-Cadbury's factory at Rathmore provided steady employment in a part of the country where such jobs were in short supply, and the government had naturally determined that the "public interest" would best be served by preserving those jobs. In the end, the agreement that was negotiated contained a clause that obliged Kerry to "take all the necessary steps to ensure that there will after the possession date be no diminution of the milk supply (as in 1973)" to the Rathmore factory.[9] In its broadest terms, then, the agreement seemed simple and relatively unambiguous: Kerry had a continuing obligation to assure a milk supply to Rathmore. In its particulars, however, the agreement was more than a little vague. For instance, although the price was to be "comparable to that receivable from potential other purchasers", this could obviously be subject to a fair degree of interpretation.[10] The fact that the term of the obligation itself was unspecified added further ambiguity. Finally, while Kerry appeared to have an obligation to provide a supply of milk to Rathmore, there was no note of Rathmore ever having any similar obligation to accept it![11] All in all, this conditional clause that was added by the government to protect Rathmore's milk supply had enough manoeuvring room within it to drive several large lorries.

Legal quibbling aside, however, the relationship between Fry-Cadbury and Kerry Co-operative proceeded in a professional and businesslike manner for the better part of the first six years of the Co-op's existence. Generally, the quantity of milk to be supplied each year, and the price, were arrived at through the "give and take" of negotiations. Each year, negotiations would commence in the spring, different positions would be taken, a series of meetings and correspondence would ensue, and eventually a compromise would be reached. Of course, the fact that Dick Godsil (the man responsible for the location of the plant at Rathmore in the first place) and Denis Brosnan had an excellent personal relationship probably greased the wheels somewhat. In any event, they always arrived at a compromise agreement. Rathmore got its milk, and Kerry got a return for its farmers that it considered acceptable.

In early 1980, however, this changed. Godsil by now was with Fry-Cadbury in Dublin and not directly responsible for the Rathmore–Kerry negotiations. There was now a new team of Fry-Cadbury executives involved, who had a distinctly different view of the original agreement. When the negotiations commenced that year, Kerry and Fry-Cadbury were apart by a penny a gallon on the milk price, and Kerry was actually prepared to compromise for a ha'penny. Typically, such a concession on the part of both sides would have led to an agreement. This year, however, Fry-Cadbury dug in their heels, refused to compromise, and instead fell back on the original agreement. But their interpretation of that agreement was that Kerry had an obligation to supply the set quantity of milk, at some specific price to be arrived at by a particular formula. To them, there was no bargaining involved. At a last meeting in Killarney, Fry-Cadbury made their challenge clear: "You (Kerry) are obliged to supply us, and we will take you to court to make you do so."

The words "we'll see you in court" are fighting words and Kerry came to the litigation with all guns blazing. The time for compromise was now over, and the issue for Kerry was perhaps a larger one. They were committed to fighting this case in court to the fullest extent, and appropriated the resources to do so. Kerry argued that the clause in the original agreement with the DDC did not have any "business efficacy", that is, it could not be applied as a template or a guideline as to how future business relationships should be ordered. Fry-Cadbury, for their part, argued that Kerry was required to provide the quantity of milk at the "formula" price that Fry-Cadbury had determined. For good measure, they also argued that Kerry was in beach of Article 86 of the Treaty of Rome (the formation of the EEC) that forbade firms to abuse a dominant market position "within the common market". Finally, they also held the Dairy Disposal Company as a defendant in the case, arguing that the DDC had certain fiduciary responsibilities to Fry-Cadbury by virtue of their sale of DDC assets to Kerry Co-operative in 1974.

The case was heard by the High Court, and a judgment rendered by Justice J. Barrington on 17 July 1981. In a nutshell, the judge dismissed all of the plaintiff's claims, and threw the case out of court. He found that Fry-Cadbury and Kerry were essentially engaged in a "series of bargains arrived at by parties engaged in an ongoing business relationship rather than a series of determinations of milk prices in accordance with a preordained formula".[12] But, for Fry-Cadbury, the outcome of the court case went even further to their detriment. The court, in fact, found that "Cad-

burys have failed to prove that they have any rights under clause
19" [the clause of the agreement governing the sale of DDC assets
to Kerry Co-op that dealt with the Rathmore "issue"].[13] In other
words, Kerry had no obligation to supply milk to Fry-Cadbury at
all!

Given the outcome of the court case, Kerry could have cut off
the supply of milk to the Rathmore factory and perhaps found more
profitable outlets for their milk. But the Rathmore factory was still
an important element in the economy of Kerry, with lots of people
dependent upon it for their livelihood. Even if there were no legal
obligation to supply the factory, most people in Kerry would have
agreed that the Kerry Co-op still had a moral obligation to supply
the milk, not for any commercial purpose, but purely (as the DDC
had always intended) in the *public interest*. So the relationship with
Fry-Cadbury went back to what it had always been, a normal
trading relationship, and Kerry continues to supply milk. Denis
Brosnan remembers a moment during the trial when Dick Godsil
was in the witness box, and Counsel posed a question to him:
"What would you have done, Mr Godsil, if you were still responsible for all the Rathmore facility?" Dick said, "I've spent the last 25
years haggling with co-ops in Kerry, but we always settled."[14] To
this day, there is a negotiation every year over quantity and price,
and an agreement is always hammered out.

In this case, Kerry's combative approach to litigation gave them
a clear, and one would imagine very sweet, victory. They would
pursue other cases with similar energy and commitment, although
not always with the same result.

The Break with Bord Bainne

Kerry's relationship with an Bord Bainne, the Irish Dairy Board,
had always been strained. Even back to the days before the construction of the milk processing factory in Listowel, some of the
major promoters of the project had complained, rightly or
wrongly, that Bord Bainne had been less supportive than they
might have been in getting the project, at long last, off the ground.
Nevertheless, with the construction of the factory and the subsequent formation of the Kerry Co-operative in 1974, the co-op developed a very active trading relationship with Bord Bainne, becoming at one point their largest supplier of export butter (sold

under the *Kerrygold* label), and a regular supplier of milk powder and butter oil.

Bord Bainne, originally formed in 1961 as a "semi-state" body charged with the marketing of Irish dairy products abroad, had converted to a co-operative form of organisation in 1972. This was done in preparation for Ireland's accession to membership in the EEC, which took a dim view of government meddling in agricultural markets. The Board's membership was composed of Irish dairy co-operatives, which paid a nominal subscription for shares allocated to them on the basis of their milk volumes. In addition to the issue of shares, Bord Bainne raised money through levies placed on milk suppliers, as it sought to build up some level of capital. The purpose of the Board was to maximise the return to its shareholders for the sales of dairy produce throughout the world. In other words, its job was to shift Ireland's milk as best it could. The guiding principle was one of co-operative marketing, so that Irish firms could avoid counterproductive competition in the export markets, while reaping the benefits of marketing scale that Bord Bainne could offer. Bord Bainne also played a leading role in building a high quality image for Irish dairy produce throughout the world.

All member-suppliers to the Board were paid the same price for the same product produced at the same time, regardless of the actual market price that any specific transaction generated. According to these operating principles, all members were obligated to export their products through Bord Bainne. Failing that, they could be expelled from the organisation. This, however, may have been honoured as much in the breach as in the observance. Many of the co-operative members of Bord Bainne seemed to have "escape clauses" — various arrangements (already in place before they joined Bord Bainne) that the Board recognised, and allowed them to maintain direct supplier relationships with certain customers for particular products. In this, Kerry's arrangement with Erie Casein for casein exports to North America was no exception.

Originally, Bord Bainne was primarily concerned with moving butter, skim milk powder and other commodity products. For these products, Kerry and others were happy enough to avail themselves of Bord Bainne's services. But in the early 1970s, the number of products were increasing, as were the squabbles over what products could, must or should be marketed through the

Board. These sorts of disputes, of course, were inevitable. Bord Bainne's task was to maximise an average price that would apply to everyone, while individual firms would take the average price when it suited them, but would try to maximise their individual prices when they could. Kerry, for its part, dutifully sold its butter and milk powder through the Board, and its casein and other products outside the Board. The relationship, however, grew more complex as Kerry's R&D team began to develop more "added-value" products that, in Kerry's view, were not the type of commodity products best marketed by the Board.

The relationship between Kerry and Bord Bainne, despite lots of ups and downs, persevered well into the late 1980s. Kerry continued to market all of its "technical" or "value-added" products outside the Board, and its skim milk powder, butter, and butter oil through the Board. In early 1987, however, a serious row broke out between Kerry and the Board about the low-fat butter spread (*Sunglow*) that Kerry had developed exclusively for Marks & Spencer in the UK. This was the spark that ignited the fuse for the eventual break between Kerry and the Board. The dispute was over whether it (*Sunglow*) was a butter product or not. The Board believed that Kerry had an obligation to market it through them (since it contained butterfat) and they in turn would supply it to Marks & Spencer. Kerry, with its focus on forging direct relationships with its customers in the UK, found such an idea completely unpalatable. Both sides stood their ground, and Kerry continued to sell the spread outside the Board. But, in reaction to the dispute, it also began to significantly reduce the quantity of butter and skim milk powder it marketed through the Board, finding its own markets for the butter, and funding the working capital to store the inventory (most butter is produced in the summer in Ireland). By late 1987, the relationship was heading for a new low.

At this point, Bord Bainne upped the ante considerably. In reacting to those firms (and Kerry was not the only one) that they saw as developing their own businesses in competition with the Board (even while still members of it), the Board moved to adopt new rules to improve the position of those firms that traded exclusively with it. They took the view that it was now time to redefine its status as a co-operative organisation, and to create rules to ensure that those who traded through the Board were the ones who owned the Board. In

November 1988 at a special general meeting, the membership approved a number of rule changes concerning voting rights, the issue of bonus shares and processes for electing a board of directors. These changes would have the effect of seriously diluting Kerry's share of Bord Bainne (since they were now trading with the Board at a very low level of volume). Kerry, joined by Avonmore Foods plc, initiated legal proceedings challenging the new rules.

The question put to the court was fundamental. What is the value of a co-op share? Is it, and does it remain, only the nominal amount (typically £1 per share) that was invested initially? Or is it more appropriately the shareholder's relevant percentage of the underlying value (e.g. net asset value) of the co-operative? In this case, the relevant value of the shareholding of Kerry approximated £10 million. Kerry's argument was that, while it had been a member of the Dairy Board during the time when that net asset value had been built, it would never see that value returned to it. Under the new rules, its shareholding would be gradually diluted until its percentage of ownership in it was minimal.

There were opportunities to settle out of court, and several of the principals may have been inclined to do so. However, as there were multiple parties involved in the suit, this proved too difficult, and the case went to trial. Quite simply, Kerry lost the case, and lost the appeal, and that was that. As Noel Cawley, by then the Managing Director of Bord Bainne, remarked:

> Once and for all we defined what the nature of a co-op was, and put a value on a co-op share, at least in law. But it [the court case] is nothing I'd want to go through again.[15]

There was little ambiguity in the court's finding:

> Assets required by an industrial and provident society are the property of the society and no shareholder has a legal right to any specific portion thereof. Such a society is also free to issue shares to new members or to allot new shares to existing members even though the effect is to reduce the fractional interest of existing members in the capital of the society. There is no implied term in the contract between a shareholder and the society of which he is a member that the fractional interest he has in the society's share capital will remain constant.[16]

Kerry contemplated taking the case on to the Court of Justice of the European Community, but ultimately decided against it. With the loss of the court case, Kerry resigned from Bord Bainne, and its break with the Board was now complete. Although Kerry, in the years since the court case, still trades with the Board from time to time, it is strictly a normal, arms-length trading relationship.

1996 — The Reduction of Kerry Co-operative's Shareholding in Kerry Group and the "Unlocking" of Value

In 1986, when the Kerry Co-op agreed to float the enterprise on the stock market and create Kerry Group plc, it also created a complicated rule structure that stipulated that the Co-op would continue to own at least 51 per cent of the new public company. This provision, in fact, was critical in assuaging farmers' fears of losing control of the enterprise. Without it, it is doubtful that Kerry farmers would have approved the flotation. In the ensuing decade, however, a great deal had happened. Kerry Group's success, through acquisitions, diversification and expansion, had effectively changed the nature of the organisation. Several factors in particular led to a new proposal on the part of Kerry Group's executive team that the Co-op further reduce their shareholding in the group to below 50 per cent.

Firstly, the Kerry Group's rapid growth had required a high level of borrowing. This, in turn, left the firm highly geared (or "leveraged"), with more and more of its productive capital funded by borrowings rather than shareholder equity. Although a high gearing level itself was not necessarily a cause for concern (financial institutions were more concerned with cash flow and "interest cover", that is, the firm's ability to service the debt), neither was it perceived as ideal. Although there was no evidence to suggest that Kerry had bypassed any growth opportunities because of it, there was a perception in some quarters that its high debt and the limits on its ability to raise further equity acted as a more generalised constraint on its financing opportunities.

Secondly, the farmer-owners of the Co-operative, with their 51 per cent stake in the Group, owned an asset of some considerable value, but had no liquidity since co-operative shares did not trade on the market. However, the shares that they *directly* owned in the Kerry Group traded, and had an objectively determined (market) value. Most of these co-operative shareholders had taken advantage of the opportunity to buy Kerry Group shares in 1986, and subsequently as opportunities had come up. The fact that these shares had appreciated rapidly in value was also not irrelevant! At the end of 1995, the share price for Kerry Group was £4.90, which (including the impact of dividends) represented a total shareholder return of £4.76 to those who had participated in the initial offering to co-operative shareholders (at 35p) in 1986.

Kerry farmers were thus confronting a stark dichotomy. On the one hand, their direct investments in Kerry Group plc had provided them with quite significant and, importantly, very tangible returns. For farmers who had traditionally been "land rich and cash poor", this was also not irrelevant. On the other hand, their "investment" in the Kerry Co-op did not offer them the same sort of capital appreciation. Even though the market value of Kerry Co-op's 52.2 per cent ownership stake in Kerry Group was worth approximately £420 million at the end of 1995, the co-operative shareholders could not get at it. That value was securely "locked away" within the overall co-operative society. There was no way for farmer-shareholders to *realise* any of the gains in the value of their Kerry Co-op (and thus Kerry Group) holdings.

Of course, this was a philosophical and legal difference in the nature of co-operative organisations compared to publicly owned companies. This had been given added and vivid emphasis by the 1991 decision in the *Kerry v Bord Bainne* case. Just as Kerry had no right to any of its proportional share in the underlying value of Bord Bainne, so farmer-suppliers had no right to any of their proportional share in the value of the Kerry Co-op (i.e. its £420 million investment in Kerry Group). Just as Kerry's investment in Bord Bainne would be gradually liquidated as it ceased trading, so the investment of many of the original suppliers to the Kerry Co-op would be similarly liquidated as they retired from farming. At least some farmers wanted something to be done.

In July 1993, the Kerry Co-op had approved a share conversion, transferring 5 per cent of its investment in Kerry Group directly to its co-operative shareholders. Its investment, at this point, still remained over the 51 per cent threshold, so there was no requirement for any rule changes. In this conversion, Kerry Co-op shareholders received 10.91 Kerry Group plc shares for each of their

Kerry Co-op shares. As might be expected, this proved to be a very popular move, with no controversy attached to it. Any further conversions, however, would have to be accompanied by a rule change approved by the co-operative membership.

Kerry executives developed a proposal that they offered to the Co-operative membership in the spring of 1996. On the table was a plan for the transfer of 21.4 million shares in the Group, now held by the Co-operative, directly to the Co-op's shareholders. This would have the effect of handing over Kerry Group shares, valued at roughly £130 million, to some 6,000 Kerry Co-op shareholders. Local newspapers reported gleefully that over 100 of Kerry Co-op's shareholders would become "paper" millionaires overnight. Accompanying this share conversion would be a rule change creating a new minimum share holding in Kerry Group (the level below which Co-op holdings would not be allowed to drop without a further "rule change") of just under 20 per cent. This would enable the Group to issue up to a further 148,000,000 new shares in the future. Additionally, they asked for a reduction in the number of Kerry Co-op Directors on the Kerry Group Board of Directors from 15 to 9, with the six vacancies filled "by six people whose expertise is of major value to the plc".[17] This new Board configuration was in recognition of the re-alignment of the shareholdings in the group, and the need to begin to diversify the composition of the board away from purely farmer representation. Finally, the proposal also provided the Kerry Co-op with an option to purchase the Agribusiness segment (exercisable between 2001 and 2020), so that the farmers (if they chose) could maintain control of those assets most directly related to them in the event of any further decline in Co-op ownership of the Group. Table 7 details the potential gains for Kerry Co-op shareholders.

Table 7: Value of Kerry Co-op Shareholding

	£m
Dec 1974	1
June 1986	31
June 1996	441*
Nov 2000	1,035**

Notes: *includes 5 per cent share exchange executed in 1993; ** includes (1993) 5 per cent exchange and (1997) 25 per cent share exchange.

Denis Brosnan had been quoted as saying:

> I look at things very simply. Is the important factor that
> they have at least 51 per cent of a public company, or is it
> that they have increased their investment from £35 million
> to £420 million? In my view it's the latter.[18]

Although Kerry Group management had done their homework
thoroughly, believed in the proposal fully, and had communicated
the proposal personally to farmers at local shareholder meetings
throughout the county (with little apparent objection), there *were*
some who objected to the proposal. The opposition centred on
philosophical rather than practical grounds, and focused upon the
issue of continuing farmer control of the enterprise and adherence
to fundamental co-operative principles.

The general concern centred upon the evolution of the Group
from a co-op to a plc, and the continued dilution of "farmer control" of the Group. More and more, shares in the Kerry Group
were seen to be controlled by "outside" shareholders, particularly
large financial institutions. As one farmer who campaigned against
the proposal said, "what do these institutions know, or care, of the
concerns of small farmers?" Some farmers, as they watched the
number of people involved with agriculture in Kerry dwindle
(from 17,000 in 1980 to 12,000 in 1995), worried that as the emphasis at Kerry Group changed to being a global player in food ingredients, its commitment to local farmers and, indeed, to farming as
a way of life in Kerry, would weaken. As Donal Hickey reported in
The Cork Examiner:

> When co-ops changed to plcs this was a worry that both-
> ered many farmers: would they lose control of their own
> enterprises to financiers who would henceforth be calling
> the shots? . . . Not so long ago, the Kerry Group (still re-
> ferred to by farming folk as the more intimate Kerry Co-
> op) was regarded as the saviour of dairy farmers in the
> widely-scattered county, but many men of the land now
> have grave reservations. . . .[19]

Opponents, with more than a little hyperbole, suggested that
farmers who voted for the proposal would be "selling out" the co-

operative for "thirty pieces of silver". Mundy Hayes, a prominent dissenter (and the eldest son of Eddie Hayes), said:

> It's just not right. They are appealing to no more than people's greed. After the deed is done, what will the farmers of Kerry have left but a few bob in the bank?[20]

Yet the more reasoned core of such emotional objections can be found in basic co-operative tenets, which hold that:

- Owners are members of the co-operative, and they retain control of the enterprise. With the conversion, the co-operative members were taking their shares from the co-operative holding and becoming direct owners of the public limited company, Kerry Group. They were moving, said opponents, from "co-operators to capitalists".

- Co-operative members control equally, that is, one member, one vote. This "one member, one vote" applied to decisions involving the co-op's 51 per cent stake in the plc. With the conversion, control of the plc will increasingly be based on "one share, one vote".

- There should be limited returns on capital. To pay a large return on invested capital is anathema to co-operative thinking — yet in this case, co-operative shareholders would be receiving a substantial return on their original investment in the co-operative.

Many of the objections, explicitly or not, also focused upon fears concerning the future of farming in Kerry. Would Kerry Group continue to help the farmers of Kerry, even when those farmers no longer held substantial control of the enterprise?

> Many rural communities are gravely threatened by current farming trends. Townlands in remote parishes, once densely populated by growing families, are now practically deserted, with derelict homesteads and overgrown farm buildings bearing mute testimony to policies devoid of any social feelings. [21]

Phil Healy, former President of the Kerry branch of the Irish Farmers Association, summed it up succinctly:

> The lack of confidence among many farmers is frightening and there's a terrible fear among the smaller men that they're on the way out.[22]

There were concerns that as the Kerry Group matured into an increasingly large and diversified multinational firm, with large blocks of shares held outside of County Kerry, the embeddedness of the Group in Kerry, and the strength and extent of its roots in this rural Irish county, would weaken.

In the run-up to the vote, however, it seemed that such sentiments were very much in the minority. Some opponents suggested that few farmers in Kerry were anxious to openly cross the management of Kerry Group. If this were true, they hoped that, since the proposal would be voted upon by secret ballot, enough farmers would side with them to vote down the proposed rule change. After all, rule changes could be made only with the approval of at least 75 per cent of the membership at two special general meetings spaced two weeks apart.

The first of the two required meetings was scheduled for Monday, 15 July 1996. Most uncharacteristically for County Kerry, it was a sweltering summer day, and the Brandon Conference Centre (a few doors down from Kerry Group Headquarters in Tralee) was not air-conditioned. Even though a large attendance had been expected, the turnout exceeded expectations, with about 2,400 people crowded into the ballroom. There were already traffic tie-ups outside the conference centre an hour before the start of the meeting. It was obvious that the exhortations (from both sides) to shareholders to attend the meeting had been heeded. It should be remembered that, for a rule change such as the one proposed, it was only those members who actually attended the meeting who would have a vote. Interestingly, many wives accompanied their husbands to the meeting (this was scarcely ever the case at the AGM). This fact alone demonstrated the serious nature of the meeting for, as one wag at the hotel bar suggested, "The wives are there to make sure they vote the right way!"

The meeting was long (over four hours) and hot, and the final vote was 1,109 (85 per cent) in favour and 199 (15 per cent) opposed. Subsequent to that meeting, however, anti-agreement groups mounted a very intense effort by telephoning or personally canvassing almost all Kerry Co-op members. For the second meeting, held two weeks later, over 3,000 people crowded into the Brandon Conference Centre, the biggest attendance in Kerry Co-op history. Conor Keane, of the newspaper *The Kerryman*, provided the following account:

> Mr Brosnan, chief executive of the co-op and managing director of Kerry Group, made an impassioned plea at the outset to co-op shareholders to vote in favour of the proposals. He retraced how Kerry Co-op had a turnover of just £1 million in 1972 and today has evolved into Kerry Group with a turnover of £1.2 billion. "I am asking not for an 85 per cent majority but I ask for a unanimous vote in favour of these proposals so that we can walk out of here united and on the right way forward," he said, his voice quivering with emotion.

Two hours later, after the votes were counted, he got the overwhelming majority he wanted. But the "no" campaigners had done their work and with an extra 600 votes present, the winning margin was cut from 85 per cent to 80 per cent with 20 per cent against. The votes were counted and the bar at the Brandon Hotel was packed five deep at the counter as the farmers celebrated backing the right horse 24 years and 7 months ago when they selected Denis Brosnan as their chief executive.[23]

So with a vote of 1,457 in favour and 375 opposed, the rule changes were approved, the restructuring was put into motion, and the "swap" of shares was executed in the first quarter of 1997.

Although the importance of the reduction in the Kerry Co-op shareholding may pale in comparison to other milestones in the life of the Kerry organisation, it accomplished many things. First, it "returned" to Kerry Co-op shareholders some portion of the value that, in the view of many (but not all) was rightfully theirs. It should be emphasised that this was by no means a symbolic return, but a tangible, material amount of wealth that could, and did, make a real difference in people's lives. This was not an exercise in "funny money". The recipients of these plc shares now had some measure of liquid wealth that they could allocate according to their individual needs. For many shareholders, it was the first time in their lives that they had had such options. It made the difference in the retirement planning of more than one Kerry farmer! For the Kerry organisation, it not only provided it with new options to raise equity finance to fuel future growth, it also sent a message to the financial markets that Kerry would continue to innovate and grow. In this, as in others, Kerry was among the first. Others would follow.[24]

Opponents of the conversion have not necessarily changed their minds, and continue to lament what they consider the "loss" of the co-operative. It is unlikely, however, that this issue will raise its head again until the Kerry Group begins to near the 20 per cent co-operative shareholding level. When that time comes (and it may not be for years), the Kerry Co-operative will have an even more dramatic decision to make. Will it "cash out" its investment entirely? Will it buy back its "Agri-business" segment, and does it even want it? These will be interesting questions, but it is unlikely that the original executive group who pioneered these changes will be the ones pushing any such agenda in the future. That will be up to a new generation of leaders.

In the meantime, some 55 per cent of the shares of the Kerry Group continue to be held in County Kerry (37 per cent with the Kerry Co-op, and the remainder owned directly by suppliers, directors, employees and others in the county). These shares represent a market value of approximately £1.1 billion at the end of 2000.

Notes

[1] Michael Hanrahan, personal communication, 25 October 2000.

[2] It has had several names over the years. Initially, under the leadership of Tim Lyons in the early 1970s, it was known as the Farm Services Unit.

[3] Liam Chute, personal interview, 28 March 2000.

[4] Donal Hickey (1990), "Kerry Group AGM likely to be a stormy get-together", *The Cork Examiner*, 28 May 1990.

[5] I have intentionally avoided dealing with the politics of farm organisations in Kerry. To address the topic intelligently would take a book in itself.

[6] Donal Hickey (1990), op. cit.

[7] *Kerry's Eye*, "Counter-Attack by Co-op", 17 May 1990, p. 1 and p. 5.

[8] Dick O'Sullivan, quoted in *Kerry's Eye*, op. cit., p. 5.

[9] ILRM. 1982. *Cadbury Ireland Ltd. v Kerry Co-Operative Creameries Ltd and Dairy Disposal Co Ltd*: High Court 1980 No. 3732P, p. 81.

[10] ILRM, op. cit., p 81.

[11] ILRM, op. cit., p. 81.

[12] ILRM, op. cit., p. 83-84.

[13] ILRM, op. cit., p. 78

[14] Denis Brosnan, personal interview, 1 June 1999.

[15] Noel Cawley, personal interview, January 2000.

[16] ILRM (1991), *Kerry Co-operative Creameries Ltd. and Patrick O'Connell v An Bord Bainne Co-operative Ltd and Avonmore Creameries Ltd, Avonmore Foods plc and John Duggan v An Borde Bainne Co-operative Ltd*: Supreme Court 1990 No. 227 and 234, p. 852.

[17] Brendan McGrath (1996), "Co-op to Cut Stake in Kerry Group to 39 per cent", *Irish Times*, 16 May 1996.

[18] John Murray Brown (1996), "Farmers to cream off profits? — Kerry's plan to change its share structure", *Financial Times (London)*, 6 March 1996.

[19] Donal Hickey (1990), "Kerry Goup AGM likely to be a stormy get-together", *Cork Examiner*, 28 May 1990.

[20] Mundy Hayes, personal interview, 12 October 1999.

[21] Donal Hickey (1990), op. cit.

[22] Donal Hickey (1990), op. cit.

[23] Conor Keane (1996), "Kerry farmers vote themselves £130m", *The Kerryman*, 30 July 1996.

[24] It should be noted that IAWS Co-op, a co-op owned by a group of co-ops, actually reduced its co-operative shareholding to below 51 per cent a few weeks before Kerry, although Kerry initiated its process of share dilution sooner.

Chapter 13

Global Expansion in Food Ingredients

Kerry ingredients sales are about £1.6 billion. I am not sure if we are number one today, but I certainly don't know of anybody that is any bigger than us. I would be very surprised if anyone will be as big as us in two or three years time, because Kerry has been the growth phenomenon [of the industry]. — Denis Brosnan, speaking at the 1999 Annual General Meeting[1]

A Global Strategy in Ingredients

The successful consolidation of the Beatreme and Kerry ingredients businesses in the US provided a solid foundation from which to launch further development activities. Although organic, internal growth in ingredients was proceeding well, Kerry remained focused upon external growth through acquisition. The confidence generated by success in the US now encouraged Kerry to think bigger and look even further afield as it sought to expand its ingredients business. Additionally, the firm's publicly articulated commitment to achieving a doubling of sales revenue every five years added impetus to the search for external acquisitions.

This acquisition strategy was part and parcel of Kerry's ultimate goal of becoming a global, and not merely international, player in the food ingredients industry. The difference is important. An international firm in any industry reflects a firm that maintains operations in many countries, but is generally compartmentalised in the sense that each national market, and the firm's subsidiary that serves it, stands alone. This is also termed a multi-domestic strategy, and is often employed by consumer product firms that must be particularly responsive to the widely varying consumer markets in each country. In such industry or organisational structures, there is little integration among the various national subsidiaries. Global industries, however, are quite different, insofar as there exist myriad opportunities to integrate operations on a global basis, reaping major benefits from scale and scope economies, learning and transferring knowledge from one part of the firm's global operation to another, yet still remaining attentive to changes in domestic markets.

The structure of the specialised food ingredients industry clearly suggested that only global firms would be able to develop the necessary economies of scale in research, development and manufacturing, combined with the world-wide learning and technology transfer capabilities that are the critical success factors in the industry. Additionally, as the customer base of food ingredients companies themselves became increasingly global, ingredients companies would have to follow suit. In other words, if a firm supplies McDonalds in North America, it will be expected to be able to supply similar ingredients to McDonalds' operations in South America, in Europe and in the Far East. Kerry Ingredients' aspiration was unambiguously to achieve such global stature; indeed, to be a successful player in this industry, it would have no choice.

Certainly, the large, affluent and nearby European market, with its 320 million consumers, was a natural target. With its exports of milk protein powders from Listowel, Kerry had always had a tangential involvement with the food ingredients sector in Europe, but it had yet to evolve into a serious business for Kerry. Indeed, the industry was considerably different from that in North America. For one thing, the prepared foods industry that Beatreme primarily serviced in the US scarcely existed in Europe, and popular convenience foods like macaroni and cheese or "hamburger helper" had yet to surface on European supermarket shelves. What Europe did have in common with the US, however, was the snack food industry, and this would be the first "loose brick" that Kerry would focus upon as it sought to build an ingredients business in Europe. Already, with the purchase of Beatreme, the technology for spray-drying specialty food ingredients had been transferred to Listowel. Leading further trailblazing efforts for ingredients expansion in Europe was Finbarr O'Driscoll, who had returned to Ireland to take up the position of Director of European Sales in 1991. His brief was a simple one: to build a European ingredients business. Interviewed by a reporter at the 1992 International Food Technology Fair in New Orleans, O'Driscoll said:

> "There are 350 million people in Asia/Pacific and 320 million in Europe, not to mention the teeming millions in China and they must all be fed. The next two or three years will be most interesting from our point of view." His aim now [said this reporter] is to ensure that Kerry grows in Europe just as it has done in the US.[2]

With the purchase of Milac GmbH in 1990, Kerry had already made its first investment beyond the borders of Ireland, the UK and the US. Milac, located in Wadersloh, Germany, was a small manufacturer of dairy and specialty food ingredients. This was followed by the acquisition of Eastleigh Flavours in the UK in 1991, which expanded Kerry's in-house flavour capability for its (slowly) growing European customer base in the snack foods category. Eastleigh, which had been buying cheese powder from Denmark, now sourced these same materials from Listowel. Listowel, for its part, was now switching its focus from dairy products to other spray-dried food ingredients. The acquisition of Tingles Ltd. in 1993 provided Kerry with a further presence in supplying the growing UK snack food industry. Located in Portsmouth, England, Tingles was a small but profitable flavour supplier with a successful track record of consumer acceptance of its new flavourings.

Meanwhile in North America, the Kerry Ingredients team, headquartered in Beloit, engineered two acquisitions in 1993 with the purchase of Malcolm Foods, based in St. George, Ontario and Research Foods, located in Toronto. The consolidation of these two businesses established Kerry as the leading supplier of specialised food ingredients to the Canadian snack food industry, further solidifying the range of products and service provided to major food manufacturers in the snack, dairy and convenience food sectors throughout both North America and Europe. The purchase of Malcolm Foods was interesting in that it had, like Beatreme, been a

Beatrice company, and had actually at one time reported directly to Beloit. Later, when Beatrice began to re-organise, it was made into a separate Canadian division. With the break-up of Beatrice it was sold to TLC, then spun off, then sold again, and then put up for sale to the highest bidder. Kerry bid $4 million, while the owners wanted $10 million, but there was a complication. Kerry believed that Malcolm was actually using Beatreme's technology (from the time when both were Beatreme companies), using the same formulas and the same equipment. Kerry filed and secured an injunction that prevented Malcolm from being sold. As was typical of Kerry's general approach to litigation, it approached it with terrier-like perseverance. Kerry would simply not let go. After some four years of depositions, and two months before coming to trial, Kerry bought Malcolm for $7.5 million. By the end of 1993, then, Kerry Ingredients' expansion plans were travelling down a two-tiered track, with further ambitious expansion plans for both North America and Europe. South America and the Far East were also, by this stage, being served by a new international sales and marketing team with newly established offices in Buenos Aires, Taiwan and San Juan, Puerto Rico.

Just five years after the acquisition of Beatreme, Kerry Ingredients returned 1993 sales of £343 million, or some 39 per cent of the total Group turnover. Fully 28 per cent of total Group sales were now represented by ingredients sales in North America.

A "Greenfield" in Mexico

In 1993, it was decided to turn the focus of attention away from Europe for the moment and look "south" in North America. By 1993, the Mexican market was, in a word, "hot". The North American Free Trade Area (NAFTA) had been approved and was to go into effect on 1 January 1994, creating what at the time was the world's largest free trade area. With the promise of dramatic growth within the Mexican economy, as well as low production costs and unfettered market access throughout the North American economy, foreign direct investment began to flood into Mexico. It would be a logical extension of Kerry's growing ingredients business. A move into Mexico would be a particularly critical development for Kerry, in that for the first time it would be entering a newly emerging, developing market.

Through most of the 20 years of the Kerry Group's history, it had evinced a very strong preference for acquiring existing, if underperforming, businesses. It would throw its organisational resources into straightening out these operations, integrating them with existing Kerry units, and then using them and their existing customer base as a platform for continuing new business development. At times, however, such a strategy was not practicable. Kerry searched high and low in Mexico for a food ingredients company to buy, without success. There simply were none. There were distributors and traders, but no one actually manufacturing for a customer base with which Kerry could get started. Just as had been the case in North America, when it had seemed that neither Beatreme nor any other large ingredients company would ever be available, Kerry eventually bit the bullet and built what was essentially a "greenfield" site in Mexico. Stan McCarthy went to Mexico and negotiated the purchase of a company, Productos Vegetales de Mexico, a unit of Basic American, with an excellent manufacturing plant for sale in Irapuato, about four hours north of Mexico City. Situated on the Panamerican Highway, Irapuato was a hub situated between the three primary commercial centres in the country — Mexico City, Monterey and Guadalajara — where the major customers in the country were based. Irapuato was already home to other major food processors that served the North American market.

In January 1994, the first Irish Trade Mission to Mexico, led by the then Taoiseach Albert Reynolds, announced Kerry's investment plans to an audience, including major customers and government officials, at a function hosted by President Salinas at the Presidential Palace in Mexico City. The facility in Irapuato was in excellent condition, with good services and sound structure, and about 250 acres for expansion. It had not, however, been a food ingredients plant, but simply a plant for drying and processing vegetable products. Kerry planned a massive investment there. Said Jerry Henchy, later to be plant manager in Mexico and Brazil:

> It was a matter of taking all the processing capabilities we
> had for the global core technologies around the world
> and weaving them into one very large site in Mexico.[3]

Kerry installed two large spray-dryers, dry-blending capabilities, and wet-processing technology. It had to literally raise the roof to accommodate the dryers. Since the facility had offices, Kerry moved the administration centre there, and added warehousing space, an R&D facility and a Pilot Plant. All told, the investment came to approximately £30 million. Clearly, the Irapuato facility was not intended to be at all a peripheral operation, for it had under one roof elements of each of Kerry's core technologies. If anything, it was to be a centrepiece and an example of the route Kerry would take in the emerging markets.

Kerry's new state of the art, 150,000 square foot plant was commissioned in June 1994, at a ceremony attended by Governor Vincente Fox (today the President of Mexico). Of course, like most expensive start-ups, it was under pressure from the start, particularly since the business had to be built from scratch. Unfortunately, the start-up was confounded by serious difficulties, and Kerry's initial experiences in Mexico were quite harsh. Experience is, however, the best teacher, and the value of what Kerry learned in Mexico can scarcely be exaggerated.

Although it had already been supplying customers in Mexico from its operations in the United States, Kerry would quickly need to build the business in order to utilise its Irapuato facility effectively. As one step, Kerry bought out a firm of commodity traders in Mexico City, hoping that the trading house would bring with them the right connections to potential food ingredients customers. The logic appears to have been similar to the way Kerry had proceeded in the States, leveraging Kerry's commodity sales of casein to build customer relationships with blue-chip clients that later brought some early and important accounts to Kerry's nascent ingredients business. Of course, Kerry already had somewhat of a customer base in Mexico, particularly with the multinational food companies that dealt with Kerry in the United States. In any event, it didn't appear to work so neatly in Mexico. Kerry's purchase of the trading house had only limited success. It was one of the first lessons Kerry learned about the ways in which business in the developing world differed from that of the more advanced economies.

Another big issue was that of personnel. It was critical to get the right people in place quickly, but being new to the culture it was a

huge challenge and quite easy to get wrong. Management techniques for employee selection and retention, organising, direct-
ing, motivating, communicating, evaluating and leading others do
not necessarily travel well. Techniques, styles and processes that
worked in Europe or North America meant little in Mexico. Very
much, it became a matter of trial and error. In fact, Kerry changed
tack several times. The original idea had been to use local Mexican nationals to manage the enterprise, but this did not initially
work. It was imperative that the distinct organisational culture of
Kerry imbue this new operation, and neither the culture nor the
sense of urgency that is so deeply embedded in it transferred easily. A full-scale transfer of expatriate experts from North America
and Europe then took place, but this was also only partially successful. They ran into many of the same issues that bedevil expatriates everywhere: some adapted well to the very different social
and business culture in Mexico, and many did not. Perhaps even
more importantly, if the right local employees were not in place to
be trained, it would not work. Eventually, Brosnan tapped a veteran Kerry manager, Dick O'Sullivan, to go to Mexico. Essentially,
O'Sullivan was given a clean sheet of paper and based on what
Kerry had so far learned in Mexico, the hard way, proceeded to
diagnose the problem, prescribe a solution and make a list of the
things that would have to be done. Simplistic, but effective.
O'Sullivan, on the surface, seemed an unlikely choice to remake
the Mexican operation. He was a native Kerryman who had been a
practising large animal veterinarian for years. He had served the
organisation as the manager of the AI Station at Castleisland and as
the General Manager of Kerry Agribusiness. However, O'Sullivan
was nearing retirement age, did not have a background in manufacturing, and had never had an overseas assignment. But Brosnan
had confidence in him to help transfer the Kerry ethos and culture
to the new Mexican venture. Granted, Brosnan's track record of
choosing the right people for the particular tasks at hand was not
at all bad.

The Mexican culture was very much relationship-based, and
such relationships took time to nurture and develop. It took time,
but O'Sullivan was able to build the basis of a team, of a business
standard, and of a business. What was needed in Irapuato was
neither an Irish culture, nor an American culture, nor a purely

Mexican culture. What was needed was a Kerry culture, adapted to the Mexican context. To achieve this, employee selection, retention and training were emphasised, so that locally trained Mexican managers could not only run the Mexican operation, but could be moved anywhere throughout Kerry's world-wide operations. This, in fact, has happened, as some managers trained in Mexico later moved to Brazil to assist with the start-up there.

O'Sullivan's difficulties, however, were compounded by the devaluation of the peso in 1995. Although the Mexican operation was *selling* well in pesos, *purchases* of ingredients from the States were denominated in dollars. In order to counteract the deterioration in buying power, Kerry de Mexico began to export tomato powder under the *Trumato* label to the States. This was eminently sensible, given the large supply of tomatoes in the area, and exports of tomato powder, begun as a way to cover exchange rate variations, have since become a major business. Eventually, operating profits began to take off and the Irapuato operation became one of the better performing plants in Kerry Ingredients' worldwide operations, providing a convenient springboard for continuing expansion into Latin America.

The lessons learned in Mexico would later be applied in Brazil and elsewhere, as Kerry continued to expand further in the developing markets of Latin America and the Far East. Kerry's Mexican operation demonstrated to the international food companies that were its premier customers — the Frito-Lays, the Pillsburys, the Krafts and others — that Kerry would supply them with the same high standard of service, reliability and innovation that they required anywhere in the world. This was one more important rung on the ladder to becoming a global enterprise.

The Acquisition of DCA and Golden Dipt

During mid-1994, even as the new venture in Mexico was struggling to overcome massive start-up difficulties, Kerry was hot on the trail of another, and far larger, acquisition target. The food ingredients businesses of Allied Domecq plc, DCA Food Industries (Donut Corporation of America) and Margetts Foods in the UK, had been placed on the auction block, and a number of major international food organisations, including Kerry, were very interested. Given the wide interest, and with Goldman Sachs orchestrating the sale, the price was likely to be high. DCA, headquartered in Garden City, New York, had operations in five countries and specialised in the provision and application of food ingredients for the baking, dairy, food processing and food service industries. Its product lines provided a very neat complement to those of Kerry, particularly its food coating, bakery mix and fruit preparations products. Relative to Kerry, DCA was a massive operation, with some 20 manufacturing facilities and 2,200 employees around the world. Importantly, its Margett's subsidiary in the UK offered the opportunity to make further inroads into the UK ingredients market, while its ventures in Australia and Poland provided entrée into still newer markets for Kerry. By far, however, the greatest attraction to Kerry was the "Golden Dipt" business, a provider of food coating applications to large industrial processors of seafood, poultry and vegetables. The "Golden Dipt" business brought with it a blue-chip line-up of customers like McDonalds, Burger King, and Kentucky Fried Chicken, and immediate access to the giants of the quick service restaurant industry. It was an entrée that Kerry had been seeking for years.

But there were problems as well, and not everyone in Kerry thought DCA would be a good acquisition. Before actually bidding, Brosnan, Finbarr O'Driscoll, Stan McCarthy and Bob Kasik took a whirlwind tour of DCA's facilities in North America, "from New York to California to Toronto to Vancouver".[4] Unlike a similar inspection tour that they had taken six years before, prior to the purchase of Beatreme, they travelled this time in a small chartered airplane rather than a GMC Suburban truck. The manufacturing plants had been starved of investment for years. They were, said Brosnan, "as bad as we thought they were going to be".[5] Stan McCarthy remembers that:

> Our impressions were mixed, to say the least. There was a perception in the industry that the bakery business was a tough business, providing nowhere near the returns to which we had grown accustomed. We definitely had some degree of optimism on coatings, but we were worried about the bakery side, and the equipment business. DCA had the reputation in the industry, being owned by Allied Lyons who just drew money out of it, that they didn't invest

in people, assets, or the business. You could see that on
the trip around. The world was moving a lot quicker than
DCA, from an industry perspective. So, to say that we were
all enthused about the business, that wouldn't be the
case.[6]

Still, while investment at the manufacturing level had been low,
and there may have been management issues, DCA brought
strengths to the table as well. Its excellent customer mix was very
attractive. Its coatings business offered Kerry a completely new
business, and one that had excellent growth prospects. Finbarr
O'Driscoll remarked that "Americans like coating on everything,
on their chicken, on their shrimp, and on their fish".[7] In assessing
the value of DCA there were many trade-offs, but Brosnan was already convinced and relentlessly drove the acquisition. He was
nothing if not a risk taker, and his 20 years of leading Kerry had
not diminished it. Ultimately, the acquisition was his call.

   Randy McIntyre, now the Senior Vice President of Sales for
Kerry Ingredients in North America, discovered this the hard way.
He and a number of colleagues in Beloit had been asked to evalu-
ate DCA and report back to Brosnan with their recommendations.
It was a meeting that McIntyre never forgot. Brosnan and Friel
were there, along with Jack Warner, McCarthy, Mark Earley and
Steve Foley.

> A colleague and I made a very negative presentation in
> terms of DCA. We talked of concerns with a bakery mix
> industry with limited growth prospects because frozen
> was taking over from mix. We noted that Golden Dipt
> had lost its ground to Newlyweds. There were also hu-
> man resource issues. At the end of all this, Denis not too
> politely dismissed us with the commentary, "Randy, you
> wouldn't buy anything unless it was perfect. You are
> waiting for the perfect acquisition and the perfect acqui-
> sition isn't going to come along." He kind of booted us
> out of the room, and from what I hear the other three got
> an earful.[8]

DCA had sales of $375 million in 1993, with operating profits of $36
million. In the not so distant past, however, its operating margins

had been even better. Brosnan was not put off by the negatives, and was convinced that Kerry could harness the many capabilities of DCA to great effect, while managing, minimising and finally eliminating many of its shortcomings. For all his confidence, however, he acknowledged that it would be a tough row to hoe.

> I remember very well a lot of our own senior managers saying that it was just too big. Not from a size perspective, size didn't enter into it, but everyone knew it was an organisation that was in decay, inasmuch as nothing had been spent on it for a number of years. The administration systems were collapsing. Key MIS systems were non-existent. A lot of the managers were de-motivated. It was an organisation that, in our opinion, had been "milked" dry. It had been giving back to its parent who demanded it all the monies that had been created there for quite a number of years, and they had actually run it into the ground. So, the question at the time was not whether it was the right or wrong company for Kerry to buy, but whether or not Kerry in fact had the resources to be able to turn it around fast enough to stop the decay.[9]

In the bidding for DCA, however, Kerry had to deal with another suitor, Dalgety plc, a European food group that was more than twice the size of Kerry and had an ingredients business of its own. But Brosnan, over the years, had cultivated a reputation for paying above the odds for acquisitions and then making them work. After all, the $130 million paid for Beatreme in 1988 included a premium of about $92 million over the net asset value of the firm, and more than a few eyebrows were raised at the time. Six years later, however, the Beatreme purchase was widely acknowledged to be a bargain. Said Brosnan about the bidding for DCA:

> We weren't afraid. Kerry almost created the concept of paying big dollars for what is now referred to as goodwill. But goodwill in the food ingredients business was technical capability and certainly customer listings.[10]

Unlike the Beatreme deal, however, Kerry did not have a "first mover" advantage. They and Dalgety were literally neck and neck in their bidding competition for DCA. Some newspaper reports suggested that the management of Allied Domecq favoured Kerry over Dalgety because they "preferred Kerry's way of doing business".[11] In the end, however, it came down to price. According to Brosnan:

> We were both there at the finish, and our offer wasn't that much better. They were willing to pay approximately the same money. Dalgety probably just couldn't make up their minds, or just regarded the task as too big for them. They pulled out at the very, very end. They just couldn't finish it.[12]

Dalgety was also distracted at the time by another potential acquisition. A pet food business in Europe was up for sale, and Dalgety was evaluating it at the same time as DCA was on the block. They could not do both. Eventually, Kerry made a bid that Dalgety did not counter quickly enough, and the purchase was agreed.

The announcement of the purchase was made on 7 November 1994. Kerry would buy the food ingredients business of Allied Domecq plc (DCA Food Industries Inc. in the US, and Margetts Foods, headquartered in the UK) for $402 million (approximately £250 million). The purchase was to be financed by a share placing in November that yielded £26 million and bank borrowings for the remainder. With Dalgety in the picture to the very end, the negotiations over the purchase had been stressful and the closing itself difficult. Nevertheless, the deal was closed in New York in November. Ned O'Callaghan remembers looking out the window of the New York skyscraper with other bank representatives and lawyers at the conclusion of the closing and seeing a helicopter heading for the building (which had a landing pad on the roof). One of the assembled quipped that "it's Dalgety" coming in to make a final bid. The comment generated a bit of laughter, but it was nervous laughter. For all they knew, perhaps it was Dalgety, but it was too late. Kerry had won by a nose. The general consensus at the time was that Dalgety's failure to get DCA represented a fatal blow to its ingredients business. In an industry where firms would have to grow increasingly global to thrive, or even survive, Dalgety had missed a rare opportunity to join the ranks of global food ingredient players. This would have serious consequences for Dalgety, as well as Kerry, later.

Reflecting on Kerry's successful pursuit of DCA, Finbarr O'Neill of the Bank of Ireland, one of Kerry's principal bankers, said this:

> They simply inspire confidence in people. They are very professional, reliable, timely and accurate with their work. Their speed of response and sense of urgency is something that you get a feeling for, always, in the case of Kerry. They have a capacity to make things happen and to get inside the skin of things. Things that would be too untidy for others, they do. All of this inspires people to work with them.[13]

The $402 million purchase, more than three times what Kerry had paid for Beatreme only six years before, was one of the largest acquisitions ever made by an Irish company at that time. It more than doubled the size of Kerry's ingredients business in one fell swoop, brought it into new product categories and several new geographic markets, and promised its own share of problems and integration issues. Kerry's much vaunted strengths in turning around poorly performing businesses and optimising good businesses would be put to the test yet again.

The Integration of DCA

Until the acquisition of DCA, Kerry Group had had no presence with the quick service restaurant (QSR) chains that were experiencing rapid, and global, growth. Now, since the QSRs were big users of coatings provided by DCA, Kerry had the opportunity to develop important relationships with the biggest players in the food service industry. Strategically, this was of immense importance in positioning Kerry for further significant growth. Additionally, it was Kerry's first foray into a completely new technology, one that was flour-based (as opposed to Kerry's traditional dairy and seasoning-based technologies). This technological leap was also of no little importance.

Brosnan himself was to oversee the integration, but it was to be implemented on the ground by Kerry's US and UK teams for DCA and Margetts, respectively. Kerry took over in January 1995, and

Stan McCarthy, Mark Earley, Randy McIntyre and others from Beloit almost immediately moved out to DCA's headquarters in Garden City, Long Island (just outside of New York City). As it turned out, they were to commute back and forth to Garden City for the better part of the next six months. The initial thinking had been that Kerry would run all of its North American ingredients business out of Garden City, and with that in mind David Lipka (the President of DCA) was put in charge of all of Kerry's businesses. Early on, however, the wisdom of this early decision was called into question. DCA's corporate culture, and particularly the corporate culture at the Garden City headquarters, was profoundly different from Kerry's. Right away, there were serious problems with integrating the management teams.

One should realise that Kerry's organisational culture, initially bred in County Kerry, Ireland, had transferred very well to Wisconsin in America's heartland. Both Kerry and Beloit, Wisconsin were rural areas with a tradition of dairy farming and a work force who were seriously committed to their communities and their employers, with a very solid work ethic. Separated by national cultures, Wisconsin and Kerry people were nevertheless similar in many ways, and the moulding of the two cultures into Kerry's organisational culture of drive, achievement and success had been remarkable. But now Kerry's *organisational* culture, as embodied by the firm's American and Irish employees, was proving difficult to graft upon DCA's Garden City headquarters. Stan McCarthy, who played perhaps the primary role in the DCA integration, said that:

> It was just such a change, a different world from a business perspective. The mentality that existed in that corporate office was so different from that we were used to, it was quite a culture shock. They used to say in Garden City that when they crossed the Hudson River, they were "roughing it".[14]

Of course, the first job in integrating the businesses was to get familiar with DCA. It was, after all, a very new business for Kerry. For one thing, on the operations side Kerry had always been involved with seasonings, dairy processing, and "wet" processing activities. DCA was flour-based, baking-based, with "dry" processing activities. Kerry would have to build new competencies in these areas and DCA's technical people would be key to such learning. In the areas of systems and management, however, the more Kerry saw the more they disliked. DCA's information systems were poor and its management autocratic. All decisions came out of Garden City, and the manufacturing locations merely took orders with little by way of collaboration or teamwork. Gradually, it became clear that the Garden City headquarters was providing little value-added, and the original plan to base the North American headquarters there was reconsidered. Plans for any permanent relocation of people to Garden City were shelved. By the middle of 1995, it was decided that Beloit was probably the better location in which to base Kerry's North American ingredients operations. Nevertheless, the decision to close Garden City was not easy and implementing it was not pleasant.

There was no manufacturing done in Garden City, just the headquarters office and a small research facility. As it turned out, few of the staff, with the exception of a couple of salespeople, transferred to Beloit. It was also decided to close the Golden Dipt Divisional Headquarters in St. Louis, and consolidate technical activities in a newly enlarged facility in Beloit. Although it was a tough sell in many cases, a good number of the technical people from St. Louis did agree to relocate. Steps were also taken to consolidate DCA's Canadian operations into an existing Kerry facility in Toronto, and to close the Jessup manufacturing plant in Maryland.

In Europe, the integration process proceeded even more quickly, with the closure of a DCA plant at Whitburn in Scotland and the consolidation and reorganisation of activities into Listowel in Ireland, and the Aylesbury and Fareham technical centres in the UK.

The integration of DCA was a difficult, costly and painful one, with the local American and European ingredients division managements playing the key roles. It would also be wrong to suggest that the effort went precisely according to plan; it went, in fact, quite differently to what had been originally envisioned. Despite the success that Kerry had had, and continued to have, in integrating its acquisitions, it was almost always a messy process. Yet

Kerry, as an organisation, had developed a facility, an organisational competence, of being able to push through. Kerry's philosophy of integration echoes Shakespeare, where he wrote (and I
paraphrase), "If it were done, then 'twere well it were done
quickly!" Brosnan has made this clear:

> The difficulty is that we've nearly always bought compa-
> nies that give lots of opportunity for cost reduction and
> rationalisation. So, the very difficult decisions made by
> our front team are that a certain number of people have to
> go. They have only a matter of months to make that deci-
> sion, to choose those who will work to drive the business
> forward under our principles and goals, and very quickly
> take out those who have become accustomed to running
> the business in the old way. There will be the first few cru-
> cial and difficult meetings. Within a few short months,
> you've got to see who has actually bought into it, and who
> doesn't want to hear about it. You work with the former, and
> get rid of the latter. We certainly take out numbers, includ-
> ing people who would have played a very useful role for
> Kerry, because we simply don't have time to wait . . .[15]

In commenting on the outcome of the DCA acquisition, Randy
McIntyre had cause to reflect on some of the initial doubts about
the wisdom of the purchase:

> We acquired DCA and we made it work. Of course, it was
> everything we said it was, and it was a very hard row for
> all the reasons we identified. There were people issues,
> market issues, lack of investment. But it was also every-
> thing that Denis expected it would become. Both sides
> were right. Denis' vision and perseverance in being able
> to achieve it made it work. But it was damned hard! I'll bet
> nine out of ten companies would have failed.[16]

The DCA acquisition did work, although Brosnan will admit today
that he probably underestimated the task.

> You must realise what it took out of Kerry. All the senior
> people in Beloit disappeared for months, and Beloit suf-
> fered that year, inasmuch as there were only two people

left in Beloit to run it . . . which was Jack Warner, Michael Leahy and all the second-line management. Everyone else had gone . . . we had to take out every single one.[17]

It took an enormous investment in assets, in systems, in people, and in management time and attention, but the operation turned around. Brosnan and others in the Kerry organisation speculate that for any other organisation, the acquisition of DCA would have left them with a huge problem. Perhaps so. Kerry's single-minded commitment to successfully integrating its acquisitions, regardless of the short-term costs, manifested itself again with DCA. Certainly, more aggressive pricing was a part of the equation as well. Finbarr O'Driscoll had returned from Europe to work on the sales side of the integration, and had immediately initiated a re-examination of prices in response to increases in the price of their raw materials. With the rationalisation and consolidation effort well on its way by the end of 1995, Kerry was now the dominant specialty food ingredients company in North America. It was time now to focus attention on ingredients markets elsewhere. Margett's in the UK, along with their subsidiary in Poland, were providing a larger platform from which to grow the ingredients business in Europe, and DCA's joint venture in Australia brought Kerry for the first time to the land "down under". Both platforms would very shortly be put to good use.

Other Acquisitions

1996 — Ciprial S.A.

With the integration and rationalisation of the DCA businesses in North America and the UK well on their way, Kerry's Ingredients business was now organised into three distinct operating groups: Kerry Ingredients North America, now headed by Jack Warner; Kerry Ingredients Europe, led by Jerry Houlihan; and Kerry Ingredients International, headed by the peripatetic Finbarr O'Driscoll. O'Driscoll returned to Europe late in 1995, and turned his attention to the further expansion of the ingredients business there. His first stop was France, where he negotiated the purchase of Ciprial S.A. for IR£54 million in January 1996. Ciprial was a leading supplier of specialty fruit-based ingredients to European luxury ice cream and yoghurt manufacturers, and bakery and confectionery companies. It was a market leader in candied fruits and specialised fruit ingredients for cakes, desserts and other sweet snack items. With modern production facilities in Lyons and Apt in France, and near Naples and Rome in Italy, the acquisition of Ciprial broadened Kerry Ingredients' geographical base in Europe considerably, marking the Group's first major European foray out of the British Isles. With 1993 sales of £70 million and operating profits of £4.9 million, its margins were reasonably good and Kerry felt they could only be improved upon.

Ciprial also presented some unique, if not particularly critical, challenges. For one thing, it was the Kerry organisation's first major encounter with developing pan-European teams, as it combined people from Ireland and the UK, France and Italy in the integration and reorganisation efforts. Cultural, linguistic and social differences soon surfaced, highlighting the fact that even within the European Union there remained a diversity of national business cultures. For his part, O'Driscoll found the language issue the most daunting. Despite some weeks spent in Paris to learn what French he could prior to the integration of Ciprial, he found the net result to be that:

> I learned how to order wine properly. I learned how to pronounce guys' names properly. I learned how to pronounce the names of cities. That was it. I couldn't manage any more![18]

In any event, the difficulty in creating effective cross-European teams created an interesting counterpoint to the undeniable commercial benefits of the acquisition, and raised questions regarding just how far Kerry could stretch their managerial resources over an accelerating and geographically expanding range of acquisitions.

Said Brosnan:

> We would have been happier if Ciprial came in late 1996 or 1997, but it came on offer and it had to be bought because it gave us size and scale in fruit ingredients. Companies like that don't come on the market very often, and when they do you have to move. Taking Ciprial has stretched us; we don't have unlimited resources.[19]

Of course, being aware of the problem, or the challenge, was one thing; passing up an important strategic acquisition would be something else again.

1996 — DCA, Solutech, Australia

Once the purchase of Ciprial was finalised, attention reverted to Asia. The first order of business was to secure full control of So-lutech DCA, a 50 per cent joint venture with Cerebos Australia that had come to Kerry in the DCA deal. Kerry had never been comfortable with joint ventures and had never believed them to be an appropriate way of utilising the organisation's distinctive competencies in application-specific solutions for the food industry. Nor would Kerry ever be anxious to give away its technologies, its formulations or its processes. It acquired Cerebos' 50 per cent equity in March 1996. The acquisition of Solutech provided the Group with both a manufacturing capability in food coatings, marinades and seasonings within Australia and a platform for its planned expansion into the booming Asian market. Kerry was now serving that market largely through exports from its North American and European units. As the market grew, however, a stronger presence in Asia would be necessary.

1997 — SDF Foods, Malaysia; GR Spinks, UK

In early 1997, Brosnan, O'Driscoll and a number of others took a major tour of Asia, stopping in Shanghai, Hong Kong, Tokyo, Singapore, Bangkok, Jakarta and Kuala Lumpur. Kerry was beginning to feel pressure to follow its global food company customers to Asia, and it had decided that expansion in Asia could not be postponed. In particular, the spread of the major food service brands to Asia was making it less and less feasible to continue supplying them only from the US and Mexico. The question was where to invest. Certainly China was a possibility, but Kerry had already concluded that it should not, at the moment, enter China. Despite the general rush to invest in China, few Western companies were actually making money there, and the business environment was extremely difficult. The probable necessity of having to team up with a local partner in a joint venture also served to cool Kerry's ardour. Of course, Kerry never said it would "never" enter China; it was a question of timing, and the timing was not yet right.

They did, however, open an office in Singapore to serve as the headquarters for Asia-Pacific operations. In late 1997, Kerry agreed to the purchase of SDF Foods, a small Malaysian food ingredients company owned by a consortium of Asian and Danish investors (including Fuji Offset, Niro Industries BV and Eng Lian Enterprises Sdn Bhd) for £6.6 million. Even though the original investors had suffered persistent losses, SDF had a modern and relatively under-utilised manufacturing facility in Johor Bahru (near Singapore), built in 1993, that offered Kerry the necessary room to expand the facility rapidly. Although SDF had been producing relatively unsophisticated food ingredients, Kerry planned on transferring its processes, technology and equipment into the plant quickly. This would enable it to begin producing the more sophisticated ingredients that its food processing and food service customers demanded.[20] In addition, coming on the heels of the "Asian flu", the Asian fiscal crisis of 1997 and the subsequent devaluation of the local currency, the purchase was a bona fide bargain, at something less than 89 per cent of the annual turnover.[21] Kerry's annual report for 1997 stated that the factory would benefit from:

> Malaysia's rich raw material resources including palm oil and starch [and] approximately 90 per cent of SDF's production is exported to growth markets in the food processing and food service sectors in the region.[22]

Kerry made several other smaller acquisitions in 1997. In December, it announced the purchase of GR Spinks & Co. Ltd. from Gist-Brocades, NV. Spinks, located in Bingham and Okehampton in the southwest of England, was a manufacturer of various fruit and confectionery ingredients used by dairy dessert and ice cream manufacturers.[23] According to Kerry:

> Spinks' unique enzyme and process technologies, dedicated to the fruit preparations and confectionery sectors, combined with Kerry's existing fruit technologies, will give Kerry an unrivalled position in the European industry

in terms of total fruit processing systems from fruit sourcing, processing and applications.[24]

This purchase, combined with strong organic growth and development of new products and applications at Kerry's applications research centres in Apt, France, Tenbury Wells, UK, and Italy and Poland, firmly established Kerry as the premier supplier of fruit preparations in Europe.

Dalgety Food Ingredients (DFI)

It was the fourth quarter of 1997, and nearly three years since the purchase of DCA. It had been a very big bite to take, had caused some anxious moments and taken time to digest, but had ultimately proven itself to be an eminently wise decision. Certainly, Kerry's management had been stretched thin attending to the DCA integration, the plant in Mexico, and the acquisitions in France, the UK and Asia (not to mention acquisitions on the consumer foods side of the house!). Yet these most recent experiences, combined with the earlier challenges at Denny's and then Beatreme, had led to the development of a distinct organisational competence. Kerry knew how to acquire and integrate a business as well as or better than anyone else. They had proven this time and again. Now that things had settled down a bit, the organisation was ready for another major acquisition. Coincidentally, a major strategic acquisition candidate had just come on offer. Dalgety plc had put its specialty food ingredients and flour businesses on the auction block.

For Dalgety, its own failure to outbid Kerry for DCA three years earlier effectively excluded it from the ranks of the global players in specialty food ingredients. DCA would have provided them with the North American presence they lacked. They had been involved in the bidding until nearly the end, and had lost to Kerry by the slimmest of margins. Some suggested that it was a loss of nerve on Dalgety's part, that they just could not go the extra mile or that they had too many other alternative acquisitions distracting them at the time. Could Dalgety have done with DCA what Kerry did? That would remain a highly debatable question. Subsequent to Kerry's purchase of DCA, Dalgety had finalised a £440 million purchase of Quaker Oats' pet food business in Europe, a step that would ultimately lead them to refocus their business on the pet foods category. The writing was on the wall even at that point; the pressures for consolidation in the food ingredients industry would likely lead Dalgety to exit the business.

Dalgety's performance had, for years, been lacklustre, and the newly acquired pet foods business had not yet produced the expected returns. Three years of restructuring had failed to resolve the problems, and its chief executive, Richard Clothier, resigned in September in favour of Ken Hanna, who had recently joined the group as finance director. On the advice of its outside consultants, Bain & Company, Dalgety announced on 15 September 1997 that it would put its food ingredients and flour businesses up for sale in order to concentrate on its pet foods and agricultural supplies activities. Its target for the sale was approximately £300 million.

Dalgety was a very attractive target for Kerry, perhaps as important as DCA. The strategic fit was a near perfect one. Dalgety had a strong presence in ingredients in the UK, precisely where Kerry was weakest. It had an excellent customer base throughout Europe, with a business that dovetailed nicely with Kerry's global ingredients operations. Conversely, it had no significant presence in North America, so any overlap of activities would be minimal. Nevertheless, Kerry's planners saw some opportunities for synergy, particularly in research and development activities. Dalgety, however, insisted on selling their ingredients and flour milling businesses as a package. Flour milling and the baking industry in general were generally commodity businesses with low margins in which Kerry had scant interest. Yet in order to get at the ingredients piece, the entire package would have to be purchased, with flour milling spun off at a later date. Kerry, unlike some other suitors, was willing to do this. The businesses on offer had 1997 sales of Stg£359 million and operating profit of Stg£29.9 million.

There were reportedly at least six bidders who submitted offers by the deadline of 19 December. Kerry was clearly the most committed to the purchase, expressing strong interest from the very beginning. After the announcement of the offer they rented offices in London and assigned roughly 20 people there for the duration of the negotiations, due diligence and closing. This team stayed with it throughout. Nothing was being left to chance. There were reportedly three rounds of bidding, beginning in October and culminating in a final round in December. Kerry was clearly not going to be denied. The agreement was signed at 1:30 in the morning on 26 January, simultaneously with Dalgety's agreement with Du Pont on the sale of certain intellectual property rights and research unrelated to Kerry's food ingredients business.[25] Kerry had agreed to purchase Dalgety Food Ingredients (DFI) for Stg£335 million, a price with which representatives of Lazard's, Dalgety's investment bankers, were reportedly "enormously pleased", and considerably higher than the £300 million that had been expected.[26] Once again, some suggested that Kerry had paid a high price for the acquisition, at roughly 12 times operating earnings. Yet such criticism was "old hat" to Kerry by now. For their part, and underlying the entire process, was the sheer conviction that they, Kerry, could and would get more out of the Dalgety business than anybody else.

The purchase, which was conditional upon shareholder approval from both parties, provided Kerry with operations in the UK, France, Germany, Italy, Ireland, the Netherlands, Poland and Hungary. Included in the purchase agreement was the Spillers Milling business in the UK and its eight flour mills. Under a separate agreement on 12 February 1998, Kerry announced the sale of Spillers Milling, consisting of six of the eight flour mills, for a consideration of Stg£92 million to Tomkins.[27] This sum was used to reduce the debt incurred in the acquisition. In the prospectus provided to shareholders before the Extraordinary General Meeting in March, the Board outlined the rationale for the purchase as follows:

> Your Directors believe that DFI is a good strategic fit for Kerry and meets Kerry's stated acquisition policy objectives. In particular, the acquisition allows Kerry to broaden its spread of ingredients technologies and extends its potential to develop additional innovative products. In addition, DFI has positions in a number of product categories in Europe. The combination of DFI and the Group's existing ingredients operations and technologies will help consolidate Kerry's position as a global ingredients business capable of servicing the requirements of major international food manufacturers and food service companies. Specifically, the proposed acquisition will help Kerry to expand in a number of fast growing European food industry sectors through the provision of innovative

and advanced technologies and additional European
manufacturing, technical and distribution facilities.[28]

Addressing the Extraordinary General Meeting of Kerry Group
shareholders in March, Brosnan noted that the acquisition:

> . . . makes Kerry by far the leading seasonings and coat-
> ings company in the world. Nobody else has anything like
> the same global presence.[29]

In particular, Brosnan noted that Dalgety had saved Kerry a
great deal of trouble, in that Dalgety had been acquiring companies in Europe for the five years prior to the acquisition.[30]
Dalgety, said Brosnan, did the painstaking work of finding,
buying and integrating the various European operations. Not
only did it save Kerry trouble, but more importantly, it saved
Kerry time while it was busy building in North America. In its
drive for international expansion, as it strove to achieve the
necessary scale and scope that would enable it to compete with
the biggest and best in the world, time was surely of the essence.

Kerry took over Dalgety in March 1998, after the shareholder
approval of the acquisition. The target was to get in, integrate the
operation, and hand it back to its own local management group
within 12 months. Dalgety, however, proved to be an uncommonly
smooth transition, and most of Kerry's team was back out again
within nine months. Denis Brosnan appreciated the benefits of a
relatively quick integration.

> You cannot keep the acquisition in a state of turmoil for
> too long. The longer you keep it in turmoil the slower it
> will be to come to ultimate success, which only comes
> from an absolutely stable management. The sooner you
> can move it out of turmoil and into stability, the sooner you
> will get the profits back. Either we've got better at it, or
> else Dalgety was a very easy subject.[31]

Of course, Dalgety was far closer to "home" in Tralee as well, and
more compact in its operations, than DCA. In any event, by the

middle of 1999, Dalgety was well integrated into the Kerry organisation.

As Jerry Houlihan observed:

> The additions of DCA and Dalgety gave us geographic spread and scale, and provided us with the opportunity to start to develop a business in continental Europe. With manufacturing locations in Italy, France, Holland, Germany, Poland and Hungary, it gave us a base around which we could grow.[32]

Entry into Latin America

As Kerry was finalising its takeover of Dalgety's ingredients business in Europe, it was also concluding negotiations for its first acquisition in South America — Star & Arty Ingredientes Alimenticios LTDA of Brazil, a provider of specialty food ingredients to the ice cream, food processing and convenience foods sectors in South America. Kerry had been prospecting for potential acquisitions in both Argentina and Brazil, looking to gain a foothold in the growing South American ingredients market. Star & Arty, with a good technical reputation for its production of various emulsifiers and its location in Brazil with its huge population of 160 million, was a particularly attractive target. Further market access was also assured under the Mercosur Free Trade Treaty between Brazil, Argentina and Chile. With more and more major food processors expanding throughout South America, Kerry had to follow. Star & Arty appeared to offer at least the beginnings of a good foundation for the servicing of this business, particularly in view of its existing customer base, and Kerry purchased it for £7.3 million in February 1998. It was headquartered in Sao Paolo, with a production facility located in Valinos, about an hour away. This facility, however, would clearly be inadequate to service the extent and scope of business that Kerry envisioned.

In November 1998, Kerry bought a manufacturing plant from Nestlé, located in Tres Coracoes, Minas Gerais, about four hours drive from both Sao Paolo and Rio de Janiero. Nestlé had used the site for the production of infant formula and various powdered beverages, but was in the midst of a rationalisation campaign to consolidate their operations down to only a few plants. It had two spray-dryers that Kerry planned to modify and enlarge to meet expanding production requirements for specialty food ingredients. Kerry planned to consolidate all production and technical development for their South American markets in this modern facility, which they commissioned in August 1999 at a total cost of some $20 million. With things much improved in Mexico, Dick O'Sullivan, by now ready to retire back home to Kerry, was asked by Brosnan to do one last chore for the organisation — to move down to Brazil for the start-up of the new facility.

Of course, there were challenges, but the situation was vastly different from that which had prevailed in Mexico. For one thing, Kerry was able to employ an excellent operations staff that had been left behind by Nestlé, with workers already well versed in the standards and operational routines of food ingredient processing. Although Kerry had to train the new employees on their unique processing systems, the former Nestlé staff themselves were able to pass along valuable technical knowledge to Kerry. It was a useful synergy.

Fresh from its experience in Mexico, Kerry knew that it was critical to have the right organisational structure in place, and the right people on board. Considerable effort went into building the right team with the right mix of people. To that end, Kerry was able to poach some excellent talent from its competitors in Brazil and from among Kerry and former Dalgety employees in Europe. Interestingly, a number of employees in Mexico transferred to the Brazilian start-up, including both Kerry expatriates and Mexican nationals.

In Brazil, Kerry would have to compete with imported products to work itself into a position of leadership in the Brazilian market. It would have to show technological improvements and begin to demonstrate to its customers in South America the full range of technical possibilities, basically by changing people's thinking. Finally, the management of currency exposure in Brazil, as it was in Mexico, was critical. It was all-important to be able to buy raw materials in the local currency, the real, and to export products denominated in dollars. Still, the start-up in Brazil was far less difficult than Mexico, due partly to local circumstances and to some extent by what Kerry had learned in Mexico.

At the official inauguration of the facility at Tres Coracoes, Denis Brosnan said:

> When this investment programme is fully commissioned, the Tres Coracoes plant will be one of Kerry's most technologically advanced and diversified facilities in the world. The technical facilities at this site will also form an important part of Kerry's global R&D network, bringing Kerry's leading ingredient technologies and research expertise to the Group's large customer base in Argentina, Chile and Brazil. Some of Kerry's Brazilian team have already been trained at other Group sites in the US and in Europe. We are confident that we can continue to build our market presence so that our sales in the Mercosur region will grow from a current level of US$20 million to US$200 million over the next few years. Under the guidance of our excellent management team, technologists, sales and customer service people, we have every confidence that Kerry do Brazil's strategic plans will be fulfilled.[33]

As one more piece in the jigsaw of Kerry's continuing international growth, Brazil was so far proving enormously successful. Nevertheless, it represents only the opening chapter of the story of Kerry's South American operations.

Burns-Philp & Co., Ltd. (Australia and New Zealand)

In early 1998, Star & Arty had just been bought in Brazil, and the search for a suitable plant location had already begun. It was acknowledged that a substantial investment would be required. The Dalgety acquisition was about to go to the shareholders, and no one was certain how difficult the integration and consolidation of Dalgety's operations would be. The only certainty was that Kerry's managerial resources, if not its financial resources, were already under considerable strain. These were not the ideal circumstances under which to contemplate yet another acquisition, but the fact was that Burns-Philp & Co., Ltd., the giant Australian food group, had put its food ingredients division in Australia and New Zealand up for sale. The businesses had annual sales of £80 million, and represented in many ways a very attractive acquisition possibility to Kerry. First, Kerry had only a minor presence in Australia through its purchase of the DCA-Solutech joint venture the previous year. As its big customers continued to expand globally, it was important that Kerry expand its reach to service them anywhere in the world, but Kerry did not yet have this capability in Australia. Secondly, Kerry had always had a marked preference for buying existing businesses with not only facilities, but more importantly, a solid customer base and a distribution system. Burns-Philp presented just the sort of opportunity Kerry preferred.

Burns-Philp itself was conducting an ongoing rationalisation of its operations and sell-off of its non-core business assets in a desperate attempt to stave off bankruptcy. Its attempted management buy-out in 1997 had failed, its shares were trading at approximately one-tenth of their previous year's value, and it was reporting losses again for the year 1998. (The food ingredients businesses, however, appeared to be profitable.) There was some debate over whether the bakery and seasonings business were "core" or "non-core", but as one Australian analyst put it at the time:

> A sale at the right price for the company would be good
> at this stage. With no certainty they will still be trading at
> all in six months, it's still a question of whatever it takes.[34]

Brosnan, at least publicly, initially downplayed Kerry's interest in Burns-Philp. He was quoted as saying, after the EGM that approved the Dalgety purchase, that "it's a good fit but it's in the wrong place at the wrong time".[35] With the Dalgety acquisition and major investments in Malaysia and Brazil, Kerry's management resources were stretched very thin.[36] Nevertheless, the strategic fit of the Burns-Philp businesses trumped Kerry's operational concerns, and Hugh Friel was dispatched to Australia in late April to negotiate the acquisition. Regardless of the unfortunate timing, it was simply too good an opportunity to pass up. An additional attraction was the fact that it could be bought very cheaply.

Certainly, there were a number of potential buyers for the Burns-Philp businesses, but eventually the other suitors ran into problems and fell by the wayside. Kerry was left as the only potential buyer. Alex Aramenko, then the Managing Director of the food ingredients division of Burns-Philp, and currently the Managing Director of Kerry's operations in Australia and New Zealand, remembers that,

> We were very interested in Kerry. The combined ingredients businesses, when added to our Pinnacle bakery ingredients business, could gain from our national distribution system, and we could gain critical mass for our five factories.[37]

The purchase was confirmed on 19 May 1998 for an unannounced price. With the addition of the Burns-Philp businesses, Kerry now had an ingredients business in Australia spanning a range of seasonings, flavourings, coatings, sauces and bakery ingredients. In addition to its existing facility in Sydney (acquired through the buyout of DCA), it now had manufacturing plants in New South Wales, Queensland, Victoria and in Auckland, New Zealand.

With the closing of the transaction in June 1998, Kerry was faced yet again with the now familiar challenge of bedding down a new acquisition and integrating it into the Kerry organisation. But each integration effort, of course, was unique and integrating the Burns-Philp acquisitions in Australia and New Zealand presented its own particular challenges. For one thing, the geography and the vast distances in Australia, with its scattered population of 18–19 million, made it a very difficult and expensive country for product distribution. Additionally, the manufacturing facilities were rundown and starved of capital investment; costs of production at the Australian sites were in some cases three times more than costs in Kerry's US facilities.

Alex Aramenko observes that:

> Within six months or so of Kerry coming in, profit began to pick up. We began to realise cost reductions in our factories, with the closure of three of them and the expansion of two others, and became the low-cost producer in the industry. We were able to derive advantages from Kerry's global purchasing power in sourcing our raw materials. We benefited from fresh capital investment. But we also allowed Kerry to begin to roll out their core tech-

nologies to customers who they otherwise wouldn't have
been able to get to.[38]

Liam Chute, another long-time Kerry executive who had already
served Kerry in the Dairy business and the Agribusiness in Ireland, and had then gone to Canada to handle DCA's American
bakery operations, was asked by Denis Brosnan to spend a year in
Australia to work with the integration effort. His primary task was
to help develop a plan for how to proceed with the business and to
put a team in place to execute that plan. Of course, another large
task was to introduce to the new operation something of Kerry's
organisational culture. Chute says that:

> They were bad at what we were good at. We were always
> good at being the low-cost producer. We had a bit of
> technology. So we worked on becoming more efficient,
> brought in our technology, improved distribution, and
> branded our products.[39]

Factories were rationalised, construction on a new factory was underway, and stores throughout the country were consolidated.
More importantly, Kerry's planning process was initiated and a
new leadership team of local managers was put in place. Aramenko notes:

> We (Burns-Philp) came with tired assets, and people
> struggling with massive disruption, a lack of capital, and
> underlying structural problems. We are now going
> through a period of structural change, one that will go on
> for some time. Nevertheless, we are starting to grow.
> Kerry has come in and made change as painless as possi-
> ble and the integration has gone as smoothly as could
> have been expected. It really has been a change in the
> culture, a culture that has an expectation of achieving what
> you say you will achieve.[40]

The integration of the operation into the global network of Kerry's
worldwide ingredients business continues.

Further Acquisitions

Kerry has continued on the acquisition trail. In September 1999, it purchased the SFI Group of specialty food ingredients business comprising Shade Foods Inc. in the USA and Specialty Food Ingredients (SFI) in Europe. These businesses, leaders in flavoured particulates, high protein inclusions, and specialty chocolate and compound coatings, employ approximately 400 people in three plants in the United States and one plant in Europe. The total purchase price was $80 million.

The Group has since added to the Shade Particulates business through the acquisition of Harald LTDA, located near Sao Paulo in Brazil and though the acquisition of York (UK) based York Dragee.

In October 2000, Kerry announced a further expansion of its US food ingredients business with the acquisition of Armour Food Ingredients (AFI) from ConAgra, Inc., for a total consideration of $35 million. Said Stan McCarthy, CEO of Kerry Ingredients Americas:

> The AFI business complements the Beatreme business acquired in 1988 and further strengthens our leadership positions in the snack and convenience sectors of the US market. This acquisition is a perfect fit in respect of the Group's core speciality ingredients product portfolio and US customer base.[41]

Kerry's global expansion in specialty food ingredients continues apace.

Notes

---

[1] Denis Brosnan, remarks made at the 1999 AGM and quoted in *Kerry's Eye* (1999), "Companies acquired in 1998 Greater than Total Size of Kerry Group plc", 27 May 1999, p. 18.

[2] Donal Hickey (1992), "Finbarr Travels the Globe for Irish food industry", *The Cork Examiner*, 2 July 1992.

[3] Jerry Henchy, telephone interview, 16 June 2000.

[4] Denis Brosnan, personal interview, 1 June 1999.

[5] Ibid.

[6] Stan McCarthy, personal interview, 6 December 1999.

[7] Finbarr O'Driscoll, personal interview, 14 July 1999.

[8] Randy McIntyre, personal interview, 7 December 1999.

[9] Denis Brosnan, personal interview, 11 October 1999.

[10] Denis Brosnan, personal interview, 1 June 1999.

[11] Brian O'Mahony and Ralph Riegel (1994), "£250m takeover by Kerry", *The Cork Examiner*, 8 November 1994, p. 12.

[12] Remarks made by Denis Brosnan at a press conference after the 1999 AGM, 25 June 1999.

[13] Finbarr O'Neill, Personal Interview, July 1999.

[14] Stan McCarthy, personal interview, 6 December 1999.

[15] Denis Brosnan, personal interview, 1 June 1999.

[16] Randy McIntyre, personal interview, 7 December 1999.

[17] Denis Brosnan, personal interview, 11 October 1999.

[18] Finbarr O'Driscoll, personal interview, 14 July 1999.

[19] Brendan McGrath (1996), "Kerry to expand its borders to the Far East", 31 May 1996, *The Irish Times*, p. 18.

[20] Mary Canniffe (1997), "Kerry Group spends £6.6m on Malaysian acquisition", *Irish Times*, 6 November 1997, p. 20.

[21] Mary Canniffe (1997), op. cit., p. 20.

[22] Kerry Group 1997 Annual Report, p. 12

[23] *Extel Examiner* (1997), "Gist-Brocades to sell Spinks & Co. to Ireland's Kerry Group", 18 December 1997.

[24] Kerry Group 1997 Annual Report, p. 10–11.

[25] John Willman (1998), "Dalgety sells its food arm for £359m: Kerry Group acquires bulk of ingredients operation", *The Financial Times*, 27 January 1998, p. 23.

[26] Ibid.

[27] This purchase ended on a very sour note for Tomkins. Their purchase of the mills from Kerry had *not been made conditional* on approval by the UK competition authorities. After the deal closed in March, the purchase of the mills was referred to the Monopolies and Mergers Commission who, later in the year, ordered Tomkins to divest itself of four of the mills. Tomkins was compelled to do so at a substantial loss.

[28] Kerry Group plc, Prospectus on the proposed acquisition of Dalgety Food Ingredients, p. 7.

[29] Brendan McGrath (1998). "Kerry Eyes Burns-Philips as EGM backs Dalgety", *The Irish Times*, 14 March 1998.

[30] Brendan McGrath (1998), op. cit.

[31] Denis Brosnan, personal interview, 7 October 1999.

[32] Jerry Houlihan, personal communication, 25 October 2000.

[33] Address by Denis Brosnan on the occasion of the Official Inauguration of Kerry do Brazil's Processing and Technical Facilities at Tres Coracoes, Minas Gerais, Brazil.

[34] Andrew Hobbs, *AAP Newsfeed*, 27 April 1998.

[35] Brendan McGrath (1998). "Kerry Eyes Burns-Philips as EGM backs Dalgety", *The Irish Times*, 14 March 1998.

[36] Ibid.

[37] Alex Aramenko, personal communication, 25 October 2000.

[38] Ibid.

[39] Liam Chute, personal interview, 28 March 2000.

[40] Alex Aramenko, personal communication, 25 October 2000.

[41] Kerry Group Press Release dated 17 October 2000, "Kerry acquires Armour Food Ingredients in the US."

Chapter 14

Kerry — The Multinational Enterprise

In the second half of 2000, Kerry Group received two awards that recognised and highlighted its impressive performance since becoming a public company in 1986. The first was its selection (for the second consecutive year) by *Industry Week* magazine for its "100 Best Managed Companies" award, given by a panel of expert judges to those firms (from among the world's largest publicly held manufacturing companies) that had shown superior performance on an array of financial and operational criteria. Among the performance measures used were growth in sales, profitability, earnings per share and margins. Judges also considered such financial ratios as return on equity and return on assets. Finally, they reviewed information on the firms' management, management practices and processes, new market development, research and development efforts, and importantly, social responsibility and performance.[1] Appropriately enough, since the award was not based exclusively on narrow financial criteria, the judges also gave significant weight to the contribution made by top firms to their employees, and to the communities in which their operations were embedded. In the case of Kerry Group, its activities in its various communities, and particularly in County Kerry, have always been a noteworthy dimension of their overall corporate performance.[2] Although companies from some 14 different countries

were included in the "top 100", Kerry Group was the only Irish
company so honoured. Says John Brandt, the publisher and editor-
in-chief of *Industry Week*:

> *Industry Week's* 100 Best Managed Companies are the
> world's leaders in innovative management strategies.
> Their emphasis on long-term growth makes them models
> for every corporation.[3]

A second distinction was Kerry Group's Number 1 ranking (for the
second consecutive year) in total shareholder return (TSR) in the
Financial Times' annual European Company Survey (for the Food
Producers and Processors Sector). Total shareholder return, which
reflects both the changes in share price and accumulated dividends, is generally regarded as the most appropriate measure of
financial returns to individual shareholders. Kerry topped the list
with a five-year TSR of nearly 226 per cent, followed by somewhat
lower returns for the far larger European food companies Cadbury
Schweppes, ORKLA, Nestlé and Unilever.[4] Certainly, no one could
suggest that Kerry's high TSR was the result of any sort of aberra-
tion, for its TSR for the full 13 years since it went public was 1,773
per cent! A share that cost 52p on initial issue in 1986 was trading
at £11.70 at the end of July 2000. A chart of share price (to the end
of October 2000) follows.

Figure 1: Kerry Group Share Price

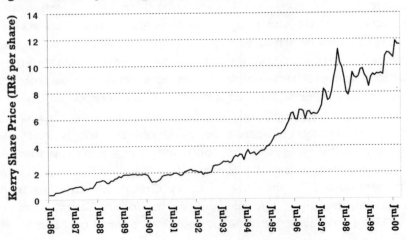

By any standard, such returns are impressive. For the period 1995–1999, Kerry's growth in sales revenues averaged 17.1 per cent annually, and its annual earnings per share (EPS) growth averaged 19.8 per cent. In fact, its EPS growth since flotation in 1986 has averaged 19.1 per cent annually. At the end of October 2000, Kerry's market capitalisation totalled IR£2 billion (€2.5 billion), with over 172 million shares on issue and approximately 18,000 shareholders. It has grown to be the fourth largest Irish industrial company (in market capitalisation) quoted on the Irish Stock Exchange. As one reviews the Kerry Group "numbers" today, it is difficult to imagine back to the beginnings of the organisation in January 1974, when it began trading as the Kerry Co-operative with £9 in share capital, 9 shareholders, and £2.85 million in borrowings.

Table 8 provides a summary of Kerry Group's financial results since its flotation in 1986. Consistent with its strategic plan, it has exceeded its goal of maintaining growth in profitability of at least 15 per cent annually. The organisation's sales in 1999 totalled IR£2 billion (€2.5 billion), with operating profits of £160 million (€204 million). It is very telling of Kerry's growth as a global enterprise that turnover and profit from activities within Ireland, while continuing to grow in absolute terms, now account for only 25 per cent and 17 per cent, respectively, of total Group results (see Figure 2).

Table 9: 14-Year Statistics for the Kerry Group (All figures in IR£)

	1986	1987	1988	1989	1990	1991	1992
Turnover	265,242	291,289	396,721	559,551	584,099	754,931	826,737
Operating Profit*	11,157	11,397	17,906	31,397	31,963	42,084	46,403
Earnings per Share*	6.01p	6.63p	9.98p	12.8p	13.9p	16.6p	18.1p

	1993	1994	1995	1996	1997	1998	1999
Turnover	879,975	882,697	1,199,093	1,233,253	1,344,129	1,732,642	1,934,534
Operating Profit*	50,196	55,549	85,739	90,594	104,891	136,547	160,359
Earnings per Share*	21.2p	23.5p	30.1p	33.9p	39.4p	48.1p	58.0p

Note: *(Before goodwill & exceptionals)

Figure 2: Geographical Analysis of Turnover and Operating Profit (by Origin) 1999

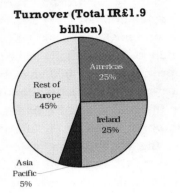

Turnover (Total IR£1.9 billion)

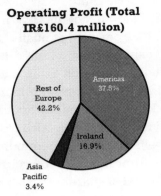

Operating Profit (Total IR£160.4 million)

The Kerry Organisation Today

Mission

The fundamentals of the Kerry Group mission statement have been essentially unchanged since the mid-1980s. Today, it reads as follows:

- The Kerry Group will be a major international specialist food ingredient corporation.

- It will become a significant supplier of added value brands and customer branded food products to Irish and UK retail outlets, while at the same time expanding its consumer foods business in selected European countries.

- Kerry will be a leader in selected markets through
    - Technological creativity
    - Superior product quality
    - Superior service to its customers, and
    - The unique wholehearted commitment of each employee.

- The Kerry Group will continue to grow its earnings at an annual rate of 15 per cent over each five-year period.

Cynics, often with good reason, may dismiss the importance of a company's mission statement as merely an exercise in maintaining good public relations. At its worst, it can be a vague, amorphous, and vacuous "feel good" statement of how an organisation prefers to depict itself to its constituencies. At its best, however, a statement of mission can simply and crisply communicate the motivating life-force of an organisation. At Kerry Group, the mission statement is at the very core of what the organisation is and what it does. It is more muscle than fluff. It supplies a hard-edged, tangible vision of *where* the organisation is to go, *how* (broadly) it is to get there, and *what results* the organisation *commits* to deliver. It is the very first step in the planning process, the essential "clarity" that has imprinted itself upon the collective psyche of the organisation, and the lodestone from which the specific goals and objectives of the organisation emanate. If the goals and objectives developed by Kerry Group during their continuous planning and budgeting cycles are the *road maps*, then the mission statement is clearly the *compass* that sets the broad direction.

Ownership, Control and Board of Directors

Despite the dilution of the Kerry Co-op shareholding, a significant holding of Kerry Group shares remains in County Kerry. In addition to the Co-op's 37 per cent share, it has been estimated that a further 20 per cent of the Group's shares are held individually by Kerry Co-op members. It is interesting to note that, although the Kerry Co-op's shareholding has declined to 37 per cent (and may be further reduced to as low as 20 per cent with additional share conversions), the *market value* of its total shareholding has continued to *rise*. The market value of Kerry Co-op's holding in late 2000 was approximately £1,000 million, a far cry from the roughly £31 million value of its 83 per cent shareholding in June 1986. In addition to the Co-op holding, a number of financial institutions have taken significant positions in Kerry Group stock, including the Bank of Ireland, AIB Investment Managers,Irish Life Assurance, and Trimark Investment Management Ltd. Kerry shares have had a history of thin trading, as the Co-op shareholding does not trade and Kerry farmers have been as loathe to sell their shares as to sell their land and farmsteads. If anything, financial institutions have often considered themselves to be "underweight" in Kerry Group shares and unable to acquire them in the quantities that they might prefer.

Managers in Kerry's Agribusiness Division continue to maintain extremely close ties with the supplier-shareholders of the Kerry

Co-op. They attend regular meetings of the Area Advisory Committees, communicating to farmers the latest company results, addressing operational issues, and importantly, listening to and attending to farmer concerns and questions. Although there are many alternative communication channels available for disseminating information and getting feedback, there is often no replacement for direct, face-to-face contact. Attendance at these local meetings enables Kerry managers to "keep their ears to the ground" at farm level. Although the agribusiness itself may be less and less material to the success of the organisation, the status of these suppliers as important shareholders provides a clear incentive to be well acquainted with their concerns. Additionally, the recognition that these Kerry farmers were responsible for giving the organisation life to begin with is never far from the surface. The Kerry Group's connection with its farmers is not one driven exclusively, or even primarily, by pounds and pence. In another unusual twist, it should be noted that Denis Brosnan generally makes it a point to address each of the nine advisory areas, individually, on an annual basis. He typically presents the Group's annual results, entertains questions, and will have a few pints with the farmers after the meeting. This might be considered highly uncharacteristic behaviour for the managing director of a major industrial firm, but it is absolutely in character within the context of the Kerry organisation.

The Board of Directors of Kerry Group, for its part, has undergone a very gradual evolution from exclusive control by Kerry Co-op directors, to (presently) one with majority co-operative representation, to (eventually) one in which the Kerry Co-op representation may be further diminished. At the moment, the rules call for 15 non-executive directors, nine of whom are appointed by the Kerry Co-operative. Thus far, however, only two Directors with a non-farming background have been appointed to the Board. Michael Dowling, former Secretary of the Department of Agriculture and Food in Dublin and Dr Ivor Kenny, Senior Research Fellow at University College Dublin and a Director of other Irish public companies, were both appointed to the Board in 1998. The Executive Directors are Denis Brosnan (Managing Director), Hugh Friel (Deputy Managing Director), Denis Cregan (Deputy Managing Director), Michael Griffin (CEO, Kerry Foods) and Stan McCarthy (President, Kerry Americas).

That the structure of the Board will change over time is clear. (Denis Brosnan, for his part, has made it clear that the structure will "mature" over time.) How quickly that will happen, and the extent to which it will happen, remains to be seen. Only one thing is certain, that the transformation process will be one of *evolution* rather than *revolution*. Changes in ownership structure and control have, thus far, occurred slowly and gradually over time. The various constituencies are typically given more than adequate time to get accustomed to and comfortable with new arrangements. Changes are signalled long in advance, ideas are floated and reactions gathered, and often when the change finally comes it has already been long anticipated. This is one more aspect of the Kerry way.

Employment

The Kerry organisation has grown from its initial (and still active) facility in the 22-acre Canon's Field in 1972 to encompass manufacturing, sales, R&D and marketing and sales facilities in 15 nations on five continents. From the "gang of eleven" who began work in a muddy field at North Kerry Milk Products in April of 1972, Group world-wide employment grew to approximately 14,000 by November 2000. As late as 1985, Kerry's last full year before becoming a public company, its total employment of 1,400 (except for a few sales people) was wholly located in Ireland. By 2000, however, the picture had changed considerably. Irish employees now constitute a distinct minority of overall Group employment (although interestingly, the numbers employed at the original Listowel site still number approximately 500, on average), and Kerry employees are increasingly dispersed around the globe, as follows:

Ireland	3,157 (incl. 1, 028 in County Kerry)
United Kingdom	6,168
Continental Europe	1,862
Americas	2,196
Rest of World	617

Kerry Ingredients

With estimated 1999 sales of £1.3 billion (€1.6 billion), or 66 per cent of total Group sales, Kerry Ingredients maintains a portfolio of more than 9,000 products and currently markets its products in 80 countries. Although Kerry no longer reports profitability on a divisional basis (it prefers to report on a geographic basis), analysts have estimated Ingredients' contribution to overall group profitability at 74–76 per cent of overall Group profits, with operating margins in excess of 9 per cent. It has 25 technical centres manned by some 350 food scientists, and 57 manufacturing facilities located throughout the world.

Kerry Ingredients' core technologies are uniquely suited to the evolving global market for specialised food ingredients. Markets for ready-to-use foods, and snacking and convenience foods, continue to grow. Indeed, the desire for convenience drives the food industry, as more consumers live in single parent and dual income families where time available for the preparation of meals has itself become a scarce commodity. Additionally, consumers are increasingly demanding food products that exhibit high flavour "impact" over a wide range of tastes, from savoury to sweet, traditional to ethnic tastes, as food tastes have become increasingly internationalised. Consumer demand is also highly sensitive to concerns over the safety and nutritional content of foods, its appearance and its freshness. All these market "drivers" are operative in a dynamic and highly competitive environment of proliferating new product development.

Kerry Ingredients' core technologies include expertise in providing cheese and dairy flavourings, coating systems, sweet and savoury flavourings, and specialty lipid systems to a wide range of top-tier customers. Indeed, a listing of customers sounds like a "Who's Who" of the food industry, including Genreal Mills-Pillsbury, Unilever-Best Foods, Kraft-Nabisco, Kelloggs, Heinz, Quaker Oats, Burger King, McDonalds, Tricon, Frito-Lay and Proctor & Gamble.Of particular importance is the highly specialised, engineered nature of the ingredients Kerry provides to each customer. Most products are highly customised to the specific needs of each customer, and once an ingredient has been "spec'd in" to a product formula, it is very difficult to switch.

Kerry, in fact, considers itself to provide "application and customer specific food technology solutions" rather than merely food ingredients.

Importantly, in specialised food ingredients, Kerry has no one obvious competitor. Although it competes with many companies who employ various food technologies, no other firm has the same range of technologies, or competes as broadly on a regional basis, as Kerry. Uniquely, it is a certifiably "global" provider of the very widest array of specialty food ingredients.

Kerry Foods

Kerry Foods, with estimated 1999 sales of IR611 million (€784 million) (32 per cent of total Group sales), commands a portfolio of leading Irish and UK brands, as well as a wide range of own-label products sold into selected markets. Foods' contribution to overall Group profitability is estimated by analysts to be in the 25–26 per cent range. It has 22 manufacturing facilities in the UK and Ireland, a dedicated distribution network in both countries, and is a supplier to all major supermarket groups, convenience stores and independent retailers in both national markets. Its range of food products includes pork and poultry products, dairy products, juices and mineral waters, convenience foods, savoury products and home-baking products.

Product innovation and exceptional customer service have been prime components of Kerry Foods' success in the highly competitive consumer foods segment. Kerry continues to follow a dual strategy of investment in its premier brands such as Denny. Ballyfree, Mattessons, Wall's, Dawn, Millers, Richmond, Homepride, Low Low, Move over Butter and Kerrymaid, while continuing to supply the multiples with their customer-label requirements. Such an arrangement, in fact, is much to the taste of the major retailers, since only the presence of strong brands can ensure the success (and margin contributions) of their own-label brands. Although to a certain extent this dual track is a synergistic one, Kerry is geared to increasingly focus upon the development of its branded products where margin opportunities are much enhanced.

Although consumer foods activities, to date, have been limited to the Irish and UK markets, Kerry continues to evaluate expansion opportunities in "selected markets". All signs point to these "selected markets" as being the newly emerging market economies of Eastern Europe.

Kerry Agribusiness

Kerry Agribusiness remains firmly rooted in Kerry, focusing its efforts upon servicing the needs of Kerry's local milk suppliers in terms of farm inputs, technical assistance and milk assembly and collection. In the context of Kerry's organisational goals, Agribusiness is considered a "service provider", oriented towards efficiently providing a range of services to its farmer/suppliers, most of whom hold shares in Kerry Group. It is decidedly not a profit centre.

Other Functional Areas

R&D activities are dispersed throughout technical centres around the world in all of Kerry's major markets, including Beloit (USA), Listowel (Ireland), Bristol (UK), Sydney (Australia), Apt (France), and Tres Coracoes (Brazil). This is certainly consistent with Kerry's core competence of supplying "food technology solutions" for highly focused and specialised applications. Research and development activities are clearly focused upon product development rather than "pure" or "blue sky" research. Kerry may acquire promising basic research from universities or other companies, develop it, and apply it to new products or to more promising "solutions". It is, after all, knowledge itself that Kerry is selling. As Denis Brosnan says, "We are selling a small amount of material, and a great amount of technical development."[5] Of course, any research can be imitated over time, so it is important, to keep margins intact, to keep pushing the boundaries, even to the extent of making one's own products obsolete. Given the fact that most of Kerry's competitors are spending similarly large funds on research and development activities, the rate of product improvement, development and introductions has been dizzying. It can be a very dangerous world for any firm that does not, at a minimum, keep up with the cutting edge of product and technology development.

Although Kerry's various business units, and individual operations, are headquartered throughout the world, the corporate headquarters remains in Tralee, in the same building it first occupied in 1978, when it was still the Kerry Co-op. The home office staff remains relatively small and highly focused, with departmental support teams covering the range of disciplines. At present, it houses approximately 80 employees.

Stages of Kerry Group's Development

Like most organisations, Kerry Group has progressed through a series of distinct stages in its organisational life. Yet even today, looking back upon a history that, while short, has been remarkably eventful, Kerry Group remains an aggressive, acquisitive, growth-oriented organisation, far more prone to looking forward than looking back. Although it clearly has achieved some measure of maturity in its systems, processes and goals, it can scarcely be considered a "mature" organisation in the life-cycle sense. If anything, its focus upon continued growth in sales and profitability has now been stepped up a notch and extended to a new level. The focus today is upon expansion of the enterprise to a size and scope that will enable Kerry to compete effectively and efficiently in a global food industry that is rapidly consolidating.

In examining the current phase of Kerry's growth and development, it may be helpful to summarise its earlier phases:

- **Phase 1 — Getting Established (1972–1979).** This was the start-up phase of the organisation, a time when the primary goal was, literally, organisational survival. Indeed, the long, frustrating but ultimately successful crusade of a small number of promoters to give birth to the organisation was, of itself, a remarkable success story. The very early days of the manufacturing facility in Listowel were the crucible in which the essentials of Kerry's distinct organisational culture were forged. The focus on survival evolved to an understandable focus on achieving security. Co-operative in its structure, the organisation "stuck to its knitting" in the milk sector, built a track record and cultivated strong support from its natural constituency of Kerry farmers, and expanded somewhat opportunistically in the liquid milk business. At the same time, it began to differentiate itself from the herd, developing a highly "commercial" orientation that was different than the prevailing co-operative "ethos" of other dairy co-operatives. It developed something of a reputation as a disruptive influence within the co-operative movement in Ireland. Yet, this would have been a subtle difference. In its essentials, Kerry Co-op was not all that different from other co-operatives. It focused on farming, on expanding milk production, and on maximising returns for its members. It focused on the familiar. Nevertheless, it could be considered to be co-operative in structure, but with a strong and developing public company ethos.

- **Phase 2 — Diversification (1980–1988).** The first phase of Kerry Group's organisational saga ended with a jolt, as the firm's total dependence on its milk supply was clearly, if not cruelly, exposed. The firm literally redefined itself, resolving to reduce or eliminate its vulnerability to the commodity milk business. The formal strategic planning process was initiated, leading Kerry to diversify into the branded consumer foods market in Ireland, and ultimately into changing its organisational structure. Realising that growth required levels of capital not available to co-operative organisations, Kerry became the first co-operative to convert to a public company. This was the culmination of a fundamental philosophical change that had been in the works for some time. Kerry Group would achieve the best returns for its shareholders, *whatever* the business. The business need not have been agriculture. Kerry's "equation for growth" was put into balance, as the firm focused upon its clear strategic objective to become a "substantial international food organisation", built the capability to achieve it, and located pools of capital sufficient to fund it.

- **Phase 3 — Going International (1988–1998).** The beginning of this period is best marked by the purchase of Beatreme Food Ingredients, which provided the first concrete manifestation of Kerry's ambition to become a multinational food ingredients company. A decade of continuous, and related, acquisitions followed, as Kerry built a significant presence in both the global specialty food ingredients markets and consumer foods in the UK and Ireland. Growth was focused and highly disciplined, and Kerry's unique ability to both integrate new businesses, and in a number of cases to turn them around very quickly, surfaced as a distinctive capability of the organisation.

- **Phase 4 — Global Scale, Scope and Spread (Present)**. Kerry's aggressive growth orientation continues, no less urgently than before. Although, in the context of Irish companies, Kerry Group can be considered large, in the context of the global food companies that dominate the world's markets, it is still relatively small. Given that the industry is continuing to consolidate, and the most competitive firms reap the optimal efficiencies that come with size and scale, Kerry must grow still larger to compete effectively. As expansion continues, naturally, the organisational processes, structures, and indeed culture, must stretch to encompass it. The propagation of the distinctive Kerry culture will be a singular challenge during this period. Similarly, as the senior executives who have led the Kerry organisation for nearly 30 years begin to reach an age when retirement may not be out of the question, the issue of succession assumes a critical importance.

This short chapter has taken a snapshot view of the Kerry organisation today. In the next chapter, we will review the Kerry story over the nearly 30 years of its organisational life, and search for the lessons that may be derived from "the Kerry Way".

Notes

---

[1] See *Industry Week*, 21 August 2000, for additional details regarding the selection process and criteria.

[2] Corporate performance, of course, is not exclusively measured in financial terms, despite a sometimes depressing tendency for evaluators to believe so.

[3] John Brandt, quoted in a Kerry Group press statement dated 23 August 2000.

[4] *Financial Times*, "European Company Performance Survey", June 2000. Full details are also available on Kerry Group's website (www.kerrygroup.com).

[5] Denis Brosnan, personal interview, 7 October 1999.

Chapter 15

The Kerry Way: Strategy, Structure and Culture

The steps we are taking now to continue building a profitable, stable business are no different to those we have taken over the past decade. Others may find that different ways work better for them. I will confine myself to the Kerry way. . . . — Denis Brosnan[1]

There is a Kerry way of thinking, and a Kerry way of doing things. One of them is "second best is not an option". If you are in a business, you are the best, or you are out. That's where they strive to be, the main player. It stems from part of the football code of the County. We've got to be the best! — Conor Keane, journalist[2]

In business, no less than in the greater human community, there is a natural temptation to study closely those who have been particularly successful in their chosen pursuits with the goal of unlocking the "secrets" of success that they are thought to possess. Yet this can be a dangerous game. Though such prescriptions can be deceptively simple, rarely does "one size fit all", and what works wonders for one organisation may spell disaster for another.

The Kerry organisation's success, over the nearly three decades of its history, makes it a tempting target for such emulation. Of its success, even in the context of the currently roaring "Celtic

Tiger" Irish economy, there can be little doubt. That it has developed its own unique approach to achieving organisational success is difficult to dispute. That its "rags to riches" story is at least interesting, and perhaps even inspirational, is generally accepted. These factors, combined, have led to the gradual development of a reputation, or perhaps more properly a "mystique", that surrounds the organisation. But what can be learned from "the Kerry Way"?

This chapter examines some of the distinctive competencies of the Kerry Group, the explicit as well as implicit skills and capabilities that have distinguished it, the vision and focus on planning that have guided it, and the pride of the people and the county that have built it and nourished it. Clearly, some elements of "the Kerry Way" may prove instructive, but they must be viewed with a full and fair measure of circumspection. The ethos and culture of the organisation are in many ways the products of its own unique history. It is a history that no other organisation can expect to duplicate; they must find their own way. Henry David Thoreau, in discussing what might be learned from a reading of his classic book *Walden*, once said that he hoped the reader would "not stretch the seams in putting on the coat, for it may do good service to him who it fits". The same admonition may be given to any reading of the Kerry Way.

Using some degree of metaphorical licence, the chapter is broken into three sections on strategy, structure and culture, and subtitled *The Head*, *The Hands* and *The Heart*. This format has been appropriated from the educational institution at which the author currently lectures, where it has been accepted as an article of faith that the faculty will endeavour to educate students intellectually (the head), emotionally and aesthetically (the heart) and practically (the hands). It is, I believe, a format not ill-suited for a discussion of the Kerry Group.[3]

Vision, Leadership and Strategy (The Head)

In assessing the success of the Kerry Group, it is difficult to overestimate the immense contribution made to the organisation by three extraordinary leaders, Eddie Hayes, Frank Wall and Denis Brosnan. Hayes had a vision that he kept alive through sheer force of will, throughout years in a virtual wilderness, a vision dismissed by most as wildly impractical and unlikely to see the light of day. He persevered for years on a quixotic quest for a milk processing factory for County Kerry, and Denis Brosnan gave that initial vision its practical manifestation. Wall, for his part, threw his considerable support behind the move to form the all-county co-operative. His belief that such a co-operative would allow Kerry farmers to at long last gain some modicum of control over their economic destiny carried considerable weight in Kerry, and allowed Brosnan to choreograph and implement a plan to accomplish it. Finally, Brosnan himself, as a prominent "wunderkind" in Irish business, has demonstrated time and time again an incredible foresight and an uncanny, instinctive ability to divine future trends in business. This sense of vision, married to a unique talent for harnessing the utter loyalty, energy and commitment of others, has shaped the Kerry organisation since its creation. His imprint is in evidence throughout the history of the Kerry Group. No one's shadow looms larger.

Although clearly visionaries, Hayes, Wall and Brosnan were also nothing if not practical, hard-edged, commercially minded men with few illusions about the difficulties involved in acting upon and achieving their visions. This was not "pie-in-the-sky", woolly-eyed idealism; it was idealism with a pick and shovel, well grounded and concrete. It is this sense of strategic vision, the legacy of the founders, which permeates the organisation even today.

Eddie Hayes

Hayes spent a good part of his life involved in politics, yet was scarcely a "political" man. Michael Quill, himself a native of County Kerry and later the leader of the Transit Workers Union in New York, once unkindly characterised a New York politician as one who "could talk out of both sides of his mouth and whistle at the same time". Eddie Hayes was never that sort of politician, for he pulled few punches and said what he thought straight out. Indeed, whatever political ambitions he had were unfulfilled. He led through sheer, unadulterated perseverance and force of will, yet he was never the leader of a popular crusade. Indeed, prophets are seldom recognised in their native places! As many friends as he had, politically, he probably had as many enemies. If he believed something was right, and he was set upon a goal, he was tenacious and unswerving in his pursuit of it. It was not unusual that he would step on a few toes in the process. In any event, Hayes quite simply never knew what it was to quit. Somehow, in some way, this same tenacity came to permeate the Kerry organisation, and was particularly obvious in the early days when the word "failure" was not even permitted in the vocabulary. Many will argue that this same ethic characterises the Kerry organisation to the present day. As one reviews the history of the organisation, one can see the same willingness to rock the boat, absorb criticism, and "take the road less travelled" in the pursuit of a strategy or goal that is deemed to be right.

In the years leading up to the founding of the Kerry organisation, it was Hayes who carried the torch the longest, and kept it lit in the darkest of times. It was Hayes who knew of, believed in, pursued and wooed Denis Brosnan. Indeed, his approach to staffing the new Kerry organisation was a highly enlightened one for any business person of the time, let alone for a Kerry farmer. It was quite simply that one should search for the most capable people, pay them well enough so that they did not have to worry about how much money they were earning, and allow them to concentrate on the job at hand. This was the approach taken in hiring Kerry's key executives.

Clearly, the founding of Kerry and the hiring of Denis Brosnan are the two critical contributions for which Eddie Hayes will be long remembered. But he possessed another quality, demonstrated during the very early years of the organisation, that had an equally important effect upon the subsequent performance of Kerry Group. It is a quality, and an approach, that other business leaders may still find particularly instructive in the new commercial environment of the twenty-first century. Simply put, he knew when to step in to protect his staff, and when to back away and let them get on with the job. For example, when Denis Brosnan was hired, more than a few feathers were ruffled; there were many capable, qualified, experienced, and far more senior people (generally creamery managers) interested in the post, and the creamery managers in particular expected it would be "one of their own". Hayes, and a few of the other more progressive of Kerry's farming leaders such as Frank Wall, stepped in to take the brunt of the abuse and opposition, leaving the new executive to get on with the hard task of getting the operation off the ground. Similarly, when the controversy over whey disposal, effluent and then the "odour problem" at the Listowel plant literally threatened to halt operations in the summer of 1972, Hayes stepped in forcefully. He acknowledged the "teething problems" of the new facility, went to the community and elected officials counselling patience, and gave assurances that the problems would be worked out. There was no search for a scapegoat, no blame-mongering. On the other side of the equation, Hayes also knew when to back off. Having hired Brosnan, he allowed him to select his own staff. He then got out of the way while the new team began to run the operation. There was no peering over the shoulder, second-guessing, or uninvited interference. The executives and managers were given room to execute the organisation's strategy. For someone like Eddie Hayes who had pioneered the entire idea of a milk processing plant, virtually alone, for so long, it is remarkable that he was able to step back from the day-to-day running of the operation as he did. He was there for support when needed, and out of the way as the management team got on with the job. Such wisdom is an essential, and often underrated, component of effective leadership.

Years later, one senior executive at Kerry lamented the fact that so many of the younger managers and employees in the company had only known Eddie Hayes in his later years, as a Board member, at a time when he was somewhat diminished by age and sickness. He died in 1997. It was unfortunate that they had not seen at first hand Eddie Hayes' seminal contribution to the organisation, and indeed to all of County Kerry.

Frank Wall

Frank Wall and Eddie Hayes were a study in contrasts. Wall was seen by most as a Fianna Fáil man, while Hayes was Fine Gael. Wall was a leader of the ICMSA, while Hayes was staunchly IFA. Wall was a high profile supplier to the Listowel DDC creamery, while Hayes chaired his own local co-operative. Hayes was a national Board member of ICOS, while Wall was one of the key players in the founding of Bord Bainne and sat on the Board for many years. Hayes hired Denis Brosnan, while Wall was involved in the decision to hire Tony O'Reilly as the first Chairman of Bord Bainne. Hayes was blunt, and Wall was, as they say in Ireland, "cute".

Wall, in fact, was a consummate politician, able to navigate the contentious waters of farming politics in County Kerry with great effectiveness. This innate ability, combined with the serious level of respect that people in the Kerry farming community had for him, was his greatest strength. People looked up to him and came to him with problems or for advice. He was also a businessman as well as a farmer. He had been a salesman for a company that manufactured agricultural equipment, and had travelled extensively through Ireland and the United Kingdom.

Wall's organisational skill was unmatched, for he never blundered into events, issues, meetings or decisions without a plan. Before any meeting or decision, he would have a strategy in place. He would know who had taken a particular position, the particular concerns held by people, where the balance of power lay, and where the majority fell on the issue. A prudent man, he would make certain that he had sufficient support on his side. If not, then there was more work to be done.

In the drive to form the Kerry Co-operative in 1973, Frank Wall was looked upon to deliver the votes of the DDC farmers, and he did not disappoint. Later, as the first chairman of the Kerry Co-operative, he stepped aside after the 1974 election and passed the chair to Eddie Hayes. Some suggest that he might have remained as the chairman for some time, that he "had the votes" if he wanted them. Others say he that he didn't. These are matters for conjecture. But, in the early years of the co-operative, what was needed was "balance", between those in the north and south of the county, and between the rival farming organisations, the ICMSA and the IFA. What is clear is that in those early days of the co-operative, Wall helped not only to maintain that "delicate balance", but helped mightily to forge the bonds of loyalty and trust that have come to characterise Kerry Co-op's relationships with its farmer-shareholder constituency.

Denis Brosnan

John B. Keane, writer, publican, raconteur and passionate observer of all things Kerry, is not often prone to undue circumspection. Indeed, he has been known to be extravagant with both his condemnation and his praise. His comments on Denis Brosnan are no exception:

> Denis Brosnan is a genius, pure and simple. He can get people to do things. He takes calculated risks. He is extraordinarily talented. I wouldn't say that about anybody else in Kerry, except maybe Mick O'Connell the footballer. He is the most surefooted Kerryman of all time.

> The farmers of Kerry are a proud, wonderful people who had the courage to invest, and believed in Brosnan when they wouldn't believe in others. He was one of them. He had to convince people, of course, but he had the facts behind him. They had great faith in him. Brosnan showed them what they could do. History will be very kind to Brosnan, for he has made Kerry a better place.[4]

Readers may judge this to be hyperbole, or at least exaggeration. It may be. Not everyone would agree with any assessment that has Denis Brosnan virtually walking on water. Yet, it *is* significant that a sizeable portion of the Kerry Group's constituency *would* agree with it! When asked about the reasons for Kerry Group's record of success, invariably the first answer given by most observers is the leadership and vision of Denis Brosnan. His imprint is everywhere. He has been, and remains, the dominant influence in the birth, growth and continued development of the enterprise.

That he is an effective leader is unquestioned. His subordinates, colleagues, various publics and competitors attest to it, and his record of accomplishment supports it. However, identifying the quality of leadership is one thing, and decomposing it into its constituent parts is quite another. In doing so, one begins with another anomaly, for Brosnan is a quiet leader, not given to emotional exhortations or theatrical displays. Yet he is possessed of an undeniable charisma. Webster's Dictionary defines charisma variously as "a special quality conferring extraordinary powers of leadership and the ability to inspire veneration", and "a personal magnetism that enables an individual to attract or influence people".[5] The loyalty and commitment of his managers bear testimony to the fact that Brosnan has it. They will go through walls for him. Their willingness to follow his lead, commit to objectives, pursue them relentlessly and accomplish them in the face of substantial challenges is derived in some large measure from his understated, but inspirational, leadership.

His leadership style is singular, in one way, because he is far more prone to listen than to dictate. A number of Kerry executives have related being at meetings where presentations have gone on for hours, followed by discussion and debate, and Brosnan has sat attentively, but quietly, taking it all in but scarcely contributing a word himself. He allows his subordinates to talk it out, weigh the options and fully explore an issue. At the end of it, if necessary, he will make the decision or propose the solution. One manager related how, after hours of discussion of a particularly thorny issue, Brosnan finally spoke up and made the decision. "We all looked at each other," he said, "wondering why we had not seen that ourselves in the first place. It was clearly the best solution."

Brosnan exudes a quiet, matter-of-fact confidence. There is little false bravado or braggadocio, but there is plenty of intensity. He may listen well, but if someone comes to Brosnan for a decision, he will get it, and quickly. He often sees things in clear black-and-white terms. Visionary that he is, he also has a bias for action, and is nothing if not decisive. He will follow his instincts. Says Brosnan:

> I don't have any problem in someone telling me, "You're not right." The only thing is that there are times when I say, and this is horrible to say, that I *know* I'm right, when I say, "Just believe it, this is the right thing to do." I will listen to everybody; I have no problem with advice of any description. Still, there are times when I've had to take it alone and say, "I've something of a sixth sense that this is what needs to be done."[6]

Of course, confidence and trust are based upon past performance, and Brosnan has consistently delivered. But it is a curious prescription for leadership, perhaps akin to American President Teddy Roosevelt's admonition to "speak softly and carry a big stick". Brosnan himself says:

> To be Kerry . . . is certainly to be simple, courteous and polite, while at the same time knowing that we have a lot of skills and strengths, and that we are the best at something, or the biggest at something.[7]

Doubtless Kerry's competitors over the years might take exception to this characterisation, since it seems very much at odds with Brosnan's reputation for bold, brash and even ruthless action in the commercial sphere. This is the root of another apparent contradiction, for how can a soft-spoken introvert and listener, with a penchant for aggressive and decisive action, inspire such awe? Perhaps it is his equally conspicuous reputation for being a man of remarkable prescience and vision. Ivor Kenny, perhaps Ireland's foremost management thinker, has quoted Brosnan as saying that "a chief executive has to 'sense the future'".[8] No one has demonstrated that ability better than Brosnan, or been able to harvest the benefits of such vision as well. Kenny has called Brosnan "the best strategist I've met".[9]

Certainly in County Kerry, farmers have credited Brosnan with having "the Midas Touch", as if the success of the Kerry Group were the result of one person's magic elixir. Anyone who knows the organisation well, however, knows that is not true. The critical success factors of any organisation are far more extensive and complex than the contribution of one leader. Still, Brosnan, if not the elixir, has been the catalyst. He makes things happen. With his vision and energy, he has embodied and symbolised "the Kerry Way". It is perhaps illustrative that today Brosnan spends a great deal of time travelling to Kerry's increasingly far-flung outposts, inspecting the facilities, encouraging the troops and attending the review meetings. Before these "flying visits", as Kerry managers scurry about with preparations, they talk of having the "PBs" (the "pre-Brosnans"), for a visit from "the chief" is, like an act of nature, intense, swift and uninsurable.

Even today, it is not unusual for commentators to speculate on what might have happened if Denis Brosnan had gone somewhere else but to North Kerry Milk Products in 1972. Joe Rea, a popular agricultural journalist who has covered the agricultural scene in Ireland for over 30 years, spoke of this with tongue only slightly in cheek:

> One can only wonder, what would have happened if somehow Denis Brosnan had been deposited in the rich dairy lands of the Golden Vale, rather than the green fields of North Kerry nearly thirty years ago.[10]

Fortunately for Kerry, this thought need only provide an opportunity for idle, if interesting, speculation.

The Discipline of Formal Strategic Planning: Clarity and Purpose

It is not unusual for many business enterprises to pay lip service to the idea of serious strategic planning. Targets may be arbitrarily set by upper management, with lower levels of the organisation consigned to retrofitting action plans to attain "the number". In others, it is an informal process, limited to the very few who "by the seat of their pants" develop a general direction for where they think the organisation is going. At Kerry Group, however, the process of strategic planning is formal, rigorous, participatory and dead serious. One should particularly emphasise that it *is* in fact an *ongoing process*, not a discrete, spasmodic activity that rears its head once a year, is grudgingly addressed and promptly put in the drawer until the following year. It is a central organising principle of the Kerry enterprise, a lynchpin in its growth and development and a prime mechanism in its execution of programs, its integration of acquisitions, and its overall conduct of the business.

Certainly, the art (or science) of formal corporate strategic planning attained prominence in the 1970s, as many firms embraced planning as a panacea, capable of solving a myriad of ills. Too often, however, it was not integrated into the fabric of the organisation but was treated as a "standalone" component, separate, apart and compartmentalised from the rest of the organisation. It was an ivory tower approach, for "planners" naturally did the planning. Implementation, on the other hand, was done by someone, or everyone, else, few if any of whom had been involved with the planning in the first place. All too often, this resulted in plans that were utterly unrealistic, "pie in the sky" exercises that were not grounded in reality. The whole notion of strategic planning itself suffered as a result.

But strategic planning can, and should, happen on many levels. In Kerry, planning is ingrained in the fabric of all levels of the organisation. The process is not confined to a select few. If Kerry's organisational culture is the "heart" of the enterprise, and if the capabilities of Kerry's people are the "hands", then to continue the analogy, Kerry's strategic planning process is the "head". Although the process is critical, demanding and detailed, it is not necessarily extraordinarily complex. Kerry, in fact, has adopted a very simple definition of planning, attributed to the late Michael Killeen:

> Strategic management is about how one gets an organisation from where it is now to where, after careful planning, it decides it wants to be in a period of years from now ... [11]

Key to Kerry's practice of strategic management is the critical importance of *clarity* in the mission, in the goals and objectives and in the implementation steps. Again and again, in conversations with Kerry managers, the term "clarity" (meaning the ability to "see clearly") or "lucidity" or "transparency" dominates discussions of strategy. There must be *clarity* in the vision. In other words, everyone must understand it. It must be agreed, written down, understood and practised. Hugh Friel explains it this way:

> Now, it [the strategic planning process] is diffused throughout the organisation. It has introduced clarity. I would hope there is a lot of clarity. If you were to ask twenty different people at different levels throughout the organisation about the organisation and where it's going, and why it does particular things, the answers you'd get should be pretty similar to the answers you'd get from the three of us [Brosnan, Friel and Cregan] in here. [12]

In addition to clarity, the Kerry organisation also serves as an exemplar of what strategists Gary Hamel and C.K. Prahalad have termed "strategic intent". Targets must be clear, objectives must be known, all must be pulling in the same direction. They also counsel organisations to "stretch" beyond the safe strategy of merely seeking objectives and opportunities that fit organisational resources. Resources themselves, in their view, should be stretched, objectives should be more aggressive and ambition should dominate. Hamel and Prahalad, in their critique of "Western management thought", describe it this way:

> Companies that have risen to global leadership over the past 20 years invariably began with ambitions out of proportion to their resources and capabilities. This concept,

fundamentally different from that which underpins Western management thought, is "strategic intent". These organisations begin with a goal that exceeds their present
grasp and existing resources. They then rally the organisation to close the gap by setting challenges that focus
employees' efforts in the near to medium term. Year after
year, they emphasise competitive innovation: building a
portfolio of competitive advantages; searching markets
for "loose bricks" that rivals have left underdefended;
changing the terms of competitive engagement to avoid
playing by the leader's rules. The result is a global leadership position and an approach to competition that has
reduced larger, stronger Western rivals to an endless
game of catch-up ball.[13]

Kerry Group has taken this counsel to heart. Since the time of the
caravan in the Canon's Field in Listowel, it has been an organisation "with ambitions out of proportion to its resources", constantly
"searching markets for 'loose bricks'". Reinforcing Kerry's emphasis (some might say "obsession") on planning, Denis Brosnan
has gone so far as to claim that "80 per cent of a company's performance is linked to strategy, and 20 per cent to operational performance".[14]

Of course, the planning process begins with the mission, and
ends only with implementation and accomplishment. Kerry's mission has remained remarkably stable: to grow in the ingredients
and selected consumer foods markets. This is far different from
those organisations with mission statements that alter with regularity. Similarly, Kerry's commitment to double sales every five
years and increase its earnings by an average of 15 per cent a
year are tangible, stable targets of which everyone in the organisation is aware. There is no confusion over where the organisation
intends to go. The strategic planning process at Kerry begins with
this understanding, this clarity (and unity) of purpose.

If Kerry has displayed an obsession for achieving its targets, it
is the planning process that has supplied a framework for doing
so. Planning is not "blue sky" theorising, but also monitoring performance compared to the plan to ensure that the organisation remains on track to achieve its goals. "Planning meetings" are an
ever present fact of life at Kerry, intense in nature and held at all

levels. At these periodic meetings, performance is reviewed and goals and priorities agreed. Each individual at these meetings is held accountable for personal goals that are quite specific, concrete, achievable (but not easy!), measurable and have completion dates! Next to every specific goal is a name, a personal responsibility. It is perhaps this absolute expectation of personal responsibility that drives the implementation end of Kerry's dynamic planning process. There is, in a sense, no place to hide.

Kerry's approach to planning and implementation, that is to say, to profitable growth, may be summed up in an "equation" or "formula" often cited by Kerry managers. It is:

$$\text{Strategy} \times \text{Capability} \times \text{Capital} = \text{Sustained Profitable Growth}$$

If any one of these factors is missing, goes the mantra at Kerry, there will be at best zero profitable growth. Certainly, Kerry has always had a strategy. Capital was more problematic, but as a publicly traded company with a stellar record of performance, capital constraints have ceased to be the limiting factors they once were. With regard to capability, Kerry's managerial and technical resources have been tested in the highly competitive global arena and have not been found wanting. It is to these capabilities, the "hands" of the Kerry organisation, that we next turn our attention.

Structure and Capability (The Hands)

Ten Simple Things

Denis Brosnan has never been accused of being overly theoretical. His prescriptions for success, as might be expected, are practical, grounded and above all, simple. Of course, that does not mean they are easy. Nevertheless, in many ways they serve to drive the business, and Kerry managers have come to know these principles well.

1. *Be clear on, and write down, your short- and long-term goals.* Short of going to the gallows in the morning, writing is another good way of concentrating the mind. On paper, goals already achieve a certain concreteness, a greater reality.

2. *Select a maximum of ten key issues which you and each of your colleagues must concentrate on in order to achieve the goals set.* Goals, and issues, must be prioritised. Having twenty priorities is the same as having none.

3. *Know your core competencies.* Focus on what you and the organisation do well, and work to eliminate your weaknesses.

4. *Continually monitor progress.*

5. *Keep things simple.*

6. *Learn how to "eat the elephant".* Dice up problems into smaller size pieces.

7. *Use the Loose Brick Theory.* Don't attack competitors with a full frontal attack that will engender a serious response; look for underdefended territory and begin to build your business in a small way, staying below the response threshold of large and powerful competitors.

8. *Would the organisation be more or less profitable without you?* This is the most important question, and one which focuses again upon Kerry's ethic of personal responsibility. It is a question that, according to Denis Brosnan, he continues to pose to himself.

9. *Clearly understand and react quickly to your business environment.* Sense the future.

10. *Remember that change is continuous. An organisation must be responsive and flexible in its management of change.*

This recipe for "getting things done" is sufficiently simple that one might consider it trite or hackneyed. The list does lack the lustre offered by extravagant words and complex, multidimensional theory. Yet it is difficult to argue with success. In what may seem to be a minor triumph for common sense business principles, the Kerry Group, at ground level, has been guided by these principles over the last two decades.

No Politics Here — The Stability of Leadership

Granted, at the start, that there is no such thing as an apolitical organisation, nevertheless the Kerry Group, at least at certain levels, appears to have avoided the political infighting and jockeying for position, particularly in the upper echelons of management, that seems to characterise many other organisations. Why this apparent absence of office politics? Certainly, County Kerry and its citizens are scarcely apolitical! One major reason, it seems, is that there has never been any serious question as to who is ultimately in charge. Denis Brosnan has been acknowledged as "the chief", and his leadership has never been questioned. There are simply no challengers.

There are other factors. One is that there is simply no time for plotting. The pace of activity is so fast, and each individual shoulders enough responsibility, that there is simply no room for Machiavellian machinations. Another may be that the top people in the organisation simply do not tolerate it. A final contributing factor is that, as Brosnan suggests, although many managers have remained in the same positions for some time, their accompanying responsibilities have continued to change along with the organisation:

> Kerry has been so different during the three decades, changing many, many times. I think it's a fact that everyone has been managing a different part of a different organisation every two, three or four years. Looking back, what have I done these past two years? I have devoted most of my time to either Asia or South America. So it means that somebody else is doing what I did four or five years ago, which is looking after other parts of the organisation. You can see that in a total role reversal with Denis Cregan. He was asked to take over all of Kerry Ingredients Europe in 1999. So, he is doing a very different job in 1999 than he did in 1997 or 1998.[15]

The wrong impression should not be given. Kerry Group is a social, that is to say a human, organisation. It has its own internal politics, important and petty, throughout all layers of the organisation. To claim otherwise would be absurd. Yet the executive suite has apparently been spared the worst effects of politics, bickering and manoeuvring. The troika at the head of the Kerry organisation is not only remarkably competent, they are also remarkably complementary in their approaches. They are very, very different people, with contrasting personalities, strengths and weaknesses. Says Brosnan:

> We *are* very different in what we do well. For instance, I just spoke of Denis' [Cregan's] role in the current year. He will do a far better job than I would in making a solid, secure business of Kerry Ingredients Europe. The reason is, it is a very new, emerging part of Kerry with a lot of acquisitions, so the first time around Finbarr O'Driscoll and I swept it, and did the broad brush stuff. Our style is to do that and move on to the next stage. Now, Denis Cregan has a very different style of getting very deeply involved and maximising the profits. Hugh Friel is very different, also. I won't use the phrase "he likes to stay at home", but he does keep the show totally tied together even at times when I have disappeared for weeks or months altogether.

> We were fortunate that three different talents came together, each one perhaps with his own expertise. Often in organisations there can be overcrowding, and maybe skills are negated because people at the top are of the same skill and the same focus. In us, it's been the absolute opposite, because three people can use all their talents and create a situation where one and one and one give you far more than three.[16]

There is also a description that is more to the point. There is a story widely retold in County Kerry that Denis Brosnan once gave a talk and declared something to the effect that "it takes three people to run a company successfully: a dreamer, a businessman, and an SOB. And I'm the dreamer." Observers generally agree that Brosnan *is* the dreamer, but that Cregan and Friel deserve serious accolades for negotiating the deals, running the business and taking care of the details. Some say that while Brosnan is eager to get a deal or an acquisition done with and move on to the next one, Friel and Cregan may be more prone to say, "Toughen up, we can get a better deal than this." For nearly three decades, since the muddy spring of 1972, the complementary skill sets of this trio have been at work in the executive suite at Kerry. Unusual in these times of executive mobility, this stability in the ranks of the top management has evolved into one of Kerry's unique strengths.

Organisational Culture (The Heart)

An organisational "culture" or "climate" is not designed and engineered. Nor is it carefully considered and crafted as part of an explicit business plan. It cannot be conjured up overnight. Rather, it emerges over time as the outward manifestation of the organisation's collective personality. The culture, or the ethos, is the core personality of the organisation; it carries the values and principles that drive it, and reflects the collective norms and expectations of those who toil within it. The culture at Kerry reflects the personality and the personal ethic of the organisation's founders, the circumstances of the organisation's birth, infancy, and growth, and the historical, social and economic context of its times. It is no easy matter to dissect an organisation's culture. One searches for outward signs, the processes, structures, attitudes and values that provide a hint of the deeper, implicit but dimly perceived heartbeat of the organisation that lies below.

The young managers who first joined together in the muddy field of the Listowel factory's construction site in April 1972 forged the foundations of Kerry's organisational culture. The determination to achieve the objective, the refusal to accept failure, the willingness to work audaciously hard, the ability to deal with adversity and the necessity to rely upon each other, all came to characterise the organisation. These managers, and the colleagues who joined them during the following few years, formed the essential core of the Kerry organisation. Given their youth and energy, and the fact that so many of them chose to remain with the organisation for their entire careers, they have had an unparalleled opportunity to imprint upon the entire organisation those elements of their shared experience of the early days. This heritage, and the culture that it spawned, remains a prominent and important component of the Kerry story.

Those very early struggles in the Canon's Field in 1972, when the success of the enterprise was clearly in doubt, defined an attitude that endures today. It is simply this: *failure is not an option*. Nor does it exist in the organisational vocabulary. Just as it was inconceivable in 1972 to shut down the factory in order to take care of the painful problems of whey disposal, effluent issues and the famous odour problem, so it has been nearly inconceivable in later years that the organisation will not achieve its objectives. Kerry is a consummate "can do" organisation. Says Brosnan:

> Obviously there has to be a vision of where you want to be in five years or ten years, and this vision has to be "bought into". The senior executives at Kerry, they all believe it, and once they believe it they start making plans as to how it can be achieved. So, I haven't had any of my colleagues, whether they are my nearest colleagues here or elsewhere throughout the organisation, who have ever said to me, "It can't be done." Everybody has said, "Let's find a way by which it can."[17]

It is also an enterprise that has not been averse to taking risks. The start-up of the factory before its completion, the formation of the co-operative with all of £9 of share capital and huge debt, the purchase of Denny's, the rough times of the "Milk Wars" and the huge leap represented by the purchase of Beatreme, all offer testimony to this. Kerry has also never hesitated to invite criticism about an orientation that some saw as too combative for what was (at the time) a co-operative organisation. Indeed, the very existence of the organisation was something of a rebellion against an establishment that was ready to consign the dairy farmers of Kerry, and their milk supply, to the tender mercies of neighbouring, out-of-county, co-operatives. The court cases with Fry-Cadbury and Bord Bainne were as symbolic as they were practical matters. Its willingness to adopt a position counter to that of ICOS and most, or all, of the other Irish dairy co-operatives demonstrated an independent streak unusual for the time. The first co-operative to diversify successfully out of its core food business, the first to become a public company, Kerry has remained aggressive, acquisitive and, to many, threatening. Although no longer the brash "upstart" it once was, Kerry's drive does not appear to be in any sense diminished. It is almost as if there is still something to prove.

Seamus McConville, a former editor of *The Kerryman* newspaper and a close observer of the Kerry phenomenon, has commented upon this:

He [Denis Brosnan] didn't mind kicking the establishment. Bord Bainne, ICOS, he had his rows with them. He said, we'll do our own thing, and obviously, he was supported. Now, some people might consider this arrogance, but in retrospect he was right. Bord Bainne was run by people who represented the other co-ops, and they saw this bloody upstart, and they didn't want the boat rocked too severely. They didn't like the sound of this guy because he was talking revolution. They felt that he, and the Kerry Co-op, were dangerous, and I'd say they tried to put him down. He was the big, bad wolf. But for the farmers in Kerry, he led them into a certain amount of freedom, he taught them how to look after themselves. They had been completely dependent. We had a dependent culture in this county, and we'd had it for years. But I think we are emerging from that, leaving it all behind us, and I'd say he's one of those who has taught us to think for ourselves, act for ourselves, be ourselves. Yes, he broke the rules. But who made the rules? Those same fellows who were minding their own patch.[18]

Another factor that has contributed to this attitude is the tendency of Kerry's managers to see themselves as underdogs. This predilection clearly characterised the early days of the organisation, and not without reason. Kerry Co-op was born amid the hostility or passivity of other co-operatives, and in the early years was often dismissed out of hand. In this "mythology", Kerry Co-op was surrounded (in their view) by hostile and predatory co-operatives eager to siphon off whatever portion of Kerry's milk supply they could. With their backs to the North Atlantic, and with a geography and climate less hospitable than that of their neighbours, Kerry cultivated the myth of being an organisation battling against the odds, against the elements, against the fates. To survive, they had to work harder, be smarter, go farther, be more audacious, take chances and simply be the best many times over. In this mythology, there was no chance to sit back and rest upon one's laurels. There were always more dragons to slay.

Whether or not Kerry's underdog status was real or imagined is perhaps of little consequence. There is power in myth. Myths may endure long after the conditions that gave rise to them have disappeared. This may be the case in Kerry, for the notion of being an underdog continues to colour the culture of the organisation. With Kerry now the premier specialty food ingredients company in the world, and a bona fide global player, one might reasonably expect this idea to diminish. But, says Brosnan, it is a question of where the goals are set:

> Back then, when Kerry was the smallest of the Big Six co-ops, our goal was to find our way out of that and make sure we moved up the ladder. But as things moved into the 1990s, particularly in our worldwide ingredients business and in consumer foods in the UK, Kerry was still the underdog because we had simply moved into a bigger marketplace. I think it was about 1995–96, where Kerry was awarded the Supplier of the Year in the UK, that I thought "at last we have arrived". But you will always be the underdog if you set your goals on a higher plane. We are still the underdog, still small, when you look at somebody who has $5 or $10 billion in sales. So it is really where you set those goals.[19]

This aspect of the Kerry culture, surviving intact somewhere in the organisational memory, has manifested itself clearly in an almost terrier-like perseverance to complete the task. Many Kerry managers refer to this as one of their prime organisational attributes. Michael Drummey describes it in this way:

> The fact that we'd come from nothing, and had to fight our way here, has helped us in everything we do. If we go in to win something, just like you go to win the All-Ireland, certainly the Kerry people, the Kerry followers are not too happy if you come home a loser. Equally, if Kerry Group plc goes to buy DCA or Dalgety, it isn't going to lose them. So, I suppose it comes from having been underdogs for so long.[20]

All this leads, of necessity it seems, to a formidable work ethic. Says Denis Brosnan:

> All those who work at Kerry work very hard. I'm not sure why they still do so, but perhaps we [the top executives] lead it from here.[21]

On the other hand, critics suggest that "you have to sell your soul to work for Kerry". Indeed, some have found the pace and intensity of work to be too demanding, and they will normally not tarry too long with the organisation. Kerry, for its part, has made particular efforts to ensure that it can fill the ranks of its employees with the best and brightest. They have been one of the most active recruiters of third-level graduates in Ireland and are actively recruiting on a global basis. These new graduates may expect that responsibility can come very early at the Kerry Group. Said one young manager, "You'll be given enough rope to hang yourself!"

One of Kerry's major organisational tasks is to support the development and diffusion of its unique organisational culture around the world. The next generation of Kerry managers are today learning, and themselves re-inventing, the Kerry Way. Perhaps the drama of the Canon's Field is being played out by young and energetic Kerry managers in Mexico, Brazil, Malaysia and elsewhere. If so, one can only imagine that it will become a better culture because of it.

Ultimately, of course, the Kerry culture is a results-driven culture. One never takes one's eye off the ball. Ivor Kenny once described an organisational culture (much like Kerry's) as:

> . . . a strong, recognisable one with a tendency to see life in simple, "common sense" terms. The predominant characteristics of the culture were loyalty, energy, adventurousness/risk-taking, pride, buzz and discipline.[22]

It describes the Kerry culture well.

The Kerry Way

The well-balanced individual nurtures and balances the needs, and contributions, of the head (intellect), the hands (practical capabilities) and the heart (emotions). Kerry Group, throughout its organisational history, has proven itself well able to balance, nurture and harness its own capabilities of strategy, structure, people and culture. Its commitment to strategic planning and implementation, its technical and managerial capabilities and its distinctive culture have thus far yielded a rich bounty of organisational success.

Notes

1 Denis Brosnan, addressing the Deloittes/IDA Forum for Chief Executives, Royal Hospital Kilmainham, 9 November 1989. Reported in *Co-op Ireland*, "Building an Irish Multinational: Brosnan says sales target of £1 billion 'Well Within Our Reach'", undated copy, p. 5.

2 Conor Keane, personal interview, 27 June 1998.

3 The institution is Skidmore College in Saratoga Springs, New York. The founder, Lucy Scribner Skidmore, was motivated by a desire to educate young women liberally and broadly, and to arm them, additionally, with the very practical skills they would need to be successful in a sometimes inhospitable social environment.

4 John B. Keane, personal interview, 29 March 2000.

5 *Webster's College Dictionary*, New York: Random House, Inc.

6 Denis Brosnan, personal interview, 7 October 1999.

7 Ibid.

8 An interview with Ivor Kenny in *Spotlight*, an online publication of the HR Global Network edited by Sarah Powell. (http://www.mcb.co.uk/hr/current/spotlight/spotlight2.htm)

9 Ivor Kenny, personal interview, 9 July 1999.

10 Joe Rea, personal interview, May 1999.

11 Attributed to Michael Killeen, IMI Conference, 1984.

12 Hugh Friel, personal interview, 31 May 1999.

13 Gary Hamel and C.K. Prahalad (1989), "Strategic Intent", *Harvard Business Review,* May/June 1989, p. 63.

14 Internal Kerry Group briefing materials.

15 Denis Brosnan, personal interview, 11 October 1999.

16 Ibid.

17 Ibid.

18 Seamus McConville, personal interview, 27 May 1999.

19 Denis Brosnan, personal interview, 11 October 1999.

20 Michael Drummey, personal interview, 6 January 2000.

21 Denis Brosnan, personal interview, 11 October 1999.

22 Ivor Kenny (1999). *Freedom and Order: Studies in Strategic Leadership*, Dublin: Oak Tree Press, p. 150.

Chapter 16

The World of Kerry

I would hope to be remembered for having helped put County Kerry on the map, internationally. I would hope that those who live here, or who travel from here, could take great pride in saying they are from County Kerry, and that it is the headquarters of the Kerry Group. — Denis Brosnan

No one ever expected that Kerry would stop anywhere. You'd never see a day when someone would say, "That's enough!" There was always another step, and there was massive support for that. At the end of the day, the county is a better place for it. — Denis Buckley, Chairman of Kerry Co-operative Creameries, Ltd. and Vice-Chairman of Kerry Group

The Celtic Tiger

Ireland, with an average annual growth rate of 9.9 per cent for the past three years, has achieved the status of the fastest-growing economy not only in the EU, but in the entire developed world. Christened the "Celtic Tiger", it has cut a broad swath through much of Irish society, with economic and social effects reaching into every corner of the Irish nation.

Ireland's economic buoyancy reinforces a new self-confidence. In marketing terms, Ireland is changing its homely, bucolic image into an international brand increasingly recognised in business and the arts. The changes have been tumultuous. Dublin's skyline is being

> transformed by new hotels and apartment blocks. Car
> sales are at record levels. The new affluence is evident in
> shops selling foreign-made luxury goods. . . . Ireland has
> rarely had such a benign economic climate.[1]

Powered by an influx of foreign direct investment, particularly
from US-based multinational corporations, Ireland has at long last
emerged from the economic doldrums. It is a very different place;
to some, it is almost a different country. Its largest single trading
partner is no longer the UK, but the US. Agriculture, once dominant, now contributes little more than 5 per cent of the nation's
GDP (it was 16 per cent as late as 1973) and 10 per cent of the nation's employment (it was 24 per cent in 1973). Unemployment in
Ireland today (the end of 2000) is 3.7 per cent, a figure that some
suggest is the equivalent of structural full employment. The number of working people has increased by over 370,000 in the period
1994–1999. By 1999, GDP per capita had reached a par with the EU
average. Exports have grown by an annual average rate of 16 per
cent since 1993. Housing starts and construction are booming, and
there is a new air of optimism in Ireland that is quite at odds with
its dismal economic past. Ireland today must grapple with an array
of issues for which it has been unprepared by experience. Tight
labour markets and their attendant cost pressures are beginning to
chip away at the broad consensus of the "social partnership" that
characterised the earlier years of the "tiger economy". As in many
other developed and developing economies, prosperity has been
uneven, tending to centre in and around Dublin and bypassing in
great measure other parts of the country. Most telling of all, perhaps, is that Ireland is now a net *importer* of labour, appealing to
those in the Irish Diaspora (with the right skills) to return home,
and scouring the world for other immigrants to Ireland who may
help to continue power the engine of economic growth. If the
problem of "Irish immigration" has been at issue for over a century and a half, it now has a profoundly different cast. *Inbound* immigration has led, in some quarters, to a backlash on the part of
some Irish, and raised very serious questions as to what it means
to be "Irish" in the new millennium. As the Celtic Tiger roars its
way through the global economy, the Irish must grapple with their
own sense of national identity.

This sea change in the economic fortunes of Ireland did not happen by accident. If there were any such thing as "the luck of the Irish", history would testify that it would be very bad luck indeed! The "opening" of Ireland to the global economy that began with Seán Lemass, the IDA's successful wooing of foreign investment, and Ireland's pivotal accession to the EEC in 1973, all played their part. Similarly, the strengths of Ireland's system of national education have finally come to the fore. In addition to their expected production of scholars and literary genius, Ireland has increasingly focused on training in science and technology, producing graduates particularly well equipped to function successfully in the "new economy" of high technology, instant communication and global competition.

In many ways, the story of Kerry Group is emblematic of the "Celtic Tiger" economy itself. Although its roots are firmly embedded in the agricultural tradition of "Old Ireland", Kerry quickly turned its attentions beyond the confines of Ireland's small, island economy. As Ireland itself began to industrialise, Kerry moved beyond commodity food production into the added-value sphere. Utilising the resources and capabilities available in its home country, Kerry Group used Ireland as its platform for growth into first an international, and later a global, corporation. Denis Brosnan has called Ireland a "crossroads" between North America and Europe. In a speech to the Ireland United States Council for Commerce and Industry in 1994, Brosnan said:

> Over the past two decades, we have looked both east and west to exploit the opportunities awaiting us. If Ireland were not our headquarters, we might have looked to the east or to the west, but I am quite sure never to both. Ireland was and is the ideal crossroads for Kerry to build an international food business, and biased though I may be, I cannot think of any better location to have a corporate and major base. . . . We did not choose it, but this act of God, or of history, has enabled us to exploit the opportunities both to the east and to the west.[2]

People at Kerry Group like to note in passing that Tralee is actually closer to Brazil than is Chicago. Centrality aside, Kerry has benefited from many of the same factors that have attracted foreign multinationals to set up operations in Ireland, including a well-educated, skilled and enthusiastic workforce, EU and government support, high quality raw materials and a high standard of living. In other respects, however, it has itself contributed to the further development of those same attributes. As an indigenous success story, Kerry Group has demonstrated that the recent successes of the Irish economy are not solely related to the influx of foreign investment and multinationals, but are also reflective of dynamic, outward-looking Irish firms. The confidence and maturity that have so recently surfaced in the Irish commercial sector are the fruits of international successes such as Kerry's. There must be considerable national pride in sending Irish people abroad as "global managers" employed by an Irish-based multinational, rather than as the misty-eyed economic exiles of the not-so-distant past.

Kerry Group gives evidence of a new commercial ethos in Ireland, one characterised by self-confidence, independence, productivity, innovation and high levels of both aspirations and expectations. The age of economic stagnation, dependence and emigration appears, at long last, to be over. Ireland has taken its place in the integrated, interdependent global economy of the new millennium. Although economies may cycle through periods of boom and bust, and the fortunes of individual companies wax and wane, it is difficult to imagine that Ireland will ever return to the economic doldrums of the past. Kerry Group has been a beneficiary of, and a contributor to, this *wirtschaftswunder* that is the new Irish economy.

Kerry Group — A Stakeholder Approach

There are many ways to measure an organisation's performance. Financial criteria are perhaps the most straightforward, and measures of the Kerry Group's financial performance, including total stockholder returns, have been amply reviewed already. The returns to investors in Kerry Group have been extraordinary. Yet financial returns are not the sole means of assessing the overall performance of any company. All companies, in fact, have many "stakeholders", that is, all those who are affected in some way by the activities of the company and/or can somehow, themselves, have an effect upon those same corporate activities.[3] All of these stakeholders, or constituencies, in turn have different interests in the various outcomes of corporate activities. Customers, employees, governments, interest groups and communities all have various interests and "stakes" in corporate activities, some of them complementary and others in conflict. Successful corporations need to successfully balance the sometimes-conflicting needs of their various stakeholders in order to ensure organisational survival and success. The overall performance of any organisation must be measured by its success in meeting these multiple expectations. Kerry Group, throughout its short but eventful history, has shown an uncanny ability to satisfy the demands and interests of its many constituencies.

One important constituency is that of its *customers* and *consumers*. Kerry Group intensively focuses upon the satisfaction of customer and consumer expectations. These customers, many of whom are themselves global players of considerable size, geographic scope and technical sophistication, expect — and accept — nothing less than high-quality, low-cost products, dependability of supply and technical leadership. In fact, as these customers grow larger and more complex, they are seeking suppliers who can match their own scale and meet the full range of their diverse needs. Customer relationships increasingly reflect a longer-term, relationship-based partnership rather than the old transaction-based buyer/seller arrangements. Specialty food ingredients, as produced by Kerry, are increasingly customer *and* application-specific, and encompass research and product development efforts as well as manufacture and delivery. As it broadens and deepens its core technology capabilities on a worldwide basis, Kerry has increasingly become a "one-stop shop" for its customers, achieving status as a preferred supplier to many multinational food companies. In consumer foods as well, Kerry has built strong and enduring relationships with major retailers, providing leadership not only in the processing of quality food products, but also in research of consumer trends and preferences. With its focus on "category management", Kerry has built its knowledge base and ability to assist retailers in meeting the changing demands and preferences of consumers for convenience, variety and quality. For Kerry's retail customers, that also means assisting them in marketing their products effectively and profitably.

Another important stakeholder group is that of suppliers and employees. Kerry Group, at the end of 2000, has approximately

14,000 employees around the world (nearly 3,200 of them in Ireland) and thousands of suppliers, running the gamut from the largest global players to small, local suppliers. Additionally, its original and most important suppliers, the dairy farmers of County Kerry, remain much in evidence, although their numbers have declined to approximately 3,500. The employees, of course, remain the heart of the organisation — the ultimate, unique, inimitable sustainable advantage that will power the enterprise through the rough, globally competitive waters of this new millennium of challenge and opportunity. As such, considerable time and effort is being expended on improving management capability, developing strategic management skills and linking and harnessing the skills, motivation and wholehearted commitment of each individual to the achievement of Kerry's organisational goals. This emphasis on personal responsibility and the "unique, wholehearted commitment" of each individual has been, and remains, a distinctive characteristic of the Kerry organisation.

Finally, with over 80 manufacturing facilities now located in 15 countries around the world, 25 technical centres, and international sales offices in many others, Kerry Group has begun to expand its role in various communities around the world. As Kerry continues its global expansion, it will need to further define itself as a global corporate citizen. At the moment, however, as one examines the impact of nearly 28 years of organisational existence, it is clear that nowhere has the Kerry Group's influence been as strong as in County Kerry, Ireland. It is where the enterprise was founded, where it is headquartered and where the majority of its stockholders still reside. It is only appropriate that this story end where it began, in the "Kingdom County" of Kerry.

The Kerry Group and County Kerry

In some ways, County Kerry today is not so different from 1972. The landscape remains a dominant presence, with a spectacular natural beauty that consoles the native and attracts the tourist. Gaelic football is still played and followed, at every level in every parish, with an all-consuming passion, and the Sam Maguire Cup (awarded for the All-Ireland Championship in football) has returned again to Kerry, for the 32nd time, in the first year of the new millennium. Most in Kerry would agree that this is only as it should be. Kerry, although having failed in its attempt to achieve "Objective One" status within the EU (which would have provided privileged funding as a "disadvantaged area"), remains, at least in its own eyes, a "peripheral area", the westernmost outpost of the EU. Agriculture, although not the dominant activity it once was, remains a vitally important part of the economic life of the county and the 120,000 people who reside there.

Yet, in so many other ways, County Kerry in the year 2000 is a far different place from that of just 30 years ago. It is no longer a sleepy, insular backwater, so far from cosmopolitan Dublin as to be casually dismissed. The ripple effects of Ireland's "Celtic Tiger" economy have reached Kerry, and the economy of Kerry has revived along with the fortunes of Ireland itself during the 1990s. Emigration rates have declined and the population of the county has stabilised. Although many young people still leave the county, their destination now is less likely to be England or America than Dublin and the booming east and south-east of Ireland, where jobs are going begging for lack of qualified applicants.

The connections between the Kerry Group and the community of County Kerry are strong and myriad and not easily untangled. In its numerous sponsorships, its philanthropy, the spillover effects of its economic activities and the wealth it has generated for its shareholders in the county, many of its impacts are concrete, tangible and explicit. Some, however, are not.

Even as the Group has grown from a simple regional milk processor to a diversified international food products company, its ties to Kerry have in many ways grown deeper and more varied. Certainly, the Kerry Co-operative shareholding in Kerry Group (presently at 37 per cent) and the plc shares owned directly by suppliers, employees and others in County Kerry (an estimated further 18 per cent) have kept Kerry Group well rooted in its native soil. The involvement of Kerry farmers with the Kerry Group (through the Kerry Co-op) has been continuous, direct and influential. It might also be added, in view of the success of the Kerry Group, that they too must have been doing something right. Said Denis Brosnan:

> The farmers are very involved here, and as management
> we enjoy it, and the farmers do as well. We listen to the

farmers at area advisory meetings and have a pint in the pub afterwards, and that keeps one's feet on the ground.[4]

The support of both the farming community and the community at large has been a critical element in the Group's success. Throughout the Group's history, from the construction of the Listowel factory to the formation (and financing!) of the co-operative, to additional calls for capital for expansion, to the decision to go public, to the imperatives of growth and diversification, Kerry's management has always been able to count upon the strong support of its natural, and original, constituency. Such loyalty, and faith, is nearly unprecedented. Michael Hanrahan, the chairman of Kerry Group since 1981, notes that:

> They invested in Kerry, believed in Kerry and appreciated Kerry. And Kerry has given back to the community what the community has given to them, and continues to . . . [5]

Arising from this heritage, the Kerry Group's contribution to economic development in Kerry has helped to transform the county. At present, Kerry employs in excess of 1,000 in the county, with a further 3,500 milk suppliers and their families dependent upon the income derived from selling milk to Kerry. It is the largest industrial employer in Kerry. The economic impacts, in turn, cascade down to other local suppliers, lorry drivers, local retail stores, construction and countless other commercial activities. The wealth derived from the appreciation of Kerry shares, as well as dividend payments to shareholders (in both the Co-op and the Group), have also made a profound difference in the everyday lives of people who, for too long, had done without such economic benefits. Kerry Group has unquestionably led the economic revival in Kerry, and the effects of this sea change have been felt by almost everyone in the county, not just a scattered and fortunate few.

In the area of philanthropy, Kerry Group has also not been found wanting. It has contributed financially to a full range of causes and local amenities. As one local Kerry politician noted:

> As the largest and most successful company in the area it is inundated with requests for sponsorship. All are considered, and very few of merit go unaided.[6]

It has contributed, in a major way, to the Kerry Cultural and Literary Centre, Writers' Week in Listowel, the Kerry Hospice Foundation and hospitals throughout the county (e.g. Cahirciveen), St John's Centre, Samhlaíocht Chiarraí (a county-wide community arts initiative), the Festival of Kerry, the reconstruction of the famine ship *Jeannie Johnston* and many, many others. One of the more telling examples of Kerry's philanthropy was its contribution of £250,000 to the Kerry Parents and Friends of the Mentally Handicapped in December 1997. This contribution was actually made by the Kerry Co-op to commemorate the 25th anniversary of its founding and, as the amount suggests, was more than just a noble gesture. What better commemoration of organisational success than the opportunity to give back to the community that had faithfully supported it through the years? In Kerry, as in few other places, memories are very long. Sometimes this is a good thing.

Kerry Group and many of its executives have been involved in some manner with the development of most of the major amenities built in County Kerry during the past several decades. The Aqua Dome in Tralee and the Kerry Airport at Farranfore come immediately to mind. No doubt there are others. Suffice it to say that Kerry Group has been involved with numerous public/private partnerships, and continues to play a lead role in fostering economic development in the county. This has also taken the form of encouraging tourism. Kerry has done this through its support of *Swing*, a programme to promote tourism centred on the fine golf courses located in the county, its recent sponsorship of the Irish Open at Ballybunion, and continuing sponsorship of the horse racing meetings held in Killarney, Tralee and Listowel every year. Involvement in such public/private partnerships, of course, goes well beyond the confines of the county. Denis Brosnan, for example, has served as the Chairman of the Irish Horse Racing Authority for many years, devoting a substantial portion of his time to the many reforms and activities associated with the further development of the racing industry in Ireland.

Finally, the Kerry Group's sponsorship of the Kerry football team goes back over many years, and is perhaps the most visible manifestation of the pride, and passion, of both the county and the Kerry organisation. There are certainly parallels. Both the team and the Kerry Group are held to high expectations and are committed to excellence. Both are known for their tough work ethic, their spirit and enthusiasm. If ever there were a sponsorship "made in heaven", the Kerry football team and Kerry Group match may come close.

Some say that with great power comes great responsibility. To whatever extent Kerry has come to be the dominant enterprise in County Kerry, it appears to have shouldered its appropriate responsibilities well. They have helped to make Kerry a better place.

Concluding Words

The story of the Kerry Group is not yet finished. It is unfolding daily in the cut and thrust of the global marketplace, in the actions of its managers and employees, in its relationships with customers and suppliers and in its impacts on the many communities in which it operates. Certainly, there is ample reason to believe that it will have a long history indeed. Yet the story of the Kerry Group as it has unfolded thus far is already an instructive one. It is the story of a people, and a place, and a time. It is the story of a dream that became a reality, far beyond the imaginations of those who gave birth to it. It is a story of patience and persistence, and a group of people, rewarded. Perhaps the twenty-first century will have little need for morality plays in business. If it does, however, the story of the Kerry Co-op and the Kerry Group may be read, perhaps with no little profit.

Notes

[1] *The Financial Times*, 30 July 1997.

[2] Address by Denis Brosnan to the Ireland United States Council for Commerce and Industry, 15 July 1994.

[3] For the seminal work on stakeholder theory, see R. Edward Freeman (1984), *Strategic Management: A Stakeholder Approach*, Boston: Pitman Publishing Inc.

[4] Woulfe, J. (1994), *Voices of Kerry*, Dublin: Blackwater Press, p. 231.

[5] Michael Hanrahan, personal interview, 25 October 2000.

[6] Carroll, B. (1997), "Listowel honours Kerry Group for 25 years of excellence", *The Kerryman*, 26 September 1997.

Index